THE BOOK

ON THE

BOOK

THE BOOK
ON THE
BOOK

A Landmark Inquiry into
Which Strategies in the
Modern Game Actually Work

Bill Felber

Thomas Dunne Books
St. Martin's Press 🜍 New York

Since baseball is a game for fathers and sons, it is

only appropriate to dedicate this book to the memory of one

Frank Felber, and to the future of another

THOMAS DUNNE BOOKS.
An imprint of St. Martin's Press.

THE BOOK ON THE BOOK. Copyright © 2005 by Bill Felber. All rights re-
served. Printed in the United States of America. No part of this book may be
used or reproduced in any manner whatsoever without written permission except in the case of brief quotations embodied in critical articles or reviews. For
information, address St. Martin's Press, 175 Fifth Avenue, New York, N.Y.
10010.

www.stmartins.com

Design by Nancy Singer Olaguera

Library of Congress Cataloging-in-Publication Data

Felber, Bill.
    The book on the book / Bill Felber.
        p. cm.
    ISBN 0-312-33264-5
    EAN 978-0312-33264-8
    1. Baseball. 2. Baseball—Statistics. I. Title.

GV867.F45 2005
796.357—dc22
                                                2004051445

First Edition: May 2005

10 9 8 7 6 5 4 3 2 1

CONTENTS

ACKNOWLEDGMENTS

The author is indebted to many people whose faith, cooperation, and effort helped make this book a reality.

The first and foremost bow must go to John Thorn, a friend for nearly two decades, who had the confidence to say to someone otherwise relatively unknown in the world of baseball publishing, "Go for it and I'll go with you." When John was able to go no further, Rob Wilson and Peter Wolverton took up the cause. Lots of excellent ideas never become books for the absence of that simplest of all backings.

In the same context, I want to express appreciation to Gary Gillette, a trusted advisor on this volume. Gary filled a most important role, rigorously challenging premises while at the same time maintaining an unflagging confidence in the author's ability.

Many of the arguments put forward herein are at their base statistical. In the field of baseball math, Pete Palmer is king. I wouldn't have a tenth of the guts it would take to discuss the relationship between payroll and victories in the context of regression theory if Pete Palmer hadn't held my hand through the process. Working with him is a great joy and an honor.

Joy Hayes possesses only a pedestrian knowledge of baseball; her professional field is actuarial studies for the state of Illinois. But she is a genius at statistics, and that is in addition to being my sister. When I wanted to know whether any of my several wild-hare ideas could be demonstrated to be true or false through use of formulae, she pointed the way. In the same vein, she is one reason a lot of my dumb ideas—and there were many—never saw print.

There are a handful of really useful baseball research libraries in America: the Library of Congress, the New York Public Library, the National Baseball Hall of Fame Library, the SABR research library . . . and Dean Coughenour's basement. How fortunate for this book that I live about a mile from the latter. In addition to being a collector of records and publications dating back to the game's founding, Dean is tirelessly cooperative, a heartful critic, a sagacious analyst, and occasionally even a booster. To hear Dean say, "I think I know where you're going with this . . . and I think you're right," is the equivalent of a month's worth of adrenaline.

Many people affiliated with the Society for American Baseball Research provided assistance, in the form of data, argumentation, inspiration, critical analysis, or in other means. Some did so without even knowing. They should not go unrecognized. Among them: the late Doug Pappas, Cappy Gagnon, Lloyd Johnson, Bill James, Don Zminda, John Jarvis, Phil Birnbaum, Bill Gilbert, Neal Traven, and Peter Bjarkman.

THE GAME
ON THE FIELD

PREFACE TO PART I

When Albert Spalding wrote one of the first histories of baseball in 1911, he deliberately sidestepped any discussion of strategies. Said Spalding, "The opinions of up-to-date, scientific experts so widely and so honestly vary as to what really constitute important methods that there is no intelligent hope of bringing them together."

If he were alive today, Al Spalding couldn't get away with that dodge for two reasons. First, virtually every fan has an opinion on strategies, and fans are not at all shy about sharing their wisdom. But second and more relevant to Spalding's point, today we often do have the tools to determine which strategies work and which don't. We can tell through computer analyses precisely how frequently a stolen base must be successful in order to help the offense. We can develop statistical models to determine how much money is too much to pay Alex Rodriguez. We can determine exactly—if only in retrospect—how large a budget any team must have in order to be competitive in the pennant race.

In other words, we can gauge what works and what doesn't.

Spalding's reticence notwithstanding, the merits (or demerits) of particular strategies have always fascinated fans, players, and owners alike. Spalding himself was not immune from this reality; witness a comment from the 1885 edition of his *Official Baseball Guide* regarding baserunning:

> Each season's experience only shows more and more the fact that good baserunning is one of the most important essen-

tials of success in winning games . . . Any soft-brained heavyweight can occasionally hit a ball for a home run, but it requires a shrewd, intelligent player, with his wits about him, to make a successful baserunner. Indeed, baserunning is the most difficult work a player has to do in a game.

The importance of baserunning was one of the principal tenets of the original "Book"—by which is generally meant the common understandings that have governed baseball strategies. "The Book" became fixed in the minds of the game's cognoscenti over a period of decades, although in fact it has undergone a constant process of reform and revision. Over time, entire chapters governing on-field play—on topics as diverse as the wisdom of the sacrifice, playing for the long ball, the arrangement of a lineup, expectations for the starter, the use of relief pitching—have been written, erased, and rewritten. Just as managers of the 1950s would have viewed strategies of earlier generations as dated, some of their assumptions seem unfathomable today.

Those changes may be driven by alterations in rules or playing conditions, such as improvements in the manufacturing of the baseball around 1910 that made for a harder product capable of being driven farther. They may also occur due to external demand: When Babe Ruth proved that fans loved a slugger (and would pay to see one), the long ball became a marketing device as well as a strategic tool. And as often as not, the on-field "Book" is rewritten due to simple copycatism. If one manager tries a new strategy and enjoys success, it is a virtual certainty that within a short time the idea will be widely pilfered, whether the pilferage actually makes strategic sense or not. For evidence, just look into the nearest bullpen.

It is one thing to say that strategies have changed through the years—driven by wisdom, popular tastes, rules, legal judgments, or other factors—and another to assert that the changes have represented constant improvement. "The Book" as it is commonly understood today represents nothing more than the collective judgment of the game's managers and general managers. The very fact that it has undergone constant revision strongly argues that "The Book," in the sense of representing the statistically ideal way of logically playing the game, has never been "written." And if that is the case, why would one deduce that "The Book" is "written" today, that strategic knowledge has reached its apotheosis, or that improvement has even necessarily taken place in a straight line?

What we do know is that, more than ever, we are equipped to assess "The Book," to judge its legitimacies and weaknesses, and determine the extent to which big league teams do (or ought to) govern themselves by it. Which is joyous news to long-suffering fans of numerous perennially hapless teams: Maybe those bums of ours can't win, but at least we can figure out why not.

A side note: Because the data do not exist for it to do so, neither this book nor any other explores one potentially vital aspect of modern "strategy" (if strategy it be), and that is the impact of performance-enhancing drugs. To the extent it is a factor, that factor is miasmic. We know from 2003 testing results that between 5 and 7 percent of players were using some type of improper, if not always illegal, performance enhancement. We don't know for how long, nor do we know the extent to which (if any) that use has affected the game.

But simply because research into the impact of performance enhancements is not presently possible, we should not proceed as if those enhancements do not exist. In retrospect, the evidence of the impact of their use seems clear. For years experts have mumbled that there is "something different" about the modern game—generally this occurs in the context of the growth of offense during the most recent decade—and they have done so seemingly against all logical evidence. The flailing toward a theory at times sounds almost comical. Expansion? But why should expansion dilute only the pitching, while actually improving batting? Greater racial diversity? Oh, so what you're saying is that minorities can hit but not pitch? Fitness regimes? As if pitchers don't work out. Each of those pseudo-theories tumbles one by one, and what remains is the one surreptitiously spoken theory that cannot be disproven because it cannot be factually addressed: juice. For the good of the game, let us hope that theory as well is eventually undermined by evidence.

1

THE COMPONENTS OF PLAYER VALUE

Even before the result was announced, conventional wisdom conferred the 1998 National League Most Valuable Player Award on Sammy Sosa rather than Mark McGwire.

The argument for Sosa and against McGwire could be heard that fall on the evening sports shows and read in the national newspapers. *USA Today*'s National League columnist justified his selection of Sosa on the basis that McGwire's accomplishments—which, it should be noted, include setting the all-time record for home runs—came on behalf of a non-contender. In his mind this posed the question, "Valuable to what?" The previous night, an ESPN analyst backed Sosa's candidacy for the same reason precisely one breath before naming Ken Griffey, Jr. the American League's MVP. Griffey's Mariners finished nine games below .500 and in third place in the four-team AL West that season.

Another ESPN commentator said he would vote for McGwire as Player of the Year, but not MVP. This is the smarmy new parsing. In baseball there is no such thing as player of the year. But what of it? ESPN pays its on-air personalities to be advocative and entertaining; commentators are not required to be reality-based.

The cavalier dismissal of McGwire based on his team's non-standing—which, by the way, received nearly unanimous ratification when the official vote was announced—logically reduces as follows: he's not the MVP because Ron Gant, Donovan Osborne, Jeff Brantley, and Kent Bottenfield stunk.

Yet in that befuddling reasoning, the vote also frames a fascinating and broader question: What precisely is value? As the baseball experts saw it in 1998, Sosa had value because his team won; McGwire lacked value because his team didn't.

The way we define "value" is the linchpin of much of "The Book" about baseball strategy for the simple reason that strategies are inevitably focused toward maximizing "value." Yet in the modern game, value analysis is often subjective and thus prone to error. Sports commentators commit this error as do team executives. As we consider the relevance of the modern baseball "Book," one of our foundations has to be an understanding as to what constitutes "value." In forming that understanding, we have to be careful that our trendy definitions don't confuse the ends with the means.

THE FORMULA FOR SUCCESS

One of the singular beauties of baseball is that the components of success can be quantified. Relating the value of a basketball player to scoring average is too one-dimensional; football rotisserie leaguers don't even try to assess the value of a pulling guard. It's hard to reduce to a numerical formula the components that make a great professor, a great lawyer or, for that matter, a great book. The measure of a corporation's success can be stated on a bottom line, but can one devise a formula accurately presenting the relative contributions of all the corporation's accountants, salespeople, engineers, production line workers, and officers to that bottom line?

This can be done in baseball because we have a very measurable result—namely a victory—which is created by means of a second entirely measurable occurrence, that being runs.

Thanks to the intervention of computers, we know—and I do not use the word "know" loosely—that in the modern game the average base hit produces forty-six one-hundredths of a run; the average double produces eight-tenths of a run, etc. Conversely, we know that the average out reduces production by one-quarter of a run.

All that being the case, and setting aside only the intangibles and uncountables, determining the MVP at season's end is a deceptively simple task. Count the singles, doubles, triples, home runs, walks, steals, and outs made by each player, apply the proper run-producing value of each event, add proper fielding and baserunning quotients, and you can define any player's value in the appropriate context of games won. (The same process works essentially in reverse, by the way, for pitchers—with equal validity.)

The Most Valuable Player Award is a frequent backdrop for value-related arguments. Sometimes it takes the McGwire-Sosa context. At other times, the debate focuses on whether a pitcher should be eligible to win the award. None has since Dennis Eckersley won with Oakland in 1992. In the case of pitchers, the disqualifier tends to be twofold: First, they have their own award, the Cy Young; and second, they don't play every day. Of the first, little need be said in refutation beyond that it is plainly silly. So what if pitchers have their own award? In the NHL, defensemen have their own award . . . did that stop hockey writers from voting for Bobby Orr for MVP all those seasons?

The second argument, that pitchers' value is diminished because they are not everyday players, is superficially more appealing. Yet given a tinge of thought, that argument, too, quickly collapses. The essence of baseball is the pitcher-batter matchup, and it is not a vast oversimplification to say that the fellow who wins the greatest number of those matchups over the course of a six-month season is the most valuable player. There are, of course, degrees of "winning" and "losing" such matchups: While both a walk and a home run qualify as "wins" for the batter, one carries a substantial number of bonus points. But we can adjust for those variations.

It is certainly true that an everyday position player has the opportunity to impact four or five times as many games as, for example, a starting pitcher. At the same time, a starting pitcher's impact on the game in which he appears is several times more significant than the impact of any individual position player. This is so for an obvious reason. In the typical game, a position player gets four or perhaps five opportunities to "win" or "lose" a pitcher-hitter matchup—and by doing so, influences the game's outcome. In a stretch of five games, that might amount to participation in between twenty and twenty-five such confrontations.

A starting pitcher would only pitch one of those five games, but he would be involved in every one of the pitcher-hitter confrontations for the duration of his tenure in that game. Pedro Martinez may have only made 29 starts in 2000, but he pitched 217 innings, averaging seven and one-half innings per start. Since we know that Martinez allowed 160 base runners by either a hit or a walk, we can state the proposition in another and more precise way: Martinez influenced 811 pitcher-hitter confrontations in 2000, and he won 80 percent of them. The average American League pitcher won 65 percent; Martinez's edge over the field was 15 percent.

Jason Giambi, the writers' choice for the 2000 MVP Award, certainly had a fine season. But Giambi was a part of only 647 pitcher-hitter confrontations—influencing the outcome of games 164 fewer times than Martinez. He did win 47 percent of those matchups, 12 percent more than the 35 percent league-wide average for batters. But still, his advantage was less substantial than Martinez's advantage

(A side note: Seen in this context, the 1992 MVP Award to Eckersley—or to any relief pitcher—is plainly silly. In 1992, Eckersley won 77 percent of his pitcher-hitter confrontations . . . but he only engaged in 313 of them. More on the frivolousness of considering relievers as MVP candidates in a subsequent chapter.)

Our cursory examination of Martinez versus Giambi has not thus far taken into consideration the supplementary factors we cited above. Giambi, for example, hit 43 home runs; Martinez allowed just 17. Giambi drew 137 bases on balls; Martinez issued just 37. Giambi piled up 73 extra base hits; Martinez allowed 36.

We can't accurately weigh those numbers in our minds, but statistical analysis can. In fact that's precisely what Pete Palmer's Batter

Fielder Base Stealer Wins and Pitcher Wins* does: Weigh all those factors and reduce them to a comprehensible sentence. When you do that, this is the result. In 2000, Pedro Martinez improved the Red Sox by a factor of 8.4 victories, the highest total in the American League. Rodriguez actually stood second, improving the Mariners by 6.8 victories. Giambi was the league's third most valuable player, improving Oakland by 5.2 victories.

SPINNING THE TRUTH

The point of this exercise isn't solely to criticize the thought processes most voters apply in considering their MVP selections—although that alone would be a constructive exercise—but to underscore the true concept of value. Recognition of the rough equilibrium between the importance of pitching and hitting—as expressed in the MVP voting—would be a step in that direction. A second step, illustrated by the debate between the credentials of Sosa and McGwire in the 1998 NL race (or the mirror debate involving A-Rod and Miguel Tejada in 2002), would involve recognition of the importance (or lack of same) of winning in the context of individual awards.

Because baseball is a team game, not an individual one, it is impossible to fairly overlay team performance onto matters of individual accomplishment. No single player is good enough to merit that sort of accolade. The Sosa versus McGwire scrum illustrates the failure of

---

*BFW (and its companion for pitchers, PW) are terms used to express in a single number the impact of contributions by an individual player to team success. They were devised by baseball statistician Pete Palmer and author Gary Gillette. BFW stands for Batter Fielder Base Stealer Wins, and may be read as an expression of the number of games a position player won or lost for his team—through batting, fielding, and baserunning—compared with an average player. PW stands for Pitcher Wins and does the same thing for pitchers. More detailed definitions of the terms can be found in the 2004 edition of *The Baseball Encyclopedia* by Palmer and Gillette.

such logic. Sosa's 1998 achievements added up to a Batter Fielder Base Stealer Wins of 5.0. To put it another way, a team comprised of 24 completely average players plus Sammy Sosa should (pending the intervention of luck) have finished the season five games above .500 (86–76). But McGwire's achievements equate to a BFW of 7.1; a team of 24 average players plus McGwire should have finished 88–74 and beat out Sosa's crew by two games. To argue anything else is to visit Bottenfield's sins on McGwire.

These debates concerning value are a fascinating and ongoing part of baseball, and they are also—hopefully happily—much of what this book is about. Perhaps it is his personality as much as his performance, but in a recurring way, Sammy Sosa often finds himself personifying one aspect or another of that debate.

In June of 2000, when the Chicago Cubs briefly put Sosa on the trading block, the issue was all about his value to the team.

That seemed a silly argument to Sosa, and to a lot of Cub fans. Consecutive seasons of 60-plus home runs, nearly 300 RBIs along with an MVP Award and a spot in the playoffs (in 1998), and the guy needs to defend his production? "I don't know what more I can do," complained Sosa when Chicago management sniped at him.

His manager, Don Baylor, along with some of the Cub brass, had a few suggestions. The critique as management saw it: He struck out too much, didn't use his speed, had become increasingly one-dimensional, and was a liability in right field. "He drives in 160, but lets in 45 on defense," went the now-famous anonymous remark from the unnamed team official.

The Sosa Affair represented an especially prominent instance—only one of many in baseball (as in life)—of both sides engaging in selective truth-telling. When they put you under oath in court you are sworn to tell "the truth, the whole truth . . ." but nobody takes an oath during meetings with the press, certainly not ballplayers or club executives. Therefore what often emerges is a process of limited truth-telling. In the matter of Sosa's value to the Cubs in the summer of 2000, not a single word presented by either side could have been argued to have been spoken in error. But neither was either side's version accurate in the sense of being a full, honest, or complete assessment: "the whole truth," as it were.

The facts are that by June 2000, Sammy Sosa had become everything both his supporters and his detractors said he was. Sammy Sosa could make a clear and compelling case for his accomplishments. One does not devalue a home run; there is no such thing as a cheap or empty one. Runs batted in are a bit more problematic—the situation dependency of their nature can compromise their value as an index of production. But even so, 158 of them (in 1998) followed by 141 of them (in 1999) is pretty tough to argue around.

Nor could there be any question of Sosa's credentials as a gamer. Between 1997 and 1999, he missed only four of Chicago's 487 games. He also started every Cub game in 1995, and would have done the same in 1996 had not a fracture sustained when he was struck by a pitch cost him that season's final six weeks.

As might be expected, Sosa's Batter Fielder Base Stealer Wins— the best single-number gauge of all-around contribution—was superb in both 1998 and 1999. Following his 5.0 rating of 1998, his BFW slid in 1999, but only to 4.4, still a substantially positive figure.

Yet to Sosa fans, there ought to be something unsettling in that 4.4 BFW rating. It came, after all, during a season in which he delivered 63 home runs, a figure at the time surpassed by only McGwire in all of baseball history. More than that, Sosa counted for a league-leading 397 total bases, adding 24 doubles, 2 triples, and 91 singles to his 63 blasts. That sounds like it ought to produce a mega-mega season, not merely a very good one.

For purposes of comparison, here are some of the other players who rated within a few fractions of a 4.4 BFW in 1999: Craig Biggio (4.3), Brian Giles (4.1), Mark McGwire (4.2), and Robin Ventura (4.5). The best mark in the National League, by the way, belonged to Houston's Jeff Bagwell (5.3).

Well, the company Sosa kept at that rating level in 1999 certainly is nothing to be ashamed of. At the same time, when a similarly productive player is Brian Giles (24 fewer homers, 26 fewer RBIs, 77 fewer bases), it is fair to suspect that there are, indeed, gaps in Sosa's all-around play, and that some of those gaps are reflected in his BFW. Which means the Cubs, too, may have been telling at least some of the truth.

SOSA AND GILES MANO A MANO

If we can identify those gaps in such an obviously talented player, they may shed light on the less readily obvious yet important aspects of talent as it contributes to what baseball is all about: winning games.

What in the heck did Brian Giles do in 1999 to help the Pittsburgh Pirates win games that Sammy Sosa didn't do for the Chicago Cubs?

First, he got on base more . . . and it was a lot more. Savvy fans today recognize that if on-base average isn't the most important single statistic, it's in the top two. Giles collected 164 base hits in 521 official at bats for a batting average of .315. Sosa had 180 hits—16 more than Giles—but he burned up 104 additional at bats in getting them; that's 88 more outs laid at Sosa's feet than at Giles's. At three outs to an inning, it's fair to say that Sammy Sosa killed a lot more innings than Brian Giles did.

Giles then compounded his on-base advantage by drawing 17 more walks than Sosa, and by doing it in that same 104 fewer plate appearances. The impact of a walk on potential run production, which goes unrecognized by many sluggers, is effectively doubled by this reality: Batters who draw a lot of walks do so by not swinging at pitches that batters who draw few walks *are being retired on*. Should it be viewed as coincidence that in 2004 Barry Bonds batted .370 while at the same time drawing more than 100 unintentional walks? Not in the slightest; they are in fact very closely related. What do you suppose is the normal batting average on pitches thrown out of the strike zone that are put into play? We've no way to truly tell, but a pretty good guess would be about 150—after all, that's why they make pitchers throw the ball over the plate. The consequence of patience thus is that not only is a player more likely to reach base, he is *at the same time* less likely to be put out. Without even swinging, the on-base average and batting average both look better, the one because of the walk, the other because of the out he didn't make.

In the cases of Giles and Sosa, we can apply the time-tested Linear Weights formula to parse the data. Sosa's 63 home runs produced 88.2 runs; Giles's 39 produced 54.6. Sammy also out-singled Giles, 91–89. At .46 of a run per single, that's an additional run in Sammy's favor, moving his edge to 34.6. But it's about the only edge Sosa has.

Giles hit 33 doubles (good for 26.4 runs) while Sosa hit 24 (good for 19.2 runs). That reduces Sosa's edge to 27.2 runs. Giles had three triples (3.06 runs), Sosa had two (2.04), costing another run.

The differences in walks and outs erode most of the rest of Sammy's advantage. At a cost of a quarter run per out, Sammy's additional 88 outs erase 22 runs. Sammy's edge over Giles in value falls to 4.2 runs. Giles's 95 walks amount to 31.4 runs; the 78 walks Sosa drew only count for about 25.7. Suddenly Giles measures as the better batsman by a factor of about a run and a half.

In days past, Sosa could have counted on his baserunning speed to boost his rating. But not lately. In 1999, he only tried to steal 15 bases, and only succeeded 7 times. That performance is a net cost to the Cubs of 2.7 runs. Giles only stole 6, but he only tried 8 times, meaning that he created 6 fewer Pirate outs on the bases. His baserunning net: just over a half a run. Add them all up, and offensively Giles actually produced about 5 runs more for Pittsburgh than Sosa did for Chicago.

Their performances in the field continue the effective standoff. Sosa (2.41) showed better range in right than Giles (2.38) did in center; that's a clear plus for Sammy. On the other hand, Giles committed only two errors, while Sosa made eight. Giles also rang up six assists, one more than Sosa. Considering that Sosa played 300 more innings in the field, that can't be overlooked.

When the Cubs filed their brief against Sosa with the ticket-buying public, they were largely taking issue with his defensive performance. Part of what bugged Cubs management can be measured, and its impact on run-prevention quantified. The quantifiable elements include put-outs, assists, errors, and range. Playing mostly in right in 1999 (he also played 195 innings in center), Sosa registered 322 put-outs, translating to that rather high range factor. It was in fact fifth best in the majors (behind Michael Tucker, Jermaine Dye, Mark Kotsay, and Tim Salmon). That also represented a significant upgrade from Sammy's far more average 2.17 range factor of 1998. In that very measurable and meaningful sense, Sammy had become a more complete "go-getter" type player.

That improvement was not reflected, however, in two other signposts of defensive acumen, assists, and errors. Sosa committed eight errors in 1999, a total exceeded among right fielders only by Vladimir Guerrero. His .976 fielding average was below the .982 average that was par for regular Major League right fielders in 1999. In fairness to Sosa, it is dangerous to indict him too harshly—as some might interpret the Cubs as trying to do—for the subpar fielding average. Playing a position where few errors are made by either the best or worst fielders, small events carry great statistical weight. If, for instance, Sosa had committed just two fewer errors (six rather than eight) his fielding average would have precisely matched the Major League average. It would be hard to argue that the occurrence of two errors over a season is enough to differentiate between an average fielder and a poor one.

His assist total is another matter. Sosa posted five assists in right field in 1999, three fewer than the Major League average for his position. But he significantly trailed many of his contemporaries. Mark Kotsay led the majors with nineteen, nearly two and a half times as many as Sosa. Jermaine Dye and Albert Belle also had more than twice as many as Sosa, while Guerrero, Magglio Ordonez, Paul O'Neill, Larry Walker, and Matt Stairs all reached double figures. Only the previous season Sosa had run up a much more representative total of fourteen. (The trend has continued since 1999, by the way. In 2003, Sammy recorded just two assists. Among regulars in right field, nobody got fewer than that. By 2004, Sosa's liabilities were viewed by many as offsetting his strengths.)

LESSONS FROM LITTLE LEAGUE

Why fuss over a few assists? If that's indeed what got under the skin of Baylor or the rest of Cubs' management, it might well justify their pique with their star outfielder. For starters, let's keep in mind what an outfielder's assist does. It is more than merely an out. In virtually every case, it both posts an out and erases a base runner, often at the plate, and it often follows on the heels of another out—a caught fly ball. An outfielder's assist is the very definition of a rally killer.

When an outfielder's assists decline, it's almost certainly for one of a handful of reasons, the majority of them bad. Granted, it is plausible that an outfielder's assists might decline for the same reason Paul LoDuca threw out nearly three times as many base stealers in 2003 as Ivan Rodriguez: Everybody thought they could run on Paul LoDuca, but hardly anybody even tried to run on Ivan Rodriguez.

But as it pertains to Sammy Sosa, a question inevitably follows: Do you think base runners are afraid to run on him? Do you think base runners view him as the new Roberto Clemente? Because unless you do, there has to be a more onerous answer.

That's the judgment Cubs' management presumably came to. Its indictment: That Sosa became a classic "scatter-arm"; he too frequently overthrew the cutoff man, allowing trailing runners to take extra bases when he had no chance to retire lead runners. That he threw wildly up or down the line, especially on throws to home plate. That he gave runners too big a head start by the simple act of taking too long to throw.

This list of grievances is interesting to baseball statisticians for one commonality. All three of the on-field "crimes" mentioned in the paragraph above are recognized to occur, yet not a single one of them can be reduced to a number. Unless they are formally scored as an error—and they routinely are not—no scoresheet, data service, or record book will maintain them under the heading of "throws offline," "runners unretired," or "poor execution."

That means we have no way of closely approximating the legitimacy of the Cubs' complaint as it pertains to the impact of Sosa's defensive deficiencies on Cub fortunes. Yet every one of his presumed flaws leads to runs being scored. Since these results often occur on plays at the plate, the damage can in fact be instantaneous.

In the absence of hard data, let's play a few "what-if" games. What impact might Sammy Sosa have on run production if he were a more polished player in these impossible-to-quantify ways? One of his deficiencies—it's a common one at the Major League level—is simply that he catches the ball with one hand. Since their introduction to Little League, fielders are taught to "use two hands," but that's generally on the rationale that they'll drop it if they do otherwise. The admonition falls by the wayside somewhere around the American Legion level, and by the big leagues few managers would have the nerve to order outfielders to use two hands to catch the ball.

Yet there's a perfectly valid reason, one which has nothing at all to do with the likelihood that a fly ball would otherwise be dropped, for even the most reliable of Major League outfielders to use two hands as a matter of routine.

How many times in the course of a ball game does a "bang-bang" play occur at a base? That's a play in which the ball and the base runner arrive at virtually the same time, and the umpire's call could be either safe or out. The result is determined by literal fractions of a second.

Here's the follow-up question: When Sammy Sosa, or any other outfielder, catches a fly ball with one hand, how many tenths of a second does he waste getting his ungloved hand up from his side and into position to remove the ball from his glove in preparation for a throw? Five tenths? Three? Let's say it takes Sosa an extra three-tenths of a second, once he catches the ball, to position his throwing hand, which until that moment has been resting languidly at some locale other than adjacent to his mitt. How many bang-bang plays do you suppose occur during the course of a season in which the result is decided by a matter of three-tenths of a second?

Well, even the slowest base runner can cover the ninety-foot distance between bases in about five seconds, a pace that translates to eighteen feet per second, or about five and a half feet in three-tenths of a second. So the question really is: How many tag plays at a base are decided by a distance of five and a half feet or less? Virtually all of them; such a play probably comes up multiple times a week for every Major League team. So let's shorten the time: Let's say Sosa can shift his throwing arm from at rest into position to grip the ball in one-tenth of a second; that still translates to nearly a two-foot edge to the base runner, more if he has any speed at all. How frequently is a play at a base decided by two feet? Once again, while we don't have numbers, instinctively we'd say it happens on many plays involving a sliding runner.

That lapse in positioning his throwing arm to make a throw—not the prospect that he might need it near his glove to prevent dropping the ball—is part of the reason Cubs' management instinctively landed on Sosa for defensive deficiencies. (It's also the real reason why all outfielders—not just Little Leaguers—ought to make it a lifetime habit to catch the ball with two hands with runners on base.)

THE PERFECT SAMMY

Let's say we created the perfect Sammy Sosa . . . what difference would it make? We've just described a circumstance related to arm positioning for a throw that probably comes up several times in Sosa's week, several chances to improve his prospects for retiring a runner on the bases. But there are many variables in throwing a ball, and even a well-positioned Sammy isn't going to make a perfect throw every time. So let's say—it seems a minimalist argument—that Sammy's revitalized arm positioning technique merely results in retiring one additional base runner at home plate every two weeks. What difference would that make to the Cubs' fortunes?

Over the course of a twenty-six-week season, it would add 13 assists to Sosa's total, and he would instantly soar to the very top of the Major League charts for right fielders. Let's say such a play occurred with a runner on third base and none out. According to Pete Palmer's base-out situation, the beginning run potential in that circumstance is 1.277; that is, the offensive team could expect to score on average

1.277 runs. Once the ball is hit, there are three possible outcomes. Here is how the run potential is affected by each possible outcome:

1. The runner tags. Using his normal form, Sammy makes his usual throw and the runner scores from third. With one out and nobody on, the offensive team's run potential decreases to .249. However, since a run already has scored, the inning's true run potential is 1.249.
2. The runner tags. Using his revised and quickened form, Sammy pegs the runner out. Now instead of a runner at third and none out, there is nobody on and two out. Sammy's arm has reduced the inning's run potential from 1.277 to 0.095, less than a tenth of a run per inning. That's a swing of more than a full run.
3. The runner tags but, respecting Sammy's newly won reputation as a gun, doesn't try to score. The offense still has a runner at third, but this time with one out. Its run production potential declines from 1.277 to .897 runs. Without even making a throw, Sammy has crimped the other guy's offense by about four-tenths of a run.

In other words, if Sammy's revised arm positioning resulted in the erasure of thirteen runners from the bases over the course of a season, it could reduce opposition run production by a projected 15.4 runs. Those numbers change depending on the number of outs in the inning. If, for instance, Sosa makes his play on a fly ball with one out instead of none, a runner thrown out at home attempting to score reduces his team's expected run production for the inning to zero—because the play ends the inning. But as a general guidepost, a swing of 15 runs would not be out of line for such a change in performance. And even in these days of high-octane offense, a swing of 15 runs translates to an improvement of a game or two in the standings. That's a big reward for simply raising your hand when you're told to.

Sammy Sosa commits other unmeasurable transgressions—so do all outfielders. The most common involves overthrowing the cutoff man. It's a macho thing, don't you know? "I don't need no stinking help throwing this guy out." But even great outfielders are taught to hit the cutoff man for three reasons, all of them valid:

1. The cutoff man can redirect a throw that is in time, but flying off-line.
2. The cutoff man can intercept a throw that will be late, and do so in time to retire some other base runner or at the least prevent that base runner from attempting to take the extra base.
3. Even if the cutoff man doesn't touch the throw, the mere possibility of his cutting off the throw may deter adventurous trailing runners.

The value of the first reason is an extension of our earlier point. It translates to additional runners retired at home or third. Instead of five assists our real-life Sammy recorded in 1999, a perfect Sammy employing good positioning technique and hitting the cutoff man might (gunning out one additional runner every two weeks) throw out eighteen runners, or possibly more.

The second and third points translate to reducing the odds of other runners scoring. Let's say Sammy always hit the cutoff man. We have no way of measuring the impact such a perfect Sammy would have on defense, but let's say such a perfect Sammy erased from the bases one runner trying to advance from first to second every other week, and kept one additional runner per week from attempting to advance. If this always occurred in a one-out situation, and employing Palmer's base-out chart, the impact on run production would be as follows:

1. The run production potential of a runner at first with one out, the situational starting point, is .478. If one such runner were thrown out every other week (thirteen occasions over the course of a season), thus changing the situation to none on and two out (.095 run production potential), the reduction in offense would project to 5 runs.

2. If one such runner were prevented from advancing each week, the situation would be changed from runner on first, one out, to runner on first, two out. The run production potential of a runner on first, two out, is .209 runs. Occurring 26 times, such an event would decrease projected offense by about 7 additional runs.

In other words, allowing those two circumstances only, our perfect Sammy would decrease the other guy's run production potential by an additional 12 runs. Along with the projected 15 runs he's begun to erase at the plate, Sammy now crimps the other guy's offense by an additional 27 runs. That's a three-game improvement in the standings. Sammy's BFW, by the way, would climb from 4.4 to about 7.3, giving him a legitimate claim to the 1999 Most Valuable Player Award.

And that improvement would occur at the mere price of catching the ball with two hands and hitting the cutoff man. So when Don Baylor and the Cubs argued—against all Sammy's home runs and against all his RBIs—that he let in too many runs by sloppy defensive play, their case was not without merit.

Much of what has preceded in this chapter falls quite firmly within the realm of raw speculation. The fact is that while we can calculate the value of a strikeout and a walk, we cannot assert with finality how many would-have-been walks end up as strikeouts. Too, while we can measure the theoretical value of a poor throw, just as we can measure the value of a home run, we can't translate that theory into practice because we can count only the home runs, not the poor throws. Doing the latter would require making a judgment that a throw that did not retire a runner *would have* retired the runner had it been executed with greater propriety and precision. That isn't done. Keep in mind that we are not talking about errors here, at least not as baseball recognizes errors; we are, instead, talking of mistakes.

The limitation of much of statistical analysis—including much of what follows in this book—is that it is necessarily founded on that which *can be* measured. It must inevitably exclude from consideration that which cannot be measured but which exists notwithstanding. When Sammy Sosa argues that he is a great ballplayer, his defense consists largely of that which can be measured and quantified. When the Cubs argue against his case, their defense is more esoteric and less substantive. That is not to say it is either more or less true.

Statistics can aid us in sorting out selective truth-telling from the opposite. We ought to pursue that sorting process—and we will in the pages of this book. But our pursuit remains limited by the constraints of our knowledge. Our search for the perfect statistic, like the Cubs' search for the perfect Sammy, is not yet fulfilled.

1.1 *A Diversion into Win Shares and Loss Shares*

In the field of assessing player performance, the big recent development was the unveiling of Bill James's Win Shares formula. Bill got a full book out of it in 2002, and his seasonal *Handbook*s contain the Win Shares ratings for players based on subsequent seasons.

There is no need to go into the theory or substance of Win Shares in detail in this space; Bill has done so with his characteristic thoroughness and elan in *Win Shares* itself. Because it is one of the few efforts extant to try to synopsize the sum total of a player's contribution in a single number—a sort of Grand Unified Theory—Win Shares is worth noting. Because Bill James is the brain behind it, Win Shares is worth taking very seriously. But Win Shares should be analyzed warts and all. To date—particularly in the reviews that followed the theory's initial publication—there was far more paean than pan. Since we are on the prowl for ways to assess player performance, and since Win Shares is the vogue new tool, Win Shares deserves a more objective review.

That review starts with the underlying premise, which Bill himself states (on page 347 of his 2004 *Handbook*) as follows:

> The Win Shares credited to the players on a team always total up to exactly three times the team's win total. . . . If a team wins 80 games, the players on the team will be credited with 240 Win Shares, always and without exception. Nothing—not even a rounding error—is allowed to disrupt this relationship.

As a general rule of life, it's a good idea to beware of absolutes, and this is one of those moments. So the first critique of Win Shares as a tool for assessing overall player performance is this: It is based on a fixed and unyielding artificial stricture. For Bill, who has contributed so much to the statistical and mathematical contribution of baseball (and, by extension, beyond baseball), that is a shockingly non-mathematical constraint to insist upon.

There is no reason why one should be able to force any valid assessment of relative player performance out of such a stricture. If a team wins 80 games, why does it follow that 240 points of responsibility ought to be assessed, much less subdivided? Why not 238, 239, 243, or 300? If one team wins 80 games and another wins 79, why—in a mathematically valid system—should the first team's players get three more Win Shares than the second team's players? Bill's answer is the triumph of functionality over science: Because it works out, that's why.

Well, there's certainly something to be said for things working. You probably won't know the answer to this one, but just for fun take a guess: What's the standard deviation for wins by a team in a season after all the measurable skill factors are considered? In other words, how many games are decided essentially by luck? The answer is plus or minus 6.35 games. That means that if one team won 80 games, the only thing you can really, truly say about the skill levels of the players involved on that team—expressed mathematically—is that those skill levels should have resulted in between 73.65 and 86.35 victories.

So even if you buy Bill's premise of three Win Shares per team, the most you can say mathematically is that the team's players should receive somewhere between 220.95 and 259.05 Win Shares . . . not precisely, eternally, and unbendingly 240.

There is a second basic flaw to the underlying logic of Win Shares, namely its presumption that all games are won. This is manifestly and obviously not so. At a statistical level, a team that wins 80 games also loses 82 games. Shouldn't we have Loss Shares? I suspect that Bill's initial response would be to note that the outcomes of those games are accounted for in some other team's Win Shares, as of course they are. But that is based on another instinctively bad presumption, namely that the outcomes of games are determined by the positive actions of the winning team as opposed to the negative actions of the losing team.

In the long ago of baseball, this was a commonly held notion. We can see it in the evolution of record-keeping. In baseball's Great Big Book of Everything, you can find records of stolen bases dating in an unbroken chain all the way back to 1886. Harry Stovey of Philadelphia's American Association team led the majors that year with 68 swipes. How many times did they nail old Harry back in the summer of '86? Excellent question; if you find out, let us know because although baseball started counting successful steals in 1886, it didn't start counting unsuccessful ones until 1914, twenty-eight years later. The point is, though, that it did eventually start because it dawned on somebody that counting successes only told half the story.

No one can say precisely how often game outcomes are determined by some incompetence, either of strategy, tactic, or execution. But instinctively (this may come from being a Cub fan), I'd say it happens fairly often, and maybe routinely. That's what "don't beat yourself" is all about. In Bill's Win Shares system, however, incompetence does not exist, because literally every player who is rated gets a positive rating. This takes place, in turn, out of some abhorrence Bill has developed for the concept of zero as an average. He says so in his book.

> The fatal error in the method of measuring players as better or worse than .500 is that it forces one into the assumption that value consists in being better than average. That is NOT what constitutes value. What constitutes value in baseball is being good enough to play at this level. What constitutes value is being good enough to help the team win some games.

Bill goes on at some length on this subject—he's been known to do that—and when one extracts a single paragraph from such an epistle, the inevitable hazard is of quoting out of context. I hope that's not too greatly the case here, but in any event you would neither be harmed nor bored by reviewing Bill's full argument as outlined in *Win Shares*. When you do so, you will still have to confront the reality that—if Win Shares considers malperformance at all—it does so only in the most flawed way possible.

There are scads of ways to illustrate the problem, one of which is to take two players at the same position on the same team. Let's take Jeff Cirillo and Willie Bloomquist of the 2003 Mariners. Cirillo was the third baseman at season's start, but he slumped out of the gate and never did get on track. Eventually, the Mariners, struggling to keep pace with the A's in the divisional race and with the Red Sox in the wild card race, benched Cirillo. Down the stretch they turned to Bloomquist, who got in 37 games at the position. Just looking at their lines, you'd say it was an improvement, although unfortunately for the Mariners not a decisive one in terms of the pennant race. Cirillo had batted .204, Bloomquist hit .250. In about 215 trips to the plate—65 fewer than Cirillo—he posted slugging and on-base averages that were both also significantly higher than the man he replaced. Cirillo was the better fielder, although his .978 percentage (very good) and 2.33 range factor (bad) merited a mixed critique.

In sum we have two players, one playing poorly and the other so-so, the key difference being that the fellow who played poorly was on the field more. How should those players be rated?

Since he was worse over a longer period of time, there is no good reason why Cirillo should rate on a par with Bloomquist. Yet because it considers only positive accomplishments—of which an important one could essentially be described as hanging around—Win Shares rates Cirillo and Bloomquist dead even. Both get three Win Shares in the James system. Given his part-time status, it would indeed be surprising had Bloomquist gotten more than three Win Shares. Even a really good occasional player would not get the opportunity to move very far up the Win Shares hierarchy.

When I think of really good part-time players, I think of Manny Mota, the great Dodger pinch hitter from the 1970s. In 1977, Mota batted .395 for the Dodgers, almost entirely while coming off the bench in key pinch-hitting situations. He only played one game in the field, got fewer than 50 plate appearances, but delivered 15 pinch hits and posted an OPS above 1.000. How many Win Shares did Manny Mota get in 1977? Two, that's how many. Do you know who else on the 1977 Dodgers got two Win Shares? Lance Rautzhen did. Rautzhen was a rookie fill-in pitcher who made 25 appearances out of the bullpen with a 4.29 ERA that was about a third of a point above the league average. In other words, relatively speaking he was pretty bad. Do you know who else got two Win Shares on that 1977 team? Glenn Burke did. A utility outfielder, he only hit .254, but he batted nearly four times as often as Mota so he had a lot more chances to pile up the Win Shares. Do you know who got more Win Shares than Manny Mota? John Hale did (he got three). Another utility outfielder, he only batted .241, but again he racked up substantially more plate appearances. Take a look at the stat lines for 1977 and tell me who was more valuable to the Dodgers: Manny Mota, Lance Rautzhen, Glenn Burke, or John Hale? Win Shares picks Hale, largely because Tommy Lasorda played him more.

Because they recognize the importance of malperformance in assessing player value, zero-based systems do not succumb to these flaws. Palmer's BFW/PW system, for example, determines that while Bloomquist (−1.3) was hardly an asset to the 2003 Mariners, he was significantly less of a liability than Cirillo (−2.7). BFW/PW, which gives no particular credit to hanging around, rates Mota's 1977 season at +0.5, a net contribution of a half game to the Dodger cause. Rautzhen, by comparison, receives a −0.2 PW. And for burning up far more at bats than Mota while producing far less, Hale and Burke both get what they deserve: a −2.0 BFW in Hale's case and −2.5 in Burke's.

So in Win Shares we have a system that uses as its foundation a sweeping and statistically unsupportable generalization about how to ration value, that argues against the significance of zero, and that recognizes Win Shares but not Loss Shares.

Which is why Palmer's system, possessing none of these flaws, is the one I prefer to rely upon in this book.

2

THE MOST UNDERAPPRECIATED WORDS IN BASEBALL

"In pitching success, 0–2 works better than 2–0."

Jim Kaat, former pitcher and current telecaster, offered that observation in explaining Sydney Ponson's mastery of the Yankees during Baltimore's 7–0 victory on September 4, 2004. It is one of the few assertions by on-air baseball personalities that does not deserve to be challenged outright. But it does deserve to be expanded upon, for it tells only a small part of the story. As related to the count, the question isn't whether 0–2 works better than 2–0, but how much better?

And the most amazing part about the answer is that nobody's ever really tried to provide it.

It's not as if the topic is obscure. In the situational aspects of pitching and hitting, there are only a couple of essentials. One is who's doing the pitching or hitting? In 2004, the typical Major League hitter batted about .267. But the typical hitter was only rarely at the plate. Sometimes Ichiro stepped in for the Mariners; at other moments the guy with the stick was Willie Bloomquist. There is little need to reexamine the profundity of this variable, for baseball long ago developed a yardstick. It is called batting average. (The corollary—whether the pitcher is Pedro Martinez or Brian Anderson—is equally central.)

The second variable was enunciated loudly and often by Ted Williams, who credited Rogers Hornsby for passing it to him. That's two prominent endorsements for the wisdom of "getting a good pitch to hit." By that, Williams meant swinging at strikes . . . not all strikes, but strikes he could do something with. Unlike the first differential, baseball's never done anything to measure this one, because the task is impossible. After all, who's to say whether a pitch was "a good one to hit?" The batter? Lots of batters swing at "bad" pitches. Ever seen Vladimir Guerrero? The umpire? No again. Even if umpires' judgment in such matters is exemplary, as Williams often noted, not every strike is the kind you want to go after. Questrec? Let's ask Curt Schilling about using that tool. In the end, "getting a good pitch" is one of those subjective considerations that we recognize instinctively to be true, but whose measurement frustrates our full comprehension of the differences between success and failure.

That leaves us with a final variable, the count. It is central to the question of situational batting success because the count is the leverage the batter and pitcher wield against one another in the fight for dominance of the plate. As we will momentarily show, that leverage is profound. That's why no pitcher should ever take the mound, no batter should ever stride to the plate, without a firm grasp of the material to follow. And there is one more salient preface to our discussion about the count: As opposed to the other essential variables of situational hitting, we can learn about it because the count is objective.

How can we deconstruct the count? By watching baseball.

The methodology of such a study is as simple as it is meaningful. You need the following: an armchair, a pen and pad of paper, and access to ball games. Lots of them, the more the better. For this study, I collected data on five thousand batter-pitcher confrontations during the 2004 season. In each case, I asked three basic questions: 1. Was the first pitch a ball or a strike? 2. What was the count when the "action pitch" was delivered? ("Action pitch" is defined as the pitch on which the ball was either hit into play, or the batter was struck out, walked, or hit.) 3. Did the batter reach base, how, and how many bases?

Then I harvested and categorized the data according to the field of potential ball and strike counts, of which there are a dozen. Broadly speaking, those dozen can be subgrouped as "pitcher ahead in the count" (0–1, 0–2, 1–2); "batter ahead in the count" (1–0, 2–0, 2–1, 3–0, 3–1); and "even" (first pitch, 1–1, 2–2, 3–2).

The sample data should—and happily does—conform pretty closely to the typical Major League performance. For purposes of validation of the broad conclusions, here's the relevant comparison:

2004	Batting Avg.	On Base Avg.	Slugging Avg.
Actual	.267	.332	.429
Study (5,000 PAs)	.267	.336	.433

STEE-RIKE ONE!

One of the governing assumptions of the ball and strike count is the primacy of the first pitch in determining the overall success or failure of the at-bat. That assumption turns out to be only "somewhat true." As a broad rule, and allowing for obvious variations depending on the pitcher, about six of every ten pitches in a Major League game are strikes, either because the umpire deems them to be so or because the batter swings at them. For the 60 percent of occasions when the first pitch was a strike, the batting average in our sample was .262. That's 5 points below the industry-wide standard, a 2 percent reduction in performance I'd classify as marginally worth noting, but not worth losing sleep over.

When the first pitch was a ball, the group batting average rose to .274, a 7 point (2.55 percent) performance increase. Personally, I'd rather hit .274 than .267, but either way if I'm in the box I've got what could reasonably be characterized as a fighting chance. The same is true for slugging average, by the way. If the first pitch is a strike, the group slugging average falls to .421, 8 points (2 percent) below the norm. If the first pitch is a ball, slugging performance rises to .455, 26 points (6 percent) above the norm. As with batting average, I'd rather be 6 percent better than normal than 2 percent worse, but neither is the difference between being in the majors and being in the minors.

The one area where the fate of the at-bat can be said to be

strongly influenced by the first pitch is on-base average. This should not come as a surprise, walks being the major add-on in the formula. When the first pitch is a strike, the group on-base average in our sample was .296, 36 points (11 percent) lower than the MLB norm. By contrast, when the first pitch was a ball, on-base average rose to .395, a nifty 63 points (19 percent) above MLB norms. We have, to a degree, just discovered the obvious: that you're less likely to walk a batter if the first pitch is a strike than if it's a ball. At the same time, in contrast with all the other first-pitch data, the difference between reaching base 30 percent of the time and reaching base 40 percent of the time *is* profound. In our study, pitchers throwing ball one eventually issued 243 percent as many bases on balls (or hit batsmen) as those whose first pitches were strikes, and that's in spite of the fact (noted earlier) that pitchers were half again as likely to throw strike 1 as ball 1.

THE MOST UNDER-APPRECIATED WORDS IN BASEBALL: STEE-RIKE 2!

It is easier for the pitcher than the batter to use the count to his advantage for the simple reason that the pitcher controls (or is supposed to control) where the ball goes. To the extent his skill permits doing so, the pitcher can decide whether to throw a pitch in the strike zone, and—sometimes more importantly—whether to throw a pitch outside the strike zone at a time when the batter is influenced to hack at it. We can't precisely quantify the difference between a great pitcher and a run-of-the-mill one at this level. But it probably equates in a substantial degree to the ability first to put himself in a position to force batters to swing at bad pitches, and then to throw those bad pitches. Most of that logically flows from getting ahead in the count.

We would assume that when the pitcher is ahead in the count, favorable (for him) results follow. In some cases, the advantage is probably even larger than we would think. In our sample, the batting average when "action" occurred with the pitcher ahead in the count was only .216; that's about 51 points (19 percent) worse than the

sample average for all situations. Slugging average was reduced by 105
points (24 percent), from .433 for all situations in the sample to .328
when the pitcher was ahead.

The striking (and I think unexpected) thing about the sample
data is that this pitcher advantage is not uniform; in fact, it varies dramatically depending on the extent to which the pitcher is "ahead."
And in 1 of the 3 instances in which a pitcher can be ahead, he was,
for reasons we can only speculate upon, actually at a significant disadvantage.

The baseball shibboleth is that the most important pitch in the
game is "strike 1." Let's slow that talk down a bit. In the 2004 sample,
batters who did something when the count against them was 0–1 rang
up a .341 batting average with a .523 slugging average. That is not a
typographical error. At 0–1, batters actually produce a 74 point (28
percent) improvement in batting average from the overall sample with
a 21 percent improvement in power.

How can this be?

I don't know, at least not in the sense of being to empirically improve any particular theory. But I think the data encourages a little
speculation. First and most importantly, the collected wisdom of more
than 125 years has tended to over-emphasize the importance of strike
1, at least as it relates to hitting safely. We noted earlier that in all situations when the first pitch is a strike, batting average only declines by
about 5 percentage points . . . hardly a ride off a cliff. So a batter with
a first strike against him probably starts from a less disadvantageous
position than we would assume. Aggressiveness may have something
to do with it. In an 0–1 hole, a batter's tendency may be not to worsen
his circumstance by letting the count go to 0–2 (more on that in a moment). Maybe, given one pitch to study the pitcher's stuff, batters are
putting that information to good use. Perhaps pitchers, emboldened
by having gotten ahead, become careless and groove more pitches.
That leads to what seems to me to be the most likely explanation: that
with a one strike count pitchers are simply giving batters pitches they
can hit . . . and batters are doing so. By this explanation, rules that will

govern subsequent pitch counts—like getting hitters to swing at pitches that are off the plate—haven't yet kicked in.

It's possible that a more detailed study of strike 1 might yield some clarification of the degree to which each of these theories plays a role in the fact that batters are actually better with one strike against them than they are overall. This study isn't sure why that should be so. But it is so. And it leads to the first profound lesson of the count. At 0–1, pitchers need to be careful, for there is more danger ahead than they realize. Batters, by contrast, should repeat this mantra: I am not in trouble, I am not in trouble, I am not in trouble.

The most important pitch in baseball is not, as it turns out, strike 1. It is in fact strike 2.

While batters mysteriously operate at an advantage with one strike against them, that advantage vaporizes if the count shifts to 0–2. We would of course assume 0–2 to be a very bad circumstance for hitters, but I think a lot of good baseball minds would be surprised to see how correct the assumption is. With two strikes and no balls, batting average in our sample careened to .148. That was 119 percentage points (45 percent) lower than the sample average for all counts. Slugging average declined to .250. By the act of declaring the count to be 0–2 instead of 0–1, umpires in our sample decreased the batter's prospects of getting a hit by 193 points (57 percent), with changes of a similar scale in slugging average. The sample encompassed 427 instances where something "happened" with an 0–2 count; in more than half of those instances, that "something" was a punch-out. By contrast, the sample recorded only 62 0–2 hits, only 26 of them for extra bases.

Explaining this swing, while again speculative, seems a far less profound task. At 0–2, batters must be going out of the strike zone in order to protect themselves and pitchers are letting them. What do you suppose is the batting average of a typical player when he swings at a low-outside slider? I don't know either. But if you forced me to write down a figure, I'd write down something around .150; in other words, what turns out to be the normal batting performance with an 0–2 count.

CALL ME CRAZY . . .

You know what I might do if I managed a big league team and I knew that batters in an 0–2 hole typically hit .150? I might put the take sign on, that's what I might do. Crazy? Not necessarily. At a point where the odds are seven-to-one that my batter will be retired, and fifty-fifty that it will happen without him making contact, an 0–2 take sign could be construed as perversely sensible. Together with the likelihood that pitchers holding an 0–2 count are probably going to go off the plate, I might actually succeed in my goal, which is to maneuver my hitter into a more favorable pitch count.

A reminder is again in order that this needs to be read for what it is, namely a broad-scale assertion. To say that Major League hitters facing an 0–2 count bat .148 does not mean that all Major League hitters in an 0–2 hole bat .148. Maybe Ichiro bats .248 with two strikes on him, maybe even .348. The sample did not attempt individual case studies. So yes, an 0–2 take sign might be wiser with less-disciplined hitters than with guys who've demonstrated a knowledge of the strike zone. Think any manager would have the guts to try it?

I probably wouldn't either. If the batter was called out, he'd be coming back to the dugout looking for me . . . and he'd have a bat in his hand.

The second downside to an 0–2 take sign is its "upside," which is a 1–2 count. Compared to 0–2, batting performance does improve at 1–2, but hardly by leaps and bounds. In a 1–2 situation, Major League hitters carry a .170 batting average. That is 15 percent better than when they're hitting 0–2, but it's still 37 percent below league-wide averages. At 1–2, the slugging average is .239, about 45 percent below the sample average for all situations.

WHY MORE BATTERS DON'T HIT .350

You may find this odd (I do) but—excepting prospects for an eventual base on balls—it appears to make little difference to the outcome of an at bat whether the first pitch is a ball or a strike. It was noted earlier that when "action" occurs with a one-strike count, batters hit .341. At 1–0, the average is about the same, .348. This should not be read as a blanket dismissal of the importance of being at one ball and no strikes as opposed to no balls and one strike. Walks are not unimportant, the prospect of getting one soars at 1–0 as opposed to 0–1. More critically to an aggressive hitter, at one ball and no strikes you're more than one pitch away from being up against two strikes, and we've already looked at the problems that situation presents. Power is another consideration. The slugging average of Major League hitters at one ball and no strikes is .649, 216 points higher than the MLB overall average and 126 points higher than the slugging average at one strike and no balls.

Once a batter is ahead in the count, the sample puts the average batting average at .350 with an accompanying .600 slugging average. Whereas only three counts plainly favor the pitcher, five—1–0, 2–0, 2–1, 3–0, 3–1—plainly favor the hitter. Why, then, is the average batting average .270 instead of closer to .370?

The simple reason is that far fewer things happen when the batter is ahead in the count than when the pitcher is ahead. One of the reasons for this seeming disparity has already been noted: About 60 percent of pitches are strikes. That fact alone dictates that the count will favor the pitcher more often than the hitter. But there's probably more to it than that. Of the 5,000 batter-pitcher matchups in our sample, only about one-fifth ended with the batter ahead in the count. Since we are dealing here with a sample of the season rather than the entire season, our data is subject to "margin of error." If we ran the numbers for literally every at bat of the 2004 campaign, the data might come out a bit differently. But the differences likely would not be profound. So we may wish to look for other factors.

As we do so, one other note should be considered: the shortfall of "events" with the batter ahead in the count does not occur evenly across the spectrum of possibilities. Instead it is concentrated in certain counts. In fact, the more favorable the count is to the batter, the fewer times an at bat is settled. With a count of 1–0, for example, there is really no shortfall of occurrences at all. Based merely on what we know about the occurrence of balls and strikes, we could expect "action" (either a ball hit into play or a hit batter) about 350 times for every 5,000 plate appearances. In fact, "action" occurred 348 times at 1–0.

That changed dramatically when the count moved to the most favorable iterations for a batter, 2–0, 2–1, 3–0, or 3–1. At 2–0, "action" occurred just 136 times in 5,000 cases. Just 2.1 percent of the study's outcomes occurred with a count of 3–0.

When the number of events doesn't meet our standards or expectations, we may wish to resort to "bundling" data in an effort to build the sample size to a more acceptable number. So rather than attempt to estimate performances at the individual counts, we'll instead assess performance when the batter is "significantly ahead in the count," by which we mean any situation better than 1–0.

Our bundled data indicates that batters who are "significantly" ahead in the count can expect to hit about .352 with a .564 slugging average.

A second concern is to try to figure out what forces are skewing those frequencies. In other words, why are so few at bats settled at a 3–0 count? Aside from the relative infrequency of balls, I can think of three possibilities. But all of them require speculation. Even worse, two of the three are contradictory.

One possible reason is that, when they are ahead in the count, batters become more aggressive, swinging (and missing) at pitches they really should have laid off. By transforming 2–0 and 3–0 counts to 2–1 and 3–1 counts, this might account for the shortage.

A second explanation, the opposite of the first, is that batters in very good hitting counts might become too selective. The 3–0 count is the pristine exhibit on behalf of this argument. There is a consensus in baseball that the 3–0 take sign has gone the way of flannel, but the study yields pretty fair evidence that this either is not so or at least not effectively so. Of the mere 108 "events" at 3–0, only thirteen involved a ball being hit into play; all the rest were walks or hit batters. Thirteen 3–0 contacts in 5,000 pitcher-batter confrontations does not exactly suggest an onslaught of wild swinging.

These two explanations, of course, are not mutually exclusive; they both could be true, the first for some batters and the second for others. But it would take a more detailed study to ascertain the degree to which either is valid. And since such a study would require measurement of the subjective—whether the batter swung at a pitch out of the strike zone—I'm not personally persuaded that one could be fairly constructed.

The third factor is more insidious, and since I can't prove it, you could argue that I shouldn't bring it up. Umpires could have something to do with the shortage of favorable counts for batters. The theory would be that some umpires—not all of them—may be reticent to decide at bats themselves, causing them to adopt a wider strike zone at, for example, 3–0. (In other words, to give the "automatic" strike.) Again, you can't count "bad" called strikes any more than you can count "bad" swings. But if I'm right then some umpires—in their desire to defer the outcome of the at bat to the batter or pitcher—may be party to a reduction in the number of 3–0 or 3–1 events. This, concurrently, would lead to an increase in the instance of 3–2 events and, as we'll soon see, 3–2 events are in fact among the most common.

The other striking thing about the performance of batters who were "significantly ahead" in the count is that they did not do any better than batters in other counts we've already identified as being advantageous, namely 0–1 and 1–0. The collective batting average of hitters who made fair contact while significantly ahead in the count (2–0 or better) was .352. In one sense, Everyman became Ichiro. But that .352 average was just 11 points better than the performance at 0–1, and it is just 4 points better than at 1–0.

Given the decided advantage produced for a batter who is ahead in the count, why don't more hitters bat .350? Because they're too timid. Because they're too aggressive. Because the umpires don't let them. Or possibly all of the above. Is that sufficiently clear?

WHEN EVEN IS NOT EVEN

For purposes of this exercise, I considered four counts to favor neither the batter nor pitcher. Those four are 0–0 (first pitch), 1–1, 2–2, and 3–2. Collectively, they do in fact appear to favor neither. The batting average of the typical major leaguer in these counts is .274, very close to our .267 average for the sample. The .446 slugging average for this segment of the sample also comes relatively close to matching the sample and MLB norms.

Since these four counts amount to exactly one-third of the possible count situations, since we know that pitchers throw strikes about 60 percent of the time, and since these counts are definitionally balanced between balls and strikes, we could expect them to occur slightly more than one-third of the time. In other words, in a sample of 5,000 they'd comprise a few more than 1,667 events. In our survey, the actual figure was much higher—2,311 events, or 46 percent of the whole. That's another unprovable inference that there is a deferential streak to umpires; some of whom may be more likely to widen the zone when the batter is ahead in the count or narrow it when the pitcher is ahead.

The more demonstrable and tangible aspect of even counts is that while they collectively mirror Major League results, this is not at all true of the individual counts themselves. Remember the rule we enunciated earlier in the chapter: that the most important pitch isn't strike 1, but strike 2? We are about to get back to it in a big way.

At even counts with fewer than two strikes, the advantage is solidly with the batter. When the batter puts the first pitch in play, he hits a very rewarding .354 with a .571 slugging average. In a 1–1 count, the average falls, but only to .335. The slugging average, meanwhile, rises to .573.

But once that second strike crosses the plate, things change. At two strikes and two balls, batters hit .203, improving only to .224 at three balls and two strikes. In our sample, slugging fell from .573 at a 1–1 count all the way to .303 at 2–2, and rebounded only to .379 at 3–2.

The calamitous consequences for the batter at the knell of strike 2 can be portrayed in either of two ways. First, let's look at a ranking of the favorability of all possible pitch counts based on the sample batting average in each count. (For purposes of this exercise, 2–0, 2–1, 3–0, and 3–1 are bundled as "Better than 1–0.")

Count	Batting average
0–0	.354
Better than 1–0	.352
1–0	.348
0–1	.341
1–1	.335
Sample/MLB average	.267
3–2	.224
2–2	.203
1–2	.170
0–2	.148

Literally every possible pitch count with fewer than two strikes results in a batting average significantly above the sample (and MLB) average. Literally every pitch count involving two strikes results in a batting average significantly below the sample (and MLB) average. Not a single one of the pitch counts could be said to produce even an approximately "average" performance.

We can see the same thing through a slightly different lens by "bundling" all pitch counts into two classifications: "fewer than two strikes" and "two strikes." In the four counts involving two strikes (comprising 49 percent of all sample events), the collective batting average was .186 with an accompanying .289 slugging average. In the eight other counts (51 percent of the sample), the collective batting average was .346 with a .572 slugging average.

PATIENCE IS ONLY A LIMITED VIRTUE

Staring at this study, I am drawn to one conclusion . . . the role of aggressiveness in offensive success. That would not have been my anticipation going in to it. Like, I think, a lot of people, I would have counseled patience at the plate. Wait the pitcher out, let him get himself into trouble, take your time, don't be in a hurry to make an out.

But as the discussion relates to batting or slugging average, the evidence argues to the contrary. Based on the data, the most hittable pitches are very likely to be among the first two a batter sees.

Batters who wait patiently, by contrast, seem to substantially diminish their prospects of getting a hit.

That conclusion comes with one strong caution. Because bases on balls can only occur in certain counts, their impact will always be distorted, either positively or negatively, in a study of this type.

Plainly walks are a significant offensive component. But the only thing the study is capable of saying about walks is that a batter's on-base average is about 100 points lower when the first pitch hits the strike zone than when it doesn't (.296 vs. .395). Beyond that, if I have given walks short shrift in this discussion, it is because I am forced by the constraints of the study to do so.

At the same time, I think it's fair to say that the study betrays a sense, based on the relatively small number of events in decidedly "hitter's counts," that batters in such counts appear to disproportionately play for walks at times when the odds might be most favorable to hitting.

The danger with doing so is that one or two called strikes could shift them into a very disadvantageous circumstance *vis a vis* the pitcher. We often hear that batters who get significantly ahead in the count are encouraged to "look in a zone"; in other words, to become more selective in what they swing at. Based on the sample data, I'd be inclined to urge that approach right out of the gate . . . to tell batters to "look in a zone" on the first two pitches, and to be very aggressive within that zone. If I had a lineup of .340 batters—a good approximation of the norm prior to strike 2—I'd want those bats in motion. I'd also want to do what I could to prevent my .186 hitter—the norm after strike 2—from spending too much time at the plate.

3

THE VOGUE ERA OF BAD SWITCH-HITTERS

In 1999, the Seattle Mariners would have increased their run production by benching Ken Griffey, Jr., against left-handed pitchers in favor of a run-of-the-mill Major League hitter.

Since Griffey was one of the game's stars in 1999, and also the Seattle franchise, that's a pretty heavy statement, and we want to be careful not to read too much into it.

It does not say the Mariners would have increased their run production *very much*—about two and a half runs over the season, actually.

It does not say the Mariners should have known that Griffey would be a relative offensive liability against lefties. Indeed, they had no way of knowing it. Although Griffey hit just .229 in 190 plate appearances against left-handers in 1999—with just 8 of his 48 home runs and a .412 slugging average that was 164 points below his overall 1999 slugging average—the numbers were, for him, an aberration. In 1998 he had batted .299 against same-side pitching with a superb .701 slugging average. He hit .270 and slugged .536 in 1997, .297 and .741 in 1996.

Nope, in 1999 Griffey had a bad year against lefties, pure and simple.

Finally, the statement does not say that the Mariners should have platooned Griffey. Defense and intimidation still count in baseball, and at the time Griffey provided plenty of both.

Nonetheless, the fact remains that the Mariners would have

scored more runs in 1999 with Joe Average playing center field against left-handers than Ken Griffey, Jr. We can ascertain this by comparing the offensive Linear Weights Griffey actually produced in 1999 with the offensive Linear Weights that would have been produced if he had kept his at bats against right-handers, but yielded his at bats against lefties to a replacement-level major leaguer. (In this instance, "replacement level" is defined as a player who would have hit 5 percent below the average performance level for the league: the kind of outfielder called up from the minor leagues all the time.)

Griffey's Actual 1999 Linear Weights	57.00
Griffey's Right-handed 1999 Linear Weights	55.43
Replacement Level Player's Linear Weights (using Griffey's 190 plate appearances)	4.31
Total	59.74
Difference	2.74

If judicious platooning can increase run production even from a player of Ken Griffey's stature, think of the possibilities.

Those possibilities have intrigued baseball theoreticians for decades. When he managed the New York Yankees to pennant after pennant between 1949 and 1960, Casey Stengel was often thought of as a genius for his use of "platooning." Here's only a partial list of his favorite pairings: Gene Woodling with Johnny Lindell in left field in 1949; Billy Johnson with Bobby Brown at third base in 1949–50; Brown with Gil McDougald at third in 1951; Irv Noren with Elston Howard in left field in 1955; Bill Skowron with Eddie Robinson or Joe Collins at first base in 1955; Collins with Skowron or Howard at first in 1956; Enos Slaughter with Howard in the outfield in 1957; Tony Kubek with McDougald at shortstop in 1957; Howard with Yogi Berra or Norm Siebern in the outfield in 1958; Jerry Lumpe with Andy Carey at third base in 1958; and Berra with Hector Lopez in the outfield in 1960.

All that on a team that won ten pennants in twelve seasons and it's little wonder platooning developed a sort of karma in the baseball world. Sounded awfully good.

In a 1960s book titled *The Thinking Man's Guide to Baseball,* Leonard Koppett gave intellectual weight to the concept of platooning. "It has been proved again and again that intelligent platooning enhances the career and the total income of players who are not solid stars, and that it helps a team win," wrote Koppett, who then proceeded to prove it. (Koppett's book was reissued in a revised and updated form by Total Sports Illustrated in 2001.)

Bill James delved more deeply into the platoon issue in a number of studies in the 1980s. His key finding was that the vast majority of players have an inherent platoon differential; that is, the ability to hit better against off-side pitching than against same-side pitching is one of the most commonplace of attributes. "It is simply a condition of the game," James wrote. "Almost every hitter and every type of hitter hits better over a period of time with than against the platoon advantage—good hitters, poor hitters, young and old, left and right, high-average hitters and power hitters."

Based on mid 1980s data, James found that the normal platoon differential was 24 points in batting average, 53 points in slugging percentage, and 34 points in on-base average.

With those kinds of differences constituting the norm, all that's required for an effective platoon is a pair of players—one right-handed and the other left-handed—who play the same position comparably and who both fall within the vast range of "decent" hitters.

For reasons we'll get into later, there are no good recent examples of the judicious use of platooning. But the 1993 Phillies provide a relatively recent case study. Under manager Jim Fregosi, the Phillies achieved a 27-game jump in the standings, soaring from last place in 1992 to the World Series, and they did so—it could be argued—in no small measure due to Fregosi's generous use of platooning. Here's what he did.

1. He alternated left-handed hitting Milt Thompson with right-handed Pete Incaviglia in left field. Thompson played in 106

games and hit .260 in 311 at bats; he was a .279 batter against right-handers. Incaviglia saw action in 96 games and hit .278 in 317 at bats. Against left-handers he hit .278, but he added 13 home runs and 42 RBIs, an average of a home run every 13 plate appearances and an RBI every four times up. Combined, they accounted for 27 home runs and 119 runs batted in, 6 more homers and 58 more RBIs than they had totaled the previous season.

2. He alternated left-handed Jim Eisenreich and right-handed Wes Chamberlain in right field. Eisenreich played in 137 games and batted 337 times, hitting .323. Against righties he was formidable with a .322 average. Chamberlain saw action in 76 games and batted .288 in 264 at bats. Against left-handers he really fattened up, a .328 average and an extra base hit every 7.5 plate appearances. Together they hit 19 home runs with 95 RBIs, 8 homers and 26 RBIs more than in 1992.

3. He often also platooned left-handed Mickey Morandini with right-handed Mariano Duncan at second base. Philadelphia faced 113 right-handed pitchers in 1993; Morandini started 84 of those games, Duncan 29. But in the 49 games against left-handers, Duncan made 32 starts, Morandini only 17. Morandini, by the way, batted .258 against right-handers (.247 overall) while Duncan hit .273. (He also hit .282 overall, which explains why he also saw time at shortstop.)

THE PLATOON COEFFICIENT

Yet despite the substantial intellectual and statistical evidence supporting the idea of platooning, Major League teams today seem to platoon at a diminishing rate compared with a decade or a generation ago. The modern Major League manager platoons at the equivalent of just under one lineup position per season, a contemporary rule of thumb being 10.15 percent of non-pitcher at bats. We may consider this figure the standard "platoon coefficient," by which we mean the frequency with which a player is sat down rather than allowed to face a pitcher who throws from the same side as the player bats. In 1999, the range of this platoon coefficient varied per team from 22.4 percent for the Arizona Diamondbacks, the most platoon-conscious club in the majors, all the way down to 3.2 percent for the Texas Rangers. The average rate in 1999 was below the five-year average, at 9.72 percent, (accurately) suggesting a downward trend. (The formula for calculating the platoon coefficient is contained in Appendix I.)

These are not the salad days of platooning. A generation ago, between 1980 and 1984, the Major League platoon coefficient was 13.26 percent; the difference is the equivalent of a spot in the batting order. In 1980, the Minnesota Twins rang up a platoon coefficient of 31 percent, meaning that the Twins routinely platooned at two and a half positions.

We can see this same trend among players as well as teams. In 1999, there were 149 Major League players who started a minimum of ten games while achieving a platoon coefficient of 15 percent or better; that is to say, they were platooned at least semiregularly. That's almost precisely five players per team. The average platoon coefficient of those 149 players was 27.7 percent. In 1980, there were 145 such players (5.6 per team . . . remember that there were four fewer teams), and their average platoon coefficient was 32 percent.

Platooning reached its zenith in the mid 1980s. In 1986, 165 players (about 6.3 per team) carried platoon coefficients of 15 percent or higher. The following season, the platoon coefficients of the parallel group of players maxed out at 34.8 percent. Under Jimy Williams, the 1987 Toronto Blue Jays practiced platooning to a fare-thee-well. At DH, Fred McGriff made 88 starts, 87 of them against right-handers, while Cecil Fielder started 49 games, all against lefties. Rance Mulliniks got 92 starts, most of them at third base and all but two against right-handers; Kelly Gruber was the regular at third. But his 83 starts included 42 of the 50 games in which the Jays faced a left-hander, just 41 of the 112 in which they were pitted against a righty. And behind the plate, right-handed hitter Charlie Moore made 35 starts, all against lefties. His platoon partner, Ernie Whitt, started 110 of the 112 games against right-handers, just three of the 50 against left-handers.

The trend began to decline after 1987. The table of numbers below are the team-by-team platoon coefficients for two groups of seasons; the first is for the 1980–84 seasons, and the second is for the 1995–99 seasons. If you sense a greater disparity within the first group of numbers, you're right. The standard deviation for that 1980–84 set is about 5.37, nearly 50 percent greater than the standard deviation for the more recent set of numbers (3.59). Translation: Managers did things differently a generation ago; today they pretty much all manage the same—and it doesn't involve platooning.

PLATOON COEFFICIENT PER TEAM

Team	1980–84	1995–99
Atlanta	8.42	7.21
Arizona		16.85
Anaheim (California)	11.44	4.67
Baltimore	17.52	6.99
Boston	13.03	6.21
Chicago Cubs	8.24	7.05
Chicago White Sox	10.78	7.13
Cincinnati	10.02	7.41
Cleveland	13.60	5.23
Colorado		10.16
Detroit	20.02	5.38
Florida		7.48
Houston	15.64	6.02
Kansas City	15.56	7.57
Los Angeles	9.34	5.17
Milwaukee	11.30	8.22
Minnesota	15.52	6.75
Montreal	9.20	3.54
New York Yankees	17.66	6.34
New York Mets	10.34	5.48

Oakland	17.38	5.61
Philadelphia	9.50	5.62
Pittsburgh	16.22	6.46
St. Louis	15.72	4.33
San Diego	13.90	6.67
San Francisco	10.76	4.77
Seattle	12.18	5.72
Tampa Bay		7.00
Texas	11.50	5.62
Toronto	19.92	6.42

In the 1980–84 period, 16 of the 26 Major League teams platooned between 6 and 14 percent of their at bats; a range that could be considered the "norm" at the time. That means 10 teams platooned outside that "normal" range, either higher or lower. By 1995–99, the "norm" had declined to between a 4 and 12 percent platoon rate, and every team except Arizona and Montreal fit within that range.

If platooning—properly done—is a good idea, why is there less of it today than in years past? There's no way of knowing with certainty, but we can hazard a couple of educated guesses.

Guess 1. In the early 1980s, the normal twenty-five-man roster was typically composed of ten pitchers, eight regulars, two reserve catchers, and four (in the DH American League) or five other players. In today's era of bullpen specialization, however, no team would think of taking on the regular season with fewer than eleven pitchers, and often twelve. That eats up one to two roster spots that might in olden days have been devoted to the second half of a platoon.

Guess 2. The decline in classical platooning has been mirrored by an increase in switch-hitting. If they are competent, switch hitters are effectively one-man platoons. In 1980, there were forty-eight switch hitters in the major leagues who started at least ten games; about 1.85 per team. In 1999, there were eighty-seven such players; nearly three per team.

A SWITCH TO SWITCH-HITTERS

So what we may be seeing is a trend toward compensating for expanded bullpens and squeezed rosters by an increased reliance on switch-hitting.

If so, the question becomes whether those switch-hitters are "effective" platoons. What are their "platoon differentials"? James asked this question of non-natural switch-hitters (those who attempted to learn the art after becoming professionals) in the 1980s, and decided they often did more damage than good. He found huge platoon differentials among the group of converts, resulting in a net diminution of run production as compared with the run production those players would have created if they had hit from their best side only.

Today we can ask the same question of all switch-hitters. For the past several seasons, there have generally been about seventy Major League players who fulfilled two conditions necessary to be included in a study that might answer this question. They were switch-hitters, and they got at least twenty-five plate appearances from each side. (The latter condition is necessary to give the data some minimum level of legitimacy.) The seventy divide fairly neatly into three groups: the good, the mixed, and the ugly.

Of the ugly, little need be said. These players tend to be subpar (using batting average as the yardstick) from both sides of the plate. They switch-hit in order to make themselves attractive in some sense to their employers.

The "good" switch-hitters are far more substantive, but equally uncontroversial. This group, generally of about two dozen players, hits above average from both sides of the plate, and in some instances, well above average. Most are regulars or soon-to-be regulars, and several rank among the game's frontline players. Bernie Williams and Chipper Jones fit this category, as do Dmitri Young and Carlos Beltran. Possibly without exception, these players would be regulars—often stars—no matter whether they switch-hit. In their cases, the attribute becomes a bonus.

The middle group is far more interesting. These are players who hit relatively well from one side of the plate, relatively weakly from the other. In 2003, this group numbered twenty-two regulars or semi-regulars such as Roberto Alomar, Coco Crisp, Josh Bard, Mark Teix-eira, and Scott Spiezio. In cases such as theirs, the price paid by the team so it can carry one switch-hitter rather than two platoon players is relevant.

Superficially, the data against these twenty-two players comes across as indictable. Swinging from their better side, they batted .291; turned around to their weaker side, they plummeted to .223. From their bad side, they homered at a rate one-third below the Major League pace. Against left-handers, Crisp batted .321; against righties, he hit .245. Bobby Kielty was a .300 hitter against lefties, but when he faced a right-hander Kielty hit just .216. Teixeira lost 52 points against right-handers; Desi Relaford lost 62.

Most of the twenty-two did far better batting right-handed against lefties than vice versa, but there were exceptions. Roberto Alo-mar hit .285 against right-handers, but a mere .189 against left-handers. Rafael Furcal fell from .306 to .247 against left-handers. Orlando Hudson, the Toronto phenom, hit .297 against right-handers. But in 100 cuts against lefties, Hudson got just 16 hits, only three of them for extra bases, and all of those being doubles. His on-base percentage, a delightful .356 when facing a right-hander, fell to .222 against left-handed pitching.

All of that makes it sound like the modern reliance on switch-hitting as a form of a one-man platoon is injuring run production. But the evidence is at best mixed. A telling statistic in gauging run pro-duction is extra base power. To measure the impact of platooning on that facet of the game, we devised a test of our twenty-two suspects from the 2003 season. First, we counted the total number of bases they produced while batting from their "weak" side. Then we com-pared that to the number of bases we projected a replacement (batting five points below the league average and at league norms for extra base hits) would have generated.

Rule of thumb: It takes about three bases to generate one run, and about nine runs to produce one victory. So a player who produces on the order of twenty-five or so bases fewer from his "weak" side than a generic replacement could be expected to produce is probably costing his team a game in the standings. Perhaps surprisingly, of our twenty-two "suspect" players only four hit the twenty-five-base threshold. That seemingly modest number may be due to a couple of factors. Ten of the twenty-two were notably weaker against left-handed pitchers, but since left-handers are far less common than righties, those ten batted far less frequently from their weak side. Furcal only had 154 official at bats against left-handers; he got more than 500 from his stronger side. The Orioles only spotted David Segui against lefties, giving him just 50 official at bats (he hit just .200). But against right-handers, Segui got 174 official trips and batted .282. Jose Valentin only hit .131 against lefties—134 points lower than his average against right-handers—but the White Sox quickly caught on and only gave him 107 official at bats when a left-hander was on the mound.

A few hitters compensated for their declines in average by maintaining some semblance of power production. Teixeira only hit .242 against right-handers (he batted .295 against left-handers), but he still managed 39 extra base hits including 15 home runs in 356 official swings. Those power numbers aren't great, but they're better than replacement level.

The four players against whom the evidence of crimes against switch-hitting most strongly accumulated were Gary Matthews, Crisp, and Kielty, all at minus 27 bases, and Relaford, minus 26 bases. They shared several traits that we may consider to be warning signs.

First and most obviously, all had trouble with right-handed pitchers. Matthews batted .287 versus left-handed opponents, but fell off to .233 against right-handers—and he got about 225 more cuts against right-handers. Relaford was a .300 hitter in 130 at bats against lefties, but only a .238 stick in 370 tries against right-handers. For Kielty the differences were .300 in 140 at bats versus left-handers but just .216 in 287 swings against right-handers. Crisp? The Cleveland leadoff man batted .321 in 112 official trips against left-handers, but slumped to .245 in 302 tries against right-handers.

Second, whatever extra base power they had—and it generally

wasn't much—really dried up when they hit from their bad side. To-gether they combined for just 17 home runs and 90 extra base hits in 1,298 wrong-sided at bats. That's a fraction better than one homer and 7 total extra base hits in 100 swings. From their good sides, they only hit 12 home runs and 52 extra base hits, but only needed 511 swings to get them. That's about double the home run pop and a 30 percent increase in extra base power.

Finally, we cannot dismiss the simple aspect of random chance working on our averages. It's a frequently ignored problem in baseball statistics, and one that often leads to overly weighty conclusions. What we have to keep in mind—in this and other endeavors to ana-lyze baseball numbers—is the impact of sample size. For the most part, we are looking at a couple hundred bits of data, and despite what we might like to think, that simply isn't enough to remove the play of chance in the equation. In 2003, Coco Crisp couldn't hit right-handers. In 2002, he batted a respectable .256 against them. Kielty only hit righties for a .216 average in 2003, but in 2002 his average against right-handers was .303. In 2003, Relaford batted .300 against lefties and .238 against righties. But in 2002 he hit .202 against lefties and .292 against righties. The more deeply one examines switch-hitting data for great truths, the more one is inclined to remember Twain's admonition to readers of *Huckleberry Finn*. Persons attempt-ing to find . . . a plot in it will be shot.

Still, considering the net potential gain of more aggressive pla-toons and the offensive drain created by using less-competent switch-hitters instead, a good guess is that some clubs could improve by one to two victories per season through a bolder and more frequent use of platoons. This is especially true of AL teams, where modern roster flexibility is doubly squeezed by the presence of DHs who can't play the field and twelve-man pitching staffs.

3.1 *A Diversion on Platoon Managers*

Managers, like players, have platoon coefficients, and they distinguish those who like to platoon from those who don't. Between 1980 and

2000, forty Major League managers worked the bench for the preponderance of at least five Major League seasons. Here are the managers, the number of seasons (in that period) that they managed, and their average platoon coefficient. Examine the list and come to your own conclusion whether platooning is inherently advantageous.

Manager (Yrs)	Platoon Coefficient
Billy Martin (5)	22.29
Sparky Anderson (16)	18.30
Bobby Cox (15)	15.72
Whitey Herzog (9)	15.67
Dick Howser (5)	14.97
Jimy Williams (6)	14.79
Chuck Tanner (8)	14.65
Buck Rodgers (9)	14.54
Jim Leyland (13)	14.05
Jim Lefebvre (5)	13.86
Dick Williams (7)	13.44
Jim Riggleman (7)	13.29
Tommy Lasorda (15)	13.16
Frank Robinson (6)	13.08
Jim Fregosi (11)	12.95
Davey Johnson (11)	12.95
Lou Piniella (12)	12.72
Bobby Valentine (9)	12.55
Tom Trebelhorn (6)	11.98
Bruce Bochy (5)	11.62
Gene Lamont (6)	11.59
Roger Craig (7)	11.55
Pat Corrales (5)	11.03
Art Howe (9)	10.81
Tom Kelly (13)	10.76
Cito Gaston (8)	10.76
Don Zimmer (5)	10.70
Phil Garner (8)	10.02

Mike Hargrove (10)	10.01
Don Baylor (6)	9.88
Johnny Oates (8)	9.68
Tony LaRussa (19)	9.40
Joe Torre (13)	8.93
Rene Lachemann (6)	8.77
Dusty Baker (7)	8.34
John McNamara (8)	8.08
Felipe Alou (8)	8.01
Terry Collins (5)	7.82
Dallas Green (5)	7.33

4

THE STRATEGICAL MORASS

Of all the diverse topics covered in baseball's *Book*, this is the most difficult to judge. That's not a new opinion. Leonard Koppett, baseball author-analyst, asserted it in the 1960s. Bill James repeated it in the late 1980s. A manager, James estimated, made about eleven thousand judgments that could fairly be described as strategy during any given season: Everything from setting up a pitching rotation and a lineup to defensive substitutions. "With the very rare exception of a case in which a manager does something just really stupid, it is impossible to prove objectively that any game-level decision was correct or incorrect," he argued.

Koppett makes an even stronger case, in language that ought to give all couch potato managers pause. He notes that a manager's responsibilities first and foremost involve maintaining clubhouse discipline and keeping up player morale, and only as part of the task deciding whether to bunt, steal, or hit and run. "If these are a manager's legitimate responsibilities, our chances to second-guess him become unsatisfyingly meager," Koppett remarked. "About the sort of things mentioned above, the fan in the stands can have practically no knowledge."

Although Koppett's intent was to refer generally to clubhouse and off-field issues, his observation is equally astute with respect to on-field maneuvering. Other than use of a pitching staff, four on-field strategies—the steal, hit and run, intentional walk, and sacrifice—lend themselves to a greater or lesser degree to analysis. That is, we can examine the strategies and make some guesses as to which work well and which don't. But before attempting to analyze whether these are generally good strategies, let's explore one of them from Koppett's view as an illustration of what is knowable and what is not . . . in other words, the problems we are going to face.

About the sacrifice bunt, we can make a general mathematical statement that broadly ascertains the degree to which a successful bunt affects the chances of scoring a run. All we need is a computer—handy enough—and sufficient time to run a few thousand actual games through it, work which, by the way, has been done. With that as an information base, we count the number of runs scored in each "out and base" situation, derive the percentage likelihood of scoring at each circumstance, and the wisdom of surrendering an out in order to gain a base becomes more clear.

Except, of course, for one sticky little problem. Our answer is an abstraction with results linked to an average batter and/or bunter. Even a manager who understands the formula, the math behind it, and the ramifications should be so lucky as to have the right guy at the plate at the right moment in a particular game. Would the formula change if, rather than an "average" player, the one being given the bunt sign was a .125-hitting pitcher? You bet it would. How much? Again, that depends: How good a bunter is that .125-hitting pitcher? (It would also change if a very good hitter were to be given the bunt sign, but that is a problem in theory only, since it rarely happens.)

A second problem: We know little about the success rate of the sacrifice bunt in Major League games. For several years the folks at Stats Inc. have employed spotters who cull everything there is to be culled from every big league game. It is a fascinating compendium, and easily the most comprehensive report on, among other things, managerial tendencies. Here is what Stats Inc. told us about Charlie Manuel's use of the sacrifice bunt in Cleveland during the 2001 season: He tried it 67 times in 162 games. He had a success rate of 89.6 percent. His favorite inning to employ it was the first. He squeezed twice.

For Stats' purposes, a bunt is considered a sacrifice attempt if no runner is on third, there are no outs, or if the pitcher attempts to bunt.

It is considered a success if it results in a sacrifice or a hit. All very reasonable. But in terms of the most useful thing there is to know—how often Charlie Manuel attempted to sacrifice and how often he succeeded—there is a lot Stats' stats don't tell us, because nobody outside the dugout is in position to know.

We don't know, for example, how many times Manuel gave the bunt sign and his batters didn't see it, a reasonable definition of an unsuccessful sacrifice if ever there was one.

We don't know how many times Manuel put the sign for the sacrifice on and then erased it, a decision prompted either by an unfavorable (two-strike) count or to a simple change of heart. Nor do we know the outcomes of those situations.

We don't know how many times Manuel put the bunt sign on after first giving his batter a failed opportunity to swing at a pitch. The reverse of that: We don't know how many times Manuel intended to remove the hit sign in favor of the bunt, but didn't get a chance because the batter hit the ball. Perish the thought that a manager should think ahead. But that is not an unreasonable definition of an "unsuccessful" sacrifice.

We don't know whether Manuel ever tried to sacrifice with one out. Not the smartest move in the world, but it's been done.

Stats' definition appears to exclude all bunt attempts with a runner on third. From time to time, managers will sacrifice with runners at first and third, holding the runner at third. Accepting Stats at its word, those bunts would not be counted, even though they fit a reasonable definition of a sacrifice.

For that matter, we don't know whether Manuel ordered all 67 of those bunt attempts for which he was credited, or whether a batter delivered strategy à la carte.

We know Manuel's favorite inning to sacrifice was the first, but we are left to guess what to make of it . . . or whether it means anything at all. In 2001, 2002, and 2003, Lou Piniella's favorite inning to sacrifice was the seventh. But in 2000, it was the fifth. In 1999, it was the eighth. Is that information, or data masquerading as information?

Without being too picky with Stats, there are also things we don't know that it would be possible to figure out. We know, for example, that about 10 percent of Charlie Manuel's attempts failed, but we don't know how many of those failures were abject—double plays—as opposed to more routine outs. In assessing the value of Manuel's sacrifice attempts, it makes a big difference.

The same thing with the 89 percent that were successes. As James has pointed out, there are successes and then there are big successes, such as bunts that go for base hits, or that are thrown down the right field line, allowing a runner to score and the batter to reach second. That's also a factor. It would be nice to know what percentage fit into what category.

All the above isn't meant to chill the conversation about the value of sacrificing, but to give it some appropriate perspective. We can say—and we will say—that the sacrifice bunt is generally speaking a bad play. We can say that based on the statistical evidence at hand, Charlie Manuel had a better knack for knowing when a sacrifice would work in 2001 than did Tom Kelly. But if we push that data too hard, try to shape it into a mold not befitting it, we will both reach shaky conclusions and also open ourselves up to quite proper criticism.

GENERAL RULES OF STRATEGY

In a 1963 analysis of on-field strategies published in the *Journal of the Operations Research Society of America,* George Lindsey offered a series of general observations on popular strategies. I'm going to summarize them here. But before doing so, Lindsey's own admonition regarding them ought to also be offered for the record. "These calculations pertain to the mythical situation in which all players are 'average,'" he wrote. "Allowance for the deviation from average performance of the batter at the plate, and those expected to follow him, or of the runners on the bases, can be made by a shrewd manager who knows his players."

With that in mind, here are the highlights of Lindsey's findings.

1. The most valuable run for increasing the probability of winning the game is the run that would put the team one run ahead. The

run that would tie the score is nearly as valuable. All others are slightly less valuable early in the game, and become increasingly less valuable as the game proceeds.

2. Leaving aside the particular skills of individual batters, there are not many circumstances in which issuing an intentional base on balls increases the probability that the fielding team will win the game. The most favorable case for this strategy is with runners on second and third, one out, and the fielding team one run ahead.

3. With an average batter (followed in the order by other average batters), the strategy of sacrificing with only a runner on first base does not appear to be a wise one.

4. The success of individuals in stealing bases varies greatly, and the advisability of attempting to steal a base is very much dependent on the probability that the individual can complete the theft successfully. With an average runner on first only, an attempt to steal second may be justified if one run is needed to tie or go one ahead. In the late innings, the attempt to steal second is more advisable with none out than with one out, and is inadvisable with two out except when the batting team is one run behind.

Understanding our limitations, let's examine the value of *The Book* as it relates to some commonly accepted (and, within boundaries, calculable) strategic moves: the sacrifice, the stolen base, the intentional walk, and the hit-and-run.

The Sacrifice

Among those who have made either their living or an extensive hobby out of analyzing baseball strategies, the sacrifice bunt is the most universally panned. The reason lies in the odds of scoring one or more runs in each base-and-out situation, of which there are twenty-four: none on, none out, first and second, two out, etc. The odds vary through history, depending on whether we're in a high-scoring or low-scoring era. Here are close approximations of the modern-day odds.

ON BASE	OUTS		
	0	**1**	**2**
None	.537	.294	.114
First	.907	.544	.239
Second	1.138	.720	.347
Third	1.349	.920	.391
First and Second	1.515	.968	.486
First and Third	1.762	1.140	.522
Second and Third	1.957	1.353	.630
Full	2.399	1.617	.830

Research by Pete Palmer, who derived the above calculations, indicates that the "break-even" point for a sacrifice is 80 percent; that is, it has to work about 80 percent of the time to have any utility. Amazingly, as with many statistics in the highly symmetrical game that is baseball, 80 percent is almost precisely the figure at which the sacrifice does work in the major leagues. In 2003, the Major League success rate for the sacrifice was about 79 percent.

Which Major League managers are costing their teams the most runs by overenthusiastic application of the bunt strategy? Statistics calculated by Stats Inc. provide some clues.

In 2003, the honor, if one can call it that, of ordering the most sacrifices fell on Jack McKeon in Florida, with a prorated 120. (For purposes of this discussion, the following notations all are normalized as if each manager managed 162 games.) In Toronto, Carlos Tosca went the other way, asking the Blue Jays to bunt just 14 times all season, a little more than once every other week. (Tosca was also least likely to bunt in 2002.)

For reasons that are presumably obvious, National League managers call for more sacrifices than their American League counterparts. The average NL skipper in 2003 called for 92 bunts; his AL counterpart only called for 55. Alan Trammell drowned his sorrows in a veritable sea of sacrifices, calling for an AL-leading 96 of them.

Anything to jump-start the Tiger offense, not meaning to imply that such existed in 2003.

Let's see: McKeon (world-champion Marlins) was the most likely NL manager to use the sacrifice, and Trammell (119-loss Tigers) was the most likely AL manager. Don't know about you, but I'm not taking much away from that juxtaposition.

In fact, developing a precise way of measuring the number of runs produced (or unproduced) by use of the sacrifice bunt is less of a science than a guesstimate. But we can assert as a general proposition that sacrifices surrender outs and do not, on the whole, produce runs. If we were asked to develop a broad gauge of the value of a bunt, we could resort to our out-base tables for guidance. We learn that:

With a runner on first and none out, a team is likely to score .907 runs.

With a runner on second and one out (the result of the typical successful sacrifice), a team is likely to score .720 runs. That is, a successful sacrifice costs the bunting team an average of .187 runs.

With a runner on first and one out (the result of the typical unsuccessful sacrifice), a team is likely to score .544 runs. That is, an unsuccessful sacrifice costs the bunting team an average of .363 runs.

As noted earlier, these calculations are by no means precise since we can't accurately project the degree to which the sacrifices worked or failed to work. In those instances, and this is not terribly satisfactory, all we can do is assume that across the universe of baseball, those unknown matters tended to even out. If true, that means that while our numbers may be skewed, in relative terms they would establish an accurate yardstick among managers. But as a broad generalization, the data suggest that every five successful sacrifices cost the sacrificing manager's team one run, while every three unsuccessful sacrifices cost the sacrificing manager's team an additional run.

It isn't quite that simple, of course, since the alternative to sacrificing isn't to do nothing, but to swing the bat. We have to take our results and offset them against the average impact of swinging away. Looking at 2003 performances, we could make the broad statement that every five Major League plate appearances yielded roughly 3.75

outs, 1.1 hits (worth 1.3 bases), and .15 bases via other means (walks, hit batters, etc.), the sum total amounting to a loss of about a fifth of a run. That data still suggest that bunting is always a bad play. But that conclusion, too, is based on averages, when in fact managers often base their bunting decisions on something that is very unaverage, namely the below-average ability of the guy coming to the plate to hit the ball.

So what's the book on the bunt? It is this.

1. If you feel the urge to signal for a sacrifice, lie down and give the feeling a chance to pass. Statistically, the bunt is usually a bad bet, because the trade of a base for an out decreases, not increases, the likelihood of scoring.
2. The exceptions: If you've got a pitcher up with none out, or if it's the final innings of a close game, you're playing for one run, and your weak-hitting shortstop is at the plate.
3. Finally, if you absolutely must bunt, make it work.

The Stolen Base

Assessing the viability of the steal as a strategy turns on a simple question: Do you have a top-flight base stealer on your roster? By that we mean a guy who can give you a better than two-in-three guarantee of making it? If so, run him, run him, and run him some more. If not, sit tight.

There are good reasons to be cautious in using the stolen base as an offensive weapon. First, as research by Palmer, James, and others has demonstrated, it is not an especially effective way of generating offense. "Contrary to popular belief, stolen bases don't create very many runs," James wrote in a 1982 *Sports Illustrated* article that contradicted every sensory perception available in that time of Rickey Henderson's ascendancy. James was fond of pointing out that between 1961 and 1981, eight teams that led their league in stolen bases finished last in the standings. In fact, the historical correlation between league leadership in steals and success in the standings is about as weak as any statistical correlation. This may be due to another reason implied by James in that same article: Steals and home runs are competing ways of scoring runs. Teams that can't do one try to do the other. Home runs, of course, are by far the more efficient means. Ergo, teams run the base paths aggressively in large measure because they can't score runs any other way.

The Linear Weights formula reduces that instinctive assertion to a mathematical precision. It finds that while every steal increases run production by three-tenths of a run, every caught-stealing decreases run production by six-tenths of a run. You can see the same result in the run-outs chart. Presume a runner at first with two out, probably the most common single steal situation. The runner steals second. Congratulations, you have just increased projected run production from .239 to .347, a gain of .108 runs. Let the record show that to be better than nothing.

But now let us assume that calamity strikes. Your runner is thrown out. Your projected run production just fell from .239 (man on first, two out) to zero. The projected loss is more than double the projected gain. These figures vary, of course, depending on whether you attempt to steal with none, one, or two outs. But as a broad characterization, the observation is valid. Any way you look at it, the penalty for stealing is twice the gain. And the gain is more illusory than you might think.

So as a simple observation, it's fair to assert that in order for a steal to be a good idea, it has to work more than two-thirds of the time. The striking fact is that there is a vast distinction among the capabilities of base stealers. Some can virtually steal at will. Others run far too often. As an illustration, let's look at some of the more enthusiastic base stealers of recent years.

Lesson one is Brett Butler, who in sixteen seasons stole 543 Major League bases, a total that ranked him in the top twenty-five of all time. Based on that evidence alone, one might deduce that Brett Butler was a skilled base stealer and an asset to his club. Here's a dirty little secret: Butler's managers should have anchored him to first base every time he got the urge to surge. While he stole 543 bases, Butler was also caught 247 times. Using base runner Linear Weights, we can assert that while Butler's successes generated 163 runs for his team, his failures sucked back 148 of those runs. In other words, all of Butler's baserunning gyrations netted exactly 15 runs in sixteen seasons, a gain to Butler's team of about one and a half victories over the course of his career.

Beyond that, the distribution is not uniform. As with any other player, Butler had his good and bad years. In 1995, he stole 32 bases while being caught just 8 times, statistics that netted a 4.8 run contribution. That's the equivalent of about half a victory that can be attributed to Butler's flying feet. But in 1991, Butler stole successfully only 38 times in 66 tries. His base path labors that season cost the Dodgers 5.5 runs, roughly equal to two-thirds of a victory. The Dodgers lost the NL pennant in 1991 by one game. You don't suppose . . .

On the other hand, there is Craig Biggio. In 1994, Biggio stole 39 bases and was erased just 4 times, a net contribution to the Astros' offense of 9.3 runs, or one victory. You may remember 1994, the season that never ended. But it is fair to note that when play was placed in a state of suspended animation, Biggio's Astros trailed the league-leading Cincinnati Reds by just half a game. Had the race been allowed to assume its normal course down to the wire, a case could be made that Biggio's base stealing might have made the difference.

Or the difference might have been Barry Larkin's base stealing. That same season he stole 26 bases in 28 attempts for the Reds, generating 6.6 runs, about enough to make a difference of one game in the standings. Just enough to keep Cincinnati ahead of Biggio's Astros.

For a manager, making the call on whether to send a runner is not as difficult as might be thought. Sure, elements such as surprise, pitchouts, the capabilities of the on-deck hitter, and the like play a part. But the fact is that most runners fall short of the two-thirds standard that generally represents the break-even point, while a few breeze past it. In 2003, for instance, Carl Crawford stole 55 bases, got caught 10 times, netting 10.5 runs that the Devil Rays badly needed. Carlos Beltran succeeded in 41 of 45 steal attempts, contributing 10 runs to the Royals. Alfonso Soriano posted 35 steals against just 8 misses, netting the Yankees 6 runs. Rafael Furcal was 25 of 27 for Atlanta. These guys get the green light until further notice.

On the other hand, Florida's Preston Wilson succeeded in only 14 of his 21 steal attempts, a 67 percent rate that contributed precisely zero to his team's cause.

In the big picture, what should be striking about all these numbers is how inconsequential they are. That gets back to the original point, base stealing is not as big a deal as the casual fan might think. In 2003, Major League teams stole 2,573 bases and were caught 1,132 times, a 69 percent success rate that is almost precisely on the line of demarcation we delineated earlier as the go–no go point. (Aha, more symmetry.) Based on Linear Weights, National League base stealers produced a net of 37 runs in 2003, making the entire season a virtual non-event on the base paths. In the American League, base stealers fared a bit better, generating a total of 56 runs. That made the 2003 Major League net from baserunning 93 runs, or about 3 runs per team. Put another way, the combined talents of all Major League base stealers in 2003 generated about as much offense as Milton Bradley.

The Intentional Walk

One thing we know for absolute, drop-dead certain about the intentional walk: It puts a man on base at the gain of zero outs. Taken alone, that is hardly a ringing endorsement for its widespread use.

In theory, of course, the intentional walk has benefits that offset this obvious downside. Presumably, it allows a manager to finesse his way past a dangerous hitter to someone more accommodating to the defense's intentions. It may in some cases set up a double play, which could actually occur. It may improve a pitching matchup, allowing a lefty to avoid a right-handed swinger in exchange for facing someone of the same persuasion. In theory, in theory, in theory.

In his 1963 mathematical study of baseball strategies, which remains today that most analytical look at the impact of the intentional walk, George Lindsey listed two basic rationales for issuing one. The intervening years have been kind to those rationales, which continue in full vigor today. They are:

1. To avoid pitching to a particularly dangerous batter who is followed in the order by a much weaker one, or . . .
2. To set up a force play or double play.

But does the walk help teams win games?

In 1984, Palmer's simulation of games taught us a few things about the real value of the intentional pass. Here is a synopsis.

1. The intentional walk *never* reduces the expected number of runs scored.
2. In a few rare instances, an intentional walk may reduce the offense's chance of winning the game. These are always desperation, late-inning situations. Palmer found, for example, that with the score tied and one out in the bottom of the ninth, an intentional walk reduces the batting team's win probability from .825 to .806. The intentional walk was also a minor advantage in similar circumstances in the bottom of the eighth and in the top of the ninth.
3. Even when an intentional walk is issued in order to bring the pitcher to the plate, it may reduce run-scoring potential for the inning in question yet improve run-scoring potential for the game. That is because the strategy invites the offense to open the next inning with its leadoff hitter rather than with the pitcher. These are the numbers: With the number eight hitter at bat, a runner on second and two outs, a team could be projected to score .27 runs. Issuing the intentional walk—thus creating a situation with runners at first and second, two out, and the pitcher up—decreases the run potential very marginally, to .26. But as a general statement, the run potential for the following inning—when the leadoff hitter bats first—is .55. If the pitcher had led off, the run potential would have been .43. The net advantage to the offense is better than a tenth of a run.

Lindsey's 1963 study found the case to be highly dependent on who's being walked to get to whom. But generally his findings are a caution against any extensive application of the intentional base on balls. The chart below illustrates what happens to expected run production, based on Lindsey's data, when an intentional walk is issued.

Situation	Expected Runs Before IBB	Expected Runs After IBB	Change Due to IBB
Runner at 2nd, 0 out	1.194	1.471	.277
Runner at 2nd, 1 Out	.671	.939	.268
Runner on 3rd, 2 out	.297	.403	.106
Runners on 2nd & 3rd, 0 out	1.960	2.254	.294
Runners on 2nd & 3rd, 1 out	1.560	1.632	.072
Runners on 2nd & 3rd, 2 out	.687	.861	.174

In other words, the intentional walk increased the run-scoring potential in every logical on-base situation, generally by about one-fifth of a run. In 2003, the average Major League manager issued about 30 intentional walks. That's 6 gift runs per team.

John Jarvis, a professor of mathematics at the University of South Carolina at Aiken, conducted a study of the intentional base on balls that laid out what amounted to a risk-reward scenario. Studying the impact of about 21,000 actual intentional walks issued between 1980 and 1996, Jarvis deduced that they did in fact decrease the likelihood of a team scoring a single run in an inning. This was because, Jarvis discovered, that batters due up after issuance of an intentional walk hit about 11 points worse on average than the league as a whole.

However, Jarvis also discovered that while the intentional walk decreased the prospect of a single run scoring, it increased the likelihood of a multiple-run inning to a degree that basically offset the potential gain. In other words, a team protecting a one-run lead late in the game might logically risk issuing a free pass. But over the long haul, it's a neutral strategy.

A few years back, Stats Inc. kept a season-long diary-type record of the use of the intentional walk. This is what Stats Inc. found. In the American League, managers employed the intentional pass 587 times. Following the walk, a total of 521 runs were scored. In the National League, the comparable figures were 797 intentional walks and 607 runs scored. On 88 occasions in the American League, and 119 occasions in the National League (15 percent in both leagues), the intentionally walked runner scored. What do we make of that real-world data?*

We need to start with an assumption. Our assumption is that during the season in which Stats collected its data:

About 25 percent of the intentional walks were issued with a runner on second and none out.

About 25 percent were issued with a runner on second and one out.

About 25 percent were issued with a runner on second and two out.

The remaining 25 percent were apportioned evenly among the three out situations involving runners at second and third.

Combining Stats' data with our assumptions, we can make some real-world deductions regarding the value, or lack of same, of the intentional walk.

Stats noted 587 such situations in the American League during the season in question. Here's how the projected run production stacked up against the actual run production.

Situation	Instances	Runs-outs	Proj. Runs
Runner at second, none out	146	1.138	166
Runner at second, one out	146	.720	105
Runner at second, two out	147	.347	51
Second and third, none out	49	1.957	96
Second and third, one out	49	1.353	66
Second and third, two out	50	.630	32
TOTAL	587		516

---

*It would be interesting to redo such a survey based on 2004 data in an effort to determine the degree to which the results were skewed by the inordinate number of intentional walks given to one player, Barry Bonds.

In actuality, those 587 intentional walks issued in the American League were followed by 521 runs scored, a difference between expectation and reality of less than 1 percent.

In the National League there were 797 intentional walks issued. Again, assuming the validity of our scenario, here are the projections.

Situation	Instances	Runs-outs	Proj. Runs
Runner at second, none out	199	1.138	226
Runner at second, one out	199	.720	143
Runner at second, two out	199	.347	69
Second and third, none out	66	1.957	129
Second and third, one out	68	1.353	92
Second and third, two out	66	.630	42
TOTAL	797		701

In actuality, those 797 intentional walks in the National League produced 607 runs, about 13.5 percent fewer than projected based on the runs-outs data. Why the discrepancy between leagues? One possible explanation is obvious. In the National League, managers have the option of walking the eighth place hitter to get to the pitcher, presumably a much weaker hitter than pitchers in the AL would ever face. If that's actually the explanation, then one good intentional walk rule might be: Use it to get to the pitcher . . . and nobody else.

The Hit-and-Run

We probably know less about the application and value of the hit-and-run than we do about any other single baseball strategy. And that's a shame because the few studies taking up the question of its value argue for its more widespread use.

Here's what we do know of its 2003 use, virtually all of which was mined by the note-takers at Stats Inc.

1. We know that Major League managers were credited with having attempted the hit-and-run between 36 (Bobby Cox, Atlanta) and 119 (Alan Trammell, Detroit) times.

2. We know that the average "success" rate (defining "success" as the base runner advancing without a double play) was around 35 percent.

3. We know that at 50 percent, Bob Melvin in Seattle was credited with the greatest success at the hit-and-run.

That's what we know. The list of what we *don't* know—which is very similar to our questions concerning Charlie Manuel's use of the sacrifice—ought to give us proper pause for caution.

But in addition to everything else, with respect to the hit-and-run we don't even know whether the book definition of "success" is a reasonable one. When he called for the hit-and-run, what were the manager's motives? To stay out of a double play, or to open a batting hole? Depending on the game circumstances, either is perfectly logical. Yet calling a hit-and-run to open a batting hole, then claiming success because the batter was retired but the runner advanced, comes across as defining success in modest terms.

How modest? This modest. Let us refer back to the runs and outs chart. Suppose we have a runner on first and none out. We call for the hit-and-run and work it "successfully," which is to say the batter grounds out and the runner advances. Now we have a runner at second and one out. But that is the equivalent of a sacrifice bunt, and we've already determined that even a successful sacrifice is no success at all. In fact, our run potential for the inning following this "success" has fallen from .907 (runner on first, none out) to .720 (runner on second, one out). Do the same thing with one out and we reduce our likely run production from .544 to .347. As some historical figure sort of said, a few more successes of that sort and we are in last place. This all assumes that our batter makes contact on the ground. We'll get to the statistics later, but as we've already suggested, more than half of all hit-and-run tries are "unsuccessful," meaning that there is either no base runner advancement, or a double play ensues.

Managers being human, and humans being a hopeful sort, they rely on the statistically invalid belief that the next hit-and-run will work. In fact, that it will work very big. Contact will be made, the ball will find the hole in the infield, and at the expense of no outs a first-and-third circumstance is created where once there was none. If successful, the prize is substantial. Referring to the modern base-out chart, here are the relative run-production values at the onset and at the conclusion of a hit-and-run occurring with a runner on first when the batter singles him to third:

Runner on first, no out: .907

Runners on first and third, no out: 1.762

That is to say, a hit-and-run in which the batter singles and moves the runner to third base increases the run-scoring potential by nearly a full run, and does it on a one-base hit.

But look at the difference if another form of "success" occurs, a missed swing that results of a stolen base:

Runner on first, no out: .907

Runner on second, no out: 1.138

It's still a success, but our projected run production improves by only about two-tenths of a run; that is not as attractive. And of course, under the rules, a third type of "success" is possible, one in which the batter grounds out, but advances the runner to second.

Runner on first, no out: .907

Runner on second, one out: .720

Rather than increasing run production by a run, or even by two-tenths, this "successful" hit-and-run has decreased production by about two-tenths of a run.

Finally, if regrettably, we must confront failure. Many of these are harmless; the runner breaks, the runner fouls off the pitch, we start over. But some go away in more troubling ways: a runner thrown out on a hit-and-run that becomes a steal in midstride. A line drive double play. Here's what happens to run production if the first occurs:

Runner on first, no out: .907

None on, one out: .294

The hit-and-run that becomes a "caught stealing" undermines run production by more than a half run. And if, perchance, the hit-and-run creates a double play, the results are even more desultory.

Runner on first, no out: .907

None on, two out: .114

In this circumstance, fortunately rare, run production potential is virtually eliminated.

How often do each of these scenarios happen? If we knew, it would be possible to create accurate projections of the runs generated, or squandered, by each manager's use of the hit-and-run. As it is, we have no earthly idea. So the best we can do is offer generalizations.

1. It's better to succeed at the hit-and-run than to fail.
2. If you succeed a high percentage of the time, it's better to use the hit-and-run aggressively rather than sparingly.
3. But if you frequently fail at the hit-and-run, sparing use of the strategy is a plus, not a minus.

5

THE ART HOWE SCHOOL OF MANAGEMENT AND THE TACTICIAN'S RATING

In assessing managerial moves, we first must consider whether any of this means very much, whether, in fact, on-field strategy is an especially profound science or something more nearly akin to a parlor game. As we do so, let's keep Art Howe's record toward the debate's forefront.

Oakland's manager was both the most reluctant and the least effective manager in the American League in 2000 in making mileage out of the hit-and-run; it was as if he was giving the signs in Greek. Howe's A's successfully navigated the play just 15.6 percent of the time—not that Howe cared much, since he only flashed the hit-and-run sign 32 times—that's slightly more often than once a week. That was easily the Major League low. There was little change in 2001, Howe's runners succeeding just 28 percent of the time against the league average of about 31 percent. In 2002, Howe was successful on just 30 percent of hit-and-run calls. Only one American League skipper who managed more than half the season had a worse percentage. Moving to the National League Mets in 2003, Howe opened up, trying the hit-and-run 84 times (the league average was 69). But his 26 percent success rate was still well below par.

Art's use of the steal generated about four runs per season for Oakland in 2000, a very modest rate of success made even more modest by the fact that the A's only attempted 55 steals. Every other Major League manager except Jimy Williams in Boston (73) tried more than twice that many. In 2001, Art's runners nuzzled ever so gently above the 69 percent league average success rate at 70 percent. But with only 97 attempts (21 fewer than the league average), that translated to a mere three runs gained. The numbers repeated themselves in 2002. With the Mets in 2003, he was a bit below average, both in number of attempts and success.

The intentional walk is, generally speaking, a bad strategy, but Art Howe loves it. His pitchers issued 45 intentional passes in 2000, the highest number in any Major League in which walking somebody to get to the pitcher was not a viable option. In 2001, Howe issued 41 intentional passes; among American Leaguers, only Buck Martinez in Toronto allowed more. In 2002, Howe ranked third in his league in IBB frequency. Moving to the National League in 2003, Howe walked batters intentionally in a majors-leading 8.6 percent of his chances.

In sum, his incompetence at the running game strategy was offset only by the fact that he rarely used the running game, and he gratuitously put potential runs on base at a relatively breakneck pace.

All of the above would constitute an indictment of Art Howe's managerial qualifications if it weren't for the fact that his A's won the AL West in 2000 and 2002, took the wild card in 2001, and averaged 99 victories for the period. His worst failures—with the Mets in 2003–2004—came when he was most aggressive in the dugout.

Would it be possible to develop a system of accurately rating managerial on-field performance? Given what we've already acknowledged concerning the vagaries of even counting strategies much less assessing their value, any such system would have to leave plenty of room for leeway.

But if one were to devise such a system, the clearest way would be to model it after some sort of "standings" format. That's what is attempted below.

We call this a Tactician's Rating because it focuses solely on three plausibly measurable tactics: the sacrifice, the stolen base, and the hit-and-run. (Feel free to develop your own system of rating lineup construction, or clubhouse demeanor, or umpire baiting.) Here's how it is put together.

In each category, we begin by calculating the manager's success percentage as determined by Stats Inc., and acknowledging all the shortcomings inherent in that data. We use it because it is the best we have. Let's use Tony LaRussa's 2001 employment of the sacrifice bunt as an illustration of the method. That season, LaRussa asked Cardinal batters to bunt 102 times, with an 88.2 percent success rate.

The next step is to compare that success percentage to the league average for the season in question. In 2001, the National League bunting success rate was 82 percent. At 88.2 percent, Tony LaRussa succeeded 104 percent as often as the average NL skipper.

Such a rating system is easiest to comprehend when it resembles something familiar. So let's move the decimal point three places to the right and multiply all our results by five, creating ratings that very much resemble the percentage column of the everyday Major League standings in which the average skipper must and will score .500. For LaRussa, 104 percent becomes .520.

One side note: Because such a rating is based on equal opportunity, we also need to adjust the statistics of managers who were fired or hired during midseason (or occasionally for rainouts) in a fashion that assumes a 162-game season.

When we do that for the 2003 season, here's how Major League managers handled various on-field tactics. Due to the inherent league-based tactical differences created by the designated hitter rule, managers are grouped by league rather than together.

SACRIFICE (AMERICAN LEAGUE)

Torre, NYY	.546
Tosca, TOR	.534
Hargrove, BAL	.532
Trammell, DET	.532
Pena, KC	.531
Manuel, CWS	.519
Scioscia, ANA	.507
Showalter, TEX	.506

Melvin, SEA	.504
Gardenhire, MIN	.480
Wedge, CLE	.468
Little, BOS	.458
Macha, OAK	.448
Piniella, TB	.442

In considering these data, it would be useful to know how widely managerial performance varied. If every manager handled the sacrifice about as well as every other, then for purposes of that maneuver it wouldn't matter much who you had in the dugout. Standard deviation is a measurement of performance variation. In 2003, the standard deviation of AL managers in terms of their use of the sacrifice (as calculated above) was .034. For fellow non-mathematicians, that means that any AL manager whose rating was between .4665 and .5335 was essentially "normal." What mathematicians call the "empirical rule" stipulates that the first standard deviation for any set of numbers will always encompass about two-thirds of the whole; in this case, it encompasses ten of the fourteen managers. Torre was best at employment of the sacrifice while Piniella—for the second straight year—fared the worst.

SACRIFICE (NATIONAL LEAGUE)

Baker, CHC	.546
McKeon, FLA	.534
Alou, SF	.531
Howe, NYM	.531
Torborg, FLA	.531
LaRussa, STL	.528
Robinson, MTL	.524
Williams, HOU	.513
McClendon, PIT	.509
Yost, MIL	.504
Bochy, SD	.495
Tracy, LA	.488

Cox, ATL	.484
Boone, CIN	.474
Brenly, ARI	.471
Hurdle, COL	.467
Bowa, PHI	.440
Miley, CIN	.434

The standard deviation for NL managers in terms of their use of the sacrifice was .032, an even more homogenized result than in the AL. It only labels thirteen of the eighteen NL managers as "normal," but two of the five who are outside the "norm" led their teams for less than a full season, suggesting the prospect of a chance-governed statistical anomaly. But standard deviations suggest something else: the importance of the decision-maker. A small standard deviation—and the deviations we find in use of the sacrifice bunt generally are the smallest we will encounter—argue that most managers are pretty much interchangeable at this skill. Among those who managed for the full season, Baker was the best and Bowa the worst.

STEAL (AMERICAN LEAGUE)

Macha, OAK	.553
Piniella, TB	.551
Torre, NYY	.534
Melvin, SEA	.532
Pena, KC	.529
Manuel, CWS	.519
Showalter, TEX	.516
Little, BOS	.511
Hargrove, BAL	.509
Gardenhire, MIN	.486
Scioscia, ANA	.485
Trammell, DET	.435
Tosca, TOR	.426
Wedge, CLE	.418

The standard deviation for the steal in the AL in 2002 was .043, a marginally higher deviation than in the NL (see below). That suggests it was a bit more important in the AL who was flashing the steal signals. Casual baseball observers will not notice the rich irony in Ken Macha's presence atop this list given the antipathy toward which Oakland management views any tactical activity that smacks of commitment. Billy Beane needn't fret: Although his boy was the league's most efficient steal-caller, he was also anchored (with Tosca) at the bottom of the frequency list, calling only 62 steal tries all year. That's about one and a half per week, Billy, so chill.

STEAL (NATIONAL LEAGUE)

Torborg, FLA	.550
Cox, ATL	.549
Boone, CIN	.533
LaRussa, STL	.523
Robinson, MTL	.523
Yost, MIL	.521
Bowa, PHI	.518
Baker, CHC	.510
McClendon, PIT	.508
Howe, NYM	.504
Tracy, LA	.501
Williams, HOU	.500
Brenly, ARI	.485
Bochy, SD	.480
Hurdle, COL	.458
Miley, CIN	.458
McKeon, FLA	.456
Alou, SF	.428

Let's see: Jeff Torborg, managing the league's only true running team, runs at a devil-may-care pace (315 attempts when prorated over the season), succeeds a league-high 76 percent of the time, and doesn't make it through May. (Soon to be followed at the exit by Bob Boone, number three on the list.) McKeon succeeds Torborg, runs about 40 percent less often, has about 15 percent less success at it, and leads that same running team to the world championship. Further confirmation that tactical acumen is only one component of managerial skill . . . and not necessarily the key component. The standard deviation for NL managers in use of the steal in 2003 was a pedestrian .033.

HIT-AND-RUN (AMERICAN LEAGUE)

Melvin, SEA	.667
Piniella, TB	.637
Macha, OAK	.616
Tosca, TOR	.572
Little, BOS	.567
Hargrove, BAL	.561
Torre, NYY	.507
Wedge, CLE	.480
Pena, KC	.477
Scioscia, ANA	.477
Trammell, DET	.415
Gardenhire, MIN	.399
Showalter, TEX	.375
Manuel, CWS	.253

The hit-and-run is used only about half as often as the stolen base, but the standard deviation for its use by AL managers in 2003 was .110—better than twice the standard deviation for the steal. That suggests the impact on run production of the two skills is roughly equal. That standard deviation, by the way, was down a fraction from 2002 (.160) and 2001 (.166), suggesting possible skill homogenization. Given Macha's evident abilities at both the steal and hit-and-run, what would be the effect on run production of A's management unleashing him? Let's assume each success nets a base and each failure costs one (at twice the penalty in terms of run production). If Macha had used both tactics at the frequency of the league average (130 steal attempts and 72 hit-and-run attempts) with no performance decline on the part of either himself or his runners, the A's would gain seven-tenths of one run over the course of the season.

HIT-AND-RUN (NATIONAL LEAGUE)

Bowa, PHI	.710
McKeon, FLA	.652
McClendon, PIT	.609
Yost, MIL	.592
LaRussa, STL	.581
Alou, SF	.565
Miley, CIN	.554
Tracy, LA	.526
Cox, ATL	.517
Brenly, ARI	.502
Baker, CHC	.492
Robinson, MTL	.474
Bochy, SD	.424
Howe, NYM	.407
Williams, HOU	.360
Hurdle, COL	.356
Boone, CIN	.356
Torborg, FLA	.323

In the NL, the standard deviation for the hit-and-run was .091, somewhat less than in the AL, but still nearly three times the standard deviation for the steal. The top of the NL hit-and-run heap includes old managerial foxes Larry Bowa, McKeon, and LaRussa, implying that wisdom comes into play here. Jimy Williams, a veteran manager but an NL newcomer, is fourth from the bottom, four spots higher than in 2002. The rise in the standard deviation in the NL (from .081 in 2002) partially reverses a homogenization trend in place since 1999.

Until 2002, the standard deviation for the hit-and-run had been rising relatively quickly in both leagues. In 1999, it was .077 in the AL and .074 in the NL; in 2000 the figures were .109 in the AL and .086 in the NL. In 2001, they were .166 and .102. In 2002, the deviation held steady in the AL and retreated in the NL.

COMPOSITE RATING (AMERICAN LEAGUE)

Melvin, SEA	.559
Piniella, TB	.545
Macha, OAK	.543
Torre, NYY	.530
Hargrove, BAL	.528
Pena, KC	.517
Little, BOS	.512
Tosca, TOR	.490
Scioscia, ANA	.489
Showalter, TEX	.478
Gardenhire, MIN	.463
Trammell, DET	.454
Manuel, CWS	.453
Wedge, CLE	.446

COMPOSITE RATING (NATIONAL LEAGUE)

Bowa, PHI	.547
LaRussa, STL	.539
Yost, MIL	.535
McClendon, PIT	.534
Cox, ATL	.525
McKeon, FLA	.525
Baker, CHC	.515
Robinson, MTL	.511
Tracy, LA	.504

Torborg, FLA	.489
Alou, SF	.488
Howe, NYM	.487
Brenly, ARI	.486
Miley, CIN	.476
Boone, CIN	.474
Bochy, SD	.470
Williams, HOU	.468
Hurdle, COL	.435

STEADY HANDS

But are these calculations true, accurate, and meaningful reflections of tactical abilities in any kind of longer-term context? Do managers have good seasons and bad ones? Or do they manage with the consistency one assumes comes with age and experience? For that matter, does their experience give veteran managers an edge on younger ones?

There were ten managers active during the 2003 season who had been continuously active since 1999. The ten are Dusty Baker, Bruce Bochy, Bobby Cox, Mike Hargrove, Howe, Tony LaRussa, Jerry Manuel, Piniella, Joe Torre, and Jimy Williams.

The composite numbers illustrate why those 10 have hung around dugouts so long. For the half decade, their composite rating was .510, placing them notably above the Major League average. The low marks—by Howe and Williams—were respectable .489s. The champion? It's Tony LaRussa, with a rating of .546 that would make him a perennial Tactician of the Year candidate.

Our veteran tacticians were average or better at each of the three skills, and the more exotic the skill level ability (based on standard deviation) the better they stood. On what appears to be the most critical, the hit-and-run, veteran managers averaged a rating of .525, led by LaRussa's really remarkable five-year composite score of .647.

DUGOUT LEARNER'S PERMIT?

Is there a managerial learning curve? Do the tactics-related decisions of new managers improve over time? Do veteran managers have an inherent advantage over their rookie counterparts?

In 2003, there were six men managing in the big leagues for the first time. They were Ken Macha in Oakland, Bob Melvin in Seattle, Dave Miley in Cincinnati, Alan Trammell in Detroit, Eric Wedge in Cleveland, and Ned Yost in Milwaukee. Macha's A's made the playoffs, but most of the others suffered. The collective winning percentage of the six was only .448 (389–477).

But the question of the moment has to do with how they handled on-field tactics. Using our "winning percentage" model as a tool, the 2003 average of these six rookie managers was .502. That's a nudge above the Major League norm, a bit below our ten five-year managers, and also much higher than the 2002 rookie class. (Which got a collective .476 rating. About half of those 2002 rookies, by the way, did not return for 2003.)

If 2003 tactical performance is any indicator—and we'll visit that question in a moment—the futures look brighter for three members of the class of 2003 than for three others. (At least it did until October, 2004, when Melvin was fired.) As noted above, Melvin not only was the best rookie tactical manager, he was the best in the AL with a .559 score. Uncanny in his use of the hit-and-run—the tactical weapon most likely to reveal managerial skill—he had a 50 percent success rate in a league where the norm is 38 percent. If he'd hit that well in his playing days, he'd still be catching. Macha and Yost were about as good. They were also consistent: Of the three, only Macha fell below the league average in any of the three tactical areas. (His rating was .448 in use of the sacrifice. But he did that in Oakland, where the inability to use the sacrifice is considered an asset.) Macha was third best in the AL in the hit-and-run, Yost was fourth best in the NL. Macha was best in the AL in use of the steal, Melvin stood fourth, and Yost was in the top third in the NL.

The ratings hold worse news for the three remaining classmates.

Dave Miley's composite rating of .467 stood him fourth in the rookie class, ahead of Trammell and Wedge. Trammell (with a .454 composite rating) actually proved to be pretty adept at the sacrifice—he ranked third in the league behind Torre and Tosca—but giving up outs wasn't much of a problem in Detroit in 2003. When it came to moving base runners by more dynamic means, things didn't work as well. He ran a lot—his 161 steal attempts placed him third in frequency in the AL—but his 60 percent success rate was third worst. Running often and poorly is not generally a good combination. Wedge was dead last at steal success in the AL at 58.5 percent, and he too was well above the league average for trying to run. That's one key reason why his composite rating was .446, last among the rookies and last in the league overall as well.

The tale of whether the rookie class of 2003 improves will only be told over time. But we can look at previous classes for precedent. Unfortunately for logic, when we do that, the precedents are mixed. On the subject of a managerial learning curve, it appears that you are free to select the answer of your choice.

If rookie skippers of the class of 2001 and 2002 are any indication, there may be no such curve. Four of the 2002 rookies survived to manage again in 2003—Tony Pena, Ron Gardenhire, Clint Hurdle, and Tosca—and they accumulated a .476 composite rating. Not very good— and worse than their .484 composite debut in 2002. Pena was the only one of the four to exceed .500 in 2003; he rated .517 in Kansas City. Hurdle, who debuted at .498 in Colorado, fell all the way to .435, based largely on his clueless 23 percent success rate with the hit-and-run.

To date, the class of 2001 has fared a bit better. That class contained four members: Buck Martinez, Bob Brenly, Jim Tracy, and Lloyd McClendon. As freshmen, their average rating was .486, a figure they repeated in 2002. In 2003, that composite rose to .508, although predation may have been been the cause. Martinez, the class's ugly stepchild in 2001 and 2002, had been bumped off in Toronto. Of the other three, McClendon (.534) is the hot figure. His 2003 composite was 84 points above his .450 rating for 2002, which itself was 48 points above his .402 rookie score.

6

THE DECLINE AND FALL
OF THE STARTING PITCHER

Randy Johnson pronounced the perfect eulogy for the classic concept of a starting pitcher. Johnson had been brilliant for nine innings on the evening of May 8, 2001 . . . but his Diamondback teammates had not. Although he fanned a record-tying 20 opponents, the game went into extra innings 1–1. Johnson, however, retired after the bottom of the ninth, explaining to reporters why he asked Arizona manager Bob Brenly to be lifted: "I saw no point in going out there for the tenth inning. . . . What was the point? . . . The outcome is what's important."

This is a stunning commentary on pitching strategy from a man felt by many to be the best pitcher of the modern game. Even assuming Johnson was speaking merely to the pointlessness of adding to his strikeout total as opposed to his impact on the game's outcome, it is still stunning. Given the most benevolent possible spin, Johnson's comment that "the outcome is what's important" expresses his tacit assumption that the Arizona bullpen could have done a better job of winning the game than he could—on a night when he had the most overpowering stuff he ever had.

Which, if that was his attitude, may have been a more ignorant observation than the rest of his statement. Because the bullpen to which Johnson gave way on this best of all of his nights proceeded to allow two runs in two innings. The D-Backs did win the game, but only because their offense scored three runs in the bottom of the eleventh.

Johnson's problem was that he thought like a modern pitcher. In his mind, he was merely one part of a pitching "team." His role as part of that "team" was to give six or seven strong innings, but ultimately the outcome should, must, and would be influenced by the combined results of himself, a setup man, and a closer.

Seen in that context, Johnson's comment underscores a steady decline in expectation as it relates to the starting pitcher. This can be readily seen in the percentage of total innings pitched by the game's best pitchers.

Here's the trend in pitcher usage for the season ending in the number eight for each of the most recent five decades. The table illustrates the percentage of a team's total innings pitched by its top four starters—based on number of starts—and by all other pitchers on the staff.

PERCENT OF TEAM'S TOTAL INNINGS PITCHED BY EACH STARTER

	No. 1	No. 2	No. 3	No. 4	Other
1958	17.6	15.5	13.2	10.5	43.2
1968	18.1	16.1	14.2	12.0	39.6
1978	17.5	15.6	13.5	11.3	42.1
1988	16.4	14.5	13.4	10.7	45.0
1998	14.8	13.9	12.0	9.8	49.5

During the 2003 season, the four most heavily used pitchers on Major League staffs pitched an average of 50 percent of their teams' innings. That is typical of the past several seasons, but it is about 5 percent fewer innings than the average "big four" pitched fifteen years ago. At the height of the 1960s "pitching era," in 1968, the average team's four most frequently used pitchers hurled 60.4 percent of all the innings.

The average staff "ace," by which we mean the most often-used starter, pitched 210 innings, about 14 percent of his team's innings in 2003, about 30 fewer innings than the ace worked in 1988.

It's plain that less is demanded of the best pitchers today than in the not terribly distant past. But the data do not address two vital questions: 1. What, if anything, is the net impact on runs scored created by the decreased workload? 2. Is there any physical justification for it?

In the case of a few teams, this change directly costs victories. In 2002, the Boston Red Sox were one such club. A look at the usage of their three top pitchers illustrates why.

In 2002, Boston's most heavily used starter was Derek Lowe. With good reason, since Lowe won 21 and lost just 8 in 220 innings. But by even recent historical standards, Lowe was a relatively lightly used ace. He pitched just 15.2 percent of his team's innings, about 17 fewer innings than the norm for a staff ace about fifteen years before. Had he pitched those additional 17 innings, based on his 2002 ERA Lowe could have been expected to give up 5 more earned runs.

Boston's second most heavily used starter was Pedro Martinez. He pitched 199 innings. But that was about 11 innings fewer than the average number two starter worked about fifteen years before. Had he worked those additional 11 innings, Martinez could have been expected to allow 3 more earned runs based on his seasonal ERA.

Boston's third most heavily used starter was John Burkett. Applying the same assumptions, Burkett would have worked an additional 20 innings and he would have allowed 10 additional earned runs.

Of course, someone else pitched those 48 innings the Red Sox' three top starters did not pitch. The earned run average for all Boston Red Sox pitchers other than the four most-used starters was 4.58.

That translates to 24 additional earned runs, 6 more than Boston's big three would have allowed if they had pitched those same innings.

A rule of thumb is that each additional 10 runs costs a team one game in the standings; by that measurement, the Red Sox's failure to follow historical use standards in 2002 probably cost them a game.

In the ninety team seasons between 2002 and 2004, the four most heavily used starters pitched 55 percent of their team's innings just twenty-one times. Twenty of the twenty-one teams that did so (the exception was the 2004 Tigers) had winning records, the average being about 91–71. Twelve played in the postseason.

Today, the core of most teams' rotation is about seven deep: That's five starters, a closer, and a setup man. Generally in recent years, those seven slots have accounted for about 68 percent of all the innings pitched on an average Major League staff, about 1,000 innings per team overall.

But that's also why we should not really be surprised that pitching quality appears to be diluted today relative to previous years. It is diluted by the introduction of the closer and setup man into the regular workload. In 1988, the typical staff got 1,000 innings of work out of only 5.5 pitchers—and there were four fewer teams, meaning that the quality of pitching was less diluted by forty arms, or about 15 percent. In the pitching heyday of 1968, it took only about 4.8 pitchers per staff to produce 1,000 innings of mound labor, the same amount that today gets passed around among seven hurlers. And the staffs were comprised of only ten arms, not eleven or twelve as is typical today. That creates a talent dilution relative to 1968 of about 60 percent. And here a fairly obvious rule of distribution of labor enters into the equation: the more people doing the work, the less expertly the work is done.

Why would a Major League team deliberately not use its best pitchers? Three possible justifications come to mind for such a workload cutback: Fear of injury, fear of fatigue during a game, or fear of fatigue at season's end brought on by the accumulation of work. If there is a valid basis for any one of these fears, then it may make sense to use Randy Johnson less. If not, then the reduced workload carried by a modern "workhorse" is just one more of those baseball canards— and a costly one—that ought to be exploded. Let's examine each of the possible justifications.

FEAR OF FATIGUE AT SEASON'S END BROUGHT ON BY AN ACCUMULATION OF WORK

Do heavily worked pitchers tire as a season winds toward its conclusion? A traditional benchmark for heavy use is 250 innings. But that benchmark is receding. Between 1996 and 2004, only twenty-one pitchers recorded 250-inning seasons. (In 2004, only Livan Hernan-

dez did so.) The average earned run average of those twenty-one recent 250-inning pitchers on August 1 was 3.02. From that point until
the end of the season, the average ERA for those same pitchers was
2.86.

The numbers are even more persuasive against the premise than
they appear. One of the twenty-one pitchers was Jon Lieber, who in
2000 pitched 250 innings for the Cubs. Lieber's ERA as of August 1
was 3.49. He had an awful final two months and finished the year at
4.41. Virtually by himself, Lieber skewed the study.

To see how much, all we need do is remove Lieber's 2000 season
from the study. Among the other twenty heavily used pitchers, the average August-September ERA was 2.86, 14 percentage points lower
than the average for the first two-thirds of the season. Not all of those
pitchers improved as the workload built up, but most did; twelve of
the twenty had better ERAs in August and September than in April
through July. Hernandez in 2004 was one of them. His August 1
ERA was 3.65; he finished the season at 3.60.

Far larger data samples—encompassing a wider variety of pitching
talent and a larger number of innings—were available in earlier decades. The chart below illustrates the April through July and August
through September ERAs for all pitchers who met at least one of two
conditions for the 1996–2004 period as well as the other three-season
groups that are indicated. The seasons are 1956–58, 1966–68, 1976–78,
and 1986–88. The conditions: a pitcher must have worked a minimum
of 250 innings, or made a minimum of 38 starts, to be included.

Year	Apr-July ERA	Aug-Sept ERA
1956–58	3.48	3.13
1966–68	2.74	2.69
1976–78	3.07	3.02
1986–88	3.38	3.15
1996–2004	3.02	2.86

Performance improved in every multiyear period that was examined. In the 1950s, the performance of the most heavily used pitchers

improved dramatically with work. The improvement was less dramatic in the other groups of seasons. The conclusion: If today's managers believe that by cutting back on their best pitcher's innings they will keep him fresher for the stretch run, history indicates they are mistaken. In fact, by withholding 20 percent of an ace's innings in favor of a lesser pitcher, they are probably injuring their team's chances for victory.

FEAR OF FATIGUE DURING A GAME

Even so, it may make sense to remove a frontline pitcher in the later innings if the prospect is that his performance will deteriorate as the afternoon or evening wears along. It's a theory you can hear espoused on virtually any televised ballgame: "His pitch count is high, he's losing his velocity, he's tiring."

Indeed, the focus on pitch count is one of the modern game's axioms. It is universally accepted that pitchers tire after about 100 pitches; that almost no pitcher is worth a hoot after 120 pitches; and that a manager who lets a pitcher work beyond 130 pitches is foolishly risking injury. There aren't many such pitchers these days. In a modern season, there are about 4,860 pitching starts made. Yet in 2003, nobody threw 140 pitches. In 2002, just one starter did. It has happened just twenty times in the past five years.

Early in the 1990s, Stats Inc. counted the pitches for each of the majors' best arms. They found that Roger Clemens, for example, made 35 starts, but only averaged 115 pitches per start. (To put that in perspective, in the fifth game of the 1956 World Series Don Larsen threw 97 pitches . . . and he was perfect.) In only seven of Clemens' 35 starts that 1991 season was he allowed to throw as many as 130 pitches. And Clemens led the league in innings pitched.

There is one inherent problem with most pitch count–based studies; they fail to consider whether a high pitch count is the cause of a problem, or the effect of one. To put it another way, do pitchers underperform as their pitch count rises, or does their pitch count rise because they don't have good stuff? Here's a tip: If a pitcher has thrown 100 pitches by the fifth inning, it's probably because he's not getting very many people out. That being the case, a high pitch count merely tells us something we already know: the guy stinks.

There is another consideration. Randy Johnson may give up a higher on-base plus slugging average as the game goes along, but he may still be a better choice on the mound than his team's setup man, or even in some instances the closer. The real-world question managers typically face is most properly addressed this way: Who would you rather have on the mound late in a tight game: Randy Johnson facing his twenty-eighth batter, or Jose Valverde facing his first?

This was the dilemma Grady Little faced when he came to the mound during the eighth inning of the seventh game of the 2003 ALCS. Surely you recall the essentials: Pedro's gone seven and one-third, and he's held the Yankees to three runs. As the conference is held, the Sox lead 5–3 with the tying runs in scoring position. The last three batters have all hit safely: a double from Derek Jeter, a single by Bernie Williams, a double by Hideki Matsui. With Jorge Posada due up (he's batter number thirty-one for the game, and one of those "good from both sides" switch-hitters), Little has right-hander Mike Timlin and lefty Alan Embree warming up. Embree had a 4.25 ERA during the season, but in the Yankee series he'd pitched four and one-third innings without giving up a hit. Timlin, with a 3.55 ERA during the season, had pitched four innings against the Yanks and allowed just one hit.

You know what Grady Little did, and it was the last decision of significance he made as Red Sox manager. What would you have done? In retrospect of course the call is simple: yank Pedro. Posada, after all, is about to rip a game-tying double to center. But that's in retrospect. To answer the real-world question, we analyzed the actual late-game performance of two dozen frontline starters (including Martinez) using game play-by-plays from the 1999 season, as well as their usual setup men and relievers. The idea was to determine whether the trend toward more regimented use of both closers and setup men was supported by the statistical evidence, at least in the contexts of the pitchers in question. And it turns out that statistically, Grady Little faced a breathtakingly close call.

Here's how we set up the study. We broke down each starter's game-by-game performance in groups of nine batters: batters one through nine, ten through eighteen, nineteen through twenty-seven, and above. Within each group, we looked at two things, the percentage of outs recorded, and the percentage of bases allowed. Although we kept data for the first eighteen batters, we used that only as a baseline. Since our real interest had to do with determining the starter's late-game abilities relative to his likely relief, we focused on how he did against batters nineteen and above. We also threw out all of the starter's games—for these guys, there weren't many—in which the opponent scored its fifth run by the time the twenty-sixth batter strode to the plate. Why? Because we were attempting to address a confined question involving late-game strategy: When the starter is getting beaten around early, late-game strategy isn't much of an issue. We limited the study to good pitchers having good years because, let's face it, nobody cares whether Greg Swindell replaces Brian Anderson. But what if he replaces Randy Johnson? That's a far more intriguing issue.

The study is not without its biases—we just cited a couple—but in the context of the study's goals the biases make sense. We defined good seasons as an ERA below 4.00, and we defined a relatively good day as allowing fewer than five runs in the first twenty-five batters.

For the setup men and closers, we focused only on their work in those roles. To that end, we deleted any performances in which they took the mound prior to the start of the seventh inning unless—which only happened in a handful of instances—the pitchers also finished the game. In most instances, we allowed only one setup man and one closer per team, but there were exceptions for the Yankees (Nelson/Stanton) and Diamondbacks (Olson/Swindell) where the setup man roles were so assiduously divided on a lefty-righty basis. That gave us a field of sixty-four pitchers: twenty-four starters (including three each from the Braves and Astros as well as two from the Dodgers), twenty-one setup men, and nineteen closers. Pedro was in the study, paired with Tim Wakefield (the Sox 1999 setup man) and Derek Lowe (the closer).

Finally, since we were concentrating on batter-pitcher matchups, we ignored all cases involving the following: stolen bases, caught stealing, pickoffs, errors, and fielder's choices in which no out was recorded.

So who wins the Johnson versus Olson/Swindell/Mantei and Martinez/Lowe arguments? Here's how the study worked out:

Pitcher Batters Faced	Percentage of Batters Retired	Percentage of Bases per Batter
Starters (28)	.723	.431
Setup men (1–3)	.704	.463
Closer (1–3)	.714	.429

From batters twenty-eight onward for as long as they stayed in the game, our twenty-four starters faced 1,396 batters and recorded 1,010 outs, retiring batters at a .723 percentage. They also allowed 600 bases, meaning that beyond batter twenty-eight, batters got an average of 0.43 bases against the starter. (As a rule of thumb, each batter sees an average of just under four pitches; at batter twenty-eight we are talking generally about pitches 107 and above.)

That was about 10 percentage points better than our nineteen closers fresh out of the pen, whose first three opponents in the batters box amounted to 3,418 hitters. The closers recorded 2,437 outs (a .714 percentage), and allowed an average of .431 total bases (based on 1,470 bases allowed).

Even tiring, our twenty-four good starters still bettered our twenty-one fresh setup men by 19 percentage points. The first three hitters those setup men faced—there were 3,140 of them—recorded 2,209 outs, but collected 1,453 total bases, for .704 and .463 percentages respectively. Both numbers were significantly worse than the frontline starters.

Perhaps more interestingly, our starting pitchers showed little if any signs of tiring as the game moved into its later stages. Their .728 out percentage for batters twenty-eight and above was precisely identical to their out percentage for batters nineteen to twenty-seven, and their .431 total bases percentage was only slightly higher than the .418 total bases percentage against them for those number nineteen to twenty-seven hitters.

It was not actually until about batter thirty (generally about pitch 115) that the performance of good starters who had established themselves as having good days even began to decline. Against that thirtieth hitter, our starters' out percentage fell to .682, while the total bases percentage rose to .494. Posada, remember, was batter thirty-one.

So although this will come as small consolation to Grady Little, the data suggest his faith in Martinez was not without foundation. He retired 77 percent of batters beyond batter number twenty-seven, a significantly better percentage than either his setup man (Wakefield, .688) or his closer (Lowe, .773). (If you're interested, Embree's 2003 batters retired percentage was .706; Timlin's was .735.)

Of the twenty-four starters in the 1999 study, 50 percent were better bets to retire the twenty-eighth (and above) hitters they faced than either their setup men or closers were to retire their first three opposing hitters. In addition to Martinez, here are the dozen starters who had the clear edge.

Superior Starters (Setup Men and Closers)

Jose Rosado, Kansas City, .882 (Scott Service .663, Jeff Montgomery .726)

Brad Radke, Minnesota, .732 (Bob Wells .730, Mike Trombley .718)

Tim Hudson, Oakland, .767 (Doug Jones .678, Billy Taylor .701)

Jamie Moyer, Seattle, .718 (Jose Paniagua .691, Jose Mesa .634)

Randy Johnson, Arizona, .734 (Greg Swindell .707, Greg Olson .676, Matt Mantei .690)

Kevin Millwood, Atlanta, .971 (Mike Remlinger .835, John Rocker .751)

Pete Harnisch, Cincinnati, .821 (Scott Sullivan .693, Danny Graves .763)

Alex Fernandez, Florida, .714 (Braden Looper .675, Antonio Alfonseca .710)

Ismael Valdes, Los Angeles, .741 (Alan Mills .658, Jeff Shaw .705)

Todd Ritchie, Pittsburgh, .795 (Scott Sauerbeck .694, Mike Williams .665)

Russ Ortiz, San Francisco, .701 (Felix Rodriguez .644, Robb Nen .627)

Superior Closers (Starters, Setup Men)

Five of the closers proved to be a superior choice, including Houston's closer, who beat out all three Astros starters included in the survey. Although beaten by starter Ismael Valdes (see above), Jeff Shaw also made it as a superior choice to the Dodgers' ace, Kevin Brown:

Mariano Rivera, Yankees, .789 (David Cone .590, Mike Stanton .696, Jeff Nelson. 717)

Billy Wagner, Houston, .795 (Mike Hampton .761, Jose Lima .719, Shane Reynolds .636, Jay Powell .664)

Jeff Shaw, Los Angeles, .705 (Kevin Brown .680, Alan Mills .658)

Trevor Hoffman, San Diego, .749 (Andy Ashby .649, Dan Micelli .723)

Mike Timlin, Baltimore, .758 (Mike Mussina .672, Jesse Orosco .700)

Finally, four setup men emerged as superior either to the men they were replacing or to the men who replaced them. Prominent among them was the Atlanta setup man, who beat out two of the Braves' aces.

Superior Setup Men (Starters, Closers)

Mike Remlinger, Atlanta, .835 (Greg Maddux .734, John Smoltz .692, John Rocker .751)

Paul Shuey, Cleveland, .754 (Bartolo Colon .703, Mike Jackson .712)

Steve Montgomery, Philadelphia, .745 (Curt Schilling .688, Wayne Gomes .695)

Manny Aybar, St. Louis, .732 (Kent Bottenfield .632, Rickey Bottalico .611)

If these good starters are, as a group, about 20 percentage points more efficient than the setup men who replace them, and equally as efficient as the closers, then one point is fairly made. There appears to be little justification for removing a good pitcher who is having a good game prior to the thirtieth batter (115th pitch) on the context that he is tiring. Even then, given the 20 percentage point performance difference between well-worked good starters and fresh setup men, remove him only if you can go directly to your closer. Grady Little's closer was Byung Hyun Kim, and he was not warming up.

FEAR OF INJURY

The debate over whether excessive use causes a pitcher to break down (and, for that matter, what constitutes excessive use) goes back decades. Historically, those who argue the premise point to Bob Feller, Robin Roberts, Chuck Estrada, Sandy Koufax, Catfish Hunter, and the entire 1980 Oakland A's staff. Kerry Wood is a classic contemporary model: a strikeout record by age twenty; arm surgery at twenty-one.

The most comprehensive effort to determine the relationship between heavy work and injury was undertaken by Craig Wright in the 1980s. He concluded that a key element, often overlooked, is a pitcher's age. Those who consistently face a large number of batters before their bodies have fully matured break down with alarming frequency. On the other hand, Wright believed, pitchers who are nursed through their relatively tender years—until about age twenty-five—enjoy considerably greater longevity.

Wright's conclusions, detailed in *The Diamond Appraised,* are based on a calculation of the number of batters a starting pitcher faces each time he takes the mound—Batters Faced Per Start, or BFS for short. The higher the BFS before age twenty-five, the more likely it is that physical problems will overtake a hurler. If Wright's theory is correct, that is a powerful argument for removing young pitchers in the late innings of games, even if they still appear to be in command of their stuff.

To verify his thesis, Wright examined the careers of fifteen pitchers who enjoyed an exceptional season at a young age, then failed to live up to that promise. His group included such names as Larry Dierker, Mark Fidrych, Don Gullett, Jon Matlack, and Gary Nolan. He contrasted the demands placed on them during their early years with the demands placed on a second group of pitchers, these pitchers having enjoyed an exceptional season after age thirty. This group included pitchers the like of Nolan Ryan, Tom Seaver, Bob Gibson, and Don Sutton. Three-quarters of the pitchers in the first group—the young guns who burned out before their time—began pitching professionally by age eighteen; that contrasted with only one-third of the pitchers in the second group. By age twenty-five, pitchers in the first group had worked more than 200 innings above the average workload of a pitcher in the second group. They also faced more batters per start than pitchers in the second group. That's even more significant than it sounds at first, Wright argues, because several pitchers in the first group were already slowing down due to arm problems before their twenty-fifth birthdays.

Wright's conclusions about treating young pitchers gingerly have a certain appeal because they make sense. It is a sort of extension of Little League syndrome, the victimization worked on twelve-year-olds by overzealous parents and coaches insistent that Johnny throw a curve ball so his team can win the city championship.

But while Wright's data is attractive, his methodology can be laid open to question. He began by selecting fifteen pitchers *who had enjoyed exceptional seasons at an early age, then failed to live up to that standard.* That's a bias. His study might have been fairer and more accurate had he surveyed *all* pitchers of a certain age for workload, and compared that result to future injury patterns. Let's re-examine Wright's thesis, applying this new test, and see what happens.

Between 1991 and 1995, more than 115 starting pitchers age twenty-five or below pitched in the major leagues. (For purposes of this exercise we are defining a "starter" as anyone who made at least eight starts, and who started in more than half of his appearances.) In those seasons and the three subsequent seasons, what proportion of those pitchers actually sustained arm, shoulder, or elbow injuries serious enough to sideline them for an appreciable amount of time? And how did the BFS of the pitchers who were injured compare with the BFS of the uninjured pitchers?

In some respects, the results are a validation of Wright's theories. A staggering 42 percent of those young starters reported significant arm, elbow, or shoulder problems within three years of playing a starting role in the majors at/or before age twenty-five. The roster of these young starters with the conflicted careers will be familiar to anybody who has ever drafted a hot prospect in a fantasy league: David Nied, Roger Pavlik, Chris Haney, Pete Smith, Donovan Osborne, Steve Avery, Cal Eldred, Aaron Sele, Wilson Alvarez, Jack McDowell, Jason Bere, Chad Ogea, Ben McDonald, Dave Fleming, and dozens of others.

But Wright's thesis does not entirely hold up. In particular, there are valid questions whether the connection he draws between "heavy" use and subsequent breakdown is anything more than coincidental. Recall that Wright placed the danger zone at thirty batters faced per start; above that, he found, and a young pitcher's chance for injury dramatically increased.

For our 1990–1995 pitching tykes, the evidence is inconclusive, mostly because managers and pitching coaches—presumably of their own volition—stopped using young starters (or old starters, for that matter) for more than thirty batters. Of the 117 different pitchers whose charts we examined for this survey, a mere eight—just 6.8 percent—averaged a 30 BFS or higher. Four of those eight—Pulsipher in 1995 (32.2), McDonald in 1990 (32.0), Mussina in 1992 (30.7), and Fernandez in 1993 (30.2) did subsequently have problems.

Beyond that, the flip side presents problems of its own. As our data show, 109 starters age twenty-five or below were *not* required to face thirty or more batters per start, and 41 percent of them still suffered subsequent arm, elbow, or shoulder problems. In 1990, Roger Craig required his prodigy, twenty-four-year-old Trevor Wilson, to average just over twenty-one batters in seventeen starts. One season later, still just twenty-five, Wilson toiled only 23.4 batters per start on average. These are not heavy workloads; Wilson couldn't have completed a game on those terms *even if he had been perfect every day*. No matter, by 1993 Wilson missed a third of the season with a sore shoulder. And for the record, Kerry Wood's BFS for the 1998 season—the one in which he broke down—was a very pedestrian 27.0.

Here's a chart comparing the percentage of young pitchers between 1990 and 1995 within varying ranges of BFS who subsequently sustained at least temporarily disabling arm, shoulder, or elbow injuries.

BFS	Percent Injured
0–24.0	38.1
24.1–26.0	35.1
26.1–28.0	44.0
28.1–30.0	52.0
30.1 and up	50.0

The chart implies some relationship between early use and subsequent injury. But in the context of the fact that for the time period in question only about 15 percent of Major League pitchers were disabled by arm injuries, the figures for young pitchers at all BFS levels are remarkably high.

There is one more injury-related puzzle that ought to be addressed, and it is a puzzle first raised by Wright. Why all the carnage these days? After all, as he noted, it is counterintuitive. Pitchers today are bigger, stronger, better trained, both in a conditioning and baseball sense, they work fewer innings and on fewer days. Yet in 1998, eighty-six different pitchers made trips to the Major League disabled list, representing 18 percent of all the men who worked Major League games. An average team employed about sixteen pitchers during the course of the 1998 season, and lost 3.2 of them to the disabled list at some point due to throwing-related trouble. Compare that rate of failure with the rates for 1948, 1958, 1968, 1978, and 1988.

PERCENT OF PITCHERS SPENDING TIME ON THE DISABLED LIST

Year	%
1948	2.5
1958	2.4
1968	3.8
1978	7.7
1988	11.3
1998	18.0

A conspiracist could some up with many rationales for the dramatic upswing. Adopting part of Wright's earlier enunciated theory, there are no more breather games because batters are stronger. (But if so, aren't pitchers also stronger? And don't pitchers work far fewer complete games? And aren't their BFS numbers, on the whole, smaller today than ever in the game's history?)

Perhaps expansion plays a role; there are, after all, nearly twice as many teams today as in the 1950s, meaning a roughly 50 percent dilution in the pitcher talent pool. (But wouldn't there also be a 50 percent reduction in the batter talent pool, making games easier to pitch? And wouldn't all of that be offset by the greater availability of talented pitchers from previously undertapped sources: blacks, Latinos, and the like?)

Perhaps clubs today do a better job of diagnosing injuries, so players—especially high-priced pitchers—get on the disabled list more quickly. In that sense, the stats may be a chimera, suggesting a problem that actually doesn't even exist. (But shouldn't improved conditioning and treatment methods, not to mention a better understanding of the physiology of pitching, reduce those problems?)

Perhaps pitchers today simply report injuries that their brethren of prior years—out of fear of losing their jobs—worked through. Could be. The rise does roughly parallel the emergence of multiyear contracts. Maybe the game's great unspoken enemy—steroid use—plays a part.

An increasingly attractive theory points to amateur baseball as a possible culprit. Although there are no records to support this, it seems reasonable to assert that far more professional players today are products of youth baseball programs. They've often been playing competitively since they were ten, nine, or even eight years old. Almost certainly they were the best players on their teams, and almost certainly they pitched—maybe a lot. In kids' ball, teen leagues, high school, and college, they were coached by men with little training in biomechanics, and were often pushed by parents with more ego than sense. Nobody counted pitches, meaning that today nobody has a clue how many pitches those young arms have actually thrown.

In 2003, an organization known as the American Sports Medicine Institute released a study translating this theory into statistical reality. AMSI is supported by Dr. James Andrews, an orthopedic surgeon whose patient list includes many of the best-known pitchers in the majors today. Judging from the results of the study, that client list is getting younger. It found that among 476 youth pitchers (ages nine to fourteen) who took part, nearly half experienced elbow or shoulder pain at least once during the season. Andrews himself performs about 150 "Tommy John" surgeries per year, three times as many as he did less than a decade ago. And he performs them on pitchers as young as ages fifteen and sixteen.

"We don't have enough quality pitchers to go around because the good quality pitchers are being hurt in youth leagues," Dr. Andrews told Cox News Service.

Ten, fifteen, twenty years ago, far fewer major leaguers sustained serious arm injuries. Ten, fifteen, twenty years ago, far fewer major leaguers came up through extensive youth programs. That both those statements are true does not in and of itself establish a relationship—but it should be a chilling theory to any Little League parent who fancies his kid the next Roger Clemens or Randy Johnson.

Or perhaps we're going at this all the wrong way. Perhaps, seeing a rising tide of injuries in the 1970s and 1980s, we reacted by overly protecting pitchers, when we should have done precisely the opposite. Perhaps long-time pitching coach George Bamberger was right when he argued that the rash of injuries today is attributable not to working pitchers too hard, but to working them too easy. Maybe pitchers stayed in better shape a few decades back *because they pitched*. Maybe what is occurring is the result of coddling.

All of those are merely theories. The evidence does not exist to prove, beyond doubt, any of them. Perhaps they work in combination. Of all injury-related lessons, this one looms most plain: Work young pitchers gingerly. Let them grow.

7

HIGHLY PAID IRRELEVANCE

In November of 1997, the Tampa Bay Devil Rays had $25 million with which to build a new team from scratch. They invested $4 million of it—16 percent—in free agent pitcher Roberto Hernandez, who the previous season had worked only eighty innings, who had never in a seven-year career worked more than eighty-four, and who they didn't plan to work any harder.

Considering that the Devil Rays projected to play approximately 1,450 innings during their initial season, that might sound a bit extravagant. But the Devil Rays had a plan. Hernandez wasn't just any pitcher, he was a closer, and those innings he pitched weren't just any innings, they were the ninth innings. Even though he had pitched a mere eighty-one innings in 1997, Hernandez had saved thirty-one games, a nice total. By the standards of big league baseball's modern book, the ninth inning is the key one, the inning where the belts get tighter, the outs get tougher, and it takes a high-dollar specialist to perform.

Of all the various on-field strategies, only the five-man rotation is today accepted as conventional wisdom more readily than the hierarchical bullpen strategy, at whose apex sit men such as Hernandez. That strategy can be summarized as follows, and applied to virtually every Major League team.

The starter's job is to pitch seven innings with the lead.

The setup man pitches the eighth inning and holds the lead for . . .

. . . The closer, who pitches the ninth and records the save.

So ingrained has this formula become that its application is today reflexive; managers do it not out of any special thought process, but simply because they are conditioned that way. In fact, baseball watchers view it as an oddity when a team holding a lead in the late innings doesn't follow that formula. In 2004, Livan Hernandez led the major leagues in complete games—with nine. Out of almost 4,860 Major League starts, pitchers threw a total of 150 complete games, about one every thirty-two starts.

By contrast, relievers were awarded 1,230 saves.

There's no question this represents a strategy. There's also no question that it is a costly one. In 2004, Major League teams committed $283.6 million to the care and feeding of their collective bullpens. That's $9.45 million per team. The list that follows shows the percentage of each team's total payroll assets that it devoted to its bullpen in 2004.

Team	% of Payroll in Bullpen
Los Angeles	31.5
Anaheim	18.3
Cincinnati	18.0
Oakland	17.4
Philadelphia	16.6
Atlanta	16.4
Seattle	16.4
St. Louis	16.4
Pittsburgh	16.0
Florida	15.9
Texas	15.8
Milwaukee	15.1
Chicago White Sox	14.6
Toronto	14.2
Cleveland	13.9
Arizona	13.4
Baltimore	13.2
Kansas City	13.1

San Diego	12.5
Boston	12.0
New York Yankees	11.9
New York Mets	11.2
San Francisco	10.3
Montreal	10.1
Detroit	9.9
Chicago Cubs	9.4
Tampa Bay	8.9
Colorado	7.7
Minnesota	5.1
Houston	3.3

The modern day closer doesn't have the toughest job in baseball, he has one of the easiest. The number of innings worked is central to the argument. While the modern book on relief pitching casts the ninth inning as a morass for the typical starter that can only be successfully navigated with the guidance of a trained, professional closer, that premise ignores a basic rule. It is this:

Any pitcher has value only when he pitches.

You can't win the game from the bench. It is as true for pitchers as for any other player. Remember that rule for every moment of your consideration of the true value of a closer.

There is not unanimous agreement on the above. The common managerial tendency—the *Book* tendency today—is to deduce that preventing runs late in the game is more important than preventing them early, because there is less time to offset their impact. As long ago as in a 1981 article for *Esquire* magazine, and as recently as 2002's *Win Shares*, Bill James has given voice to that logic. "The value of the relief ace is greater than the relative number of runs that he saves because the relief ace prevents runs at moments of the game when the impact would be greater than normal," he writes in *Win Shares*.

James appeared to have modified that philosophy when he became an executive with the Boston Red Sox. "Using your relief ace to protect a three-run lead," James was quoted as saying, "is like a business using a top executive to negotiate fire insurance." I'd say he was more nearly right in that than in *Win Shares*. The Sox were widely roasted in 2003 after their pen under-performed, and especially after the Pedro debacle against New York in the postseason. But James, the executive, was correct. Boston's problem wasn't the logic; it was that in the great relief corps crapshoot the modern game has constructed, they had no luck.

Phil Birnbaum, chairman of the Committee on Statistical Analysis for the Society for American Baseball research, delved more deeply into this in 2003. In *Application of Win Probabilities*, Birnbaum calculates the likelihood of a team winning a game from every conceivable combination of team, inning, score, and base/out situation. There are—I am taking Phil's word for this—5,616 such situations.

Birnbaum found that most outcomes—a single, a stolen base, a strikeout—are roughly twice as important in terms of determining the outcome when they occur in the bottom of the ninth inning of a tie game as they are during the normal course of play. And when those outcomes occur in the bottom of the ninth inning with a team leading by one run—a classic "save" situation—some of the values rise to as much as four times their normal level of importance. He found the ten most "important" situations (and the relative degree of their importance) to be as follows:

1. Leading by one run, top of the ninth (+2.66)
2. Leading by one run, bottom of the eighth (+2.63)
3. Leading by one run, bottom of the ninth (+2.53)
4. Tie game, bottom of the ninth (+2.37)
5. Leading by one run, top of the eighth (+2.36)
6. Tie game, top of the ninth (+2.18)
7. Tie game, top of the eighth (+2.03)
8. Leading by one run, bottom of the seventh (+2.03)
9. Leading by two runs, bottom of the seventh (+1.93)
10. Leading by one run, bottom of the sixth (+1.93)

Just to look at this data, Birnbaum has plainly made the case for the importance of the final few outs relative to all others. Does his study undermine the premise of this chapter, which essentially is that you get an out when you can? I don't think so. And it isn't necessary to challenge either Phil's data or his conclusions in order to see how both premises can live in peaceful coexistence.

What Phil has done is calculate win probabilities based on real-game data. He has, in effect, said, "Once a game arrives at a given point, the value of a particular occurrence is inflated by that game situation." But baseball games do not arrive at particular points by fiat. Teams don't lead by one run in the top of the ninth because it was thus ordained. Ball games in fact begin zero–zero; only the accumulation of events dictates subsequent decisions, and those events can be influenced. So the notion that preventing a base hit is two, three, or even four times as important when you lead by one run in the ninth as at other times can be looked at in several ways. Phil's way—viewing the numbers as possible justification for reserving the services of highly paid and talented closers—is one. Here's another: Place greater emphasis on the earlier (and by Phil's measurement less critical) game situations as a means of avoiding the prospect of finding yourself in the situation of leading by just one run in the top of the ninth in the first place.

Didn't your mom ever tell you that the best way to get out of trouble is to avoid getting in it? Listen to your moms, baseball managers.

The great shift in game strategies in recent years has been away from that premise, and toward the approach that save situations are "inevitabilities." When one shifts pitching resources away from the early innings and toward the late innings—which is what the "closer" mentality does—the diminution of other pitching roles creates a degree of self-fulfilling prophecy. Mom be damned.

We can find evidence of that point in the historical box scores. In 1962, the first season in which every team played 162 games, the average Major League team played 40.4 games in which it led by 3 runs or fewer with two at bats remaining. In other words, the situation in which a leading manager today would call for his setup man. By 2002, the average had risen to 42.4 such games. That's a 5 percent increase in "close" games.

In 1962, the average team played 38.4 games in which it led by 3 runs or fewer with one at bat remaining. In today's game, that's the typical "closer" situation. Today, clubs play 41.5 such games per season, an increase of 8 percent.

In 1962, there were 8.9 runs scored per game. In 2002, teams scored 9.2 runs per game. That's a 3 percent increase in run production per game. Logically, as more runs are scored, one would expect that the higher-scoring team would pull away from the lower-scoring team, and the number of close games would diminish. Yet precisely the opposite has occurred. Given what we know of the change in bullpen strategy, that is evidence of a self-fulfilling prophecy.

So let's repeat, this time with specific respect to the fellow on the mound. A pitcher's value to a team is directly related to the number of innings he pitches. Theoretically, it is possible for someone to pitch a lot of bad innings, but in practice contending clubs don't allow that to happen. In fact, the best mathematical formula for measuring pitching performance—pitching Linear Weights—has only two basic components, those being earned runs allowed and innings pitched. Simply put, a pitcher who throws 225 good innings a season is roughly three times as valuable as a pitcher who gives you 81 good innings, even if the guy is Roberto Hernandez and the 81 innings are all ninth innings.

Statistically, the best that can be said for all the modern incarnations and redefinitions of the role of the pen and the closer is that they are pointless. Objective analysis of the data leads to this conclusion: No matter how you use your bullpen, you're still going to win and lose games about as often as if you did it any other way. And in recent seasons, evidence is beginning to emerge in support of the notion that today's hierarchical bullpen may actually be counterproductive.

To a generation of fans brought up to expect and admire the hierarchical bullpen, that must seem hard to swallow. So let's lay out the data.

Here's how to do it. Examine the box scores from every game played in each of several seasons over a period of decades in which what we would today recognize as a "save situation." That is, a game in which one team held a lead of three runs or fewer with six outs or fewer to go. For each season, calculate the won-lost percentage of the team leading in those games. If, over time, the new bullpen methods make sense, they ought to result in a greater won-lost percentage for the team taking the lead into those final innings.

That's what we did for ten such seasons over forty-five years, seasons rich in the diversity of the assumptions that governed bullpen use. The seasons were 1952, 1962, 1972, 1982, and 1992, as well as 1997–2000 and 2002. These seasons encompass a period that begins when starters were expected to go as long as possible, and concludes with the age of the starter-setup-closer in full flower. Here is the winning percentage in each season for teams that led in each of three "save situations" with six outs remaining.

PERCENTAGE OF VICTORIES

Situation	1952	1962	1972	1982	1992	1997	1998	1999	2000	2002
1 Run Lead	79.4	75.2	76.1	73.4	79.3	77.0	68.6	73.4	68.7	74.9
2 Run Lead	85.2	86.2	89.5	87.4	89.2	86.4	84.0	84.2	87.0	88.5
3 Run Lead	90.9	93.0	95.6	93.3	94.2	93.1	83.8	91.0	93.0	94.1
Up 3 or Less	84.3	83.7	85.6	83.6	86.3	84.3	78.0	81.9	82.2	84.7

In other words, all the machinations having to do with the bullpen that occurred between the age of Jim Konstanty and the age of Mariano Rivera had improved the likelihood of a Major League team holding a lead of 3 runs or less in the late innings of a close game barely a fraction of a percent. The difference between the highest result (86.3 percent in 1992) and the lowest (78.0 percent in 1999) is 8.3 percent of all close games. Since an average Major League team leads in about forty-three games a year by 3 runs or less with two innings to play, this means that the real on-field difference between the best result and the worst result equates to about three and one-half victories per season. The significance of that data is further tempered by the fact that the pattern is not linear. Both the best and worst seasonal performances occur within a few years of each other, and both during seasons in which fundamentally the same rules of bullpen use were in favor.

Here are the same percentages for the same years, except that these reflect the winning percentages for teams leading by 3 or fewer runs with one at bat to go.

PERCENTAGE OF VICTORIES

Situation	1952	1962	1972	1982	1992	1997	1998	1999	2000	2002
1 Run Lead	87.0	82.5	85.2	85.5	84.2	86.4	84.2	84.1	79.6	83.3
2 Run Lead	95.8	94.2	94.3	94.2	95.2	95.0	91.0	91.7	93.6	94.7
3 Run Lead	98.0	96.6	97.2	97.0	97.9	98.0	95.2	94.9	97.5	97.2
3 Runs or Less	92.3	90.3	92.5	91.8	91.4	92.5	89.4	89.9	89.2	91.2

In the ninth inning, the overall difference remains small. Teams enjoyed their best winning percentage in 1972 and again in 1997; their worst in 2000. Between 1997 and 2000, performance fell by about 3 percent; by 2002, it rebounded to a historically normal level. But that was about 1 percent worse than in 1952, when bullpens were stocked with failed starters and journeymen.

If the idea of a save artist is a good strategy, we probably would expect to see an improved winning percentage from 1982, when the reflexive use of a closer was in its infancy. There isn't any improvement. In 1982, Major League teams won 91.8 percent of the "save situation" games they played, about two points better than in 1999 and a fraction better than in 2002, but in both cases the differences being statistically insignificant. In 1982, teams won 97 percent of the games in which they led by 3 runs—fractionally less than in 2002, and 1 percent less than in 1952. They won 94.2 percent of the time when they led by 2 runs—about 0.5 percent less often than in 2002. But they won 2 percent more often than in 2002 in games in which they led by 1 run.

The reality is that you can check percentages for any of the years all the way back to 1952 without finding an overall statistical difference that suggests a pattern of steady improvement. In 1952, long before anyone thought of closers, teams won 92.3 percent of all games in which they led by 3 or fewer runs with one at bat to go, a percentage that is actually slightly higher than today.

The most interesting nugget to come out of all this is with respect to teams' performance in one-run games. Since those leads are the most fragile, the strategic application of the pitching staff may also be considered the most important in these situations. Here's the year-by-year data for percentage of victories in one-run games by the team that leads with two at bats to go.

1952:	79.4%
1962:	75.2%
1972:	76.1%

1982:	73.6%
1992:	79.3%
1997:	74.2%
1998:	68.6%
1999:	73.4%
2000:	68.7%
2002:	74.9%

If anything, one-run game performance suggests that the development of the "setup man" system in the 1990s has undermined, not enhanced, teams' opportunities to hold leads. But again, some perspective is in order. Over the course of a Major League season, teams play about seventeen games in which they are presented with the opportunity to hold a one-run lead over the final two innings. That means that an 11 percent decrease in lead-holding between 1952 and 1999 amounts to about two additional losses per team per season. It's not a big deal. On the other hand, isn't the point of changing strategies supposed to be to *improve* team performance, not *hurt* it?

Contrary to the mythology surrounding closers—that the job takes a "special" person—pitchers can and do jump into the role with relative ease. In recent seasons, converted starters Jason Isringhausen, Mark Leiter, Jose Jimenez, and Tom Gordon successfully assumed closer duties in Oakland, Philadelphia, Colorado, and Boston. Mike Jackson, an erstwhile setup man, exchanged places with Jose Mesa in Cleveland. Rookie Kerry Ligtenberg did the job when Mark Wohlers was injured in Atlanta, then John Rocker replaced Ligtenberg, then Ligtenberg, Rocker, and Mike Remlinger sort of trisected the job in 2000. Stan Belinda covered for an ailing Jeff Shaw in Cincinnati. Shaw himself had gotten the closer's job the year before when Jeff Brantley couldn't pitch. In 1999, Jose Jimenez pitched a no-hitter. But in 2001, Colorado needed a closer. Bingo, Jimenez became a closer. In

2002, much of the credit for the Minnesota Twins' drive to the AL Central pennant went to closer Eddie Guardado, who recorded 45 saves. In his nine previous Major League seasons, Guardado had worked 505 games yet recorded just 30 saves. In 2003, two of the game's most widely heralded closers were Joe Borowski of the Cubs and Mike MacDougal of the Royals. Borowski entered 2003 with 131 career Major League appearances and 2 saves. MacDougal's career totals entering 2003 were 9 and 0.

Defenders of the hierarchical bullpen would puzzle momentarily over phenomenons like Guardado, Borowski, or MacDougal . . . and then pronounce that it proves their assumption. "A born closer," they would say, as Bobby Cox in fact did say of Ligtenberg late in 1998. "He has that closer's mentality." This is the sort of standard for proof that—applied in reverse—used to get witches killed. You remember, don't you, how the good citizens of Salem determined whether somebody was a witch? They threw the suspect into a deep well; if she drowned, she was innocent. If, on the other hand, she survived, she must have used witch's powers . . . so she was hauled out and burned or hanged. Bullpens have become the witch's wells of the modern age; if a Joe Borowski emerges from obscurity to become a "closer," well, he must have the magical power. Only they don't kill him; they raise his salary. Then the newly found "closer" flops, as both Borowski and MacDougal did in 2004.

Indeed, closers not only rise quickly, they fall with equal suddenness. Of the twenty-eight closers who led their respective teams in saves in 1995, only six still functioned in a closer's role in 2000. And only one—John Wetteland—posted earned run averages in each season between 1995 and 2000 that were a half point or more below the average in his league. (The same happened to Ligtenberg, who must have lost his "closer's mentality" in 2000, when Cox gave him just fourteen save opportunities. Why? John Rocker and John Smoltz.) Considering the size of the average closer's paycheck, is an ERA a mere half point below the league average asking too much?

INVESTING LONG-TERM IN A CLOSER

Let's look at the performance of a class of pitchers who met three conditions. They worked between 50 and 125 innings in relief in 2002, had earned run averages that were a half point or better below their league's ERA, and pitched between 50 and 125 innings in relief in the same league again in 2003.

There were forty-four pitchers who fit that statistical profile in 2002–2003. Those forty-four got an average pay raise of 40 percent for 2003. But their 2003 performance, as measured by earned run average, worsened by about one-third. The cumulative 2002 ERAs of the pitchers in this group: 2.85. The comparable figure for 2003: 3.78. Of the forty-four pitchers in that group, twenty-nine had worse ERAs in 2003 than in 2002. What happened?

To a degree, the natural bias of the selected group comes into play. We did, after all, begin with a selection of pitchers whose 2002 ERAs were very low; the law of averages suggests the group ERA would tend to rise.

But the problems suffered by our group of pitchers are more real than that. In 2002, their collective ERAs were about 67 percent of the league average. In 2003, that figure rose to about 84 percent of league average. So even relative to the league, our "very good" 2002 pitchers reverted substantially toward normal. A full one-third of our sample group saw their ERAs surpass the average ERA in their league for 2003. In other words, this one-third went in one season from very good to subpar. Jose Mesa's 2.97 2002 ERA was 72 percent of the National League average. In 2003, his 6.52 ERA was 152 percent of the league norm. Mike Williams went from 71 percent of the league average ERA in 2002 to 143 percent in 2003. Luis Vizcaino and Ramiro Mendoza suffered leaps of a similar dimension.

The insidious cause of this trend was the tendency of teams in their evaluation of these pitchers to overlook two fundamentals of math—sample size and random chance. The fact that a pitcher has a very good 75 or 80 innings one season says little about how well he will pitch the following season; he simply hasn't pitched enough to establish a reliable pattern.

Sample size is something that political pollsters understand a lot better than baseball general managers. No pollster would attempt to forecast a candidate's performance on election day on the basis of eighty responses—it's simply too few bits of information. But baseball GMs stake millions on their estimate of a pitcher's prospects based on 80 innings of work.

If this is true of short-work pitchers, the data suggest it may be especially true of closers, who are the prima donnas of the group. Closers are especially vulnerable because they tend to work very few innings, generally no more than 80 or so. Of the forty-four pitchers included in the above-cited study for 1999, fourteen met an additional condition: they led their team in saves in 2002. The ERAs of half of those fourteen rose in 2003; in six cases they rose by at least a point and a half.

Despite the vagaries of their performances, the average paychecks of the forty-four pitchers included in the study increased between 2002 and 2003, by 25 percent in the American League and by an impressive 49 percent in the National League. The 2003 Phillies paid Mesa $1 million more for that 6.52 ERA; the Rockies nearly doubled Jimenez's salary—from $1.938 million to $3.6 million—and in return he nearly doubled his ERA, from 3.56 to 5.22. Jay Powell, with a 3.44 2002 ERA, got a million-dollar raise from Texas in 2003, and the Rangers got a 7.82 ERA.

If closers by themselves don't contribute to a team's chances of winning, what of the move in recent years to more structured bullpens, and specifically to the development of the "setup man"?

As a recognized and compensated position, the setup man has developed gradually over the past decade or so. As with many things pertinent to the bullpen, you can trace its emphasis to Tony LaRussa's Oakland A's teams of the early 1990s.

When LaRussa established Dennis Eckersley as his closer in the late 1980s, he did more than that. He gave every pitcher an assigned task. Jeff Nelson was the right-handed setup man, while Rick Honeycutt set up against lefties. Eric Plunk assisted Nelson, and Todd Burns filled in as needed. It became part of LaRussa's mantra: Don't ask a pitcher to do more than he's assigned to do. Given the fact that it's such a feel-good, nineties sort of notion and given the reality that LaRussa's A's won divisional titles in 1988, 1989, and 1990, the inevitable occurred. Teams copied the system.

But does the setup man contribute to victory? Or is the approximate 300 percent pay increase received by setup men over the decade of the 1990s a reward for an illusion in the same sense that the closer's paycheck is? Let's look again at the data cited at the outset of this chapter, but focusing more closely on teams that lead with two at bats left—the at bats generally dealt with today by the setup man as well as the closer.

In 2002, Major League teams won 84.7 percent of the time when they led by 3 runs or less with two at bats remaining. They won 94 percent when they led by 3 runs, 88.5 percent when they led by 2, and 74.9 percent when they led by 1 run.

Yet in 1952, forty-five years earlier, and at a time when there were no closers or setup men, Major League teams held close leads in the late innings at virtually the same rate as in 2002, 84.3 percent. It is true that 1952 teams leading by 3 runs after seven innings lost slightly more often than they do today. On the other hand, 1952 teams that led by 1 run after seven innings won 79.4 percent of the time, about 6 percent more frequently than in 2002. That begins to suggest, although it is not statistically compelling, that a manager's reflexive removal of a starter after seven innings in a close game might be slightly destructive, rather than constructive.

Why might modern bullpen strategy inhibit, rather than enhance, the prospect of victory?

A hierarchical bullpen eliminates managerial judgment as an issue. If you're paying a guy $5 million to close games, then there's not much question who's to be waved in to start the ninth, is there? As a functional matter today, this is true irrespective of whether either the guy on the mound or the closer is going well. Managers do not exercise the judgment they would exercise at other positions of judging that a closer is having a bad stretch, because the hierarchical nature of the pen is designed to eliminate judgment. Thus occur situations of the type that confronted the Chicago Cubs and Jim Riggleman in May of 1999.

The Cubs' pen was classically hierarchical, with Rod Beck at the apex. It was also the only reason Riggleman could have plausibly waved him to the mound in the ninth inning of a game against the New York Mets on the afternoon of April 23. After all, Beck entered the game with an earned run average of 11.81. His last outing, five days earlier against Milwaukee, had been a disaster: four hits and two tying runs allowed in a ninth inning save effort that was only redeemed when the Cubs scored in the tenth and Dan Serafini saved Beck. Beyond that, it had become glaringly obvious that the Cubs had better. Rodney Myers had been perfect out of the pen to that point, and Felix Heredia had allowed no earned runs in seven innings. Alas, Heredia had already pitched.

The result: Beck got fewer than half his pitches over the plate, walked two, gave up a hit and the winning run.

Two weeks passed, but Beck's fortunes changed hardly at all. Against Cincinnati on May 7, starter Kevin Tapani hurled eight innings that were good for a 2–1 lead. In the pen, Beck sat saddled with a 9.00 ERA; Heredia, next to him, could boast of a 3.86 ERA. Riggleman might have stayed with Tapani. If not, cold logic dictated a move to Heredia. But hierarchy dictated Beck, and it was Beck who got the call. He faced five batters, retired two, allowed three hits, two of them doubles, and lost the game. "I stunk," said Beck. "Beck is our closer," said Riggleman.

The Cubs moved into Los Angeles for a series with the Dodgers. Again Tapani pitched eight strong innings and left with a 2–1 lead. Again Beck came on in the ninth. Again Heredia, with an ERA less than half of Beck's—and more pertinently, a salary one twentieth the size—sat in the pen. This time Beck faced four batters, threw a home run ball, a double, and a wild pitch that cost the game.

Three games, each of them arguably lost due to an orthodox adherence to hierarchical dictates. As they left L.A., the Cubs stood two games to the bad side of .500 in the NL Central standings. Had they won those three games, they'd have been four games to the good. In the NL Central of 1999, four games above .500 was the record of a contender.

There is a second major flaw with a hierarchical bullpen, the flaw being that it functions on much the same principle as a union assembly line. There is a strong division of labor, with a concurrent detachment of responsibility. In the case of an assembly line, somebody affixes the steering wheel, another installs the doors, and a third attaches the engine assembly. If, a year after the car is on the road, something goes wrong, a lot of people can dodge responsibility.

Same thing with the hierarchical bullpen, except that the consequences are more dire to the team's fate in the pennant race. In a hierarchical bullpen, of course, the top guy's job doesn't begin until the ninth inning of a game his team leads. If his team leads in the seventh or eighth inning, well, that's work for a minion, someone perhaps given the *nomme de guerre* of "setup man," but in any consequence not the top guy. In a hierarchical bullpen, the closer's view of the situation inevitably becomes "that's not my job."

Which is fine except that the game can be won or lost by what happens in the seventh or eighth inning as well as by what happens in the ninth. Moreso, perhaps, because a game blown in the seventh or eighth *cannot* be saved in the ninth. To be fully functional, then, a hierarchical system requires that virtually every reliever be as competent as the closer—otherwise, the prospect increases that the car breaks down before it ever gets to the closer's station on the assembly line of victory. In this context, going to the pen becomes very similar to a game of Russian roulette; each time you make a programmed move, the prospect looms that you will bring in the one guy who doesn't have his stuff that night. Kansas City Royals' manager Tony Muser ran afoul of Russian roulette in the second game of a doubleheader against Cincinnati the evening of June 5, 1999. This is how Muser managed the eighth inning of a game in which the Royals led 4–3.

He opened the inning with Terry Mathews, who had pitched a scoreless seventh. Mathews retired the first batter he faced, Hal Morris.

With left-handed batter Sean Casey due up next, Muser removed Mathews in favor of his own left-hander, Matt Whisenant. Whisenant retired Casey.

With right-handed batter Greg Vaughn up next, Muser pulled Whisenant in favor of right-hander Ober Moreno. He had at that point removed two pitchers who had retired the previous five batters they had faced. Vaughn hit Moreno's first pitch over the left field fence for a game-tying home run.

Muster had pulled the trigger three times, finally found the guy who didn't have his stuff, and got blown away. An inning later, so did the Royals.

Managers once recognized the danger of this bullpen game. A quarter-century ago, it was not at all unusual for relievers of the ilk of Sparky Lyle or Rollie Fingers to be brought into a tight situation in the seventh or eighth inning and pitch to the conclusion. In 1972, the Yankees' Lyle threw 107 innings in 59 appearances, nearly two innings per appearance on average, *and* led the league in saves with 35. Fingers averaged better than two innings per appearance for Oakland in 1971 (17 saves), again in 1973 (22 saves and a world championship), and in 1976 nearly did it again, with 134 innings in 70 games. Did they wear down? Well, after averaging about 130 innings per season for seven seasons between 1970 and 1976, Fingers followed up with his two best years, leading the National League in saves with San Diego in 1977 and again in 1978. Lyle followed his 1972 workhorse performance with 27 more saves in 1973, and in 1976 he led the AL again with 23. In 1977, he worked 137 innings in 72 games, again nearly averaging two innings per game. He saved 26 more.

This is the time when somebody inevitably will say, "Well, things were different then." Okay, and just precisely what might those different things be? Was the game played at a more leisurely, more relaxed pace in the seventies? Did pitchers somehow coast through the game for long stretches? Did those long stretches include the seventh, eighth, and ninth innings, when Fingers, Lyle, and others of their kind did their work? Drugs?

Baseball researchers have been intrigued by the varying approaches to bullpen use virtually since bullpens became popular, and well before use patterns were refined to their present pattern. In the fourth annual *Baseball Research Journal,* published in 1975, Dick Cramer tackled the topic of whether relievers could be credited (or blamed, as you prefer) for a decline in batting averages. If true, the theory was plausible: Batters theretofore accustomed to seeing a tiring starter, so the logic went, were instead hitting against fresh arms.

Cramer's study was, of course, conducted during the 1972–73 seasons, when bullpen usage patterns were far less formal than they are today. Even so, what he found is instructive.

In 1972, run scoring actually increased slightly in the seventh through ninth innings. In 1973, Cramer found about a 10 percent decrease in run scoring. In both cases, though, there were disturbing random patterns to the data. In 1973, run scoring fell a full 27 percent in the seventh inning. It also fell 13 percent in the ninth inning. On its face, that might seem a powerful argument that relievers fared better than starters. But the eighth inning was a different matter: In the eighth, run scoring actually increased by 11 percent.

The 1972 data was even more contradictory. That season, run scoring increased in both the seventh and eighth innings, falling only in the ninth. Cramer's conclusion: Based on statistical criteria, differences in run production in the late innings during those seasons were more likely attributable to random chance than to any performance enhancement brought about by relievers.

As indicated earlier, the biggest problem with *The Book* as it relates to bullpen strategy isn't that it costs victories. Although there are signs of a team performance downturn, they are relatively recent and inconclusive. The problem lies in the dollar signs. If you are the 2003 Philadelphia Phillies, paying Turk Wendell, Rheal Cormier, Dan Plesac, and Terry Adams $11.23 million to do something extraneous to the task of winning games (and you fall out of the wild card race in the final week), you eventually have to ask a question. What didn't you buy with that $11.23 million? If you relinquish the wild card advantage during those final couple of weeks, and your team batting average and home run production are both in the league's lower half, would another hitter have put you over the top? Could you have gotten another hitter for half of that $11.23 million? Gee, I'm thinking yes on that one.

Those who cling against logic to that mystical faith in the closer system try to refute this evidence with several arguments, all of them transparently weak. The most common argument is the one made in 1982 by Bill James: there's just something indefinable about closers. Birnbaum's Win Probability study suggests the need for closers based on the criticality of their roles, a case that would be more persuasive if the evidence didn't suggest that those roles were self-induced.

Others argue that changes in the game since the early 1950s would have made late leads even more susceptible to being overcome had not the closer been invented. What kinds of changes? Well, baseball was virtually a lily white game in the early 1950s, so integration would be one such change. But for that to be a valid explanation, one would have to argue that the influx of minorities into the game has raised batting talent disproportionately to pitching talent; in other words, that minorities can hit but they can't pitch. Take that line of reasoning up with Juan Marichal or Bob Gibson.

Others argue that souped-up offenses account for the fact that closers don't actually save games in any greater percentage today than occurred forty-five years ago. It's true that run scoring is up; expansion and the designated hitter explain parts of this. The DH argument is plainly absurd; surely any offensive advantage gained by the trailing team's DH would be more than offset by the leading team's DH. Beyond that, late leads are blown in the American League at roughly the same frequency as in the National League. As for the general offensive explosion making late-inning comebacks more likely, that theory also assumes that only the trailing team is scoring more runs today. But why should that be the case? By definition, the leading team has had the better offense for the first seven-ninths of every game; if a generally souped-up offense helps either team, it ought to help the one that's already in front to start with.

No theory invalidates the case that the closer is an overrated and overpaid accouterment for the simple reason that the case is valid. The closer's value, then, is statistically illusory. He doesn't hold leads with any greater frequency today than starters did nearly a half century ago. He doesn't hold leads any better than less well paid relievers did a quarter century ago. If anything, he does those jobs marginally worse. The only thing he does better is get paid . . . and that he does very much better.

7.1 *The Gagne-Eckersley Diversion*

Given how little they actually pitch, it's rare for a reliever to deserve postseason award consideration. But it happens. In 2003, in the midst of a consecutive saves streak that would stretch over three seasons and reach 84 games, Eric Gagne won the National League Cy Young Award. He was arguably deserving of it. But Gagne's award also illustrates just how good a reliever has to be to stand in the front rank of value among pitchers.

Gagne pitched 82.3 innings, allowing just 37 hits, 11 earned runs, and walking just 20. Of 306 batter-pitcher confrontations, he won 259, or 81 percent. Mark Prior won 73 percent, although to Prior's credit he engaged in 863 such confrontations. Jason Schmidt won 76 percent of 819 confrontations. Gagne's PW was 4.9, identical to Prior's and better than Schmidt's 3.9. So while I might have personally picked Prior because of his considerably greater workload, the case for Gagne is completely defensible.

To consider how unusual that situation is, let's examine the last case of a postseason award–winning reliever. Until Gagne, that would have been Oakland's Dennis Eckersley, who won both the Cy Young Award and AL MVP in 1992.

Here is Dennis Eckersley's game-by-game record during that MVP season, all 69 appearances. The chart indicates the date, the opponent, the score at the time Eck entered the game (indicated by an asterisk), the number of innings he pitched and his performance, whether Eckersley figured in the decision, and the final score, if different from the score when he came in.

APP	DATE	OPPONENT	SCORE*	IP	H	R	ER	BB	SO	DEC	FINAL
1	4-6	Kansas Cy.	5-3	1	3	0	0	0	0	S	
2	4-8	Kansas Cy.	3-3	1.2	0	0	0	0	1		4-3
3	4-9	Kansas Cy.	5-2	.1	0	0	0	0	0	S	
4	4-10	Chicago	6-5	1	1	0	0	1	1	S	
5	4-16	Kansas Cy.	1-0	1	0	0	0	0	0	S	
6	4-18	Texas	5-3	1	1	0	0	0	1	S	
7	4-20	California	3-3	2	0	0	0	0	5	W	4-3
8	4-25	Minnesota	7-3	1.2	2	1	1	0	2	S	8-4
9	4-28	Cleveland	3-1	1	0	0	0	0	3	S	
10	4-30	Detroit	10-6	.1	0	0	0	0	0	S	
11	5-1	Detroit	7-6	1	2	0	0	0	3	S	
12	5-6	Detroit	5-2	1.1	0	0	0	0	1	S	
13	5-7	Detroit	6-2	1	1	0	0	0	2	S	
14	5-8	New York	8-6	1	0	0	0	0	2	S	
15	5-10	New York	5-2	1	0	0	0	0	3	S	
16	5-16	New York	6-3	1	2	0	0	0	2	S	
17	5-19	Baltimore	5-3	1	1	0	0	0	0	S	
18	5-20	Baltimore	4-2	1	0	0	0	0	1	S	
19	5-22	Boston	5-3	1.1	1	0	0	0	1	S	

APP	DATE	OPPONENT	SCORE*	IP	H	R	ER	BB	SO	DEC	FINAL
20	5–29	Baltimore	5–2	1	1	1	1	0	2	S	5–3
21	6–1	Boston	10–4	1	4	3	3	0	0		10–7
22	6–2	Boston	5–4	1.2	0	0	0	0	1	S	
23	6–3	Boston	7–4	1	3	2	2	0	0	S	
24	6–6	Chicago	6–4	1	1	0	0	0	0	S	
25	6–10	Milwaukee	5–2	1	2	0	0	0	1	S	
26	6–12	Texas	5–5	2	1	0	0	0	4		6–5
27	6–13	Texas	7–1	1	0	0	0	0	1		
28	6–15	Milwaukee	2–2	2	1	0	0	2	1	W	3–2
29	6–19	California	12–8	.2	0	0	0	0	1	S	
30	6–22	Seattle	7–2	1.2	1	0	0	1	2	S	
31	6–25	Minnesota	5–1	1.1	2	0	0	0	2	S	
32	6–29	Seattle	5–3	1	2	1	1	0	2	S	
33	6–30	Seattle	4–2	1	0	0	0	0	1	S	
34	7–1	Seattle	3–1	1	1	0	0	0	1	S	
35	7–5	Cleveland	4–2	1.1	1	0	0	0	1	S	5–2
36	7–10	Toronto	5–1	1	1	0	0	1	1	S	
37	7–11	Toronto	3–1	1	0	0	0	0	1	S	
38	7–22	New York	8–5	1	0	0	0	0	3	S	

APP	DATE	OPPONENT	SCORE*	IP	H	R	ER	BB	SO	DEC	FINAL
39	7–24	Toronto	4–4	1	2	1	1	0	0	W	6–5
40	7–27	Minnesota	5–1	1	1	0	0	0	0		9–1
41	7–28	Minnesota	12–10	2	0	0	0	0	3	S	
42	7–29	Minnesota	5–4	1	0	0	0	0	1	S	
43	8–3	Kansas Cy.	4–1	2	0	0	0	0	1	S	
44	8–5	Texas	4–3	1.1	1	0	0	0	0	S	
45	8–7	Kansas Cy.	8–5	1	2	1	1	0	1	S	8–6
46	8–8	Kansas Cy.	1–1	1	3	2	2	0	2	W	5–3
47	8–10	Chicago	5–3	1	0	0	0	0	1	S	
48	8–12	Chicago	1–1	1.2	0	0	0	2	2	W	2–1
49	8–16	California	4–4	.1	1	0	0	0	1	W	5–4
50	8–20	New York	8–6	1	1	0	0	0	1	S	
51	8–22	Baltimore	5–3	2	1	0	0	0	1	S	
52	8–23	Baltimore	7–3	.1	0	0	0	0	0	S	
53	8–25	Boston	4–4	.1	1	1	1	1	1	L	4–5
54	8–28	Cleveland	7–5	1	2	1	1	1	1	S	7–6
55	8–29	Cleveland	4–1	1	1	0	0	0	0	S	
56	9–2	Baltimore	1–2	1	0	0	0	0	2		
57	9–6	Boston	1–1	2	1	0	0	0	4	W	2–1

APP	DATE	OPPONENT	SCORE*	IP	H	R	ER	BB	SO	DEC	FINAL
58	9–9	California	3–0	1	0	0	0	0	1	S	
59	9–10	Seattle	6–3	1.2	3	1	1	0	2	S	6–4
60	9–12	Seattle	5–4	1.1	1	0	0	0	3	S	
61	9–14	Minnesota	3–2	1	0	0	0	0	2	S	
62	9–15	Minnesota	2–1	1	0	0	0	0	1	S	
63	9–18	Seattle	7–4	1.2	1	0	0	0	1	S	
64	9–20	Seattle	4–2	1	0	0	0	0	2	S	
65	9–21	Chicago	6–5	1	0	0	0	0	1	S	
66	9–24	Chicago	4–0	1.2	1	1	1	0	1	S	4–1
67	9–27	Milwaukee	3–5	1	1	0	0	1	1		
68	10–1	Texas	3–4	.2	1	0	0	1	1		
69	10–2	Milwaukee	2–1	1	2	1	1	0	1	BS	2–3

How impressive is that record? Eckersley won his awards largely on the basis of his 51 saves. But there are several ways to earn a save, not all of them as difficult as others. A few years back, the folks at Stats Inc. broke saves down into three groups: easy saves, regular saves, and tough saves. Here are the definitions:

Easy save: First batter faced is not the tying run *and* reliever pitches one inning or less.

Tough save: Reliever comes in with the tying run anywhere on base.

Regular save: All others.

How many of each type of save did Eric Gagne earn in winning his 2003 Cy Young? How many did Dennis Eckersley actually record when he piled up his 51 save, MVP, and Cy Young season in 1992? Their records above won't entirely tell us, but they give us a good idea.

In 10 of his 1992 saves—the saves of May 10, May 16, May 29, June 3, June 10, July 22, August 3, August 7, August 29, and September 9—Eckersley entered the game at the start of the ninth inning to protect a three-run lead. This is the simplest possible save situation. In 15 others—the games of April 6, April 18, April 28, May 8, May 19, May 20, June 6, June 29, June 30, July 1, July 11, August 10, August 20, August 28, and September 20—he entered the game at the start of the ninth with a two-run lead. In an additional five games—the saves of April 25, April 30, June 25, July 28, and August 22—Eckersley entered the game with the potential tying run on deck, but not at the plate or on base. In none of these 30 saves (three-fifths of his season total) did Eckersley have to face the potential tying run unless he himself brought it to the plate. Twenty-six of them—all but the saves of April 30, June 25, July 28, and August 22—fit the Stats Inc. definition of an "easy" save; the other four are "regular" saves.

In only 8 of his saves—the games of April 10, April 16, May 1, July 29, September 14, September 15, September 21, and October 2—was Eckersley asked to protect a one-run lead for one inning. He failed on one of those assignments, the October 2 game. On the five final save occasions—the games of June 2, June 22, July 5, August 5, and September 18—Eckersley was brought into the game in mid-inning with the tying run at the plate. That makes exactly thirteen times all season (including once when he was unsuccessful) when Eckersley was even required to face the tying run unless he himself brought it to the plate. The 12 saves that resulted all are classified by Stats Inc. as "regular" saves.

Was Eckersley ever called into a game in a "tough" save situation, one where the tying run was on base? (In none of his appearances was he required to get a save by working three innings.) It's possible. In nine games (the games of April 9, May 6, May 7, May 22, June 19, September 10, September 12, and September 24) we simply cannot determine from the box score whether Eckersley's save fits into the category of an easy, regular, or tough one.

But based on his usage pattern, it seems more likely that LaRussa avoided putting Eckersley into such a circumstance unless absolutely necessary. If those final 9 saves broke proportionately to the other 42, it would mean that Eckersley rang up 32 "easy" saves," 19 "moderate" saves, and 0 "tough" saves on his way to claiming the big awards of 1992.

Even though the majority of Eckersley's saves qualified as "easy," they might still have value if he replaced a faltering pitcher who was getting into trouble. But that was not often the case. In fact, LaRussa's use of Eckersley in 1992 qualifies as highly reflexive: that is, LaRussa brought Eck into the game with no regard for how well the pitcher he replaced was doing.

In two-thirds (forty-six) of his sixty-nine appearances, Eckersley was brought in to start an inning, generally the ninth. In forty of those forty-six games, Eckersley replaced a pitcher who had held the opposition scoreless the previous inning. The cumulative earned run average of the pitchers replaced by Eckersley when he was brought in to start an inning? It was 1.76. So not only was LaRussa's use of Eckersley reflexive, but in the context of winning baseball games the statistics Eckersley accumulated thanks to that use could very easily be described as gratuitous.

Even disputing the assertion that Eckersley performed a service which had actual value to the A's, you have to concede that generally he did it well. In fifty-six of his sixty-nine appearances, he did in fact hold his opponents scoreless. But it is a measure of overemphasis on the save to look at those other thirteen games—the ones where Eckersley gave up a run or two—and pose a question.

Here is the line on the thirteen games in which Eckersley was scored upon.

APP	DATE	OPPONENT	SCORE*	IP	H	R	ER	BB	SO	DEC	FINAL
8	4-25	Minnesota	7-3	1.2	2	1	1	0	2	S	8-4
20	5-29	Baltimore	5-2	1	1	1	1	0	2	S	5-3
21	6-1	Boston	10-4	1	4	3	3	0	0		10-7
23	6-3	Boston	7-4	1	3	2	2	0	0	S	
32	6-29	Seattle	5-3	1	2	1	1	0	2	S	
39	7-24	Toronto	4-4	1	2	1	1	0	0	W	6-5
45	8-7	Kansas Cy.	8-5	1	2	1	1	0	1	S	8-6
46	8-8	Kansas Cy.	1-1	1	3	2	2	0	2	W	5-3
53	8-25	Boston	4-4	.1	1	1	1	1	1	L	4-5
54	8-28	Cleveland	7-5	1	2	1	1	1	1	S	7-6
59	9-10	Seattle	6-3	1.2	3	1	1	0	2	S	6-4
66	9-24	Chicago	4-0	1.2	1	1	1	0	1	S	4-1
69	10-2	Milwaukee	2-1	1	2	1	1	0	1	BS	2-3

Nobody—not even Dennis Eckersley's biggest fan—would suggest that he pitched well in these thirteen games. Over 14.1 innings, he allowed 17 earned runs, an ERA of 10.69. He gave up 28 hits, an opponent batting average of .400. And yet, in these thirteen games that represented Dennis Eckersley at his worst, his record was 2–1 with 8 saves. So here's the question: If you subtract those thirteen games in which Dennis Eckersley plainly was bad from his season record, leaving you with 5 wins and 43 saves, do you then have a Most Valuable Player and a Cy Young Award winner? Or did Dennis Eckersley get his recognition for a save total that was to an important extent an illusion? Purely as a number, 43 saves is not especially impressive. In 1992, Lee Smith had 4 victories and precisely 43 saves for the St. Louis Cardinals. He got three points in the Cy Young Award balloting (Greg Maddux won with 112) and none at all for the MVP.

And what did the A's get in exchange for this MVP and Cy Young season? They got as few as zero games all season in which Eckersley was called upon to actually deal with a situation that involved the tying run on base, the classic "save" situation. And in case you were wondering, following his MVP season Eckersley got a 25 percent pay increase as appropriate to his celebrity, from $3 million to $3.75 million.

As noted at the outset, Gagne's 2003 line is superior to Eckersley's of 1992. Even so, it illustrates the illusory quality of saves. Twenty-five of his 55 2003 saves fit Stats' definition of "easy." Twenty-two of the remaining 30 were "regular" saves by Stats' terms. That leaves just eight games in doubt, eight cases where it would take a full review of the play-by-play to determine whether they qualified as "tough" saves.

P·A·R·T
II

THE GAME OFF
THE FIELD

PREFACE TO PART II

Who are the two most important people to the success of any baseball team? Here's a hint: They do not bat in the middle of the order, they do not lead off, pitch, manage, or wear a uniform. Their faces are rarely in the newspapers. They're the owner and the general manager. But although they're anonymous to most fans, these days, they, more than anybody they pay, dictate the success or failure of any ball club.

The chapters that follow are about the present state of the roles of these two key figures. Teams first take shape according to the dictates of ownership, which decides whether a ball club will spend $20 million, $50 million, or $100 million the following season. Not that the presence of money ensures success; in baseball, as in everything else, squandering a lot of money very quickly is easy. The real trick is succeeding with or without money.

That takes front-office sagacity, which simply means the ability to judge good players from bad ones. In recent years, sagacity as a substitute for money has paid off in Minnesota, Oakland, Florida, and Anaheim. These days, as many pennants are won in December as in September. That's the time when major player transactions occur; the time, in other words, when ball clubs take shape.

Elimination of the reserve clause, along with the advent of arbitration and free agency (all occurring in the 1970s), altered the landscape by which teams can acquire talent in ways that were once foreign, but have now become fundamental, to front-office decision-making. The same is true of long-term contracts, virtually unheard of as recently as thirty years ago, but now standard for frontline stars.

What do you suppose might have been the bidding on Mickey Mantle had he chosen—which under current player-management agreements he could have done—to declare for free agency following his 1956 MVP season? (That year Mantle won the Triple Crown, leading the league in home runs with 52, RBIs with 130, and batting average at .353.) Could he have commanded $100,000 on an open market? $200,000? If that doesn't seem like much, consider that the average team salary that season was only about $350,000.

What would the pennant-hungry Braves, basking in the financial glow of an attendance boom in Milwaukee, have bid to put Mantle in the middle of a batting order that already included Hank Aaron and Eddie Mathews? Would a Mantle free agency have effectively restructured player salaries up and down the major leagues? We'll never know, since Mantle had no such leverage. Under the premises governing baseball at the time, Mantle had only two choices: negotiate the best deal he could with the Yanks and play for that amount, or retire.

Today you don't have to be Mickey Mantle to make $5.5 million; you just have to be Roger Cedeno. That is a very good thing for Roger Cedeno; less so for the front office that persuades itself he is a player to build around. Let's see who's making the right judgments.

8

BUILDING A
WINNING TEAM

In baseball, as in any other business, the advantage is to the well endowed. Yet the rich do not always win. As long ago as 1999, Baltimore and Los Angeles each spent about $80 million to win seventy-eight and seventy-seven games respectively. That's better than $1 million per victory. In baseball as in other businesses, squandering money is the easy part. The successful franchise is usually the one that makes the most judicious use of its available resources, deploying them to their greatest effect and always, always appropriately gauging their mettle under pressure.

But unlike in other successful businesses, Major League teams seem often to be put together with little direction, plan, or forethought. Team-building strategies don't so much grow logically as they appear by accident. Looking at the allocation of team assets, a true fan might have good cause to wonder: Does anybody in the front office know what they're trying to do?

There are realistically only a few logical ways a baseball team can be constructed. It can be designed to emphasize pitching, offense, or defense; it can rely on the talents of a single megastar, or it can strive for a balance of all those factors.

True, the individual front-office decisions that come together to create each team's opening-day roster will be influenced by several factors that do not come under the realm of objective judgment: Who's free-agent or arbitration-eligible and who isn't? Who lacks trade value? Who comes up lame? How much can the team afford? What brilliant (or stupid) multiyear decisions are inherited? But whether by plan or happenstance, every Major League roster can at least broadly be characterized according to the payroll decisions that shape it, and according to the fashion in which GMs allocate those resources.

In the last six seasons, the average Major League team spent:

A fraction less than 25 percent of its overall payroll on the five men it expected to be rotation starters.

Just under 40 percent of all payroll on pitching as a whole.

About 17.3 percent of all payroll on its single best-paid player. This could be either a pitcher or hitter. (This percentage has risen steadily since 2000. In 2003, the average "star" earned nearly one fifth of his team's entire payroll, the largest percentage since 1996.)

Just under 30 percent of payroll on its "heart of the order," the three players who were expected to most often fill the 3-4-5 spots. Frequently these were its highest salaried hitters, although not necessarily. (This proportion has risen steadily since 2000.)

Slightly less than 20 percent of payroll on its middle defense—the men expected to occupy the positions of catcher, second base, shortstop, and center field.

Now for the obvious question: Are any of these team-building approaches better than others? Is there a right way and a wrong way to put a club together?

To answer that question, let's look at group profiles of teams that are put together in different ways. We've categorized every team that took the field between 1999 and 2004 by the attributes that are indicated, and, where appropriate, dug back a little deeper for interesting case studies. Playoff teams are indicated by boldface.

SINGLE STAR TEAMS

General characteristic: Highest paid player exceeds 23 percent of the entire team payroll.

Number of such teams since 1999: 19 (1999: Chicago White Sox, Florida Marlins. 2000: **Chicago White Sox,** Florida Marlins. 2001: Anaheim Angels, Cincinnati Reds, Minnesota Twins, Texas Rangers. 2002: Colorado Rockies, Tampa Bay Devil Rays, Toronto Blue Jays. 2003: Kansas City Royals, Tampa Bay Devil Rays, Toronto Blue Jays. 2004: Cincinnati Reds, Milwaukee Brewers, Pittsburgh Pirates, Tampa Bay Devil Rays, Toronto Blue Jays.)

To judge from appearances, few teams are "single star" teams because they want to be. With the notable exception of the 2001 Texas Rangers and the 2002 Rockies, these tend to be baseball's poorer relations. Since 1999, the $42.02 million payroll of the average "single star" team was substantially the smallest of any team configuration. With a few exceptions (notably A-Rod's Texas Rangers), these clubs aren't paying their top star a disproportionate amount relative to their other talent because they think it's a good way to win a pennant. They're doing it because the only alternative is to lose that star. Eventually, many do.

In fact, some do so deliberately. That's what the A-Rod trade before the 2004 season was all about. Tom Hicks wanted to trim team payroll from $103 million to about $80 million. But to do that while keeping Rodriguez would have meant tying up between one-quarter and one-third of all his payroll assets in one player, and essentially surrounding that one player with rookies and part-timers. That approach tends not to work. The Boston courtship failed because the Red Sox preferred not to court the same kinds of fiscal strictures that tied Hicks down in Dallas. (New York spends so much anyway that it is not tied down by a mere $25 million.)

Here's another intriguing trait common to these "star" teams: For the most part, the "stars" aren't necessarily stars at all, at least not by broader Major League standards. In 2003, by way of illustration, the "stars" of the three single-star teams were Mike Sweeney, Carlos Delgado, and—you'll never guess—Rey Ordoñez.

The Montreal Expos were a "star" team in 1995, but it would take a true Expos fan to identify the "star" of a club which, over the course of the strike, had shorn itself of Marquis Grissom, Larry Walker, John Wetteland, and Ken Hill. It was outfielder Roberto Kelly, whose $3.73 million contract, roughly 25 percent of their total $14.68 million payroll, the Expos were stuck with when the season started. They dumped Kelly to the Dodgers in May for Henry Rodriguez.

If you knew that the San Francisco Giants were a "star" team in 1996 and again in 1997, you could probably guess who the "star" was . . . and you'd be right. But how about the 1997 Pittsburgh Pirates? To which "star" did they give 24.29 percent of their total team payroll, a payroll that by the way amounted to only $9.33 million? It was Al Martin, to that point a career .288 hitter. In what passed then for star mode in Pittsburgh, Martin juiced his batting average all the way to .291.

Only two of the "star" players between 1999 and 2002—Frank Thomas and Barry Larkin—are still with the teams that paid them such an inordinate percentage of their purses. Most of the rest were either traded out of financial necessity or took free agency and headed off to greener pastures.

That was certainly the case in Detroit in 1996 and again in 1997, where the poor Tigers labored under some prodigious salary commitments indeed. Talk about a "star" system: In 1996, Detroit management worked a $22.3 million payroll around the mammoth financial appetites of both Cecil Fielder and Travis Fryman. Fielder commanded a gargantuan 41.25 percent of the entirety, $9.238 million. The Tigers certainly tried to move Fielder, but how did one move a player of his contractual and physical girth? After all, in return for that $9.2 million deal by midseason he was batting .248, although he did kick in 26 home runs. When the Tigers finally did find a buyer— the Yankees—they had to agree to take on Ruben Sierra in return. Some deal: Sierra was getting paid $6.2 million and hitting .258 at the time. Plus he had an attitude problem.

But even unburdening themselves of Fielder hardly left the Tiger management in maneuverable position. They still had Fryman, who earned $5.2 million in 1996 and who was scheduled to climb to $6.4 million in 1997. That $6.4 million, by the way, was exactly 38 percent of everything Detroit had in the way of payroll in 1997. Can you imagine the meeting in Tiger GM Randy Smith's office that featured this exchange:

"How we gonna win in 1997? We can only spend $18 million."

"I think we ought to give a third of everything we've got to Fryman. He hit .268 last year."

"He'll probably do better than that this year. He's a career .274 hitter, y'know."

"Let's call it a plan."

What really happened is what typically happens to "single star" teams. A GM committed to a big money, multiyear deal, presumably fearful of the public relations impact of losing the star, then the owner cut the budget and squeezed all the funds out for other players. Between 1995 and 1999, Detroit's payroll fell from $36.5 million to $34.1 million. That came at a time when average spending rose from about $20 million to about $50 million. After Fryman, the biggest "name" the 1997 Tigers could afford was (take your pick) reliever Todd Jones ($975,000) or second baseman Damion Easley ($675,000).

For the record, the Fielder-Fryman Tigers won 53 games in 1996 and finished in last place by 21 games. The Fryman-led Tigers of 1997 finished four games below .500, 19 games out of first and 3 games from the cellar.

Since 1999, only one "single star" team—the 2000 White Sox—has seen postseason playing time. That's 4.6 percent of the field, the worst performance of any of the composition patterns we'll look at. Even more indicative, only four (throwing in the Brad Radke–led 2001 Twins and the 2003 Jays and Royals) have even played winning ball. On average, "single star" teams finish ninth in their leagues in run production, eleventh in ERA, and tenth in fielding percentage. The average winning percentage for these nineteen teams? It's .457.

You paid how much for A-Rod?

MIDDLE DEFENSE

General definition: Combined payroll of middle defenders (catcher, second baseman, shortstop, and center fielder) exceeds about 28.5 percent of entire team payroll.

Number of such teams since 1999: 23. (1999: **Cleveland Indians**, Milwaukee Brewers, **New York Yankees**, Seattle Mariners. 2000: Cincinnati Reds, Cleveland Indians, **New York Mets**, **New York Yankees**. 2001: Chicago White Sox, Cincinnati Reds, Texas Rangers. 2002: Cincinnati Reds, Florida Marlins, Texas Rangers. 2003: Cincinnati Reds, **Florida Marlins**, Houston Astros, Tampa Bay Devil Rays. 2004: Cincinnati Reds, Colorado Rockies, Montreal Expos, New York Mets, Pittsburgh Pirates.)

In a subsequent chapter the data will make clear that few if any major leaguers are truly paid big bucks for their defensive prowess. Hitting and pitching get the money. That being the case, it's speculative whether "middle defense" teams are actually constructed to be strong defensively, or whether the relationship is coincidental to the fact that the club's best sticks happen to play those positions.

The 1999 Cleveland Indians and the 1999–2000 Yankees are cases in point. The Indians' middle that season consisted of the Alomar brothers, shortstop Omar Vizquel, and center fielder Kenny Lofton. Together they commanded nearly $25 million in salary, a sum that amounted to 29 percent of Cleveland's $68 million total payroll. In 1999 and again in 2000, the Yanks fielded catcher Jorge Posada, second baseman Chuck Knoblauch, shortstop Derek Jeter, and center fielder Bernie Williams. As a group, they earned $29.4 million in 2000, nearly 32 percent of George Steinbrenner's opening day budget. But did George like them for their glove work, or because they constituted the heart of New York's world championship order? Did John Hart fete his quartet in 1999 because of their defense or their offense? Roberto Alomar, a free agent signee, came to Cleveland as a career .302 batter, while Lofton had a career .311 mark. Or, and perhaps this is the correct answer, did Hart and Steinbrenner simply like their four players in every fashion possible?

Unlike "single star" teams, which almost without exception do poorly, clubs funded to be strong up the middle can point to successes. Since 1999, five have been in the postseason—that's about 22 percent of middle defense teams. Three—the 1999 and 2000 Yankees and the 2003 Marlins—won the World Series.

In the portrait of middle defense teams, there is then some reason for hope. However, the combined winning percentage for the lot of them since 1999 is only .489. Middle defense teams tend to have average payrolls (roughly $63.8 million per team since 1999), finish in the lower half in pitching, and score an average number of runs.

From time to time, teams try to focus limited resources into the middle defense slots. That was the case in Cincinnati in 1998, where Jim Bowden crafted the most outlandishly "middle defense" club in recent vintage. Working with a $22.1 million payroll, Bowden used $1.3 million of it to buy an entire starting rotation, and about $4 million to purchase a complete pitching staff. That was about $1.3 million less than he paid Barry Larkin alone. He laid out another $2.8 million to Bret Boone alongside Larkin, gave center fielder Reggie Sanders $3.7 million, and paid catcher Eddie Taubensee $975,000. Here's the math: about $12.7 million to those four positions, nearly 58 percent of Cincinnati's entire cashbox.

I'd like to report the brilliance of this strategy, but Cincinnati won 47 percent of its games in 1998.

HEART OF THE ORDER

General definition: Combined payroll for 3-4-5 hitters exceeds 39 percent of entire payroll.

Number of such teams since 1999: 26. (1999: San Francisco Giants, St. Louis Cardinals. 2000: Anaheim Angels, Chicago Cubs, **San Francisco Giants**, Toronto Blue Jays. 2001: Cincinnati Reds, Montreal Expos, Philadelphia Phillies, Texas Rangers, Toronto Blue Jays. 2002: Chicago Cubs, Colorado Rockies, Montreal Expos, **Oakland A's**, Philadelphia Phillies, Texas Rangers, Toronto Blue Jays. 2003: Colorado Rockies, Detroit Tigers, Milwaukee Brewers, Texas

Rangers. 2004: Colorado Rockies, Kansas City Royals, Milwaukee Brewers, Tampa Bay Devil Rays.)

What follows is not calculated to stir the hearts of those who believe baseball ought to be controlled by the brawnies. As a general proposition, building a team around the heart of the order—paying big bucks for big sticks in the 3-4-5 holes—is not a winning strategy.

It is, of course, fun, and it does have its possibilities. As would be expected, "heart" teams tended to rank high in offensive production. But of the twenty-six Major League teams since 1999 that fit this characterization, only two—the 2000 Giants and 2002 A's—made the playoffs. At 7.7 percent, that's the second worst mark of any category of composition; only "single star" teams do worse. Moreover, since at least as far back as 1995, no "heart" team has played in the World Series.

"Heart of the Order" teams are not plushly funded. Their average salary since 1999 has been $60.77 million, a payroll that is below the Major League "average" for the span. The group winning percentage—.460—wouldn't get you much more than fourth place in a normal season. Ironically, for a group of teams presumably built around offense, none led its league in runs scored, and as a group "heart" teams ranked eighth in their leagues. Beyond that, most "heart" teams run afoul of one of two problems: Either the sluggers they bank on get hurt or suffer through subpar seasons, or in the process of stoking their offense those teams starve their pitching. "Heart" teams do worse in ERA than teams fitting any other configuration, on average standing eleventh in their leagues. When ERAs fail, it's often the case that no amount of run production can make up the difference.

The 1999 Cardinals not only had McGwire, with his $8.3 millions salary, they also had Ray Lankford, an experienced cleanup hitter, covering him. GM Walt Jocketty added Eric Davis to bat fifth at $3.5 million. The three got about 40 percent of St. Louis's $45.2 million payroll. True to form, things rocked in St. Louis in 1999. Coming off his 70-homer season, McGwire slugged 65 more home runs and drove home a league-leading 147 runs. He also slugged .697. In some ways, Lankford helped. A lifetime .278 batter, he hit .306. But his power production disappointed. He had hit 31 home runs in 1998; in 1999 he fell off to 15. He also drove in 38 fewer runs. Davis, meanwhile, suffered a season-ending injury in late June. Suddenly St. Louis's offense, even with McGwire, was barely run-of-the-mill; the Cards finished tenth in the sixteen-team NL in run production. They were eleventh in pitching; are you beginning to get the sense of a middle-of-the-pack team? Good, because the Cardinals finished 75–86 and in fourth place. McGwire still got his $9.3 million in 2000, but the Cardinals no longer leaned on him. With a renewed emphasis on starting pitching creating a more balanced approach overall, St. Louis cruised to the 2000 NL Central title.

ROTATION

General definition: Combined payroll of expected five starting pitchers exceeds about 34.5 percent of total payroll, but combined payroll of all pitchers does not exceed about 49 percent.

Number of such teams since 1999: 11. (1999: **Boston Red Sox**, Anaheim Angels. 2000: **Atlanta Braves, Chicago White Sox**. 2001: **Atlanta Braves**, Los Angeles Dodgers. 2002: Tampa Bay Devil Rays. 2003: Anaheim Angels, Montreal Expos. 2004: Arizona Diamondbacks, **Boston Red Sox**.)

PITCHING

General definition: Combined payroll of all pitchers exceeds about 49 percent of entire team payroll, but combined payroll of rotation starters does not exceed about 34.5 percent.

Number of such teams since 1999: 9. (1999: Minnesota Twins, San Diego Padres. 2000: Minnesota Twins. 2001: New York Mets, San Diego Padres. 2002: Boston Red Sox. 2003: **New York Yankees**. 2004: **Los Angeles Dodgers**, Philadelphia Phillies.)

ROTATION PLUS PITCHING

General definition: Combined payroll of expected five rotation starters exceeds about 34.5 percent of the total payroll, and combined payroll for all pitchers exceeds about 49 percent.

Number of such teams since 1999: 18. (1999: Arizona Diamondbacks, Florida Marlins, Oakland A's, Toronto Blue Jays. 2000: Arizona Diamondbacks, Florida Marlins, **Oakland A's**. 2001: **Arizona Diamondbacks**, Colorado Rockies, Minnesota Twins. 2002: **Arizona Diamondbacks, Minnesota Twins, St. Louis Cardinals**. 2003: Arizona Diamondbacks, Los Angeles Dodgers, **Minnesota Twins**. 2004: **Atlanta Braves**, Texas Rangers.)

At first glance, the overlap between "rotation" teams and "pitching" teams is so substantial that one might conclude they are better viewed as a single entity. About two-thirds of "rotation" teams are also "pitching" teams, and vice versa. A closer look, however, brings to the surface important distinctions.

"Rotation" teams, after all, emphasize strength in the starting five, while "pitching" teams take a less-focused approach emphasizing both starters and relievers. That being the case, the most logical approach is to view this actually as three categories: teams that put the emphasis on rotation starters, teams that emphasize all pitching, and the largest category of the three, clubs that do both.

Unlike in previous categories, within the pitching-dominant categories we see clear signs of franchise-based malice aforethought: deliberate planning to win with a mound focus. Two franchises have historically displayed a strong tendency toward a rotation or pitching focus, and both have been highly successful: Atlanta and Arizona.

The Braves are the bellwether endorsement for pitching dominance. Throughout the 1990s, no franchise was a more consistent winner. No franchise had a more consistent pattern of development, either. From the ascension of John Schuerholz as GM—and especially since the acquisition of free agent Greg Maddux for the 1993 season—until the start of the 2002 season the Braves slavishly emphasized starters. Three members of the Braves rotation that broke camp in

April of 1993 were still with the team in 2002: Maddux, John Smoltz, and Tom Glavine.

This is in no small measure because Schuerholz made sure to reward them handsomely, not merely in raw dollars—although that way, too—but as a substantial portion of the overall payroll. As far back as 1993, when Atlanta's overall payroll was $37.7 million, the five Braves starters got 38 percent of that (Maddux received $5.5 million, Glavine $4.75 million, Smoltz $2.5 million). In 1994, team payroll rose to $40.5 million, and the rotation starters got 39.5 percent of it. By 1995, Atlanta starters earned 47 percent ($21.2 million) of the Braves' $45 million payroll, including $5.5 million for Maddux and $4.75 million each for Smoltz and Glavine. Result: a world title.

All this time position stars of the like of Ron Gant, David Justice, Kenny Lofton, and Fred McGriff came and went. But three of the four best-paid rotations since 1995 (as measured by percentage of the total team salary) were Atlanta teams (1995, 1996, and 1998).

With all that cash committed to starters, you'd expect the Braves to have led the National League in pitching in those seasons. They did.

Although the Braves sometimes have fit both the "rotation" and "pitching" classification, the 2000 and 2001 clubs were strictly "rotation" teams. In any event, Schuerholz's plan appeared to pretty consistently focus on the guys who gave him innings. Until the injury-forced conversion of Smoltz to relief status, and with the exception of a flirtation with Mark Wohlers in the mid 1990s, Schuerholz did not generally fall into the nasty habit of throwing big bucks at small-inning guys.

In Arizona, Jerry Colangelo and Joe Garagiola, Jr., actually set the pattern right away, paying their rotation starters 37 percent of their overall $30 million budget in 1998, the franchise's first season. That included $6.45 million to Andy Benes, which could have been viewed as a statement of priorities given the fact that Benes was coming off a 10–7 season with St. Louis in which he only worked 149 innings. (In 1998, Benes won 14 and lost 13, but he did pitch 221 innings, so it's not really fair to say the D-Backs got ripped off.)

Before the start of the 1999 season, Garagiola underscored that statement of priorities, signing Randy Johnson for $9.35 million and Todd Stottlemyre (14–13 with Texas and St. Louis in 1998) for $8 million. As a group, Johnson, Stottlemyre, Benes, Omar Daal, and Armando Reynoso earned $27.61 million, or 41.8 percent of Arizona's total payroll in 1999. That's a winner.

In 2000, the D-Backs lost Benes, but tried to bolster the bullpen with multimillion dollar arms Russ Springer, Darren Holmes, and Greg Swindell. They also beefed up the checkbooks of Daal and Stottlemyre, proving in the process that just because you pay Omar Daal and Todd Stottlemyre $11.5 million doesn't make them $11.5 million pitchers. They did, however, swing a trade with Philadelphia that netted Curt Schilling, a trade perfectly in keeping with Arizona's approach. Together, the Schilling-Johnson tandem were good for a world title in 2001.

Of all possible approaches to team-building, the two that emphasize starting pitching turn out to be the most productive. The .540 winning percentage of "rotation-pitching" teams since 1999 is unsurpassed among configurations. Eight such teams played in the postseason: Arizona in 1999, Oakland in 2000, the D-Backs again in 2001, Minnesota, Arizona, and St. Louis in 2002, Minnesota again in 2003, and Atlanta in 2004.

The Minnesota Twins seized the opportunity to convert to a rotation-pitching bias in 2001 and rode that formula to success. In 2002, the team's four best-paid players were pitchers, as were five of the six wealthiest. They included Radke at $8.75 million, Rick Reed at $7 million, Eric Milton at $4 million, LaTroy Hawkins at $2.75 million, and Joe Mays at $2.35 million. On a payroll of just above $40 million, the 2002 Twins funded their starting five at about $22 million, a sum that represented better than 55 percent of the purse. That is more than three standard deviations outside the Major League norm for the period, and makes the 2002 Twins the only team (among 234 since 1995) to pay its starting rotation more than 50 percent of its total payroll. Throwing the bullpen in, Minnesota arms collected nearly 74 percent of the total swag in 2002, an amount that was again three standard deviations outside the normal practice.

That well-paid staff led the otherwise young and underpaid Twins to a .584 winning percentage in 2002; yet, strikingly, that was the *worst* winning percentage of any of the three "rotation-pitching" teams on the field that season. The Cardinals won 60 percent of their games and the Diamondbacks nearly hit 61 percent.

Five of the eleven "rotation" teams—the 1999 and 2004 Red Sox, 2000 White Sox, and the 2000 and 2001 Braves—played in the post-season. Overall, rotation-only teams won just 50 percent of their games, but that is due in substantial part to the presence within their ranks of the 2002 Devil Rays and 2004 Diamondbacks. The remaining nine teams won a playoff-contending 54 percent of their games. Rotation teams are not cheap; at $72.54 million, their average payroll is exceeded only by pitching-only teams. But they deliver results. The average "rotation" team produces its league's sixth best ERA, the best showing of any configuration. Four—the 1999 and 2004 Red Sox as well as the 2000 and 2001 Braves—led their leagues in ERA.

Either the "rotation" or "rotation-pitching" approach turns out to be better than teams that emphasize pitching without placing a special emphasis on the starting five. These are essentially "bullpen clubs." A model for the nine that have taken the field since 1999 was the 1995 Kansas City Royals. The Royals laid out 52.5 percent of their total $27.3 million payroll on pitching that season, $4.4 million going to starter Kevin Appier, and another $3.3 million to Tom Gordon. But Kansas City basically let the other three starting spots slide in favor of maintaining closer Jeff Montgomery in the style to which he had become accustomed. At $4.17 million, Montgomery got 15.23 percent of Kansas City's total cash, nearly half what KC paid all five of its starters.

How did that work? Great . . . for Appier, Gordon, and Montgomery. They went a combined 29–25 with 31 saves, and made $11.6 million in the process. But when anybody else was on the mound, KC stood 41–49 with 6 saves. The other three projected rotation starters—Mark Gubicza, Chris Haney, and Tom Browning—

contributed just 14 victories against 19 defeats, with Gubicza getting the lion's share of both. The 2003 Yankees—with their fetish for highly paid middle relief (Jose Contreras)—did the same thing.

The group's .508 winning percentage is about the same as rotation-only teams although the performances of the 2003 Yankees and 2004 Dodgers improved the numbers. These teams tended also to rank only average in team ERA. Finally, they also fare much worse in run production, generally ranking about tenth in their league. No "pitching" team that did not also emphasize its rotation has led its league in pitching—or run production for that matter.

BALANCED TEAMS

General definition: Payroll for each of the groups outlined above fits within one standard deviation of the average.

Number of such teams since 1999: 48. (1999: **Atlanta Braves**, Baltimore Orioles, Chicago Cubs, Detroit Tigers, Kansas City Royals, Los Angeles Dodgers, Montreal Expos. 2000: Colorado Rockies, Houston Astros, Kansas City Royals, Los Angeles Dodgers, **Seattle Mariners**, **St. Louis Cardinals**, Texas Rangers. 2001: Baltimore Orioles, Boston Red Sox, Chicago Cubs, Detroit Tigers, **Houston Astros**, Kansas City Royals, **Oakland A's**, Pittsburgh Pirates, **St. Louis Cardinals**, San Francisco Giants. 2002: **Anaheim Angels, Atlanta Braves**, Baltimore Orioles, Houston Astros, Kansas City Royals, Los Angeles Dodgers, Milwaukee Brewers, New York Mets, San Diego Padres, **San Francisco Giants**. 2003: **Atlanta Braves, Boston Red Sox, Chicago Cubs**, Chicago White Sox, New York Mets, **Oakland A's**, Philadelphia Phillies, Pittsburgh Pirates, **San Francisco Giants**. 2004: **Houston Astros, Minnesota Twins**, Oakland A's, **St. Louis Cardinals**, San Francisco Giants.)

With about 30 percent of all teams between 1999 and 2004, this is the largest grouping. Some GMs show an absolute fetish for team balance. Under Ed Lynch, the Cubs took a balanced approach for six of his seven seasons, and right away you're saying, "Oops, balance doesn't sound like such a good way to go." For the record, seventeen "balanced" teams since 1999 have made the postseason, including the 2004 Astros, Cardinals, and Twins. Twenty-eight of the thirty present Major League teams (all but the Marlins and Diamondbacks) have operated out of a balanced scheme at least once since 1995.

As a group, the "balanced" approach turns out to be a pretty good one . . . if you can afford it. Twenty-seven of the forty-eight compiled better than .500 records, twenty-one did not. They win 51 percent of the time on a $69.37 million payroll that is relatively expensive. The 1998 Yanks balanced their way to 114 victories, the 2004 Cardinals to 105. On the other hand, the very balanced 1998 Devil Rays, 1999 Royals, 2001 Orioles and Pirates, and 2002 Brewers and Royals dipped into the nether reaches of sub-.400 land. Four "balanced" teams since 1999 led their league in runs scored; four led in ERA and three others led in fielding.

BORROWERS

General definition: Teams that are not above the ceilings established to fit into any of the first five groupings, but fall below one standard deviation from the average in one or more areas so that they also cannot be described as "balanced."

Number of such teams since 1999: 44. (1999: Cincinnati Reds, Colorado Rockies, **Houston Astros, New York Mets**, Philadelphia Phillies, Pittsburgh Pirates, Tampa Bay Devil Rays, **Texas Rangers**. 2000: Baltimore Orioles, Boston Red Sox, Detroit Tigers, Milwaukee Brewers, Montreal Expos, Philadelphia Phillies, Pittsburgh Pirates, San Diego Padres, Tampa Bay Devil Rays. 2001: **Cleveland Indians,** Florida Marlins, Milwaukee Brewers, **New York Yankees**, **Seattle Mariners**, Tampa Bay Devil Rays. 2002: Chicago White Sox, Cleveland Indians, Detroit Tigers, **New York Yankees**, Pittsburgh Pirates, Seattle Mariners. 2003: Baltimore Orioles, Cleveland Indians, Seattle Mariners, St. Louis Cardinals, San Diego Padres. 2004: **Anaheim Angels,** Baltimore Orioles, Chicago Cubs, Chicago White Sox, Cleveland Indians, Detroit Tigers, Florida Marlins, **New York Yankees**, San Diego Padres, Seattle Mariners.)

Think of a "borrower" as a "balanced" team that cheats the premise. Where "balanced" clubs neither exceed nor fall below one standard deviation from the norm in each of the six categories, "borrowers" allow themselves to fall below it in one category or more. That is to say, they "borrow" from some aspect—offense, defense, starting or overall pitching, or from their star—to buttress other areas just a bit.

As with balanced teams, the performance of borrowers—perhaps because they are so numerous—tends to average out. Since 1999, "borrowers" have won 49.6 percent of their games. Their record for reaching the postseason is 21 percent.

"Borrowing" can be the toy of the well-heeled; five borrowers (the 2000 Red Sox, 2001 Yankees, 2002 Mariners, and 2004 Angels and Yankees) have exceeded $100 million in payroll. But in the manic-depressive world of baseball, "borrowers" are not immune from the really low lows. In 2002, the Tigers "borrowed" their way to 106 defeats. The 2004 Mariners lost 99 games and a manager.

Does it make a difference what you "borrow" from? Absolutely. Of the eighteen borrowers who achieved better than .500 records since 1999, eleven "borrowed" from their stars. The 2001 Mariners tied the all-time record for victories while paying their highest-paid player—pitcher Aaron Sele—just 8.1 percent of their total payroll. A close look at the data, however, reveals a sort of a ruse. The payrolls of those twelve teams averaged about $88.6 million, so they could borrow from their stars while still maintaining them in fine style. In 1999, Texas's "slighted" star was Ivan Rodriguez, who only got 11.49 percent of the Rangers' stash. Any star worth his salt these days is worth better than 12 percent. But the Ranger stash amounted to $74.8 million, so Rodriguez's cut still was $8.6 million.

What did the Rangers do with that money? Beefed up their middle defense, that's what. Not by an exorbitant amount, but at 25 percent of their payroll, the payout to those four positions still amounted to about 5 percent above the Major League norm. Rodriguez, of course, was a factor. But Texas could also afford to hang on to shortstop Royce Clayton ($4.5 million), second baseman Mark McLemore ($2.4 million), and center fielder Tom Goodwin (3.2 million). The irony is that Texas's defense in 1999 was only mediocre, ranking ninth in fielding average in the fourteen-team league. You can't always get what you want.

This was a markedly different pattern from the one seen among borrowers who did not beat .500. As noted above, of the eighteen better-than-.500 clubs, eleven borrowed from their best-paid player. But of the twenty-six teams that did not top .500, only four borrowed from their best-paid player. Only two of the eighteen successful teams borrowed from their middle defense, but five of the twenty-six teams with lesser records did so. Only two of the eighteen borrowers borrowed against their pitching; and only one (the 2004 Padres) against their rotation. But of the .500 or worse borrowers, eleven borrowed against their pitching staffs and thirteen borrowed against their rotations. Four of the eighteen above-.500 teams borrowed against the hearts of their orders, nine of the twenty-six unsuccessful ones did so.

WHICH APPROACH WORKS BEST?

The question can be answered by either of two standards, but both essentially lead to the same conclusion.

We could look at winning percentage. By classification, here are the winning percentages of each group of teams since 1999:

Rotation-pitching combo	.540
Balanced teams	.509
Pitching (not rotation)	.508
Rotation only	.501
Borrowers	.496
Middle defense	.489
Heart of the order	.460
Star teams	.457

Or we could calculate the average number of games that teams in each classification exceeded or fell short of their expected win totals, given their salaries (see Chapter 9, "Faith and Hope in Baseball" for an explanation of this system). Using that method, the classification rankings are as follows:

Rotation-pitching combo	+7.2
Balanced teams	+0.6
Star teams	−0.4
Pitching (not rotation)	−0.8
Borrowers	−1.2
Rotation only	−2.4
Middle defense	−2.8
Heart of the order	−4.5

By either system, emphasizing both rotation starters and overall pitching is the superior approach in the modern game; not only do rotation-pitching teams win more games, but they are the only classification that as a group exceeds their projected victory total based on payroll . . . and they exceed it by seven games. (The numbers don't equal zero because some teams fit more than one classification.)

It may be the oldest saw in the game, but it's still true; pay for pitching—especially starters.

MIDSEASON CHANGES

In 1997, the San Francisco Giants underwent a midseason pitching makeover that played a big role in their subsequent title run.

You probably recall the key trade—especially if you're a Chicago White Sox fan. On that city's South Side, July 31, 1997 is remembered as White Flag Day, the day when Jerry Reinsdorf traded starter

Wilson Alvarez, closer Roberto Hernandez, and pitcher Danny Darwin for a half dozen prospects. The trade has been often analyzed from the Sox's standpoint: They were, you may not recall, only three games behind Cleveland when it came down. Aside from white-flagging the pennant, Reinsdorf unloaded nearly $10 million in salaries along with three free agents to be, and in return picked up several promising prospects. Three of them—Mike Caruso, Bobby Howry, and Keith Foulke—eventually made the Sox.

Nobody ever analyzes the trade from San Francisco's perspective, but the impact on the Giants' makeup was as profound as the impact on the Sox. The trade marked a change of approach as well as a change of character in San Francisco.

Brian Sabean's Giants began the 1997 season with a $34.89 million payroll that was decent but unspectacular by the standards of the time. Much of that was tied up in Barry Bonds, the slugging left fielder with an $8.667 million multiyear contract. Bonds's deal, swallowing up 24.8 percent of all of San Francisco's funds at season's start, made the Giants a "star" team. And, as we've already been through, that tagged the Giants as a loser.

The only problem was that the Giants didn't lose. They were in first place much of May and all of June and July, although usually no more than a few games ahead of Los Angeles. At the All Star break, San Francisco hit a high-water mark, standing 51–36 with a six-game advantage. The Giants still led, but only by a game and a half, when Sabean pulled the deal with Reinsdorf.

It is not easy to make such a trade, even if you are on what is popularly perceived to be the good end of it. Budget is one factor. By adding Alvarez, Darwin, and Hernandez, Sabean raised his payroll commitments from about $35 million to more than $42 million, nearly a 20 percent increase in the talent budget. That takes an understanding boss. Teams do not routinely undergo midseason shifts of anything approaching that magnitude.

But in addition to blowing up his budget and starting over, Sabean changed the face of the team. Between July 31 and August 8—in moves that included the waiver pickup of pitcher Terry Mulholland—Sabean converted his team's composition from "star" to "borrower," still a bit light on its commitment to the starting rotation, but more nearly symmetrical. "Star" clubs rarely win pennants, but "borrower" clubs do very well indeed; about 43 percent of all post-season spots are won by "borrowers."

An examination of the midseason roster moves of forty-nine teams in the running for pennants at midseason dates between 1995 and 2000 illustrates the degree to which contenders engage in such makeovers. Within that time frame, about 40 percent of the teams who were engaged in close pennant races—twenty of the forty-nine— have gone that route. In that context, it's important to note something here. When we talk about team reconstructions, we are not talking merely or specifically about trade-deadline deals. We are talking about acquisitions that alter the club's fundamental structure, trades that shift a team's basic approach from pitching to hitting-dominated, from balanced to defense, for that matter from any design component to another.

These moves did not take place without some fiscal sacrifice. Among the forty-nine contenders included in the study, the average in-season payroll increase was about 8.25 percent, from about $49.7 million to about $53.8 million. Eight of those forty-nine teams hiked payroll by 20 percent or more (the 1995 Dodgers, at 31 per-cent, made the biggest jump). Five other teams, one of which was the 1997 White Sox, actually chopped payroll. And yes, one of those five—the 1996 Cardinals—did actually reach the playoffs anyway.

Here is a listing of the forty-nine teams, their season-starting payroll and configuration, their season-ending payroll, the percent change in that payroll, and their season-ending configuration. Note: The survey excludes teams that made substantial roster changes be-cause they were out of contention. It also omits teams such as the 1996–97 Braves, 1996 and 1999 Indians, and 1998 Yankees, who were so far out front in July that their roster changes were irrelevant to the pennant race. (Asterisked teams reached postseason play.)

Year	Team	Start Payroll	Start Type	End Payroll	Percent Ch.	End Type
1995	Ana.	$29.377	Rotation	$32.709	11.34%	Rotation, Pitch
1995	*Cinc.	$41.207	Balanced	$46.688	13.30%	Rotation, Pitch
1995	*Col.	$32.453	Balanced	$38.165	17.60%	Balanced
1995	*LA	$27.570	Pitching	$36.371	31.92%	Pitching
1995	*NYY	$48.625	Borrower	$57.440	18.13%	Pitching
1995	*Seattle	$35.586	Rotation–Heart	$37.220	4.59%	Rotation–Heart
1995	Texas	$33.925	Balanced	$35.652	5.09%	Balanced
1996	*Balt.	$51.916	Mid Defense	$53.610	3.26%	Mid Defense
1996	Boston	$41.905	Balanced	$38.334	–8.52%	Balanced
1996	Hous.	$30.248	Balanced	$26.813	–11.36%	Star
1996	*LA	$34.477	Mid Defense	$37.314	8.23%	Borrower
1996	*NYY	$53.642	Borrower	$62.021	15.62%	Borrower
1996	*SD	$27.683	Borrower	$33.491	20.98%	Borrower
1996	Seattle	$40.876	Heart	$42.921	5.00%	Balanced
1996	*St. L.	$38.717	Rotation	$36.161	–6.60%	Borrower
1996	*Texas	$39.975	Balanced	$44.291	10.80%	Balanced
1997	*Balt.	$56.722	Borrower	$61.472	8.37%	Borrower
1997	Ch. WS	$56.410	Heart	$41.900	–25.72%	Heart
1997	*Cleve.	$54.886	Borrower	$58.615	6.79%	Borrower

Year	Team	Start Payroll	Start Type	End Payroll	Percent Ch.	End Type
1997	*Florida	$47.528	Borrower	$53.165	11.86%	Borrower
1997	*Hous.	$33.793	Mid Defense	$34.188	1.17%	Mid Defense
1997	LA	$45.883	Balanced	$52.279	13.94%	Mid Defense
1997	*NYY	$61.386	Balanced	$64.890	5.71%	Balanced
1997	Pitt.	$9.332	Star	$12.034	28.95%	Star
1997	*SF	$34.885	Star	$42.137	20.79%	Borrower
1998	Ana.	$36.517	Rotation, Pitch	$43.825	20.01%	Rotation, Pitch
1998	*Atlanta	$60.281	Rotation, Pitch	$61.888	2.67%	Rotation, Pitch
1998	*Ch. C	$50.753	Balanced	$51.056	0.60%	Balanced
1998	*Hous.	$40.290	Heart, Mid Def.	$47.554	18.03%	Balanced
1998	*SD	$46.307	Borrower	$53.198	14.88%	Borrower
1998	SF	$42.083	Balanced	$49.186	16.88%	Borrower
1998	*Texas	$56.156	Balanced	$60.554	7.83%	Balanced
1999	*Atlanta	$73.585	Rotation	$74.536	1.29%	Rotation
1999	Balt.	$79.002	Balanced	$70.824	-10.35%	Balanced
1999	*Boston	$59.554	Rotation, Pitch	$71.735	20.45%	Pitching
1999	Cinn.	$33.163	Borrower	$41.718	25.80%	Pitching
1999	*Hous.	$51.542	Balanced	$55.252	7.20%	Borrower
1999	*NYY	$84.640	Borrower	$86.231	1.88%	Borrower

Year	Team	Start Payroll	Start Type	End Payroll	Percent Ch.	End Type
1999	*Texas	$74.840	Borrower	$81.307	8.64%	Borrower
2000	*NYY	$92.689	Mid Defense	$110.631	19.36%	Borrower
2000	*Boston	$73.114	Pitching	$89.564	22.50%	Borrowed
2000	Toronto	$46.362	Balanced	$49.612	7.01%	Balanced
2000	*Ch. WS	$30.560	Rotation	$36.125	18.21%	Mid Defense
2000	Cleve.	$76.716	Borrower	$77.422	0.92%	Borrower
2000	*Oak.	$33.113	Rotation, Pitch	$36.933	11.54%	Borrower
2000	*Seattle	$59.241	Balanced	$61.326	3.52%	Borrower
2000	*Atlanta	$82.938	Rotation	$92.043	10.98%	Borrower
2000	*NYM	$78.797	Balanced	$80.270	1.87%	Balanced

Among the forty-nine clubs included in the survey, thirty-four of which survived to the postseason, twenty underwent midseason alterations to their basic nature. Ten of those twenty played October baseball.

When contending teams do try to change their basic makeup, and especially when they do so successfully, it's generally in one of two ways. They either beef up their pitching—often their bullpen—or they become "borrowers," drawing from one or more areas to pick up what they view as a key addition. Of the twenty teams listed above that significantly altered their roster-building approaches in midseason, fifteen followed one of those two paths.

Even so, and despite the trend that was accelerated in 2000, it remains for the most part the course set in the spring—as expressed in the payroll distribution of the roster—that holds sway.

9

FAITH AND HOPE
IN BASEBALL

The idea of contraction mutated out of a debate that dominated base-ball's off-field discussions for more than a decade—financially driven competitive imbalance.

As the chief advocate for contraction, commissioner Bud Selig gave the most direct and blunt voice to this mutation. Speaking in January of 2002 to a reporter for MLB.com, Selig put it on a "faith and hope" plane. Said the commissioner, "It's the hope and faith that the fans need to have that their team can successfully compete." As the commissioner saw it, big money—the kind spent in New York and a handful of other cities—was the pox on competitive imbalance. "Why can't the fans in a Pittsburgh or a Kansas City or Milwaukee have that hope and faith? Let the quality of management take over as opposed to just the amount of money."

Presumably, the thread leading from that philosophical posture to contraction wove around the notion that at least two teams were so financially uncompetitive that there was no hope of them ever catching up. Or, since skepticism is never out of line when considering the motives behind baseball's financial matters, contraction may simply have been a ploy to improve the owners' leverage in the discussion with players concerning a new basic agreement, a matter that was in play at the time. Whatever the motive, we are less interested here in contraction than in the underlying assumption, which is the relationship between money and competitiveness.

It is a relationship so commonly and easily assumed that it is taken for granted. There is nothing especially new about the idea that payroll disparity is ruining the competitive nature of Major League baseball. It is as old as the hit-and-run. Sometimes the complaint about "buying a pennant" is valid. As far back as 1885 league members were aghast when owners of the never-successful Detroit franchise paid the astonishing sum of seven thousand dollars to purchase the contracts of literally every member of the Buffalo franchise. Detroit actually only wanted Buffalo's star infield: Dan Brouthers, Hardy Richardson, Dave Rowe, and Deacon White; the other players were disposed of. Largely thanks to the deal, Detroit leaped from sixth place in 1885 to second in 1886, and won the pennant in 1887 with the so-called "Big Four" at its core.

In recent seasons club owners have touted the notion that payroll disparity is ruining the game as a rationale for raising ticket prices, for building new stadiums, or for seat licensing plans. The Kansas City Royals play in a park that is generally considered one of the more attractive stadiums in the American League. Kauffman Stadium was built in the early 1970s, yet it somehow managed to avoid being cursed with the cookie cutter sameness that infected other parks of that vintage. It is in good shape, has lots of parking, is clean, is blessed with excellent access and a good neighborhood—yet Royals ownership in 2001 asked the city to approve a $150 million renovation. Why? To install facilities the Royals estimate would generate an additional $30 million in annual revenues.

"If you increase your revenues, you can increase your payroll," explained club owner David Glass, whose club ranked twenty-seventh among the thirty Major League teams in payroll in 2001—and, not coincidentally, Glass would argue—twenty-eighth in victories. Their approximately $35.42 million player payroll amounted to about 56 percent of the club's total revenues of $63.7 million. (The latter is based on figures released by the commissioner's office following the 2001 season.) The Royals, said Selig, "have to improve their revenues." (He did not say *or else,* but since "contraction" was raised, the folks in Kansas City along with a few other cities presumed that those two words were implied.)

Nor are the owners alone in their pleas. "Money is not just running the game but whipping it," despaired Bob Costas in his 2000 book, *Fair Ball.* "With every season there seem to be more teams greeting Opening Day with little or no chance to compete for a pennant."

That ruinous effect of money on competitive balance was the rationale that drove the collusion argument in the late 1980s, and which led to the salary cap proposal and subsequently the players' strike of 1994. It has lain unresolved and—until the successive triumphs of the mid-payroll Angels and low-payroll Marlins—unquestioned ever since. The Major League Baseball Players Union tacitly blessed the idea by ignoring it, preferring to debate the methods of implementation rather than the premise. Until the Angels and Marlins gave them cover to do so, almost nobody in the media challenged the premise.

That being the case, several tantalizing issues and assumptions are ripe for examination. Here are a few.

What is the industry standard for the amount of revenue a team ought to put into salaries? Could small-budget teams improve their financial wherewithal simply by being less penurious?

Is the commissioner correct when he implies that the fans of a significant number of teams have no reason for "faith and hope" at the season's start due to their team's fiscal well-being? And just exactly what is a fair standard for measuring team success, anyway?

Is it possible to formulate a statistical relationship between the amount of payroll a team offers and its success on the field? And if so, is this relationship a constant or a variable?

If we can assert a financially based competitive imbalance, is this a relatively recent phenomenon or are there historical antecedents? In other words, with respect to the commissioner's wish that fans of every team could hope for a winner, was it ever thus?

PAYROLL: THE INDUSTRY STANDARD

Thanks to the commissioner's testimony before Congress in the fall of 2001, we have for one of the rare times a peek inside what Major League Baseball says are the books of its thirty teams. (Others dispute that, by the way, asserting that the numbers are cooked. For the moment, and until proven otherwise, we will assume the tenuous—that the owners are honest men.) Among other things, the data released by Commissioner Selig makes it simple to answer the first intriguing question, which is whether small-budget teams are really doing all they can to enhance their own chances of being financially competitive.

If the commissioner's data is to be believed, the average Major League team in 2001 invested 57.5 percent of its total revenues in payroll. We've already noted that the Royals devoted very nearly that slice—about 55.4 percent—to on-field talent. What of some other "small-budget" teams? In 2001, the ten lowest-payroll teams were the Twins, A's, Expos, Royals, Marlins, Padres, Phillies, Brewers, Angels, and Reds. In different ways, the A's and Expos are fascinating cases, so we will set them aside for consideration until last. Here's how the remaining seven allocated their revenues into payroll:

Reds	69.12%
Marlins	59.06%
MLB Average	57.5%
Angels	52.04%
Phillies	51.10%
Padres	48.77%
Twins	42.88%
Brewers	38.72%

Of the eight teams (counting the Royals), only the Reds and Marlins actually spent a percentage of their league revenues on salary that was equal to the league average. Selig's Brewers were toward the low end of the scale, ranking 28th in the percentage of revenues directed into player payroll. What, we might ask, would have happened to the payrolls of the six laggards if they had merely allocated the league average toward player payroll. Had they done so, their payrolls would have looked liked this (all figures are in millions):

Team	Act. Payroll	Revised Payroll
Brewers	$43.89	$65.21
Angels	$47.74	$52.77
Phillies	$41.66	$46.90
Padres	$38.88	$45.86
Royals	$35.42	$36.80
Twins	$24.13	$32.37

Since the average Major League payroll in 2001 was about $65.5 million, one club—Selig's Brewers—would have leaped into the middle tier of spenders simply by loosening their belts to the normal notch. The others would have merely moved up by degrees. But even so, these six poorer cousins would have found an additional $48.19 million—about $8 million per team on average—to spend on players if they had applied the league average formulas. (Honesty compels me to report that four of those six teams—all but the Brewers and Royals—reported operating losses in 2001 amounting to a cumulative $28.39 million. That might mitigate the idea that they could have dedicated a higher proportion of revenue to payroll . . . or it might raise questions concerning where else they're spending their money.)

THE A'S AND EXPOS

Almost universally condemned, the Montreal Expos largely operated in a fiscal world of their own, and this is as true (if one believes their revenue statement) with regard to payroll as it is of other matters. In 2001, the Expos reported overall team revenues of $34.171 million, while paying player salaries of $35.16 million. That means that the Expos claim to have paid 102.9 percent of overall revenues in player salaries. And this for the third lowest payroll in the majors. (They reported overall losses of about $12.8 million.)

Some part of the problem may be ascribable as the cost of doing business in Canada. Perhaps it is the exchange rate, but the second highest proportion of revenues paid as salaries occurred in Toronto, where the figure was a nearly as astonishing 97.99 percent. (That is 22 percentage points more than the highest percentage paid by any American-based team.)

Well before the formal announcement of their departure for Washington, most everyone in baseball conceded that the Expos were terminal. They cleared only $6.4 million in game receipts (the pauperish Twins made three times that much from the fans), and added to that just $536,000 from local television and cable. (The Marlins, not exactly a network megalith, got $15.3 million from media rights.) Spending more in salary than one takes in in revenue pretty much speaks for itself, but let's do the math anyway, this time in reverse. Assuming the Expos' figures are correct, if they had spent just 57.5 percent of revenues in player salaries Montreal's payroll would have fallen from $25.16 million in 2001 to just under $20 million.

So Montreal is the jewel in Bud Selig's argument. But Oakland is the thorn. In 2001, the A's spent just $33.81 million on player payroll, less than any big league team except Minnesota. Not only that, but the $33.81 million they did spend amounted to just 44.8 percent of total revenues, well below the league average. Had the A's spent at the league average, their payroll would have been $43.4 million, nearly $10 million higher than it actually was. Again, in fairness to the A's, they did report a slight loss (about $532,000) for the season, so it is at least arguable that the saved $10 million did not go directly into the owners' pockets. But in fact the argument does not need to be made, because as we all know the A's did not suffer through 2001. Although judging by the commissioner's "faith and hope" quotient Oakland should have been dead by April 1, the A's in fact won 102 games and made the playoffs.

For the record, the A's were one of four teams that allocated payroll at a rate below the league average and yet made the postseason in 2001. The others were the Astros, Yankees, and, yes, the Seattle Mariners. Not only did the Mariners win a record-tying 116 games in 2001, they did it while putting just 37 percent of their total revenues—the lowest percentage in the majors—into talent. And you think Pat Gillick wasn't the executive of the year?

THE BOTTOM LINE: WINNING GAMES

In addressing the matter of "faith and hope," the obvious first question is: "Faith and hope of what?" Based on his statements, we may extrapolate the commissioner's answer to this question as faith and hope of winning (or at least reaching) the World Series.

The commissioner has not addressed directly this implicit question of how one gauges success. Few in the major media have, either. But it is a vital question along the lines of "If you don't know where you're going, how can you know when you get there?" He has made several leading statements, however. One of the commissioner's revealing statistical mantras has gone like this: Between 1995 and 2000, teams in the lower half of payroll won only three postseason games. (With the Marlins' world title as well as assorted postseason wins by the A's and Twins, those figures are no longer operative.) Ergo, presumably, we are to deduce that the commissioner's standard for success is something approximating the number of postseason games won.

There is nothing wrong with the commissioner's math. Until 2003, when teams in the lower half of payroll won 14 of the 38 postseason games, anyone looking at the record would cheerfully concede that teams with low payrolls win very few postseason games, in large part for the obvious reason that they rarely play in them. But that does not establish that the commissioner's premise is the best premise.

What the commissioner's reasoning fails to take into account is the classic element of mathematical chance. Simply put, the fewer games that are played, the greater the prospect that chance will intervene in favor of the less-talented club. On any given day . . . . Conversely, the more games that are played the greater likelihood that talent will win out.

So when the commissioner stakes his judgment of the relative importance of money toward winning—the "faith and hope" quotient—on the results of postseason games, he is using the wrong basis. A far better measurement than the ability to *win* postseason games is the opportunity to *play* postseason games. Or, put more simply, the ability to win regular season games. This is the measurement that takes into greatest consideration the actual interplay between the two factors we are most interested in, money and victories. That's because it is the measurement that minimizes the luck factor.

CAUTION: MATH AHEAD

To accurately establish the impact of money on team performance, we need some mathematical formula that is designed to ascertain such relationships. We have one. It is called regression theory.

Regression theory calculates the strength of the relationship between payroll and performance, and—based on that relationship—projects how many games a team at a particular salary level ought to win. It does this by dint of a bunch of functions and chi-squares and square roots that you probably don't want to be bored with. (If you do, see note at end of the chapter.) But it does work.

Now here's the current bottom line. Between the conclusion of the 1994–95 strike and the conclusion of the 1999 season, a team's payroll could be said to be between a 60 and 80 percent factor in determining its eventual performance. In other words, during those seasons payroll was certainly the single most important factor, occasionally capable of being overcome, but substantially more important than all other factors combined. Money's influence on performance peaked in 1998, when it was an 82 percent determinant. When he talked about the doleful influence of money on the outcomes of games between 1995 and 1999, Commissioner Selig was dead on.

However, and for reasons that are not yet clear, something happened between 1999 and 2000 to undermine the commissioner's case against runaway spending. It does not appear to have been the spending itself. In 1999, the average Major League payroll was just above $48 million; by 2003, it had risen to slightly more than $71 million. Yet the mathematical relationship between payroll and victories fell from an undeniable 70.7 percent in 1999 to 51.3 percent in 2000, and then to an almost casual 31.3 percent in 2001. In 2003, the relationship was about 41 percent. This is meaningful, not voodoo, math: Between 2000 and 2003, ten teams with payrolls among the lower half in the majors (the A's all four times, the 2000–03 Twins, the 2000 White Sox and Giants, the 2001 Astros, and the 2003 Marlins) qualified for the postseason. The 2002 Oakland A's ranked twenty-eighth in the majors in payroll at $39.68 million, yet won 103 games and the AL West. The AL Central champion Minnesota Twins won 94 games with a $40.255 million payroll that was fourth from the bottom. Based strictly on payroll, neither should have been expected to win more than 73 games. Oakland won 30 more than that and Minnesota won 21 more. The world champion Marlins stood twenty-fifth with a payroll right around $50 million. That should have brought them 77 regular season victories; it actually brought them 91.

The 2002 world champion Anaheim Angels' $61.7 million payroll ranked fifteenth overall. They beat out five American League nondivision winners with higher payrolls, in some cases substantially higher. Judging strictly by payroll, Anaheim should have won 20 fewer games than the Angels did win in 2002.

Not that the big-money teams all were somehow rendered helpless. In 2002, the Yankees, Diamondbacks, Braves, and Giants did reach the postseason. All were in the top ten in spending, with New York ranking number one at $126 million. Yet in the division series the Yanks were felled by Anaheim, the D-Backs lost to St. Louis, and the Braves—seventh in spending—went down to the Giants, who were tenth. In 2003, four more top ten spending teams made the postseason: the Yanks, Red Sox, Braves, and Giants. The average position on the payroll scale of 2002–03 playoff-bound teams? It was between twelfth and thirteenth out of thirty.

At least short term, this has become a trend. In 2001, the Seattle Mariners' $74.7 million payroll was comfortable—about $7 million above the Major League average—but hardly gaudy. It ranked the M's eleventh among big spenders. Yet Seattle not only won the AL West, the Mariners equaled the all-time record for wins in a season with 116. Had payroll been the sole determining factor, based on their slightly above average spending the Mariners would have won just 82 games in 2001.

With 102 victories, the Oakland A's would have beaten any team except Seattle to the finish line in any of baseball's divisions in 2001. Yet the A's accomplished that on a $33.8 million payroll that was twenty-ninth among the thirty teams. If payroll had been the determining factor, Oakland would have won just 76 games . . . 26 fewer than the A's did win.

By applying regression theory, we can calculate how many games a ball club ought to have won at any payroll level in any given season. This allows us to examine the role played by payroll in performance in a familiar fashion. Here, for example, are two sets of standings from the 2003 season. The first set is the actual order of finish. On the right is the payroll projected standing as determined by regression theory. The lesson we should take from these tables is a simple one: When we talk about payroll disparity in the majors today, we are really talking about only one of the divisions.

2003

NL East	Actual W–L	Projected W–L
Braves	101–61	88–74
Marlins	91–71	77–85
Phillies	86–76	81–81
Expos	83–79	77–85
Mets	66–95	90–72

With a slightly greater payroll than Atlanta, the Mets finished an embarrassing 34½ games back. Can you say $12.2 million for Jeromy Burnitz, $17.2 million for Mo Vaughn, and $11 million for Tom Glavine? To the Braves' credit, they exceeded payroll-driven expectations by 13 games. Having money and also using it wisely is the best combination of attributes. The champion Marlins, by the way, overperformed by 14 games. The projected difference between the best-paid Mets and worst-paid Marlins: 13 games.

NL Central	Actual W–L	Projected W–L
Cubs	88–74	83–79
Astros	87–85	81–81
Cardinals	85–77	83–79
Pirates	75–87	78–84
Reds	69–93	79–83
Brewers	68–94	75–87

Payroll was not a major consideration in the outcome of the NL Central, where the division was bunched money-wise within eight games from top to bottom. The difference was only five games if the Brewers are set aside. In 2003, the better teams each overperformed by a few games; the lesser teams underperformed.

NL West	Actual W–L	Projected W–L
Giants	100–61	83–79
Dodgers	85–77	88–74
D-Backs	84–78	83–79
Rockies	74–88	80–82
Padres	64–98	76–86

Los Angeles began with a four-game payroll advantage over San Francisco, but played three games worse than expectations. The Giants overperformed by 17 games, the largest such achievement in the NL. Arizona did what the D-Backs should have done; San Diego and Colorado both underperformed. The projected division-wide difference: 12 games from top to bottom.

AL East	Actual W–L	Projected W–L
New York	101–61	97–65
Boston	95–67	87–75
Toronto	86–76	77–85
Baltimore	71–91	82–80
Tampa Bay	63–99	71–91

When we talk about payroll's impact on performance, as a practical matter we are talking about the AL East and the Yankees. It's fair to say that by virtue of their payroll, the Yankees began the 2003 season with an effective 10-game payroll-induced lead over the Red Sox, a 15-game advantage over Baltimore, a 20-game lead over Toronto, and a 26-game lead over Tampa Bay. Boston in turn led Baltimore by 5 games in the wild card, and led Toronto by 10. What do you suppose are the chances of a team spotting the Yanks 10 games and then overtaking them? Not likely. Fifteen games or more? No chance.

AL Central	Actual W–L	Projected W–L
Minnesota	90–72	78–84
Chicago	86–76	77–85
Kansas City	83–79	75–87
Cleveland	68–94	77–85
Detroit	43–119	77–85

Due largely to Cleveland's retreat from among the big spenders, the AL Central has become the division where payroll matters least. In 2003 the equivalent of a mere three games separated the best-and worst-funded clubs. As much as any division could be, the Central was decided on merit.

AL West	Actual W–L	Projected W–L
Oakland	96–66	77–85
Seattle	93–69	84–78
Anaheim	77–85	83–69
Texas	71–91	87–75

That's right, based on payroll Texas began the 2003 season with an effective 10-game advantage over Oakland, and lost the pennant by 25 games. The A's played 19 games above expectations based on payroll, the best performance in the majors. The projected difference between best-paid and worst-paid—10 games—meant nothing in the

AL West, where teams nearly finished in inverse order of their payroll-projected performance.

THE FAITH AND HOPE QUOTIENT

Quantifying the payroll-based projected standings also frames an interesting by-product question. If we establish that—based on payroll—the Texas Rangers ought to win 87 games, and if we also establish that the Oakland A's only ought to win 77 games, what are the chances that the A's will actually win enough games to overtake the Rangers' advantage? For that matter, what are the prospects of any team at a significant payroll disadvantage overtaking any richer rival?

That question, which is at the core of Selig's "faith and hope" argument, can be answered either by observation or logically. Since the observation-based response is the simpler, let's start with it.

What would you say would be the chances of your favorite team overcoming a 3-game disadvantage at season's start? No problem, right? Over 162 games, 3 games is less than a 2 percent handicap. How about 5 games? If your heroes started with a built-in 5-game disadvantage, would you still have "faith and hope" in the chances for victory? Personally, I'd say yes; injuries or mere bad luck could sway that many games. Seven games? This is purely a matter of feel, but 7 strikes me as about the cusp of practicality. Once we think in terms of spotting divisional rivals 8 games, we are talking about a 5 percent disadvantage over a 162-game season, and that's getting tough.

Let's now put regression theory to work. A total of 294 team seasons were played between 1995 and 2004. Applying the observational approach (as interpreted by regression theory) to Commissioner Selig's "Faith and Hope" quotient, 114 of those team seasons (39 percent) were played in utter hopelessness and despair since that percentage of teams began play with a payroll handicap that translated to 8 games or more. (The data are included in Appendix III.) Since 1995, the fans of the Expos or (since their creation in 1998) the Devil Rays have never seen the dawn of a season in which they had a chance to compete, based on this standard. Fans of the Brewers and Pirates have seen just two.

At one point or another, "hopelessness" has by this standard af-flicted partisans of twenty-four of the present thirty Major League teams in the last ten seasons alone. Based on this standard, in 1997, again in 1998, and again in 1999, the entire AL Central race was over before it started; Cleveland had the whole thing bagged. In 1998, and again in 1999, half or more of all teams in the majors were uncompet-itive. That was nearly the case again in 2002, when fourteen of the thirty teams would have been disqualified from consideration as con-tenders under the 7-game payroll-driven standard.

But there is a problem with the observational standard: It doesn't work in the real world. In 2001, the Oakland A's began the season with a 9-game payroll disadvantage to the Texas Rangers in the AL West, and with a 12-game disadvantage to the Boston Red Sox in the wild card race. By the observational standard, this should have been an insurmountable hurdle. Yet the A's surmounted it, winning 102 games and beating out Boston by 20 games. That happened again in 2002, not only in the case of the A's (who started with an 18-game handicap) but the Twins (11 games) and Angels (12 games). The A's again would have been viewed as "hopeless" in 2003, as would have been the Marlins. How'd they do?

One reasonable adaptation would be to add a performance com-ponent. This is the "logical" approach to settling the "faith and hope" question. If in any given year a team overperforms its payroll-based projected win total by a certain number of games, then it is logical to deduce that any of the other teams was equally capable of overper-forming by the same number of games in that season. Since in this re-spect the only meaningful overperformance occurs among teams in the lower strata of the payroll range, we must allow only teams in the bottom half of the salary structure to set the standard for each given season. Whichever of those lower-paying teams overperforms by the greatest amount will define the logical "faith and hope" standard for that particular season.

Here are the season-by-season results since the strike.

1995: The Mets, who should have won 61 games and actually won 69, set the standard at 8 games. Under that standard, five teams—the Tigers, Brewers, Twins, Expos, and the Mets themselves—could have been pronounced hopeless.

1996: The Expos overperformed by 15 games, winning 88 in a season in which payroll dictated they should have won 73. Fifteen games is a daunting standard. Under that standard, only the Tigers and Brewers could have been summarily dismissed from pennant consideration.

1997: Pittsburgh, which based on payroll disparities should have won 68 games, actually won 79. That's an 11-game upgrade. Even so, payroll disparities were so meaningful in 1997 that six teams could be viewed as hopeless under the logical standard. Those six were the Pirates, A's, Tigers, Expos, Brewers, and Twins.

1998: The Toronto Blue Jays won 88 games, exceeding their payroll projection by 13 games. That's a high number. But payroll's grip on the standings was a stultifying (and contemporary high) 82 percent. Consequently, even by this logical standard, money rendered fourteen of the thirty teams noncompetitive. Those fourteen were the National League's Expos, Pirates, Marlins, Reds, Phillies, Diamondbacks, and Brewers, plus the American League's Royals, White Sox, Blue Jays, Twins, Devil Rays, Tigers, and A's.

1999: Cincinnati's unexpected run at the NL postseason was the first harbinger of change in the influence of cash on results. Defying the decade's previous pattern, the Reds won 96 games (and came within a playoff game of reaching the postseason) on a payroll that should have supported 78 victories. But even that generous standard still ruled six teams out of contention in 1999, when payroll remained a major factor in performance. Those six were the Marlins, Twins, Expos, Royals, A's, and White Sox.

2000: With a payroll that should have been good for 77 victories, the Chicago White Sox won 95 games and claimed the AL Central title. In 2000, payroll's influence waned sufficiently that the 18-game "logical" standard established by the White Sox made all of the thirty Major League teams theoretically competitive.

2001: Oakland, with the majors' second lowest payroll, won 26 games more than the A's were projected to win. Needless to say, all thirty Major League teams carried payrolls that at least could project them within 26 games of a wild card spot.

2002: Again it's the A's, who should have won 73 games and ended up winning 103. That's a standard-setting 30 games' worth of overperformance. Based on that benchmark, for the third consecutive season not a single Major League team could claim to lack faith and hope.

2003: Oakland set the standard for the third consecutive season, producing 96 victories on a payroll that should have netted 77 wins. That's a 19-game overperformance. For the fourth straight season, none of the thirty teams could be dismissed mathematically—although the Jays, Orioles, and Devil Rays admittedly faced pretty steep odds.

2004: Minnesota set the standard, exceeding its payroll-projected win total by 15 games. But for the first time since 1999, some teams were disqualified by that standard. Based on their payrolls, the Orioles and Blue Jays both projected to finish 17 games behind the wild card winning Red Sox, and the Devil Rays projected to finish 22 games out.

Our logical test condemned thirty-six teams since 1995 to hopelessness. That's a far cry from the 103 that were doomed under an observational standard, but it is still 9 percent of all clubs. Notably, however, only three of the thirty-three played during the four most recent seasons.

Mathematics provides an even more scientific means of settling the "faith and hope" issue. It's called the normal distribution, and its fundamental goal is to ascertain the percentage likelihood that an event that ought to happen—such as a victory by a more fiscally endowed team—will in fact happen. Those in search of a formal explanation should consult a statistics book. For the rest of us, let's take a case in point to illustrate. Based on regression theory, we can say that Oakland's payroll was most likely to produce 77 victories in 2003, while Texas's payroll was most likely to produce 87. That's a 10-game handicap. What we really mean is that there is a 50 percent probability either team would win more or less games than that number. In that context, and considering payroll as the controlling factor, what were Oakland's chances of overtaking Texas?

The 2003 A's had to overperform by 10 victories in order to catch the Rangers, assuming Texas played as projected by its payroll. There was another possibility, of course; the Rangers could have underperformed. In real life, those sorts of things happen now and then. But the laws of probability favor the occurrence of the most likely event; that's why it's called probability. The odds of a 10-game variation from predicted performance? About 16 percent. But that variation can happen in either direction. That makes the odds of the A's actually overperforming by 10 games closer to 8 percent. They actually overperformed by 17 games, a likelihood that is barely expressable. Assuming, of course, that payroll is the driving force.

Although it works at both ends of the payroll spectrum, the law of normal distribution and probability has its most interesting application at the lower reaches. In 2003, three teams were projected to win fewer than 75 games. Those three were the Brewers, Royals, and Devil Rays. Based on normal distribution, the odds of a team that ought to win 75 games actually winning 90 games—a reasonable number to begin to speculate on October baseball—are about 6.7 percent, a little better than once every twenty team seasons.

Now you might wonder: Aren't there thirty team seasons played every year? Indeed there are. So doesn't that prove that every single season one or two of those lower-paid, 75-win teams ought to jump into the fray? No, it doesn't. Since that 15-game differential can happen in either direction, it is equally plausible that the Royals, who should have won 74 games in 2003, would win 59 games as 89. (They actually won 83.) The second problem is this: One of those three teams—the Devil Rays—was projected to win only 71 games, not 75, and with each projected loss the odds of getting to the 90-win level rise substantially. Even if Tampa Bay had beaten the financial odds by 15 games in 2003—only a 6.7 percent proposition—the Rays still would have won just 86 games. That would have been well short of the 90 needed to project them as a postseason contender

There is a third complication. As noted above, good teams may also overperform their expectations. Which means that even 90 victories may not be enough to reach the playoffs. It took 95 in the American League East in 2003.

FISCAL CENTRIFUGAL FORCE

Although both recent data and experience argue that payroll's influence on performance is on the wane, at least one measurement continues to underscore the importance of cash. Broadly speaking, there appears over the past decade at least to be an element of fiscal centrifugal force at work in baseball; a dynamic that propels the best-paid teams ahead merely by the fact that they are the best paid. Although this force does not guarantee success on an individual team, it does assert the instinctive: that being rich is better than not being rich.

In all of the past eleven seasons, teams in the upper third of payroll—as a group—overperformed their payroll-projected expectations. In 2004, those teams projected to average 89 victories, and actually averaged 92. That 3-game margin matched the peak seasonal overperformance since 1994—the margin was also 3 games in 1999. In most seasons, the overperformance averaged about 1 game. But not since 1993 have the best-paid teams as a group failed to surpass their payroll projections for wins.

This does not happen across the board. In 2004, the highly paid Mets and Yankees both failed to meet payroll-projected expectations. The Yankees are a special case, of course. Their payroll is so high that it projected them to win 106 games; that they actually won 101 is a failure in only the most technical sense. The Mets did fail; their payroll projected them to win 87 games, 16 more than they did win. But of the 106 teams in the upper third of payroll since 1994, about 60 percent exceeded their payroll-projected win total. The World Series victories of Florida and Anaheim notwithstanding, let us move slowly to dismiss the role of money in influencing season outcomes.

GRANDPA, TELL ME ABOUT THE GAY EIGHTIES

Is this a new trend, or merely a new alarm? To answer that question, let's examine an era generally viewed today as one of the game's golden ages for competitiveness, the latter part of the 1980s.

Between 1979 and 1992, no team was able to string together consecutive world championships, by far the longest such non-repeat stretch since they began playing the World Series. In those fourteen seasons, twelve different franchises hoisted the world championship trophy, and neither the Yankees nor the Braves were among them. In the decade of the 1980s, twenty-three of the twenty-six Major League franchises—all but Texas, Cleveland, and Seattle—saw postseason action at least once.

That sounds like an absolute onslaught of competitive balance. If reality is in line with our perception, then payroll was far less a factor ten to fifteen years ago than it is today.

Although reliable payroll data prior to the 1990s is scarce, we do have enough information on which to base calculations on the relationship between payroll and performance for the 1986 to 1992 pre-strike seasons, as well as slightly less reliable (but usable) data dating back to 1977.

And when we run that payroll data through the same statistical processes we used to determine the relationship between payroll and performance in the modern game, what we get is confirmation of our instincts.

We noted earlier that we can fix the relationship mathematically between payroll and performance at between 60 and 80 percent for the post-strike period up until 1999. The decline in that relationship during the past two years—to 51 percent, then to 31 percent, and to 41 percent in 2003—has been as inexplicable as it has been striking.

In fact, the last time the relationship between a team's payroll and its on-field performance ducked under 50 percent was in the strike season itself, when payroll accounted for only 43 percent of the reason why teams accomplished what they accomplished.

Now here's the interesting part: 1994 not only marks the occurrence of a strike, it also represents the midpoint of a transitional period between two distinct eras of the payroll-competitiveness relationship. Between 1994 and 2000, the relationship was always stronger than 50 percent. But for a dozen seasons prior to 1994, the relationship never rose above 50 percent. In fact, between the 1981 strike and the 1994 strike, the median of the influence of payroll on team performance ran about 30 percent; in other words, roughly the same percentage as in 2001.

In the first season following the 1981 strike, the payroll-performance relationship was as strong as it would be until 1995, about 46 percent. It dipped below 40 percent in 1983, below 25 percent in 1984, and then to an inconsequential 10 percent at its nadir, in 1987. From that point it rose slowly and randomly, but was still only a 35 percent influence on the race as late as 1993.

In this data, some may find evidence that supports another oft-made assertion related to payroll in the mid to late 1980s: that owners conspired to artificially hold it down as a check on free agency. An arbitrator made that decision in 1987, awarding millions of "collusion dollars" to veteran ballplayers. Only the owners know for certain whether they colluded, but if they did, it at least had the salutary impact of allowing lower-salaried teams to be competitive. In 1982, the Cardinals (with the fifteenth highest payroll) won the world title. In 1983, Baltimore did it with a payroll that ranked eleventh overall. The 1984 world champion Tigers stood tenth in payroll, the 1985 Royals were also tenth, the 1986 Mets were ninth, and the 1987 Twins were fourteenth. Proving that highly paid teams could also persevere, the 1988 Dodgers won despite the era-related handicap of having the majors' second highest payroll. The 1989 champion A's stood sixth in money. But then came the 1990 Reds (sixteenth), and the 1991 Twins (fifteenth). Not until the Blue Jays triumphed both on the field and at the pay window in 1992 and 1993 did the signs of the new order become manifest.

'TWAS NOT ALWAYS THUS

The differing impacts of money on team competitiveness in the 1990s as compared with the 1980s might imply that baseball turned some sharp corner early in this decade, and that the game moved in a direction it had gone never before. Sketchy published data for the seasons immediately prior to the mid 1980s suggests that may not be a valid assumption. If that sketchy data, which goes back to 1977, were all we had to use as a basis for inference, we might venture into a guesstimate that the 1980s (rather than the 1990s) were the aberration. That data suggest that payroll was a stronger factor in determining team performance prior to the 1981 strike: The relationship was 61 percent in 1981 itself, falling to only 37 percent in 1980, but climbing again to between 56 percent and 76 percent in the 1977–79 seasons. That is familiar territory for us; it is almost exactly the influence payroll exerted on performance in the late 1990s.

The payroll information that would shine light on financial competitive balance for much of baseball's history prior to the late 1970s likely is lost forever. But in 1999, Doug Pappas, who until his death in 2004 chaired the Business of Baseball Committee for the Society for American Baseball Research, uncovered what might be viewed as the question's Rosetta Stone in the archives of a Congressional hearing concerning baseball's status under antitrust laws. Pappas found team salary data for the New York-dominated 1950s, data that allows us to interpret in a broader historical context the information we already have.

Well before the onset of free agency, the seasons represented by this data (1950–58) were a time when ball clubs could hold on to their own talent forever if they chose. Players of the caliber of Mickey Mantle, Willie Mays, Duke Snider, Ted Williams, Stan Musial, Robin Roberts, Hank Aaron, Ernie Banks, Al Rosen, and Al Kaline anchored their franchises without ever changing uniforms, in part, at least, because they had no recourse by which to do so.

The impact on salaries was substantial. In 1950, the best-paid team in baseball was the New York Yankees—you might have guessed that— who made $652,000. Based on their salary relative to their competitors, that Yankee team should have won 100 games and the pennant; they actually won 98 games and the pennant. The far more competitive National League crown should have gone to the St. Louis Cardinals with 84 victories; the Cards actually won 78 games and finished fifth behind Philadelphia, whose 91 victories outperformed its payroll by a full 21 games. (The Phils were the model for the 2000 Oakland A's; they featured third-year stars Richie Ashburn, Curt Simmons, and Robin Roberts, second-year slugger Willie Jones, and Del Ennis, the veteran, in his fifth season. By today's standards, only Ennis would have even been arbitration-eligible.) But Philadelphia was the clear exception. Across the two leagues, the relationship between what a team paid and how it played on the field was a compelling and very late-1990ish 73 percent.

The pattern held for most of the decade; there were a few exceptions, but no more young upstarts disturbing the natural order of things.

In 1951, the Yankees should have won 96 games and the AL pennant; they won 98 and the AL pennant. The Cardinals should have edged out the Dodgers and Giants in the NL, but St. Louis underperformed while New York beat Brooklyn in the Thomson playoff. The strength of the payroll-performance relationship: 71 percent.

The 1952 season was something of an anomaly, but only in a predictable sense. Launching what would become a four-season financial challenge to the Yanks' supremacy, Cleveland increased its payroll to a league-high (and presumably all-time record) $443,000. That should have been good for 89 victories and the AL pennant. Indeed, Cleveland won 93 games, but it wasn't good enough to overcome New York's inherent talent edge. The Yanks overperformed their own payroll (which predicted 87 wins) by 8 games to nose out the Indians by 2. With a $358,000 payroll that looked unremarkable, Brooklyn still managed to outdo New York by 4 games in the National League. At 48 percent, the payroll-performance relationship was the decade's weakest.

Despite leading the majors again in spending in 1953 at $451,000, Cleveland again failed to unseat New York in the American League. With the fourth highest NL payroll, Brooklyn likewise won again. The relationship rose to 55 percent.

At nearly 83 percent, payroll's gravitational force hit a high for the game's recorded financial history in 1954, as Cleveland finally unseated the Yanks. Four of the season's highest paid teams were also among the five most successful; at the other end of the scale, the three worst performers (Orioles, A's, and Pirates) were also among the four worst paid. At a time when there were only sixteen teams overall, that suggests true stratification.

Payroll's pull on performance was 79 percent in both 1955 and 1956, falling to 69 percent in 1957 and again dipping below 50 percent—to 49 percent—in 1958. At that point our archeological dig concludes, at least for the moment. Absent additional data, we cannot do more than speculate on the influence of money on results for the remainder of the 1950s, the 1960s, or into the 1970s.

Who's the Oddball Here?

But a simple graph of the year-by-year relationship implies much. Here it is:

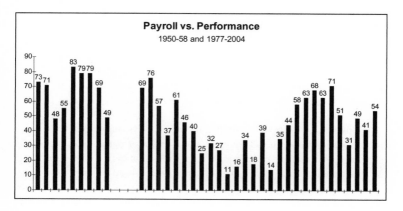

Payroll vs. Performance
1950-58 and 1977-2004

Based on the graph, there appears to be a cyclical element to money's influence on winning. In the 1950s, that influence was powerful. One can only speculate concerning the 1960s, although 1958 suggests the possibility of an incipient decline. If payroll waned as a factor during the 1960s it would fit the pattern. Regardless, payroll was a markedly stronger force in the 1970s. It receded to a deep and lengthy trough through the 1980s and early 1990s, peaked again in the mid 1990s, then engaged in at least its second (and possibly third) retreat. The 54 percent relationship for 2004 is a cusp sort of number. It could be merely a notation denoting the higher spectrum of that retreat, or it could signal that the retreat was unusually brief, and that the days of payroll dominance are about to return.

If one chooses to ascribe the unusually mild influence of money on performance in the 1980s to an illegal restraint of trade on the part of the owners, then an interesting thesis evolves. Left to its own devices, baseball is inherently predatory, allowing the rich, if uncontrolled, to feed off the poor. Only an effective means of artificial control (collusion, anyone?) can actually ensure competitive balance, thus providing a more widespread "faith and hope." Is that what happened in the era between the 1981 strike and the 1994 strike? Well, pennants and even world titles were within reach of the game's masses in the 1980s. Faith and hope abounded. Maybe collusion wasn't such a bad thing after all. Perhaps that's the commissioner's real point.

A note on regression theory:

Regression analysis seeks to find a correlation between two sets of data. The independent variable x, which could be the amount of money spent on a team, and the dependant variable y, the number of games won by the team. As the amount of money a team spends increases, does the number of wins increase proportionately?

This would be easy to answer if there were always, and in every case, a direct proportion between money spent and number of games won. We could plot the x,y points and draw a line through the points to fit the data perfectly. We could predict exactly what might happen with tomorrow's x,y data.

But the data is not always that clean and the relationship, if any, is not always that perfect. So instead of finding the line that "fits the data exactly," more often than not we have to settle for a line of "best fit." The method used is called "the least squares method" and is based on the Pythagorean logic of finding the length of one side of a triangle by taking the square root of the sum of the squares of the other two sides.

Having found the line that "best fits" the data, we need to know one more thing. Just how good a fit is this newly found "best fit" line? How well does it really match the data? To get this, we use the "Pearson correlation coefficient." In an overly simplified form, you might think of this as a sort of a way to compare the slope formed by the combined data to the slope of the "best fit" line.

10

WHAT A PLAYER IS WORTH

What's Alex Rodriguez worth? What's the right price to pay for the best hitter in the game?

The Texas Rangers, Boston Red Sox, and New York Yankees all have had to answer that question recently. The Rangers did so when they signed Rodriguez to a free agent contract prior to the 2001 season, the Red Sox and Yanks when they considered whether to trade for him prior to the 2004 season.

They arrived at different conclusions based on different judgments.

When the Rangers signed Rodriguez, they judged his value by a commonly understood yardstick: the market. Simply stated, a player is worth what he can command. By that definition, Alex Rodriguez was worth $25 million per year to the Rangers for a decade because that was the price at which a willing buyer and willing seller came to terms. At contract time, market value is the dominant standard.

At other times of the year, other standards come into vogue. In October of 1998, following Mark McGwire's history-making 70-homer season, the news media, enthusiastically abetted by fans themselves, debated McGwire's worth in terms of awards. Sure he had a great statistical season, but should he have been the MVP—his team, after all, finished down in the standings? How much value can anybody have on a fourth place club? By that yardstick, McGwire was not worth much.

There is a third aspect to a player's "value," the one relating to the number of fans he brings to the park. When Rangers owner Tom

Hicks factored into his own mind what to offer Rodriguez, no small part of the equation was A-Rod's ability to draw people to The Ballpark at Arlington. In that sense, the shortstop's own desire for a huge contract actually worked in his favor: the greater the numbers, the greater the buzz; the greater the buzz, the greater the number of fans drawn by it. If Alex Rodriguez put fannies in the seats, that enhanced his "worth."

Over time, Hicks came to re-evaluate his judgment of Rodriguez's worth; that's why he traded him following the 2003 season. Hicks came to realize that the amount he was paying Rodriguez to do things other than perform on the field—an amount we're about to establish at around $10.5 million per year—represented too great a drain on the assets he had available to make Texas a winner. In the end, Hicks was unable to trade Rodriguez to Boston because the Red Sox had come to the same conclusion. Pick up A-Rod's salary and you hamstring your ability to make any other moves. The best player in baseball may be worth $25 million per year in some market-oriented or esoteric sense, but no player could justify that salary by their contributions toward producing a winning baseball team. And winning is the best marketing strategy of all. It has always been thus.

George Steinbrenner's Yankees came to a different conclusion when they made the A-Rod deal because they were presented with a different set of financial circumstances. That different set of circumstances revolved around the salient fact that in order to get out from under A-Rod's deal, Hicks was willing to cover about about 30 percent of Rodriguez's annual salary. To Steinbrenner, then, Rodriguez was no longer a $25 million asset; he was a less egregious $18 million asset. (Hicks could cover the last $7 million, which he couldn't do with the Sox, because he wasn't picking up Manny Ramirez's almost equally outrageous salary in return.) The Sox would have made the deal, too, if they could have gotten A-Rod for $18 million a year. The Yanks probably would not have made it if they had been bound to pay his full $25 million (although with Steinbrenner signing the checks, you can never be absolutely certain).

The lesson of the A-Rod off-again, on-again deal, then, has in part to do with the contortions necessary to moving a very high-salaried player. In this most dramatic of instances, those contortions boiled down to one unavoidable fact: Nobody, not Tom Hicks, not George Steinbrenner, not Theo Epstein, thought A-Rod is worth what he is getting paid. But what then is he worth?

FRESH FISH AND SMELLY FISH

To gauge a player's value in the context of his contributions to victory, we might want to think of a marketplace in a more utilitarian fashion. The marketplace of baseball talent is very much like a food market. It is visited by customer after customer, each picking over the produce, smelling the fish or thumping the melons, and each with the same goal in mind: to gather the best ingredients using the financial resources available in each shopper's purse.

In each case, there is a very real competition that is governed by rules of nature and talent. Just as every shopper has access to the same fish and melons, every club owner has access to the same talent. Some may not be able to afford the top-of-the-line pitcher; hey, some folks can't afford lobster. Some who can afford prime beef may get stuck with a lesser grade if they're not careful. Some may buy what is marketed as a premium-priced filet of fish for its reputation, in the process failing to notice that it is well on the way to stinking. Even the richest may inadvertently purchase a few old lemons; even the poorest may find an overlooked tasty cut. The advantages lay partly with the rich, and partly with the discerning.

Most of the premier statistical researchers of baseball have addressed the question of how one assesses baseball talent in the context of winning games. Bill James has; so have Pete Palmer, Earnshaw Cook, and Tom Boswell. And their answers don't differ all that greatly; at the bottom line, in fact, they don't differ at all. Just as the shopper at the food market prowls the stands in search of definable characteristics in veal, beans, or mushrooms, so too does the sagacious baseball GM prowl the talent marketplace in search of definable qualities. Only in the case of the baseball GM, the qualities are twofold:

The ability to manufacture (for hitters) or to prevent the manufacture (for pitchers or fielders) of runs. Those are the elements that win ball games.

IT'S A ZERO-SUM GAME

The formulae for determining how a run is manufactured varies a bit from researcher to researcher, but the differences are nuances as opposed to substantive. With that background, the path to answering our question regarding a player's value becomes more clear. Here is how you measure a player's dollar value. Calculate the number of runs Alex Rodriguez, Kevin Brown, Mark McGwire, or any player of your choice prevents or produces during a given season. Make the same calculation for all big leaguers who had a similar responsibility. Then redistribute the salaries earned by all those players—including the one you are assessing—on the basis of their actual production; the greater the individual's portion of the group's total runs produced, the more money he "earned." The result is the player's actual objective "Earned Value" in terms of winning ball games above (or, in some cases, below) what others who did similar things were paid.

This approach, which is not nearly as complicated as it sounds, is valid because it is founded on an underlying and undeniable principle: Baseball is a zero-sum game. For every winner, there is a loser. Every run scored is also a run given up. The point of the game is to tip the balance sheet most decisively in your favor. The guy who does that the most has "earned" the greatest reward, which most of us measure in money.

That's also true from the standpoint of a general manager or club owner charged with acquiring talent. The trick isn't merely to ascertain what a player would cost on the open market, but also to make the most accurate estimate of whether that player is likely to contribute real value in terms of producing or preventing runs. The GM's job is to maximize the use of his resources; if those resources are reasonably close to adequate, that same GM will have a chance to construct a pennant contender.

GMs, of course, operate with a couple of inherent advantages that are dictated by baseball's contractual rules. This is the most important: For the first few years of his professional life, a ballplayer's salary is essentially based on his experience rather than his record. Because they are not eligible for free agency for several seasons—and in most cases cannot even arbitrate until they have completed three seasons—young, frontline talent can be used at "bargain" rates. Can you believe that Alex Rodriguez drew a mere $440,000 from the Seattle Mariners as recently as 1996, a season in which his .358 average led the AL in batting? It was, you see, his first full year. Or that as the reigning batting king in 1997, he made just pennies over $1 million? Rodriguez's problem was leverage: He didn't have any. (Time has since remedied that.)

ATTENTION KMART SHOPPERS

Not every GM has an Alex Rodriguez under contract to make him look good, but most have one or two talented young players who represent salary bargains. In Boston, Nomar Garciaparra played that role for three seasons. At a rookie's salary, Kerry Wood was a GM's dream with the Cubs in 1998. By the time Chipper Jones signed his first $1 million deal in 1997, he had already topped .300, 30 homers, and 100 RBIs. The Pirates paid Jason Kendall less than half the Major League average, $550,000, in 1998, fully anticipating that he would lead their team's offense. He didn't disappoint, batting .327. In Philadelphia, second-year player Scott Rolen already was recognized as the heart of the team by 1998 thanks to a 30-homer, 110-RBI season. His reward for 1999? A $250,000 raise, to $1 million, still well below the league average. Lucky GMs? No, just guys who knew how to take advantage of the rules.

These are the kinds of players general managers covet, fellows who make a big contribution for a Kmart price. Between 1995 and 2003 there were 195 player-seasons in which the player earned less than $1 million yet produced a BFW or PW of +2.0 or above. Sixty-six of those seasons were enjoyed by sixty position players, and the list includes some impressive names: Bobby Abreu, Lance Berkman, Jim Edmonds, Nomar Garciaparra, Troy Glaus, Vladimir Guerrero, Bobby Higginson, Orlando Hudson, Aubrey Huff, Geoff Jenkins, Charles Johnson, Andruw Jones, Jason Kendall, Paul LoDuca, Javier Lopez, Magglio Ordonez, Mike Piazza, A. J. Pierzynski, Scott Podsednik, Albert Pujols, Manny Ramirez, Alex Rodriguez, Scott Rolen, Tim Salmon, Alfonso Soriano, Shannon Stewart, Jim Thome, Vernon Wells, and Bernie Williams.

Indeed, you could field a prodigious starting nine out of the players listed above. And since none of them cost $1 million at the time they fashioned their exceptional seasons, it would also have been an economical team. But keep one other thing in mind: Cornering the market on a sufficient portion of the bargain-basement seasons to overcome payroll deficiencies and greatly impact a pennant race would be akin to cornering the market on gold—the commodity's too rare and there's too much competition. In 2003, there were twenty-five such players in all of the major leagues. And only ten of them—A. J. Pierzynski, Vernon Wells, Milton Bradley, Aubrey Huff, Alfonso Soriano, Scott Podsednik, Orlando Hudson, Albert Pujols, Mark Ellis, and Morgan Ensberg—played a position other than pitcher.

There's another problem. While acquiring cheap talent is always a good idea, the record suggests it isn't enough to win a pennant. Between 1995 and 2003, two teams at the top of the list of acquiring good young players were the Cincinnati Reds and Pittsburgh Pirates, who have a combined one postseason appearance to show for it. In 2003, only six teams could grab as many as two such players. The six were Houston (Ensberg and Oswalt), Arizona (Webb and Villareal), Los Angeles (Gagne and Mota), Toronto (Hudson and Wells), Minnesota (Santana and Pierzynski), and the White Sox (Marte and Loaiza). Only the Twins played in the postseason. Only seven of these "premium" players—fewer than one per team—saw postseason action. (The seven were the two Twins plus Zambrano with the Cubs, Willis with the Marlins, Soriano with the Yankees, Ellis with Oakland, and Nathan with the Giants.)

The evidence suggests that, even when it works, the "strategy" of offsetting fiscal inadequacies by building around young talent doesn't work.

It's even chancier if the young phenoms are pitchers, as a glance at the list of moundsmen who have enjoyed such a season quickly illustrates. In the case of position players, most have outgrown their sub-$1 million price tags, but the great majority continue to be frontline performers. That is far less true of pitchers who return big dividends early in their careers. Since 1995, fifty-two starters and thirty-six relievers have achieved a PW of +2.0 or higher in at least one season in which they were paid less than $1 million. Here is the complete list:

Starters: Rick Ankiel, Andy Ashby, Rolando Arrojo, Roger Bailey, Alan Benes, Mark Buehrle, Paul Byrd, Frank Castillo, Bartolo Colon, Francisco Cordova, Omar Daal, Jeff C. D'Amico, Danny Darwin, Shawn Estes, Freddy Garcia, Mark Gubicza, Pete Harnisch, Butch Henry, Dustin Hermanson, Orlando Hernandez, Tim Hudson, Al Leiter, Esteban Loaiza, Joe Mays, Wade Miller, Kevin Millwood, Mike Moehler, Matt Morris, Jamie Moyer, Mark Mulder, Tomo Ohka, Russ Ortiz, Roy Oswalt, Carlos Perez, Andy Pettitte, Joel Pineiro, Brad Radke, Todd Ritchie, Kevin Ritz, Jose Rosado, Johan Santana, Pete Schourek, Justin Thompson, Steve Trachsel, Ismael Valdes, Tim Wakefield, Jarrod Washburn, Brandon Webb, Kip Wells, Dontrelle Willis, Carlos Zambrano, Barry Zito.

Relievers: Juan Acevedo, Luis Ayala, Francisco Cordero, Octavio Dotel, Joey Eischen, Eric Gagne, Danny Graves, Chris Hammond, Trevor Hoffman, Jose Jimenez, Doug Jones, Todd Jones, Jorge Julio, Byung-Hyun Kim, Steve Kline, Billy Koch, Curtis Leskanic, Alan Levine, Derek Lowe, Damaso Marte, Guillermo Mota, Robb Nen, Troy Percival, Mariano Rivera, John Rocker, Eduardo Romero, Heathcliff Slocumb, Jeff Shaw, Ugueth Urbina, Oscar Villareal, Billy Wagner, Ben Weber, Gabe White, Scott Williamson, Mark Wohlers, Jeff Zimmerman.

Among starters, Roy Oswalt, Tim Hudson, Mark Mulder, and

Andy Pettitte are the most consistently successful. But the list is rife with pitchers who are either inconsistent (Hermanson, Wells, Millwood, Ashby), often-injured (Benes, Morris, Thompson), potential one-year wonders (Ankiel, Castillo, Ritchie), unproven over the long haul (Ohka, Willis, Webb, Zambrano, Garcia), or journeymen (Trachsel, Loaiza, Schourek, and Darwin).

Gagne and Rivera stand out as the two consistent bullpen performers. But injuries have marred the careers of Nen, Hoffman, and Wagner. And what is there to say of fellows of the stripe of Wohlers, Slocumb, Todd Jones, Williamson, Kim, and Leskanic? Only that life is never dull.

For GMs, making a budget stretch on talent of the likes of Rolen or the pre-contract Rodriguez is the easy part. The tough part is making salary decisions about the veterans. That's where the big money comes in, and it's where incentive can get in the way of performance. The same general manager who got 13 victories, 233 strikeouts, and maximum fan interest out of the $170,000 that Kerry Wood cost in 1998 also paid $5 million for the 9–14 record and 4.84 ERA turned in by Mark Clark. Was there a good Ed Lynch and an evil Ed Lynch in Chicago? Nope, merely a guy cashing one sure thing, and losing a big bet on a field horse. The real test of a great GM isn't the guy who can cash in on Kerry Wood, but the guy who knows whether to bet on Mark Clark.

AS A GROUP, GMS ARE SMART . . . NO, REALLY

Before we can proceed to assess a player's earned value, we must take one more step. We also must come to this vital, and probably controversial, understanding: Even though individual Major League general managers may make unwise, even occasionally idiotic, contractual decisions with players, as a group the GMs know what they're doing.

Let's please try to control the laughter, okay? Unless we agree to that assumption, no system of judging the relative cash value of players is worth a hoot; not this one and not any other you can devise. And the reason is disgustingly simple: We can only assess players against the salaries that were actually paid. So go ahead and debate whether the Dodgers got snookered in 1999 when they paid Kevin Brown $15 million per year to pitch for them for seven years. But you must accept the notion that the average salaries for all frontline players at any particular position are, as a group, reasonable, or analysis becomes impossible.

The easiest way explaining the concept of Earned Value is by illustration. The table on the next page presents the Earned Value of all American Leaguers who made at least 100 plate appearances during 2003 while playing shortstop as their primary position. (Since there tend to be different performance expectations for different positions, EV is a position-based calculation.) In the table, the first column lists each player's actual BFW for the season. Of all the statistical tools potentially available to measure player performance, the best and most all-encompassing is probably BFW (or its cousin, PW). The second column contains the same BFW adjusted (on the basis of playing time) to a base of zero. This step not only factors playing time as a measure of value, but greatly reduces the necessity of working with negative numbers. The third column lists the player's actual salary (in millions of dollars). Note at the bottom that these twenty-four players were paid an average of $3.62 million in 2003. Note further that they generated an average of .46 BFW points, which when adjusted for differences in individual playing time amounts to 4.29 points. Translated, the average American League shortstop in 2003 was paid about $844,000 for each adjusted BFW point he produced. That being so, calculating each player's Earned Value, the fourth column, is a matter of subtracting the player's adjusted BFW from the position average BFW, multiplying the result by $844,000, and adding the position average salary. The final column indicates the amount above or below the player's actual salary that the player "earned" during the season; a highly positive figure indicates a bargain. Deficit numbers are in parentheses.

Player	Team	BFW	Adj. BFW	Salary	EV	Gain (Loss)
Rodriguez	Tex	6.5	13.00	$22.000	$10.977	($11.023)
Garciaparra	Bos	3.9	10.40	$11.000	$8.782	($2.218)
Tejada	Oak	3.0	9.50	$5.125	$8.022	$2.897
Valentin	CWS	2.3	8.25	$5.000	$6.966	$1.966
Berroa	KC	1.2	7.70	$0.303	$6.502	$6.199
Lugo	TB	1.2	6.05	$0.750	$5.109	$4.359
Jeter	NYY	−0.2	5.20	$15.600	$4.391	($11.209)
Bordick	Tor	1.2	5.05	$1.000	$4.264	$3.264
Woodward	Tor	1.0	4.85	$0.775	$4.095	$3.320
Cruz	Bal	−1.3	4.65	$1.000	$3.926	$2.926
Amezaga	Ana	−0.5	4.35	$0.300	$3.673	$3.373
Guillen	Sea	−0.2	4.10	$2.500	$3.462	$0.962
Graffanino	CWS	1.2	3.90	$0.675	$3.293	$2.618
Vizquel	Cle	1.0	3.70	$5.500	$3.124	($2.376)
Santiago	Det	−1.8	3.05	$0.307	$2.575	$2.268
McLemore	Sea	−1.0	2.85	$3.150	$2.406	($0.744)
Infante	Det	0.4	2.55	$0.300	$2.153	$1.853
Guzman	Min	−3.6	2.35	$2.525	$1.984	($0.541)
Peralta	Cle	−0.6	2.10	$0.300	$1.773	$1.473

Player	Team	BFW	Adj. BFW	Salary	EV	Gain (Loss)
Ordoñez	TB	0.9	1.95	$6.500	$1.647	($4.853)
Sanchez	Sea	–0.4	1.20	$0.650	$1.013	$0.363
Almonte	NYY	–0.7	0.35	$0.300	$0.296	($0.004)
Eckstein	Ana	–0.7	0.35	$0.425	$0.296	($0.129)
Wilson	NYY	–0.8	0.25	$0.700	$0.211	($0.489)
Average		0.46	4.29	$3.624		

What do we learn from this list? Playing shortstop for Texas in 2003, Alex Rodriguez contributed $10.98 million in Earned Value toward whatever success the Rangers had. Measured strictly by his on-field contributions as compared with those of other shortstops, the Rangers overpaid Rodriguez by a little more than double . . . which is why they tried so hard to trade him. Since the second-highest AL shortstop EV was $2 million less than A-Rod's, it's hard to find fault either with his on-field performance or with his subsequent MVP award. The reality is that $22 million is an impossibly high figure to justify in terms of on-field accomplishment. This isn't my judgment; it's the collective judgment of Major League general managers who signed shortstops to contracts for 2003.

What else do we learn? That the pecking order in the Great Shortstop Triad, notwithstanding what the Boss of the Bronx thinks, is actually A-Rod, Nomar, a few other guys, and then Derek. Although Jeter is widely esteemed for his postseason reputation, the hard statistical reality is that in terms of on-field performance his 2003 season was mediocre. In fact the shortstop who most closely compared to Jeter in terms of on-field contribution was—hold on, George—Mike Bordick in Toronto.

Of the three, Nomar is the only one who approximately delivers equivalent value for payment received. His $8.78 million EV was about $2.3 million less than his 2003 salary, but as you scan the salary and Earned Value tables you will note that the relationship is casual at best. Of the twenty-five AL shortstops in 2003, less than a third produced EVs that were within $1 million of their actual salaries in either direction. In nine of the cases, the salaries and EVs differed by $3 million or more. Here's a theoretical question for you would-be owners and players out there: What would you say about a pay structure where the relationship between salary and performance routinely varied by a factor of $2 million . . . and could do so in either direction? More on that in a bit.

("Earned Value" tables for 2003 are in Appendix IV.)

WHAT'S A HALF MILLION DOLLARS BETWEEN FRIENDS?

Charts such as the 2003 AL shortstop Earned Value table (on pp. 194–195) are important precisely because they illustrate comparative value, which is as fair a way as any to measure a general manager's performance. That, after all, is what a GM gets paid to do: obtain the greatest return possible for the dollar spent. Does that mean the GM whose stack of talent "pluses" is the tallest will win the pennant? Not necessarily, because not all general managers begin with equally laden purses. Money is still a key factor. But money can either be wasted or taken advantage of. A GM who does a first-rate job of acquiring talent may be able to overcome a money disadvantage, in the same way that a GM who spends recklessly can fritter away a dollar disadvantage. Ask the New York Mets.

When we look at Major League salaries (and, consequently, player values) in this context, one overriding judgment becomes obvious: In the modern game, there is only an occasional relationship between a player's paycheck and his value to his team. Today, the data makes plain, players are not paid based on any accurate judgment of what they are likely to contribute to team success. And the proof of that statement is all over the place.

What percentage of core Major League players would you estimate generate a run-production value to their team that is within $500,000 in either direction of the salary they receive in return for doing it? Now that's a pretty broad leeway, $500,000 in either direction. In 2003, the average Major League salary was about $2.3 million, so $500,000 equates to roughly a 20 percent "margin of error," if you will. One measure of the reasonableness of the game's present salary structure might well be the way in which it reflects actual performance. So what would you guess that the answer would be?

There were 788 players in 2003 who could be defined as core major leaguers by virtue of having met one of the following criteria—either they got 100 plate appearances, they made at least 15 pitching starts, they pitched at least 50 innings, they accumulated at least 10 saves, or they were paid more than $500,000 above the average salary on their team. Of those 788 players, 642—81 percent—received salaries that were more than $500,000 out of line with their performance on the field. In the cases of 505 (64 percent), the discrepancies amounted to more than $1 million. For 327 (41 percent), the discrepancies exceeded $2 million. In 2003, the value of the performances of an imposing 133 Major League players (16.9 percent) varied from their salaries by more than $4 million, and there were 46 players whose values varied from their salaries by more than $7 million. The Baltimore Orioles paid Albert Belle $13 million not to play in 2003, and Belle wasn't even the game's worst value. In exchange for his $17.1 million contract, the Mets' injury-plagued Mo Vaughn made fewer than 100 trips to the plate, batted .190, and produced an Earned Value of negative $1.162 million, which translated to a remarkable minus $18.329 million return on New York's 2003 investment in him.

If that sounds like the portrait of a nonsensical salary system, consider how much more nonsensical it appears when the fringe element of our 788-player group is excluded. Of those 788 players, 143 are pitchers who are neither starters nor closers. Because they are paid relatively little, these pitchers as a group tend disproportionately to come closest to matching performance with payroll. In 2003, forty-two of those non-closer bullpen denizens turned in performances that were valued within $500,000 either way of their actual salaries.

If we remove those non-closer bullpen types from our survey, only 16 percent of the others (all position players, DHs, starters, and closers) were paid within $500,000 plus or minus of their Earned Values.

At no position other than non-closer relief specialist does the system perform especially well, but it does worse at some than at others. Of 154 pitchers who made 15 starts or more in 2003, only sixteen (10 percent) rang up Earned Values within $500,000 plus or minus of their salaries. By contrast, three times as many missed by more than $4 million. The same was true of closers. Of forty-two pitchers who earned 10 saves or more in 2003, only two (Mike DeJean and Cliff Politte) produced Earned Values within $500,000 plus or minus of their salaries. An even dozen missed by $4 million or more, led by the

Dodgers' Eric Gagne, whose $550,000 salary undervalued his performance by a fraction under $10 million ("Alors! Call my agent!"). Among 157 outfielders, thirty-three fell within the $500,000 window, but forty missed by more than $4 million. DHs and first basemen? Not even close. Of seventy-one at those positions, only seven produced value that was within $500,000 of their salaries, while 22 missed by $4 million or more.

Aside from our undesignated pitchers, catchers and other infielders were most accurately paid. But even among the 221 of them included in the survey, just forty-six (about 21 percent) produced an Earned Value within $500,000 of their actual salaries.

This gap between what a player is paid and what a player produces looks like a trend of the escalating costs of doing business that have been prevalent in baseball since settlement of the 1994 strike. During that 1994 season, the last before implementation of the new labor agreement, the patterns were vastly different. In 1994, about 61 percent of frontline major leaguers were paid within $1 million of those contributions.

The pattern began to change almost immediately with the settlement of the 1994 strike. The graph below shows the percentage of frontline Major League players whose salaries differed by more than $1 million from their performance for each Major League season since 1994.

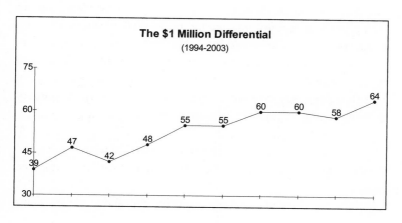

The $1 Million Differential
(1994-2003)

This is not to say that the system is more unfair either to the players or owners as large groups. Although there is little relationship between pay and performance, it is another question entirely whether one side benefits more than the other. Think for a moment of a bar with seven positions on it. One end of the spectrum—position one—represents all players who underperformed by more than $2 million. Position two represents players who underperformed by between $1 million and $2 million; position three represents those who underperformed by between $500,000 and $1 million; position four represents all players falling in the middle. This presumably expansive slot includes those who performed within $500,000 in either direction of what their salary justified.

The other end of the bar, positions five through seven, represents players who overperformed relative to their salaries by the same amounts.

How many players would be represented at each point on the bar? Where would the greatest collection of players be represented?

If the present salary structure as a broad system were unfair to players, the mass of talent would be at the end of the spectrum indicating overperformance by $500,000 or more. If the system were unfair to management, players would collect at the other end of the spectrum.

Of those 788 major leaguers who qualified as core players under our definition in 2003, about 50 percent would be placed on the "significantly overperforming" (more than $500,000) side of the spectrum, while 31 percent would be on the "significantly underperforming" side. Only the remaining 19 percent would constitute the spectrum's center. In other words, baseball has constructed a pay system that alternately takes advantage of both parties while appropriately (in terms of on-field performance) compensating only about one-fifth of the players.

On such a spectrum, 39 percent are underpaid relative to performance by amounts in excess of $1 million. Some GMs are getting real bargains out there.

Who are these most valuable (relatively speaking) players? They share several characteristics: exceptional ability combined with youth and an inexpensive price tag. In 2003, there were twenty-four major leaguers who performed at a level meriting $5 million or more above the salaries they actually earned. Only eight of those twenty-four—David Ortiz, Edgar Martinez, Frank Thomas, Esteban Loaiza, Richie Sexson, Derrick Lee, Todd Helton, and Jose Guillen—had made more than a token big league appearance as recently as 1999.

Listed in the order of their undervaluation, here are the twenty-four plus-$5 million profit players from 2003, their salaries (in millions), Earned Values, and the differences between what they were paid and what they returned in on-field contributions. (All figures are in millions; asterisks denote salary estimates where actual salaries are unavailable.)

Player, Team	Salary	Earned	Difference
L. Pujols, StL	$0.900	$12.213	$11.313
E. Gagne, LA	$0.550	$9.779	$9.229
A. Huff, TB	$0.325	$8.222	$7.897
E. Loaiza, CWS	$0.500	$7.925	$7.425
R. Sexson, Mil.	$5.125	$12.452	$7.327
D. Ortiz, Bos.	$1.250	$8.125	$6.935
M. Prior, ChC	$1.450	$7.784	$6.634
C. Zambrano, ChC	$0.340	$6.919	$6.579
T. Helton, Col.	$10.600	$17.100	$6.500
D. Lee, Fla.	$4.250	$10.625	$6.375
A. Berroa, KC	$0.303	$6.502	$6.199
V. Wells, Tor.	$0.520	$6.648	$6.128
J. Guillen, Cin.*	$0.300	$6.348	$6.048
P. LoDuca, LA	$2.637	$8.323	$5.686
B. Webb, Ari.	$0.300	$5.976	$5.676
S. Podsednik, Mil.	$0.300	$5.932	$5.632
B. Zito, Oak.	$1.000	$6.471	$5.471
M. Bradley, Cle.	$0.314	$5.753	$5.439
J. Gerut, Cle.	$0.300	$5.668	$5.368
E. Martinez, Sea.	$4.000	$9.308	$5.308

F. Thomas, CWS	$5.000	$10.285	$5.285
R. Baldelli, TB	$0.300	$5.523	$5.223
M. Giles, Atl.	$0.317	$5.406	$5.089
E. Durazao, Oak.	$1.065	$6.084	$5.019

(*Earned Value is a league-based figure. Guillen was traded during the 2003 season out of the National League. These figures are based on the NL portion of his season.)

It is worth noting that in an era when the average Major League salary is more than $2 million, most of these players were paid less than half that much. For the most part, these are pre-arbitration players who hit it very big very early.

THE RARE AIR OF IMPOSSIBLE EXPECTATIONS

Some GMs get hosed, too, and when that happens, it also happens big. In 2003, sixty-three players shafted their teams by $5 million or more. In about a third of the cases—shown in this table—injuries intervened to play at least some part.

Player, Team	Salary	Earned	Difference
M. Vaughn, NYM	$17.167	($1.162)	($18.329)
A. Belle, Bal.	$13.000	$0.000	($13.000)
M. Piazza, NYM	$15.571	$2.963	($12.608)
R. Johnson, Ari.	$15.000	$2.752	($12.248)
D. Dreifort, LA	$12.400	$1.337	($11.063)
K. Griffey, Cin.	$12.500	$1.793	($10.707)
D. Palmer, Det.	$8.500	($1.738)	($10.238)
T. Hoffman, SD	$9.600	($0.709)	($8.891)
R. Nen, SF	$8.750	$0.000	($8.750)
A. Ashby, LA	$8.500	$0.320	($8.180)
J. Cirillo, Sea.	$6.725	($0.436)	($7.161)
S. Erickson, Bal.	$7.030	$0.000	($7.030)
K. Sasaki, Sea.	$8.000	$0.989	($7.011)
R. Greer, Tex.	$7.000	$0.000	($7.000)

T. Hundley, LA	$6.500	$0.000	($6.500)
B. Wickman, Cle.	$6.000	$0.000	($6.000)
D. Erstad, Ana.	$7.250	$1.509	($5.741)
E. Milton, Min.	$6.000	$0.509	($5.491)
Average	$9.749	$0.452	($9.297)

In many of the above cases, it seems to me that we are allowing substantial leeway when we ascribe all or even most of the loss of value sustained by these players to injury. The Dodgers knew they weren't going to get value out of Todd Hundley when they traded for him. To ascribe Dean Palmer's failure in Detroit to injury is to substantially deny the miserable .140 batting average he did produce in about 100 plate appearances, not to mention his pre-injury .222 batting average in 2001. Were Jeff Cirillo's deficiencies entirely injury-related, or was 2003 the beginning of a downward slide?

Personally, I don't think there was ever any prospect Mo Vaughn would justify a $17.167 million salary. The average NL first baseman, for the record, had an EV of $3.94 million in 2003. Who's playing first in the NL? Helton, Thome, Bagwell, Sexson—it's a very strong position. The Mets agreed to pay Vaughn more than four times as much as the position generally pulls. Do you know how good your performance must be in order to justify four times the normal salary? In 2003, Helton was the most valuable first baseman in the NL. He batted .358 with 33 home runs and 117 RBIs, figures that translated to $17.1 million in EV, for a fraction less than what Vaughn made. And Helton's EV was the major-league high. Entering 2003, what were the odds that Mo Vaughn would outperform Todd Helton? His career high average was .337, but that came in 1998. He'd hit 44 home runs, but that was in 1996. In 2001, Vaughn didn't even get on the field. In 2002, he played like an oft-injured thirty-four-year-old batting .259 and lapping the league in errors with 18.

The cases of the remaining forty-four vastly overvalued players are more complex, and it is best to look at them by groups.

Premium Talent

Player, Team	Salary	Earned	Difference
M. Ramirez, Bos.	$20.000	$7.632	($12.368)
A. Rodriguez, Tex.	$22.000	$10.977	($11.023)
C. Delgado, Tor.	$18.700	$8.671	($10.029)
C. Jones, Atl.	$13.333	$6.005	($7.328)
A. Jones, Atl.	$12.000	$5.490	($6.510)
M. Mussina, NYY	$12.000	$6.034	($5.966)
Average	($16.339)	($7.468)	($8.871)

The top of the salary scale ought to be (and sometimes is) occupied by players with perfect résumés. Either they are the best at what they do, or they are nearly the best and they do it for winners, which they themselves play a large part in shaping. When they can be found, such players may be worth any price—even a price inflated to twice the player's real value. In the cases of such players, owners overspent with malice aforethought. But these players also are rare; among our fifty-six grossly overpaid players, only seven meet the criteria outlined above. A-Rod, Delgado, and Manny have the highest EVs of any player at their position. Mussina and the Joneses are near the top while playing key roles for dominant teams.

Twenty-two million dollars may seem like a lot of money for a shortstop—mostly because it is—but Rodriguez has done what he can to justify it. He has ranked first among AL shortstops in EV in 2000, 2002, and 2003, and he was third in 2001. His stats weren't too bad, either: He's averaged about .310 with 49 homers and 132 RBIs over those three years.

Mussina works in New York for a man who doesn't mind overpaying for excellence. Mussina had the seventh-best EV among all AL starters, and best among the Yankees. His $6.034 EV was twice that of the typical AL starter in 2003. Would Steinbrenner pay an extra $6 million to get a player who was $3 million above average? In a New York minute, he would.

Near-Premium Talent

Player, Team	Salary	Earned	Difference
D. Jeter, NYY	$15.600	$4.391	($11.209)
S. Green, LA	$15.667	$5.794	($9.873)
S. Sosa, Chc.	$16.000	$6.194	($9.806)
P. Martinez, Bos.	$15.500	$6.398	($9.102)
A. Pettitte, NYY	$11.500	$4.072	($7.428)
M. Sweeney, KC	$11.000	$5.179	($5.821)
T. Percival, Ana.	$7.833	$2.276	($5.557)
R. Clemens, NYY	$10.100	$4.653	($5.447)
T. Glaus, Ana.	$7.250	$2.179	($5.071)
Average	$12.272	$4.571	($7.701)

This is a roster studded with players with "star" power: they reflect the view of teams that they've got the guy worth any price as a drawing card. Sammy Sosa is a role model. He's a very fine ballplayer who produced 40 home runs, 103 RBIs, and a .279 average in 2003. That translated to $6.194 million in EV, a figure made more impressive by the fact that—as everyone knows—it came in an "off" year. Jeter is another. By the high standards of the American League, Derek Jeter is an average shortstop. I say that with the full understanding that those are fighting words in the Bronx. I have never been in a fight in the Bronx, and do not wish to be in one now—but it is true. In 2003, his EV placed him seventh in the league, just behind Julio Lugo of Tampa Bay and just ahead of Mike Bordick. Though his on-field performance has not in several seasons translated to anything approaching his salary, Steinbrenner can justify paying $7 million above performance value because he is good, flashy, and a New York attraction. The same is true of Pedro Martinez in Boston; a fine pitcher—the AL's fifth best in 2003—although overrated on the numbers. He deserves to be paid very well, but not $15 million worth of well.

Flawed Mound Gems

Player, Team	Salary	Earned	Difference
G. Maddux, Atl.	$14.750	$4.875	($9.875)
K. Brown, LA	$15.714	$7.155	($8.559)
T. Glavine, NYM	$11.000	$3.224	($7.776)
M. Morris, StL	$10.500	$4.167	($6.333)
K. Millwood, Phi.	$9.900	$4.167	($5.733)
Average	$12.373	$4.718	($7.655)

Of all positions, pitcher is the toughest to get right if your job is determining what to pay a guy. That is especially true of starting pitchers, and more so again if you're looking at veteran starters seeking or clinging to that last big contract. It's too early to say that age is catching up with Glavine, Maddux, or Brown. That might be true, although each still looked good in 2003. The rap on Brown is twofold: his injuries and his contract. The latter looks even worse when you consider that 2003 (14–9, a 2.39 ERA) was probably his best season since 1999, the first year of the mega-deal. At thirty-nine as the 2004 season began, Brown had to be considered questionable, which is why the Dodgers traded him to the Yankees. Maddux's ERA climbed three-quarters of a point in 2003, although his wins and innings totals remained impressive. He is thirty-eight. Regarding Millwood and Morris, the same question looms: Can they become anchors around which pennant winners thrive? In Atlanta, surrounded by all that talent, Millwood was occasionally brilliant. In Philadelphia as the headliner, he was just good. Nettlesome stuff limited Morris to 27 starts in 2003, and those 27 were good but not overpowering: a 3.76 ERA that was the highest of his six-season Major League career.

On the Decline

Player, Team	Salary	Earned	Difference
B. Williams, NYY	$12.357	$4.449	($7.908)
L. Walker, Col	$12.667	$4.777	($7.890)
B. Larkin, Cin	$9.000	$1.410	($7.590)
C. Biggio, Hou	$9.750	$3.453	($6.297)
A. Sele, Ana	$8.167	$1.963	($6.204)
E. Karros, ChC	$8.375	$3.030	($5.345)
M. Alou, ChC	$9.500	$4.478	($5.022)
Average	$9.974	$3.366	($6.608)

Once upon a time, not so very long ago, these contracts made sense. As recently as the late 1990s, Larry Walker and Barry Larkin were *great* ballplayers. Bernie Williams may have fit that description as recently as 2002. In baseball, the contract given to a plus-thirty-five-year-old is often inflated by reputation as opposed to expectation. Occasionally a ballplayer beats Nature's clock: Nolan Ryan certainly did it, as, to a lesser extent, has Clemens. None of these seven looks like a candidate. As a group, they returned only about one-third of their salaries in Earned Value in 2003 and, with the exception of Williams, for the most part their period of steady decline is two, three, or four years along. The problem often is that senior players achieve iconic status, especially in their home towns. Larkin is the obvious example, which is why the Reds' painfully obvious desire to release him and unburden itself of the contract in 2003 was as a practical matter doomed. The same was true of Biggio in Houston. He moved to center because Kent was plainly a better ballplayer at that stage of their careers, but it would have been unthinkable of the Astros to set him loose.

Who Made This Deal?

Player, Team	Salary	Earned	Difference
J. Dye, Oak.	$11.667	($0.903)	($12.570)
C. Park, Tex.	$13.000	$0.727	($12.273)
K. Appier, Ana.-KC	$11.500	$1.164	($10.336)
M. Williams, Ari.	$10.000	($0.519)	($9.481)
J. Burnitz, NYM-LA	$12.167	$2.799	($9.368)
D. Neagle, Col.	$9.000	($0.315)	($9.315)
J. Gonzalez, Tex.	$13.000	$3.800	($9.200)
B. Higginson, Det.	$11.850	$2.678	($9.172)
M. Hampton, Atl.	$13.625	$4.796	($8.829)
J. Mesa, Phi.	$5.200	($2.551)	($7.751)
K. Young, Pit.	$6.625	($0.996)	($7.621)
J. Hammonds, Mil.-SF	$8.200	$0.941	($7.259)
F. Tatis, Mtl.	$6.500	($0.119)	($6.619)
P. Astacio, NYM	$7.000	$0.786	($6.214)
R. Reed, Min.	$8.000	$1.818	($6.182)
T. Womack, Ari.-ChC-Col.	$6.000	$0.254	($5.746)
R. Mondesi, NYY	$8.970	$3.769	($5.201)
Average	$9.542	$1.066	($8.476)

(*Earned Value is a league-based figure. Mondesi was traded during the 2003 season out of the American League. These figures are based on the AL portion of his season.)

Thus far we have tried to rationalize the bad fiscal moves made by team GMs in their most flagrant contractual mistakes. But there is no rationalizing away these fourteen contracts. They are prismatically bad; that is, they're bad any way you look at it.

Perhaps there was a day when Juan Gonzalez was worth $13 million. (Just kidding . . . actually there wasn't.) The Rangers signed him to that multiyear arrangement before 2002, as Gonzalez came off a .325, 35-home run year for Cleveland. His was a textbook case of a player having a big free agent season. Superficially, Gonzalez being thirty-one at the time, it must have seemed plausible to John Hart that the outfielder could replicate his Cleveland numbers for several more years. But even in 2001, Gonzalez had only returned $7.17 million in EV among AL right fielders. In 2002, instead of keeping up or accelerating, his production fell off, from .325 to .282, from 35 homers to 8, and by the way, from 140 games to 70. His EV fell to a pedestrian (for Al right fielders) $2.56 million. It rose in 2003, but only to $3.8 million, far, far short of Texas's needs.

An apologist could argue that injuries prevented Chan Ho Park, Denny Neagle, or Pedro Astacio from delivering on their huge contracts, $13 million in the case of Park, $9 million for Neagle, and $7 million for Astacio. Let's take Park first: Injuries did limit him to 7 starts in which he produced a 7.58 ERA in addition to that despicable EV. But it would take an apologist to rationalize away Park's contract. In 2002, when he made 25 starts, Park produced a 5.75 ERA and a $1.257 million EV that underperformed his salary by $5.6 million. Neagle, too, was limited to 7 starts. He made 35 of them for the Rockies in 2002, and posted a 5.26 ERA. That equated to $2.925 million in EV on a $7 million salary, a $4.075 million under-performance. In 2001, Neagle made another $7 million, and returned $3.763 million in EV. Astacio? He made $7 million in 2001 and returned $3.5 million in EV. In 2002 when the Mets signed him the figures were $4 million and $2.4. Why was 2003 a surprise? So yes, Chan Ho Park, Denny Neagle, and Pedro Astacio were hurt, and yes, the deals were still awful.

Bobby Higginson worth $11.8 million in Detroit? On what basis? Here is the full roster of 2003 players worth $11.8 million in on-field production: Barry Bonds, Luis Pujols, Todd Helton, Richie Sexson, Jim Thome. If Higginson is a building block by Tiger standards, that says more about Tiger standards than Higginson. Since 1996 he's only hit .300 once. In the past five homer-happy seasons Higginson averaged 17. Go ahead, blame it on the new park. Randy Smith tied him up to a new deal that included his $11.85 million 2003 salary following a 2000 campaign that was his best. But even in 2000, Higginson was just the second-best left fielder in the AL, producing a $4.45 million EV. And it was only one year. Just the previous year,

Higginson had batted .239 and returned only $1.274 million in EV on a $3.825 million salary.

Kevin Young's last decent season for Pittsburgh was 1999. Since then he's hit .258, .232, .246, and this year .202. But when the penurious Pirates needed to throw money at somebody to maintain credibility as a Major League franchise, Young won the team lottery and a deal he'd been living off of until it finally gasped its desperate last with the conclusion of 2003.

Teams do that from time to time. They sign a player just for the waves the signing will make. They know that back home some jerk sports jock will buy the line that "the home club moved to strengthen itself today by signing . . ." How else does one explain letting Tony Womack near a $6 million deal? When the Diamondbacks signed Matt Williams to his multiyear contract, who projected that Williams at age thirty-eight would be worth $10 million? Not Matt Williams. Here's what he projected: He projected that he wanted to go home and play with his kids. Williams's average peaked with the D-Backs in 1999 and declined every season from then on until his 2003 release.

As noted in an earlier chapter, closers who are worth big bucks come along from time to time, but they are rare. Note to Philadelphia: Jose Mesa is not one of the rare ones. The Phillies gave Mesa his $5.2 million extension following a 2002 season in which he saved 45 games with a 2.97 ERA. If forced to personify closers, Mesa would be my boy; he is flighty as a hummingbird. Since 1994, when he became a full-time reliever, Mesa's ERAs have ranged from a low of 1.13 to a high of 6.52 with three stops in the twos, two in the threes, two in the fours, and one in the fives. For some reason, Ed Wade assumed that if Jose Mesa gave the Phillies a 2.97 ERA and 45 saves in 2002, he'd give the Phillies a 2.97 ERA and 45 saves in 2003 as well. What in Mesa's record made you think that, Ed? So, following the 2003 debacle, the Phillies released Mesa, who signed with the Pirates for $800,000. Which is what should happen with Jose Mesa every season.

Some part of the reason why Steve Phillips is now *former* general manager of the Mets involves the trade that brought Jeromy Burnitz to Shea from Milwaukee, in the process obligating New York to the tune of $12.2 million in 2003. What did Steve Phillips see in Burnitz that is not visible to the naked record? In Milwaukee, Burnitz had pretty consistently performed to the level of about a $4.7 million EV. To say that he was merely half as good in New York—$1.36 million in 2002 and then $2.7 million in 2003—hardly explains why Phillips thought he'd be worth three times as much.

In 2002, after acquiring Jermaine Dye in the middle of the previous campaign, Billy Beane signed him up long-term. Readers of *Moneyball* will conclude that since Billy Beane did it, this must have perforce been a sagacious move. To the contrary, Dye's performance and payroll have been on opposite tracks ever since. So much has this been true that in 2003, if players were paid based on their on-field performance, Dye would have had to give the A's nearly $1 million just for the privilege of playing right field for them. Here are the amazing payroll and performance numbers for Jermaine Dye since 2001, the year of his arrival in Oakland (as elsewhere in this chapter, all figures are in millions).

Season	Payroll	Earned Value	Difference
2001	$3.800	$3.918	$0.118
2002	$7.167	$2.603	($4.564)
2003	$11.667	($.903)	($12.570)

In short, Dye's salary has escalated by nearly $8 million at the same time the on-field value of his performance has plummeted by nearly $5 million. Billy Beane is a fine general manager, deserving—based on his performance—of all the attention he's received. But Jermaine Dye is a blot on his record.

THE ALBERT BELLE RETIREMENT PROGRAM

With occasional exceptions, good young players are habitually underpaid relative to their on-field value. The balance swings to the player at about the onset of free agency, never to return. We can illustrate the extent to which this takes place—as well as its financial significance—by two studies.

The first examines the career EVs of twenty-six of the game's current or recent frontline players. For this study, twenty-six members of the 2000 American or National League All Star teams, all of whom had been in the major leagues between four and fifteen seasons (the average was about nine seasons), were included. The players were: Jeff Bagwell, Albert Belle, Barry Bonds, Kevin Brown, Carl Everett, Nomar Garciaparra, Jason Giambi, Ken Griffey, Jr., Vladimir Guerrero, Derek Jeter, Randy Johnson, Chipper Jones, Jeff Kent, Darryl Kile, Edgar Martinez, Pedro Martinez, Mark McGwire, Mike Mussina, Mike Piazza, Alex Rodriguez, Ivan Rodriguez, Gary Sheffield, Sammy Sosa, Jim Thome, David Wells, and Bernie Williams.

This is what the study showed.

1. With a few exceptions, there was no talent learning curve among stars. Of these twenty-six players, only seven (Sosa, Sheffield, Alex Rodriguez, Edgar Martinez, Chipper Jones, Wells, and Thome) produced less in EV than they earned in salary in any of their first three seasons. Twenty-five of the twenty-six (the exception was Wells—and that but a mere $70,000) carried positive career EVs after their first four seasons. Between seasons one and four, the average EV of these players was $1.94 million; the average salary was $770,000.

2. The numbers swung closer toward equilibrium during the fifth and sixth seasons. Among these players, average EVs rose to $3.69 million in seasons five and six. But salaries rose at an even faster rate, from $770,000 to $4.05 million for these stars. This meant that during the fifth and sixth seasons the stars were overpaid by an average by $360,000. Eleven of the twenty-six players produced net positive EVs in their fifth and sixth seasons. In a few cases, the differences were substantial. Belle's average fifth and sixth season EV was $3.93 million, a handsome performance, except when compared with Belle's average $7.85 million salary.

On the other hand, Jason Giambi produced an average $7.21 million EV during his fifth and sixth seasons while being paid merely $2.68 million. Giambi overperformed by $4.61 million in those seasons.

3. After season six, the star player almost always produced less in value than he received in salary. Just three (Edgar Martinez, Giambi, and Thome) yielded a net positive career EV after season six. The average gap between Derek Jeter's EV and salary after season six was a fraction under $5.5 million. The average salary for the twenty-six stars did rise substantially—to $6.07 million. But salaries doubled, to $9.372 million after season six for players in this star group.

4. Over the long haul, the salary system biases toward star players by a factor of about 25 percent. Our twenty-six stars produced an average of $50.561 million in career EV at a cost of $65.860 million. But that was only meaningful to owners if—and this rarely happened—they held on to their young stars. Of the twenty-six, only six (Williams, Jeter, Jones, Garciaparra, Bagwell, and Edgar Martinez) were still with the teams that brought them to the big leagues through the start of the 2004 season.

5. But there was a second trick as well—picking the right player. The list is rife with big winners and losers. Over his fourteen Major League seasons, Gary Sheffield has produced $61.75 million in EV, but at a salary of about $91 million. In terms of what he produces, Sheffield has been one of the most productive players of the last fifteen years; in terms of what he's been paid, he is also one of the worst values. The same was true of McGwire. At $46.636 million, his career EV is exceeded by only a handful of players. But McGwire received about $74.7 million in pay to produce that $46.6 million in value, leaving him effectively in debt to his owners by $28.1 million. He does not lead in that category. Belle's $37.231 million career EV is considerably less than half his $94.4 million career salary, which he continued to collect from the Orioles in 2001, 2002, and 2003 despite the fact that he had retired.

Some day, perhaps soon, A-Rod may pass even Belle. In 2003, Rodriguez produced $11 million in EV, a figure that would be stunning measured against any standard except his own $22 million standard. Against that standard, it created a breathtaking production deficit of $11 million. In 2002, Rodriguez "earned" a hefty $11.53 million, but that was still $10.47 million short of what he was paid. Given the way inflation works in baseball, it's unlikely Rodriguez will maintain that kind of deficit production. In time he may even be viewed as a bargain. But if his production ratio does not improve, the first three years of his $252 million contract suggest that he will return only $120.9 million in EV to his team.

Remarkable in the other direction are the cases of Bonds, Bagwell, and Edgar Martinez. On a cumulative salary of a bit less than $45.8 million, Martinez has returned nearly $75.5 million in EV, a gain to the Mariners of roughly $30 million. Bagwell has earned $73.1 million and returned $81.3 million, a gain to the Astros of $8.1 million. Bonds has not literally been a fiscal plus to his owners, but they're not complaining. On career earnings of about $110 million, he has generated $100.1 million in EV, a 91 percent payback. During the 2001 through 2003 seasons—possibly the three best seasons any player has ever had consecutively—Bonds produced $37.6 million in EV on about $40.7 million in salary.

The second study looked at some of the same questions, but from a broader base. Focusing on the performance of between 700 and 750 players during the 1998 and 2003 seasons, we asked these questions:

1. At what experience levels did players return the best Earned Value?
2. Was there a particular experience level at which a player's Earned Value ceased favoring the team, or was the pattern more random?
3. Was there any such thing in a player's career as a "key season?"

The results fluctuated somewhat between the two studies, but maintained some essential patterns. The table below lists some results of the 1998 and 2003 studies. The first column lists the number of years of experience. For each of the two study seasons, the next column denotes the average Earned Value for all players at that experience level. The final column indicates whether, and by how much, the EV exceeded or fell short of the average salary for all players at that experience level who were part of the study group. (All figures are in millions; negative numbers in parentheses.)

Yrs	1998 Av. EV	Diff. From Sal.	2003 Av. EV	Diff. From Sal.
1	$0.800	$0.580	$1.631	$1.111
2	$1.080	$0.860	$1.802	$1.390
3	$1.460	$1.180	$2.380	$1.895
4	$1.280	$0.800	$2.264	$1.614
5	$1.210	$0.270	$2.316	$0.945
6	$1.560	$0.220	$2.391	$0.254
7	$1.670	($0.480)	$3.939	$0.517
8	$1.920	($1.010)	$2.449	($1.436)
9	$1.700	($0.710)	$2.948	($1.541)
10	$2.240	($0.920)	$2.392	($2.258)
11	$1.810	($1.260)	$2.962	($2.428)
12	$2.000	($0.950)	$2.661	($2.118)
13	$2.410	($1.180)	$3.327	($1.160)
14	$2.140	($0.850)	$3.607	($0.271)
15-plus	$1.380	($0.700)	$3.187	($3.343)

There is an odd blip in this data that shows up in year seven of the 2003 study. Notice the unusual leap in Earned Value among seventh-year players in 2003. In their first six seasons, player Earned Value essentially increases in a steady progression in both 1998 and 2003. This continues to be true in the 1998 study through season eight, when Earned Values appear to begin to fluctuate at what we might think of as a level of maturity.

But in the 2003 study, the pattern breaks at year seven with a substantial leap in EV from $2.391 in year six to more than $3.9 million.

Then in year eight Earned Value reverts to the "normal" pattern of growth at about $2.5 million.

The $3.9 million EV for seventh-season players is not only a large departure from the pattern of the rest of the study, it is in fact the highest EV generated by any group of players, period. (Based on the remainder of the study, we would have projected these players to produce about $2.45 million in Earned Value, or about $1.5 million less than they actually did produce.) It turns out that a couple of things are at work here.

First, as it happens, the seventh-season class is a more than normally talented one. Todd Helton is in that class. So is Miguel Tejada and so is Magglio Ordonez. Second, the class contains several players who had unpredictably exceptional seasons. Joe Borowski was a seventh-season player in 2003. So was Bartolo Colon. When a low-paid player has a big season, it creates EV distortions.

Finally, and perhaps of equal importance to the other factors, it happens that an abnormally large number of seventh-season players perform at unusually expensive positions, the prime one being first base. For necessary reasons we assumed at the outset of this discussion the intelligence of general managers as a group. As a group, NL GMs paid their regular first basemen nearly $4 million in salary in 2003, making it the best-paid position in the majors. In EV players are grouped and rated by position. That means in turn that the Earned Value of players at the most expensive position necessarily will be higher than players performing at similar skill levels in positions considered by GMs to be less demanding. Thus EV rates Todd Helton as worth $17.1 million in 2003. It rates Richie Sexson, another National League first baseman and another seventh-year player, as worth $12.452 million. It rates Derrek Lee, another NL first baseman and another seventh-year player, as worth $10.625 million. All of those ratings are in comparison with an average NL first baseman . . . not in comparison with an average NL player.

If Helton had generated precisely the same BFW while playing a less demanding (by GM standards) position, his EV would be less. (If he were an NL center fielder, for example, his 10.3 adjusted BFW would have produced an EV of about $9 million. As an AL second baseman, his EV would have been about $5 million.) Now you are perfectly within your rights to argue that playing second base or center field is not less demanding than playing first base; that in fact it is more demanding. Artistically, and considering only defense, I would cheerfully agree. But GMs, who consider all the components of player performance, believe the average NL first baseman was worth $4 million in 2003, while the average AL second baseman was only worth $1.16 million. And remember, as a group GMs are smart.

It's important to understand the blip in the 2003 data because we need that context to make any sense of the two studies. They do appear to show that between year six and year seven, the pendulum swings rather fully from the team's side to the player's, and that it never does swing back. Until that sixth-seventh season nexus, player performance almost always favors the club, by amounts that range from close to $2 million (for third-year players in 2003) down to about $250,000 by year six (again in 2003). The switch takes place one season earlier in the 1998 study, and appears to be a direct result of the idiosyncratic overperformance of seventh-season players in 2003.

For the most part, the patterns are one-sided and apply to stars and non-stars alike within experience levels. Among sixty-seven rookies included in the 1998 survey, almost all earning the minimum, 85 percent produced results that were a net plus for their teams. For second-year players, the comparable figure was 90 percent; for third-year players, it was 88 percent. The average third-year player got a $280,000 salary and returned $1.46 million in on-field value, a net profit to the club of $1.18 million.

Rookie results for 2003 were skewed a bit by the presence of two "rookies" in name only, Hideki Matsui and Jose Contreras. Both earned far more than the usual rookie minimum, and created an anomalous circumstance where 2003 "rookies" on average actually earned more than 2003 second-season or third-season players. Even so, the general findings of 1998 repeated themselves.

The odds began to work against the teams a bit in the player's fourth year. Still, at that level, 80 percent of players in the 1998 study (and nearly 90 percent in 2003) yielded a net plus value for their clubs. That value averaged $800,000 in 1998, and $1.614 million in 2003. In their fifth and sixth year, both arbitration seasons, players remain generally profitable to clubs, but less certainly so. Of fifty fifth-year players in the 1998 survey, only 58 percent performed at a level that was a net profit to their teams, and that level of net profit fell to $270,000. By the sixth season, the figures were both nominally break-even, 49 percent and $220,000. In 2003, relative performance still strongly (by $945,000) favored the teams for fifth-year players, but moderated to $254,000 for sixth-year players.

If one fundamental change appears to have taken place between the two studies, it is a shift toward older, more experienced players. In the 1998 study, production shifted to favor the player in the seventh season, but in the 2003 study that shift took place during the eighth season. One factor in this respect may be that the study field itself aged. In the 1998 study, the largest single grouping of players occurred in the fourth season; by 2003, the largest grouping of players represented season six. In 1998, there were only a relative handful of players in action above season fourteen, but the 2003 study found forty-seven such players, and they included many of the game's most productive performers: Bonds, Kevin Brown, Palmeiro, Sheffield, Clemens, Schilling, Johnson, Maddux, Smoltz, and Sosa.

At some point in the past couple of years, GMs have decided to pay the premium price for older talent, and they are reaping some rewards for that decision. In the 1998 study, the Earned Value of players hit its high point in the thirteenth season, declined in season fourteen, and then declined precipitously for players in seasons fifteen-plus. In 2003, that was less dramatically the case. With the exception of the seventh-season anomaly, the peak $3.607 million EV occurred in season fourteen, but then declined to a still productive $3.123 million EV in seasons fifteen and beyond.

For general managers, the problem turned out to be the price they had to overpay for that performance. In 2003, it cost the average GM about $6.4 million to sign one of those super-productive, super-senior players, meaning that the $3.123 million in EV came at a cost of about $6.4 million. That's a tough market, but it is in fact the cost of doing business with the best veteran players. It holds true both in the 1998 and 2003 studies; substantial overpayment for substantial production. In the 1998 study, players in seasons ten and above generated an average of about $2 million in EV, but cost $3 million to sign. In 2003, such players generated $3 million in EV, but demanded $5.349 million to do so.

Is there a "key" season? The two studies yield contradictory results. In 1998, the fourth season was plainly the make-or-break year, the one season when teams appear to most closely measure performance versus cost and weed out those players likely to justify extra expenditures from those who will not.

A total of ninety-three players in the 1998 study, 13 percent of the whole, fell into the four-year classification. That was more than a third again as many as any other experience level. By contrast, there were only forty-five players in the sample who were at their fifth season of experience, fewer than half as many as in the fourth-year group. Plainly in 1998, general managers used the fourth season, with its intimations of approaching arbitration and free agency, as a weeding-out year. A player made it in year four or he didn't make it.

That did not, however, hold true in the 2003 study, when both the fifth and sixth seasons produced larger fields of players. This is probably more evidence that by 2003 GMs exercised either greater patience or a preference for more experienced players.

Monetarily, players are at their most profitable to teams in their third seasons. In 1998, the third-year group (Jason Kendall, Andruw Jones, Scott Rolen, et al.) posted a collective Earned Value of $1.46 million at an average cost of $280,000. In 2003, the comparable figures (for players such as Lyle Overbay, C. C. Sabathia, and Carlos Zambrano) were $2.38 million in EV and $485,000 in salary. But as good as those third-year groups were, they trailed, in terms of cold, hard on-field production, every single experience group between years six and fourteen in both studies. So if you could afford them, you were better off selecting among the veterans.

VALUE AND ARBITRATION

Because it includes an externally imposed resolution of the best judgments of the players and management, baseball's arbitration system is
an excellent laboratory for assessing the degree to which the salary
structure is logic-based. Generally speaking, players become eligible
for arbitration following a set number of seasons when the player and
team agree that the player should be re-signed, but when there is no
agreement as to salary. At that point, both the player and management
submit their best judgment as to the player's value to a third party.
These judgments are presumed to be based on the player's value relative to other players with similar skills and responsibilities. A hearing
is held at which the two sides lay out their defense of their estimates,
and the arbitrator selects one of the figures to be the player's salary for
the year.

The arbitrator is not allowed to superimpose his or her own judgment on the process. However, the player and owner may continue to
negotiate while the matter is under hearing, and they may halt the
process at any point they reach agreement. Only at the point that an
arbitrator's decision is announced does it become final and binding.

Between 1995 and 2003, there were about sixty such arbitration
decisions issued involving a player who subsequently made a significant contribution to a Major League team while playing under the arbitrated salary.

A study of those contributions further illustrates the capricious-
ness of the game's salary structure. Simply put, in their efforts to pre-
judge what particular players deserve to be paid based on their relative
worth, both players and management are often clueless.

Of the cases included in the study, the player's arbitrated salary
came within a half million dollars of matching his actual EV less than
one-quarter of the time. There were only fourteen such instances. The
arbitrated salary landed within $1 million of the actual EV only half
the time, and the difference exceeded $2 million a dozen times.

The arbitration system was equally capricious to players and owners. Seven players underperformed their arbitrated salaries by $2 mil-

lion or more. Five overperformed by that amount, but those five included the two most egregious misdecisions of all. One was the $2 million award to Expos pitcher Javier Vazquez in 2001 (his EV was $7.869 million, a $5.8 million shafting). The second was a $1.25 million award during the same season to Diamondbacks catcher Damian Miller (whose 2001 EV was $5.29 million).

But those two decisions, while miserably unfair on their face, illustrate that the basic problem is often with the players' and teams' miscomprehension of how to measure player value. In the case of Miller, his $1.25 million arbitration award represented the value he himself put on his own services—he was, in other words, his own worst enemy. (The Diamondbacks had offered $850,000.) In the case of Vazquez, the arbitrator accepted the Expos' figure. But Vazquez himself only asked for $2.85 million; even if he had gotten it, that still would have been $5 million less than he turned out to be worth.

Stunningly, of the arbitration awards included in the study, only fifteen—that's just one-quarter—involved cases where the player's actual EV eventually landed between the team's offer and the player's demand. In other words, three-quarters of the time both player and management were either too high or too low—often way too high or way too low. In those instances, even a sagacious arbitrator is left with no valid options. In Miller's case, his EV worked out to be about 423 percent of his award. Had the arbitrator chosen the club's offer, it would have produced an award out of touch with eventual reality by 622 percent. The list of decisions contains twenty-six cases—that's more than 40 percent—in which neither player nor management gave the arbitrator an option that would have produced a salary measuring between 50 percent and 150 percent—quite a wide leeway—of the player's eventual Earned Value.

In some cases the reputations of the players alone might be the big stumbling blocks. Catcher Charles Johnson was generally perceived to be one of the stalwarts at his position. Three times—in 1998, 1999, and 2000—Johnson went to arbitration, losing twice and winning once. Yet on all three occasions, even the teams' offers exceeded Johnson's eventual EV by more than one-third. Johnson's estimates of his own worth were off by between 40 and 60 percent each time. The result: Arbitrators awarded Johnson $11.5 million in salaries during seasons in which his aggregate EV amounted to $6.4 million. Even if he had lost all three arbitration cases, Johnson still would have been paid about $4 million more than he produced in on-field value.

11

RATING THE GENERAL MANAGERS

Between their 1997 world championship and 2002, the cash-starved Florida Marlins averaged just 70 victories. (Only the expansion Devil Rays and the incompetent Tigers compiled worse records for that stretch.) At less than $50 million, solidly in the game's lower third, their 2003 payroll didn't markedly improve. But their record sure did; the Marlins claimed 91 victories, the NL wild card, and eventually the world championship.

The biggest single contributor to that 2003 success was a late-thirties used-up shortstop whose greatest previous moment of glory came when he was named All–Los Angeles County as a high schooler in the early 1980s.

Until the Marlins' sudden rise to prominence in October of 2003, it's doubtful that even hard-core Florida fans could have identified Larry Beinfest by his picture. At thirty-eight, Beinfest's background was in administration. His playing career had ended on those Los Angeles high school fields. He got degrees from the University of California and Syracuse, then gravitated into the front office of the Seattle Mariners, where for ten seasons he moved through a succession of jobs, eventually becoming assistant to the vice president. His work caught the eye of Jeffrey Loria, who chose Beinfest to be interim GM of the Expos after the 2001 season. When Loria sold the Expos and purchased the Marlins a few months later, Beinfest moved to Florida with him.

Given the impact that general managers have on the success, or failure, of their clubs, it's remarkable that their role in the game isn't more widely recognized either by the casual fan or by baseball experts—but it isn't. Until the publication of *Moneyball* cast a spotlight to Oakland's Billy Beane in 2003, no serious effort had been undertaken to study any Major League front office operation. As extensive and expansive an industry as SABR-analysis has become, this book represents the first attempt to quantify the impact of Major League front offices on team success.

Front offices are largely run by anonymous figures. The Minnesota Twins reached the postseason in both 2002 and 2003. How many Minnesota Twins fans know who the Twins' GM is (Terry Ryan), or how long he's been GM (since October of 1994)? Because of their teams' wide exposure and postseason success, fans may be familiar with Atlanta's John Schuerholz or the Yankees' Brian Cashman. But can you match up these general managers with the ball clubs they operate: Dave Littlefield, Allard Baird, Ed Wade? (Pittsburgh, Kansas City, Philadelphia respectively.)

In determining the success or failure of a club, general managers have the most important task of all, excepting possibly the guy who sets the budget. That task is talent acquisition. In baseball, it used to be that pennants were decided in August and September. Today, they are decided in November and December, when the big trades come down and the free agent deals occur. Summer may be for the players, but winter is for the GMs, and their winter performance sets the course for what will unfold in the ensuing summer.

The very best—Beane, Cashman, Walt Jocketty (St. Louis), Schuerholz, and Brian Sabean (San Francisco)—have the ability to reshape and strengthen their teams by several games. These moves, by the way, are of quantum greater significance than most of the maneuverings the field manager may engage in from the dugout. As has frequently been established, all the lineup juggling in the world has relatively little to do with improving a team's run production. Platooning is a parlor game compared with finding the right slugger or a useful starter on the open market. Effective use of the hit-and-run, the sacrifice, even the steal bear far less on a team's final record than the tinkering by a skilled GM.

Via a judicious series of front office maneuverings, many of them subtle and several interlinked, Beinfest lifted the Marlins from sub-.500 status in 2002 into contention in 2003. Not all of these moves worked; GMs, like hitters, don't bat 1.000. But the cumulative effect made Beinfest the most successful GM in the National League in 2003. Here are the highlights (numbers in parentheses denote the 2003 BFWs or PWs of the players):

1. He traded Preston Wilson (+0.1) and Charles Johnson (−0.5) to Colorado for Juan Pierre (+0.8) and Mike Hampton, then sent Hampton (+1.6) to Atlanta for Tim Spooneybarger (0.0). The swap of centerfielders cost Florida some power—Wilson hit 36 home runs in Denver—but it energized the top of the Marlins order and helped the defense. Pierre not only proved a better fit in the expansive Florida outfield, but he led the majors with 65 steals, batted .305, and provided a .361 on-base average. He also had a better range factor and a better fielding average than Wilson. Effectively trading a starting catcher (Johnson) for a fill-in pitcher (Spooneybarger) doesn't sound like much of a bargain, until you ponder the financials. Together, Johnson and Wilson earned $13.5 million in 2003; Pierre and Spooneybarger earned a combined $1.3 million. So (ignoring the Hampton pass-through), the deal not only netted the Marlins +1.2 in BFW/PW, it also freed up $12.2 million in cash, which Florida used to purchase . . .

2. One season of Ivan Rodriguez (+2.8) for $10 million as a free agent catcher.

3. Having solidified much of the middle defense, Beinfest locked in the remainder, signing both second baseman Luis Castillo (+1.7) and shortstop Alex Gonzalez (+2.2) to 2003 contracts totaling about $6.5 million.

4. With the cash left over from the Wilson-Johnson-Rodriguez maneuvering, Florida financed a swap of five pitchers with Detroit, the significant name being Mark Redman (+0.5). He made 29 starts and pitched 190 innings for Florida, winning 14 and losing 9 with a capable 3.59 ERA.

5. Minor moves followed: Gerald Williams (–0.5) and Todd Hollandsworth (–0.1) signed on as free agents. Beinfest let three potential free agents go. One, Julian Tavarez (+0.6), signed with Pittsburgh and helped the bullpen. But the Marlins were better off without the other two—outfielder Eric Owens (–1.3) and reliever Graeme Lloyd (–0.8). Chad Fox (0.6) and Jeff Conine (0.2) supplied midseason help in the bullpen and on the bench.

6. In May, in the wake of the season-ending injury to pitching anchor A. J. Burnett, Beinfest reached into the farm system and found pitcher Dontrelle Willis (+2.2), who had gone 4–0 in 6 starts at AAA Carolina. For the most part, GMs who go to the farm in midseason are merely hoping to avoid a disaster, but Willis proved to be a gem. In 27 starts for the Marlins, the high-kicking Willis won 14, lost just 6, and posted a 3.30 ERA on his way to winning the Rookie of the Year award.

7. The last piece fell into place in mid-July when Beinfest shipped three minor leaguers to Texas in exchange for closer Ugueth Urbina (+1.2). Teams don't trade minor leaguers for established closers in July unless they're trying to contend. Thus the simple act of making the deal created vibrations in Florida, where the midsummer atmosphere traditionally has been more conducive to selling talent than purchasing it. Urbina had value on the field as well as off; he saved six games with a 1.41 ERA.

The sum of Beinfest's scorecard showed a net gain of 2.7 games via trades, only partially offset by a 1.7 game loss in players who departed. The Rodriguez signing was the centerpiece of a 4.5 game improvement attributable to free agent arrivals, enhanced even more by a 1.5 game net improvement due to free agent departures. For the most part, farm system products are short-term liabilities. But thanks to Willis, the Marlins actually derived a half-game benefit from their 2003 system products. The bottom line: Between October of 2002 and October of 2003, Larry Beinfest made the Marlins 7.5 games better than they were when he began his labors. Florida's advantage in the wild card race? Four games. Larry Beinfest for MVP.

Largely because his team won the World Series, Beinfest's was the most notable performance among baseball's dress-suited players in 2003. But it wasn't the only job worthy of note. Joe Garagiola, Jr., got little attention in Arizona, his efforts to restore the Diamondbacks to the championship throne they held in 2001 hobbled with the problems afflicting Schilling and Johnson. But in one sense those problems proved to be an opportunity as well, for they forced Garagiola to dip deeply into the farm. The D-Backs brought ten contributing rookies to the majors, and their contributions amounted to a +8.4 short-term gain for the team. I don't know how far back into Major League history you'd have to go to find a more productive rookie class—I've gone back to 1986, and the closest parallel is only a +5.6 by Walt Jocketty in 2001 (when Pujols, +5.4, accounted for virtually all of it). But I'm comfortable saying you'd have to go back a long way.

Getting any positive production out of your rookie class these days is rare in itself. Of the 150 GM seasons since 1999, only thirty-six produced positive short-term values from the rookie class; that's less than one in four. Only seventeen produced values in excess of +1.0. By contrast, 106 of those seasons produced negative values, eighty-eight of those negative values exceeded −1.00, and seventeen exceeded −5.0.

So when Garagiola, in response to pitching injuries, raided Tucson for Brandon Webb (+3.1) and Jose Valverde (+1.1), right there he got more than he could have reasonably expected. When Oscar Villareal, a 2002 alumni of Tucson, kicked in another +2.7, when Robbie Hammock (+1.6), Alex Cintron (+1.0), and Stephen Randolph (+0.6) provided affirmative support, Garagiola could boast a rookie class for the ages. (When the Diamondbacks collapsed in 2004, Garagiola's reputation also nose dived. See Appendix V for 2004 GM Ratings.)

THE STANDARD ISN'T WINNING, IT'S HELPING

Although both Beinfest and Garagiola were impressive in 2003, neither ends up at the pinnacle of GM ranks for the season. That title belongs to the since-retired Pat Gillick, whose swan song in Seattle improved the Mariners' fortunes by 10 games. And since Gillick's Mariners failed to make the postseason in 2003, that in turn ought to prompt a question. How can a guy whose team did not succeed be viewed as a great success himself?

To answer that, let's consider what the GM rating does and does not do. The GM rating measures the degree to which a general manager's performance affects his team's standing from season to season. When we say Pat Gillick bettered the Mariners by 10 games, we are in effect saying that the Mariners—who finished 93–69 and two games out of the wild card—would have finished (roughly) 83–79 had Gillick done nothing at all. Since Seattle also finished 93–69 in 2002, we might also say that Seattle's talent pool was destined to decline by 10 games, and that Gillick offset that decline.

The GM rating unmasks the occasional mirage that envelopes a GM who happens to walk into a very good situation, or highlights the performance of an executive confronted with a poor one. Gillick's is an example of the latter. At the conclusion of the 2002 season, his task was to pick through the aging bones of the Mariners' roster to determine which players still had value and which did not. There were eight in particular, and Gillick exercised perfect judgment. He re-signed forty-one-year-old starter Jamie Moyer (+3.3), and Moyer went 21–7. He extended forty-one-year-old Edgar Martinez (+2.3), and Martinez batted .294. He held on to little-noticed reliever Shigetoshi Hasegawa (+2.8), a decision that proved invaluable when closer Kaz Sasaki went down with an arm injury. Hasegawa rang up 16 saves. And he retained thirty-five-year-old John Olerud (+0.4).

Who did he cut? Ismael Valdes (–1.5), picked up from Texas in the middle of 2002. Valdes signed as a free agent with the Rangers and inflicted a 6.10 ERA on them in 22 starts. He cut thirty-eight-year-old Ruben Sierra, who also signed with the Rangers and produced a –1.1 BFW. Desi Relaford (–1.1 in Kansas City) and John Halama (–.1 in Oakland) proved to be similarly fortunate eliminations.

Gillick's season was not perfect; in addition to those moves he also cut a young and little-used centerfielder named Scott Podsednik

(+2.2), who went to Milwaukee and made a name for himself. But even debiting the Podsednik decision, plus a couple of other minor missteps, Gillick still positioned the 2003 Mariners 10.7 games to the better via his free agent decisions alone. Even given modestly negative results from trades and the farm system, it still produced his overall +10 rating.

Gillick's successor in Seattle, Bill Bavasi, had far less fortune. His big move entering 2004 was to sign shortstop Rich Aurilia. He replaced Armando Benitez (he topped 45 saves with Florida) with Eddie Guardado (he got hurt). Meanwhile, all the guys with one more season left when Gillick re-signed them in 2003 (Olerud, Moyer, Martinez, Hasegawa) had no more seasons left in 2004. Those were among the reasons why one of the most popular Web sites in Seattle in September of 2004 was www.firebavasi.com.

Occasionally the GM rating exposes a GM as overhyped. In 2003, two execs received unmerited praise for improvements that were largely the products of their predecessors' efforts. In Chicago, the media spent much of August and September fawning over Jim Hendry's labors to kick the Cubs into the postseason picture. Plainly Hendry worked hard at that goal, picking Kenny Lofton (+0.8), Randall Simon (0.0), and Aramis Ramirez (+0.5) out of Pittsburgh, getting Tony Womack (−0.5) from Colorado, and Doug Glanville (−0.2) from Philadelphia. Counting preseason dealings, the net of his acquisitions via trade amounted to +1 game in the standings, augmented by an additional 0.9 game improvement attributable to the players he traded away.

But Hendry was much less of a genius at the signing table. He gave Shawn Estes (−2.8) $3 million. Bad move; Estes labored through an 8–11, 5.73 ERA season. He signed Lenny Harris (−1.50) as the team's pinch hitter; Harris produced a .183 average before the Cubs boxed him to, of all places, Florida, where he hit .286. He re-signed Antonio Alfonseca (−0.6) for the bullpen, and Alfonseca was never effective. Of twelve Hendry signings entering 2003, eight produced negative value for the Cubs. The truth is that while Hendry got the credit, the accumulation of his moves actually crippled the Cubs to the tune of those three games in the standings in 2003. Chicago won the NL Central because of the emergence of Mark Prior (+4.9), the continued development of Kerry Wood (+3.1), the acceptable if not spectacular season turned in by Sammy Sosa (+0.9), and the development of Joe Borowski (+1.7)—all of them products of Hendry's predecessor, Andy McPhail. There is such a thing as residual impact— the footprint left behind by a departed GM (more on that in a bit). In 2003, McPhail's residual impact on Cubs' fortunes exceeded 18 games to the good. What Hendry did in 2003 was bask in McPhail's reflected glory.

What Omar Minaya did in Montreal was ride a wave of talent put in place by his predecessor, Jim Beattie. Fired after the 2001 season and since co-habiting with Mike Flanagan in the Baltimore front office, Beattie actually left the cupboard well stocked for Minaya, who got the media credit when the Expos exceeded very low expectations in 2002 and again in 2003. The key parts in that 2003 success were Vladimir Guerrero (+2.6), Javier Vazquez (+3.4), Livan Hernandez (+3.7), Brian Schneider (+1.8), Jose Cabrera (+2.3), and Jose Vidro (+0.3). Of the group, only Hernandez (via a trade with San Francisco) was a Minaya production. Admittedly, the weakest part of Minaya's game—trade losses—was financially driven. The big 2003 loss in that respect was Bartolo Colon (+1.9) to the White Sox. On the other hand, he also traded Matt Herges (+0.8) and Scott Strickland (+0.7 in limited use) in moves that cannot be described as money-driven. At base, the Expos—who finished 83–79 in 2003 under Minaya's supervision—would have finished 85–77 had he slept through the winter.

WELFARE FOR POVERTY-STRICKEN GMS

The Minaya assessment prompts a close friend and highly knowledgeable baseball man to wonder whether the GM rating is deficient because it fails to consider the role of money as a driver of GM decisions. Generally speaking, you will find the name of Brian Cashman toward the top of lists (including this one) of effective general managers. Brian Cashman happens to GM the Yankees. Chuck LaMar

GMs the Tampa Bay Devil Rays, which means that in building a 2004 team LaMar made do with one-sixth of Cashman's fiscal resources. Minaya had the same problem in Montreal. Shouldn't a GM rating give Minaya or LaMar some sort of break?

It's a reasonable position to take, not that I'm going to take it, because to take it is to betray an interest in motivations. This is a book about the objective effectiveness of strategies—including team-building strategies—not about the driving forces behind them. To ponder what Omar Minaya or Chuck LaMar didn't do because they didn't have Brian Cashman's money (or his demanding boss, or his scouting system, or his whatever) may be a fair topic for debate. But it is beside the point that they did it. Since at season's end the standings are wins-driven rather than money-driven, the most meaningful measurement is of the moves that were made, not the ones that might have been made under a nonexistent set of conditions. Life's not fair, Omar . . . deal with it.

Beyond that, while nobody would deny money's influence in team-building, the relationship is far from precise. As the remainder of this chapter and associated tables will demonstrate, the hierarchy of GM excellence in the current game is a relative hybrid of big-money, medium-money, and even small-money guys. For every Cashman or John Schuerholz near the top of the list there's a Walt Jocketty or a Brian Sabean from middle-market clubs, not to mention Billy Beane from decidedly small-market Oakland.

And while the bottom end of the rankings does appear to tilt toward smaller-market GMs, the pattern again is heterogeneous. In 2003, John Hart from big-payroll Texas was the second-worst GM in the AL; Dan Evans from big-money L.A. stood thirteenth among the eighteen men (counting two each in New York and Cincinnati) who held the title of GM in the NL.

THE LANGUAGE

One reason general managers tend to be anonymous is that historically there has been no generally recognized method of assessing their contributions to their teams. In part, this may be due to the fact that the position of general manager only evolved in the 1930s, a time when baseball's basic statistical nomenclature was fully established. Strangely, although the SABRmetric revolution of the 1980s greatly refined many understandings concerning baseball stats, that revolution virtually bypassed the front office.

Yet creating such a measurement is not a difficult assignment. Two tools are needed: 1. A reasonable set of criteria; and 2. a measurement tool capable of assessing player performance. SABRmetrics provides a wide range of tools for the latter task: Bill James's Win Shares and Pete Palmer's Batter Fielder Base Sealer Wins leap readily to mind. I happen to prefer Palmer's BFW—along with its pitching companion, Pitcher Wins—for reasons described earlier in this book.

Establishing the criteria for evaluating a GM is more complex, but at their heart they can be reduced to three things, all related to the team's roster. Those three general tasks are: 1. Acquiring or moving players via dealings with other GMs—such as in trades, sales, or waiver transactions; 2. knowing which free agents to sign, and which potential free agents to release or not re-sign; and 3. producing talent from within the organization. It also must be kept in mind that general managers do these things both in a short-term and long-term context.

Here's what we mean by each significant term.

Short-term impact: The impact of any player-related move, measured in BFW or PW, that occurs during the season in which the move is made (if made in-season), or in the immediately succeeding season (if made during the off-season). If the player is acquired, short-term impact only accrues for as long as the player remains with the team.

Long-term impact: The impact of any player-related move, measured in BFW or PW, that occurs following the season in which the move is made (if made in-season), or following the immediately succeeding season (if made during the off-season). If the player is acquired, long-term impact only accrues for as long as the player remains with the team. If the player is dealt or otherwise lost, long-term impact accrues on a sliding scale over the first five seasons following the short-term loss, unless the organization reacquires the player within that time frame, in which case the calculation is halted. The sliding scale is as follows: 100 percent of BFW or PW in the first season, 80 percent in the second season, 60 percent in the third season, 40 percent in the fourth season, and 20 percent in the fifth season.

Acquisition: A player obtained by trade, sale, or waiver from another Major League team or system, assuming that player does not immediately spend at least the equivalent of one season in the acquiring club's farm system.

Trade loss: A player traded, sold, or waived directly to another Major League team or system.

Free agent gain: A player under contract by one of four means: 1. Signed on the open market after his contract with another team expired; 2. signed on the open market following his release by another team; 3. signed to a multiyear contract extension by his own team if not already free-agent eligible, or to any contract extension by his own team if free-agent eligible; 4. given a contract extension.

Free agent loss: A player whose contract expires and who subsequently signs with another team, or a player who is given his release.

Product: A player in his first five years of Major League service with the team he originally signed with, or with a team in whose organization he spent at least one minor league season prior to coming to the majors. (Note: Players with less than five years of Major League experience who are signed to multiyear contracts cease being counted as products, and are counted as free agent gains.)

The combination of those elements will in turn lead to short-term and long-term ratings. Short-term ratings can be thought of as the impact (measured in victories) of a GM's moves during and immediately prior to the season at hand on the team's performance. Long-term ratings can be thought of as the impact (measured in victories) of a GM's prior moves on the team's current-season performance. Listed below, by league, are the 2003 short-term ratings for all active general managers. (Appendix V contains more detailed ratings for general managers for seasons since 1999.)

2003 Short-term Ratings

AMERICAN LEAGUE

GM	Team	Short term
Pat Gillick	Seattle	+10.00
Brian Cashman	Yankees	+4.40
Theo Epstein	Boston	+4.10
Billy Beane	Oakland	+3.40
Kenny Williams	White Sox	+3.10
Bill Stoneman	Anaheim	+1.60
Mark Shapiro	Cleveland	0.10
Terry Ryan	Minnesota	−0.80
Chuck LaMar	Tampa Bay	−2.70
Allard Baird	Kansas City	−5.40
Flanagan-Beattie	Baltimore	−6.10
J. P. Ricciardi	Toronto	−12.70
John Hart	Texas	−12.80
Dave Dombrowski	Detroit	−14.30

NATIONAL LEAGUE

GM	Team	Short term
Larry Beinfest	Florida	+7.50
Joe Garagiola, Jr.	Arizona	+6.10
Ed Wade	Philadelphia	+1.10
John Schuerholz	Atlanta	+1.00
Jim Duquette	Mets	−1.50
Gerry Hunsicker	Houston	−1.80
Omar Minaya	Montreal	−2.10
Steve Phillips	Mets	−2.60
Jim Hendry	Cubs	−3.20
Kevin Towers	San Diego	−3.60
Dave Littlefield	Pittsburgh	−3.70

Jim Bowden	Cincinnati	−4.50
Dan Evans	Los Angeles	−5.20
Dan O'Dowd	Colorado	−7.60
Brian Sabean	San Francisco	−8.00
Walt Jocketty	St. Louis	−9.40
Doug Melvin	Milwaukee	−11.40
(Interim team)	Cincinnati	−13.40

And here is a table of the 2003 long-term rankings of general managers. (First-year GMs have no long-term rating. There were five in 2003: Epstein, Flanagan-Beattie, Duquette, Melvin, and Cincinnati's interim GMs.)

2003 Long-term ratings

AMERICAN LEAGUE

GM	Team	Long term
Brian Cashman	Yankees	+28.70
Billy Beane	Oakland	+26.50
Pat Gillick	Seattle	+9.40
Allard Baird	Kansas City	+6.70
Terry Ryan	Minnesota	+3.80
Kenny Williams	White Sox	+2.20
John Hart	Texas	+1.60
Chuck LaMar	Tampa Bay	−3.20
Bill Stoneman	Anaheim	−4.20
J. P. Ricciardi	Toronto	−5.60
Mark Shapiro	Cleveland	−6.00
Dave Dombrowski	Detroit	−10.70

NATIONAL LEAGUE

GM	Team	Long term
John Schuerholz	Atlanta	+28.40
Brian Sabean	San Francisco	+19.70
Walt Jocketty	St. Louis	+18.60
Dan O'Dowd	Colorado	+13.40
Ed Wade	Philadelphia	+12.20
Gerry Hunsicker	Houston	+11.50
Steve Phillips	Mets	+6.20
Larry Beinfest	Florida	+4.00
Dan Evans	Los Angeles	+1.80
Joe Garagiola, Jr.	Arizona	−1.90
Omar Minaya	Montreal	−3.80
Jim Hendry	Cubs	−3.90
Dave Littlefield	Pittsburgh	−4.00
Jim Bowden	Cincinnati	−4.10
Kevin Towers	San Diego	−10.30

WHAT A GOOD GM DOES

As noted above, the impact of a GM accrues both in the short term and long term, and those accruals are not necessarily parallel. If Gerry Hunsicker traded three prospects for Randy Johnson in late July of 1998, and if Randy Johnson went 10–1 for the Astros the rest of the season, that is a short-term impact—and a very salubrious one indeed. Johnson's PW with the Astros at the tag end of 1998 was +3.2, meaning that over the final two months of the season he added 3.2 victories to the team's total. Meanwhile, none of the three players traded by Houston contributed anything to anybody's Major League success. We congratulate Gerry Hunsicker on a nifty short-term move.

Whether it will turn out to be a nifty long-term move hinges on John Halama, Carlos Guillen, and Freddy Garcia. Johnson, of course, took free agency and left for Arizona, which meant that Houston's long-term gain from the trade was precisely zero. Between 1999 and

2003, Halama, Guillen, and Garcia coincidentally also generated a combined 0.00 BFW/PW for their teams, so Gillick remained ahead on the deal by 3.2 games, subject to change in either direction.

Major league general managers operate in different ways, under different circumstances, and with different styles. But if you look seriously over several years' data, patterns recur. You could think of them as the Rules for Good General Managing. Five appear to be the most important and most readily identifiable.

1. Build for the Long Term, Not for the Short Term

The defining personnel move of the 1990s probably was the signing by Atlanta of free agent pitcher Greg Maddux prior to the 1993 season. By getting Maddux, Braves' GM John Schuerholz acquired a pitcher who went 20–10 with a league-leading ERA in 1993. The record will further note that with a 6.1 PW, Maddux was the most valuable pitcher in the majors that season. But the Maddux signing is not the defining player move of the 1990s because of what it did for the Braves in 1993. Its true importance lay in what it did for the Braves after 1993. For the decade between 1994 and 2003, Maddux was worth 50.5 PW to Schuerholz's credit, and to the Braves' pennant hopes. Put another way, due to that single late 1992 signing, the Braves effectively started most of the past decade five games above .500 before Schuerholz did anything else.

GMs often are called upon for the quick fix, but quick fixes do more damage than good. The average short-term impact of all front-office moves—that includes trades, free agent decisions, and farm system promotions—made by GMs who have been active since 1999 was about −2.20 BFW/PW—that's a 2.20 game loss in the standings during the ensuing season. But the average long-term impact of those same moves is +1.83 games.

There is no better recent illustration of this fact than the championship won by the Arizona Diamondbacks in 2001. Garagiola's moves between October of 2000 and September of 2001 could fairly be described as only modestly effective. His prize signee, Mark Grace

(–0.4), produced a .298, 15 homer season that was actually a hindrance to the cause. Free agents Miguel Batista and Reggie Sanders helped, but rookies Rod Barajas (.160, 3 HR, 9 RBI), Robert Ellis (a 5.77 ERA in 92 innings), and Troy Brohawn (a 4.93 ERA in 50 innings) were liabilities. Overall, Garagiola's short-term moves yielded a 0.5 BFW/PW gain that would not by itself have been enough to lift the Diamondbacks into contention.

Fortunately for the Diamondbacks, Garagiola had already done most of the heavy rebuilding prior to 2001 by acquiring Curt Schilling, Randy Johnson, and Luis Gonzalez. Thanks to those acquisitions and a few others, the long-term BFW/PW impact of Garagiola on Arizona for 2001 was +20.7 games. Those pre-2001 moves were the reasons Arizona won its division and the World Series as well.

Even the best GMs can generally only move a club perhaps six to eight games from one season to another. Gillick's already discussed efforts represented the 2003 benchmark. In 2002, the best performance in this respect was turned in by Sabean, who upgraded the Giants by 17.9 games. The bulk of that, by the way, was represented in his re-signing of Barry Bonds (+11.7).

The only GMs since 1999 who have helped their teams short-term by an average of five games or more per season have been former Boston exec Dan Duquette (5.58), and the Yankees' Cashman (+5.04).

By contrast fifteen general managers have averaged a long-term improvement to their teams in excess of five games for the past five seasons, and the figure is often much in excess. Thanks to Maddux, Schuerholz leads that chart at +17.56. Sabean stands second at 13.46, and Beane is at 13.38. The long-term moves of Cashman and Jocketty have also improved their teams by an average of more than ten games per season since 1999.

During that five-year period, the average short-term impact of GM moves has been 5.8 games. The average long-term impact, however, has been 7.4 games.

Here are the five best single-season long-term impacts by general managers since 1999.

1. Dan Duquette, Boston, 2002, +29.60
2. Brian Sabean, San Francisco, 2000, +29.40
3. John Schuerholz, Atlanta, 2003, +29.00
4. Brian Cashman, Yankees, 2003, +25.50
5. Billy Beane, Oakland, 2001, +24.80

And here are the five worst.

1. Chuck LaMar, Tampa Bay, 2002, −21.30
2. Chuck LaMar, Tampa Bay, 2001, −15.50
3. (tie) Dave Dombrowski, Florida, 2000, −12.10
   Ed Lynch, Cubs, 1999, −12.10
4. Dave Dombrowski, Florida, 1999, and Detroit, 2003, −10.70

2. Build Through Free Agency, Not Through Trades

Those ain't rubens you're dealing with, and they don't slicker easily. As a general proposition, most trades don't greatly influence the fortunes of the trading teams. Where GMs can really swing their clubs is through the judicious use of free agent cash. And this especially includes knowing which of your own guys to keep.

Since 1999, the average short-term impact of the players acquired by trade, sale, or waiver has been about −0.75 BFW/PW. That was nearly offset by the 0.45 "gain" from players who were traded away, but the short-term net impact of all trades was still an uninteresting −0.30 BFW/PW. Factoring in the long-term impact only improved the picture by a barely noticeable 0.03. There are exceptions, but for the most part teams tend to trade weaknesses, not assets.

By contrast, the short-term impact of free agent signings, resignings, and extensions was +0.26. Meanwhile, the long-term impact of those moves amounted to +2.68 games. Free agent losses improved team prospects by an additional 1.08 BFW/PW, meaning that as a general propostion teams improved their positions long term by 3.17 games by signing the right players and cutting the wrong ones adrift.

The bottom line: Since 1999, trade activity tended to hurt teams' short-term and long-term fortunes by a third of a game, but signing activity tended to help by about four games.

This—the relative inaccesibility of the more productive free agent market necessitating a consequential reliance on less productive trades—is the real handicap under which small-revenue teams operate.

For much of his career, Schuerholz has been the master of the free agent market, and especially so with multi-year deals. Since 1999, the average long-term BFW/PW impact of his signings/extensions is +11.70 per season. (Much of that success has involved re-signing or extending players already under contract: players like Maddux, Glavine, Smoltz, Chipper Jones, and Lopez. That decade-long pattern of tying up the core, by the way, jarringly ended following the 2003 season when Schuerholz let Lopez, Sheffield, and Maddux all leave to free agency.) Schuerholz's long-term score improves to +13.44 when the players he surrenders to free agency are entered into the equation. The losses of Sheffield, Maddux, and Lopez appear to be turning this pattern. But between 1991 and 2003, Schuerholz's ability to wisely apply Ted Turner's money to the right places on the free agent market was a significant part of the explanation how the Braves dominated the National League.

It is precisely the same story for Cashman's manipulations of the Yankees. Cashman's short-term and long-term BFW/PW for trades is an unremarkable +0.32. But at the signing table, considering the short-term and long-term impact of both his signings and releases, Cashman's net score is +16.58. Part of that is his ability to retain talent such as Bernie Williams and Jorge Posada; part is the ability to reach out to a Roger Clemens or a Jason Giambi. In its totality, that's why New York is the AL's pre-eminent team.

For the most part, the GMs who have succeeded in the late 1990s and into the first year of the twenty-first century have been successful signers.

Here are the five best general manager seasonal impacts since 1999 in signing, re-signing, or extending players (combined short and long-term):

1. Brian Sabean, San Francisco, 2002, +27.60
2. Brian Cashman, Yankees, 2003, +27.00
3. Dan Duquette, Boston, 2002, +25.90
4. Brian Sabean, San Francisco, 2000, +25.20
5. Brian Cashman, Yankees, 2002, +23.40

And here are the five worst:

1. Kevin Towers, San Diego, 2000, −11.50
2. Syd Thrift, Baltimore, 2001, −10.40
3. Sal Bando, Milwaukee, 1999, −7.30
4. Kevin Towers, San Diego, 2003, −7.00
5. Cam Bonifay, Pittsburgh, 2001, −6.40

3. Anybody Seen a Wheeler-Dealer?

The ability to strike well at the trade table, especially short term, is a rare gem. Not only do you gain, you gain at the direct expense of your competitors. Traders have to work subtly, of course, since nothing is more harmful to them than a reputation. Following the publication of *Moneyball,* much of the industry table talk concerned whether Billy Beane would be ruined as an operator by its discussion of his methods. In that respect, two National League GMs may be sorry if word gets out on their abilities to fleece the competition.

Ask the Anaheim Angels about Walt Jocketty. He talked them out of Jim Edmonds for Kent Bottenfield and Adam Kennedy. In 2000, players acquired by Jocketty through trades or waiver deals improved St. Louis short term by 11.4 games, while the players he traded away improved the Cardinals by another 4.8 games. That's a 16.2 game improvement due to one aspect of a GM's job and in just one season. He was good in 2001 and 2002 as well—with overall short-term trade impacts of +4.4 and +2.4—before slumping in 2003 to a−2.0 rating. Atop that, the previous acquisitions of players such as Edmonds continued to pay dividends. In 2001, Jocketty's long-term trade score—the measure of the value of prior-season deals—was

+3.9. In 2002, it was +1.50, and in 2003 +2.00. His average trade score since 1999 is +5.32, the best in the majors. It was no coincidence that St. Louis won the NL Central in 2000 and 2002, and tied Houston for that position in 2001.

Stuck in small-market San Diego, Kevin Towers presided over the construction of Padres divisional champions in 1996 and again in 1998, displaying a keen sense of which players to acquire and which to unload. Short term, he is one of the majors' most prolific junk dealers, improving the Padres by an average of 2.56 games since 1999 just by shedding non-talent. When San Diego approached triple digits in victories and won the NL West in 1998, both sides of Towers's deals were keys.

His first, most important, and most obvious move was to acquire the ace of the world champs, pitcher Kevin Brown, from cash-strapped Florida, in exchange for Derrek Lee. Brown brought 5.20 PW with him to San Diego, while Lee contributed –.50 BFW in Florida, a short-term gain of 5.70 games. Towers made other, smaller but also significant moves as well. He picked up pitchers Dan Micelli and Donnie Wall from Detroit in exchange for reliever Todd Worrell and Trey Beamon. Combined, Micelli and Wall improved the Padres by 2.70 PW, while losing Worrell and Beamon added another 1.00— a net gain to San Diego of 3.7 games.

He sent his catcher, John Flaherty, to Tampa Bay, opening up a place for theretofore reserve Carlos Hernandez. When Flaherty produced a .207 batting average (for a minus 2.50 BFW) in Tampa and Hernandez hit .262 (0.60) in his first season as the San Diego regular, Towers had effectively improved his team by another 3.1 games.

Since 1999, budget strictures have hampered the Padres' flexibility. But for a time, Towers's skill at dealing partially offset the damage. When the Padres pared back in 1999, Towers lost players to free agency (notably Brown) that produced a negative 5.50 short-term impact. That impact was exacerbated by the fact that the bargain-basement free agents Towers did acquire—notably Dave Magadan and Eric Owens—netted his club another –1.90 short-term regression in the standings in 1999. The Padres fell from 98 victories to 74.

Only his trade skills helped Towers partly stanch the talent drain, and probably kept the team out of the 1999 cellar. His acquisitions improved the club by 3.6 games short term, while the players he traded represented another 6.1 game improvement. Short term, Towers's 1999 GM rating was a miserable −6.20, standing second from the bottom of the National League. But as a trader, his score that season was +9.70, plainly the league's best. In 2000, he posted an overall trade score of 10.80, although virtually all of that represented the long-time appreciation of previous deals. He fell to +5.40 in 2001, again scoring disproportionately with the residue of previous years' trades, particularly among players he traded away. When in 2002 Towers finally began to accumulate negative value both from previous seasons' dealings and from traded players, his overall trade score plummeted to −9.00. Shorn of his one strength, Towers in 2002 ranked third from the bottom among all general managers in terms of his short-term value to his club, and dead last in long-term value. He rebounded to a +4.00 short term and +1.10 long term as a trader in 2003.

Here are the five best general manager seasonal impacts since 1999 at trading (combined short- and long-term impact).

1. Walt Jocketty, St. Louis, 2000, +19.30
2. Kevin Towers, San Diego, 1999, +16.50
3. Billy Beane, Oakland, 2003, +16.10
4. (tie) Doug Melvin, Texas, 2002, +12.80
   and Gerry Hunsicker, Houston, 2002, +12.80

And here are the five worst.

1. Chuck LaMar, Tampa Bay, 2002, −16.50
2. Dave Dombrowski, Florida, 1999, −12.60
3. (tie) Dave Dombrowski, Florida, 2000, −11.90
   Woody Woodward, Seattle, 1999, −11.90
5. Jim Beattie, Montreal, 2001, −11.60

4. As a Rule, the Free Agents You Get Are Far More Important Than the Free Agents You Lose

Most free agent decisions are actually non-decisions. In any post-season, the list of available free agents is dotted with guys nobody wants. Following the 2003 season, for example, that list included the likes of Albert Belle, Hector Carrasco, Deivi Cruz, Scott Erickson, Brook Fordyce, and Kerry Ligtenberg . . . and that was just Orioles. Each had already become a role player or worse, and Baltimore did not for one second regret the prospect of their loss.

This is one part of the reason why successful general managers worry a lot more about who they can sign off another team's roster than who the other guy can sign off their roster.

In 2003, the average short-term value of all signings by each team's GM—that includes free agents signed off other teams, free agents re-signed from one's own team, and players receiving contract extensions—was about −1.16 BFW/PW. The average short-term value from free agent losses was +0.40. But this is a case where the averages are deceptive due to the difference between "value" and "impact." There is a significant difference. By "value," we mean the average score. By "impact," we mean the linear movement away from zero without consideration for whether that movement is positive or negative. The average short-term impact of arrivals was 2.94, but the average short-term impact of departures was just 1.97, a full game less.

The pattern repeats over time. Since 1999, the average short-term impact from all signings is about 2.93 BFW/PW. The net short-term impact created by departing players is 1.80. Among the 159 GM seasons analyzed for this study, two-thirds created a greater short-term impact on their teams by who they signed than by who they let get away.

Success at the signing table is a hallmark of the game's preeminent general managers. The top five short-term GMs since 1999 (Duquette, Cashman, Jocketty, Garagiola, Beane) average a short-term impact of 3.96 BFW/PW by who they sign. In contrast, they only impacted their teams an average of 1.59 BFW/PW in their signing losses. (Departures which, in the cases of all but Beane, by the way, were beneficial.)

One may argue that this is true because those teams have the resources to hold all of their good players. There is a chicken and egg quality to this argument: Which came first, the money or the victories? Plainly, a GM would rather have George Steinbrenner's money than Jeffrey Loria's. But the argument is not nearly that simple. Nobody has ever suggested Billy Beane operates with a padded payroll in Oakland, yet his signings alone have improved the A's short term by nearly four games per season, and those gains were only partially offset (-2.32 BFW/PW) by free agent departures. Baltimore Orioles GMs have always had plenty of Peter Angelos's money to toss around, yet neither Pat Gillick nor Syd Thrift was especially successful in free agent related work in Baltimore. The Texas Rangers franchise was considered well-heeled even before the signing of Alex Rodriguez. Doug Melvin's short-term rating for free agent signings and losses—a rating fashioned mostly in Texas although with a 2003 stint in Milwaukee added—is -1.68.

Finally, as the table below will strongly suggest, a crucial element is taking care of your own. Prior to the 1999 season, Sabean had the common sense to extend Barry Bonds's contract for three more years. Prior to the 2002 season, he had the continued good sense to re-sign him. Given that Bonds responded by generating a combined $+42.6$ BFW, those two moves virtually by themselves guaranteed Sabean's inclusion on lists of the best GMs of the past five years.

The five best general manager seasonal impacts at short-term signing or extending talent since 1999:

1. Dan Duquette, Boston, 2000, +16.40
2. Brian Sabean, San Francisco, 2002, +6.20
3. Brian Cashman, Yankees, 1999, +12.70
4. Brian Cashman, Yankees, 2002, +11.30
5. Pat Gillick, Seattle, 2003, +10.70

The five worst:

1. Syd Thrift, Baltimore, 2001, −8.00
2. Woody Woodward, Seattle, 1999, −7.80
3. (tie) Billy Beane, Oakland, 2002, −7.40
   Kevin Towers, San Diego, 1999, −7.40
4. Kevin Towers, San Diego, 2000, −7.30

5. Quick Improvement Through the Farm System Is Next to Impossible

In 2003, Joe Garagiola, Jr., brought to the big leagues the best rookie crop of any team in recent history. If that crop restores Arizona to contender status, Garagiola will have matched Walt Jocketty's deeds in improving the 2001 St. Louis Cardinals. Thanks largely to Albert Pujols, Jocketty's farmhands boosted the Cards all the way into the postseason, something Garagiola could not do in 2003. Few can.

Jocketty's 2001 Cardinals were chock full of generally low-dollar players. Some like Pujols (+5.4) were new promotions. Others, notably Matt Morris (+3.2) and J. D. Drew (+3.2), had been up a year or two, but lacked sufficient seniority to wield salary leverage against whom the game's salary structure gives the team most of the advantages. Combining short-term and long-term impacts, these recent Cardinal farmhands boosted the team's short-term performance by 13.0 BFW/PW in 2001, a stunning total that would have been even better if Rick Ankiel had been able to throw the ball over the plate. They were the biggest reason why the Cardinals reprised their 2000 playoff berth. And they made Jocketty far and away the most successful "farmer" among Major League GMs in 2001.

Dan Duquette's experience in Boston was more typical. Contrary to the opinions of most Red Sox fans, Duquette had a good year in 2001. His +4.6 short-term GM rating ranked second in the AL behind only Gillick. He was +6.1 in his short-term dealings with free agent eligibles. Although today Red Sox fans measure Duquette's 2001 efforts as a disappointment because of the Carl Everett problems, his real shortcoming lay in his failure to harvest any talent from Pawtucket or the other links in Boston's farm chain.

The Red Sox used eight fresh farmhands in 2001, and none of the eight produced a positive BFW or PW. Shea Hillenbrand (−1.8) was an everyday player and a liability, while Casey Fossum (−0.4) and Sun-Woo Kim (−0.2) hurt more than they helped in occasional pitching stints. Outfielder Trot Nixon was a plus, but the short-term farm net was −3.6 BFW/PW to the Sox' cause. In that skill Duquette ranked tenth in the league.

With only occasional exceptions, GMs who want to build around their farm system better be in it for the long haul. In 2003, the average short-term BFW/PW for farmhands not yet free agent eligible was −1.67 in the AL, −1.52 in the NL. Of the 32 GMs [counting two each in New York (NL) and Cincinnati], Garagiola's +8.40 was the only short-term score exceeding +0.60.

In contrast, the short-term scores of 17 were −1 or worse, bottoming (to nobody's surprise) in Detroit, where a legion of Dombrowski's preemies (Jeremy Bonderman, Franklyn German, Wil Ledezma, Matt Roney, Andres Torres) added 9.5 games of additional misery to the ponderous burden already borne by Tiger fans.

This obviously is a particular problem for those teams that envision themselves as cash-strapped and thus duty-bound to build from within. Terry Ryan successfully navigated such a course in 2002, riding a team largely composed of homegrown talent to the AL Central title. But he barely survived the journey. In the three previous seasons, Ryan's average short-term score for farm products was −8.2, lowlighted by a −12.8 short-term score in 1999. (That 1999 class—which included Torii Hunter, A. J. Pierzynski, Doug Mientkiewicz, Christian Guzman, Mark Redman, and Joe Mays—proved that from time to time persistence in the face of adversity pays off.) A tenet of the farm-oriented franchise is the ability to think in the long term, but during the three seasons prior to 2002 Ryan's long-term farm score was −1. Terry Ryan is one guy who should be thankful he works for a very patient and understanding boss.

This was a common thread among the game's have-nots. Among the GMs of the ten lowest-payroll clubs for each of the past five seasons—that's 50 GM seasons—only eleven posted positive short-term farm results, and just two of those seasons (Bowden +2.6 in

2002; Beane +1.1 in 1999) exceeded +1. The average short-term score of the ten was −2.8; long term, the average rose, but only to −0.2. Even as their farmhands matured, the performance of these players still caused lower-salary teams to recede from the rest of the league.

Only the very well-managed succeeded in harvesting talent on a regular basis. Again, Schuerholz and Beane stand out. Since 1999, Schuerholz has realized an average gain of 5.04 games from such players. That total does not include the production generated by farmhands such as Chipper Jones or Andruw Jones, who signed multi-year extensions. Long term and short term, Beane's farm production (Hudson, Mulder, Zito) has boosted the A's by an average of 4.94 games. In a class with those two is Hunsicker, whose Astros benefit by an average of 5.02 games annually from the short-term and long-term production of the Houston farm.

The five best general manager season impacts since 1999 at use of the farm system:

1. Joe Garagiola, Jr., Arizona, 2003, +8.40
2. Walt Jocketty, St. Louis, 2001, +5.60
3. Jim Bowden, Cincinnati, 1999, +4.20
4. Bill Stoneman, Anaheim, 2002, +3.40
5. Gerry Hunsicker, Houston, 2001, +2.70

The five worst:

1. Terry Ryan, Minnesota, 1999, −12.80
2. (tie) Dave Dombrowski, Detroit, 2003, −9.50
   Randy Smith, Detroit, 2001, −9.50
3. (tie) Kevin Towers, San Diego, 1999, −8.50
   Terry Ryan, Minnesota, 2001, −8.50

THE TEN BEST GM EFFORTS

To the extent that general managers gain any fame at all, they do so by shepherding their teams to pennants. But the GM rating suggests that while winning is in fact the important thing, it is not *the only* thing. Some GMs do fine work in obscurity, burdened by a sorry talent base and given the Sisyphian task of trying to shape it into something respectable. To a degree, the GM rating rewards these men, since it measures the impact of a general manager on team performance beyond what that performance would have been had the GM not interceded. In the GM rating, in other words, a guy who inherits a talent base that should play at 62–90 and remakes it into a 500 club has done as well as one who takes an 81–81 team and makes it a 100-game winner.

That's the theory, at any rate. In practice, it's plainly easier for a GM—especially one blessed with fiscal tools—to operate at the higher, rarer end of the spectrum. Among the ten highest single-season short-term GM scores since 1999, eight were attained by the bosses of playoff-bound teams.

Here are the ten best short-term GM seasonal impacts of the past five years:

1. Walt Jocketty, St. Louis 2000, +19.40
2. Brian Sabean, San Francisco, 2002, +17.90
3. Dan Duquette, Boston, 2000, +14.00
4. Joe Garagiola Jr., Arizona, 1999, +12.30
5. Steve Phillips, Mets, 1999, +12.20
6. Walt Jocketty, St. Louis, 2001, +12.00
7. Gerry Hunsicker, Houston, 2002, +11.30
8. Brian Cashman, Yankees, 2002, +11.00
9. Brian Cashman, Yankees, 1999, +10.30
10. Pat Gillick, Seattle, 2001, +9.70

And here are the ten worst:

1. Randy Smith, Detroit, 2001, –14.80
2. Terry Ryan, Minnesota, 1999, –14.20
3. Interim, Cincinnati, 2003, –13.40
4. Ed Lynch, Cubs, 2000, –13.00
5. Larry Beinfest, Florida, 2002, –12.80

6. John Hart, Texas, 2003, −12.80
7. J. P. Ricciardi, Toronto, 2003, −12.70
8. Dean Taylor, Milwaukee, 2002, −12.60
9. Syd Thrift, Baltimore, 2001, −11.60
10. (tie) Herk Robinson, Kansas City, 2000,
    and Doug Melvin, Milwaukee, 2003, −11.40

HERK'S TOXIC WASTE DUMP

Occasionally a GM finds it easier to improve his team by dumping players than by acquiring them. Until a better model comes along, former Kansas City GM Herk Robinson is the prototype. Coming off a 72-win 1998 season, the Royals set up as truly awful for 1999. They fell to just 64 victories. Short term, there was little Robinson could do, as reflected by his −4.0 shortterm rating. His 1999 long-term rating of +4.2 is, however, an entirely different story, leaving him with an overall impact on the 1999 Royals of +0.20. It is Robinson's long-term rating, built on the carcasses of guys he had previously unloaded, that illustrates the rippling effect of a general manager.

In Milwaukee that season, Sean Berry batted just .228 and lost his job permanently. Brian McRae batted .218 during a three-city farewell odyssey and went into broadcasting. Gary Gaetti's average fell 77 points from the previous season, to .204. That decline didn't even lead the Royals Alumni Association, because Detroit's Gregg Jefferies lost 101 points, from .301 to .200. In San Diego, Wally Joyner hit just .248. In San Francisco, Mark Gardner went 6–11 with a 6.47 ERA. In addition to dismal 1999 performances, all six of those players shared one other commonality: Herk Robinson had traded them. Between 1999 and his 2000 departure, Robinson averaged a long-term improvement to the Royals of 5.35 games just by the players he either unloaded or allowed to walk away. That is graduate-level addition by subtraction. Had Robinson been anything approaching as successful in other facets of the GM game, he would still probably be the Kansas City GM. As it is, Robinson's deficiencies in all other GM areas almost precisely offset his skill at dumping players, rendering him an overall non-factor in Kansas City's fates those two seasons.

RESIDUAL IMPACTS

Dan Duquette was fired by the Boston Red Sox following the 2001 season. But Duquette's impact on the Sox hardly ended with his departure. In fact, the core of the Boston team that went 93–69 in 2002 bore Duquette's stamp; Nomar, Lowe, Pedro, Manny, Wakefield, Varitek, Urbina, and Damon all either had been acquired by Duquette in trades or captured by him as free agents. His successor as GM, Mike Port, made very few moves, and they tended to be nondescript. We can think of the impact of Duquette's ghost on the 2002 Red Sox as a residual impact; the value of the players who are left behind after a GM departs. As those players either sign new contracts, are traded or cut, that residual impact fades until—several seasons down the road—it has evaporated altogether. But in its early seasons the residual impact—virtually entirely a long-term impact—can be substantial. In the case of Duquette, it amounted to 27.3 games, meaning that in 2002 the most impactful GM in the American League was Dan Duquette's ghost.

It would be wrong to simply discount the impact of dear, departed GMs because their successors live with the deals that they make. In 2003, no fewer than fifty-one men who no longer made decisions for Major League teams could nonetheless be said to have impacted the fates of those teams by decisions that had been made as much as a decade or more earlier.

There are two logical ways to calculate this residual impact. One is simply to apply the actual residual BFWs and PWs; the second is to apply a sliding scale in the same fashion that we do with the players traded or lost to free agency by operating GMs. Given the level of natural team-to-team movement that takes place among players, the latter method seems founded on a more logical foundation. The cases of Bill Lajoie and Ted Simmons illustrate the point. During the 1987 stretch run, with the Detroit Tigers in need of a veteran pitcher, Lajoie acquired Doyle Alexander from the Atlanta Braves in exchange for a hot prospect named John Smoltz. The Tigers did win the AL East, and Lajoie left the GM position after the 1990 season. But if one applied a straight, non-sliding scale to the residual rating, the effect would be to argue the implausible: that Bill Lajoie had a residual impact on the 2003 Detroit Tigers of 3.5 games. It's certainly possible that had that deal not been made, Smoltz would still be in Detroit today and performing at the same level. But a sliding scale seems more realistic.

The same can be said of Simmons, the general manager in Pittsburgh after the 1993 season who was forced by budget issues to bid farewell to free agent Barry Bonds. Absent a sliding scale, one would be forced to argue that Simmons, who left the GM's office that same winter, should be charged with a residual impact on Pittsburgh's 2003 season of −8.8 games as an outgrowth of that 1993 decision.

Applying the sliding scale substantially reduces such distortions by limiting the long-term impact of departed GMs to five seasons. In 2003, the most impactful tended for perfectly logical reasons to be the most recently removed from office. The Cubs' Andy McPhail, at +18.80 games, was number one, followed by Boston's Mike Port (+14.20), the Dodgers' Kevin Malone (+12.30), and Toronto's Gord Ash along with Texas's Doug Melvin (both +11.90). Port's rating is an anomaly in that he benefits from an inflexible rule of the residual rating: When a GM leaves office, all players not signed, promoted, or acquired by his successor are credited to his tenure. In Port's case, that tenure lasted only a single season, and the bulk of his 2003 residual rating is attributable to players—Nomar, Manny, Pedro—he simply inherited from Duquette and had the good sense not to get rid of. Duquette probably deserves most of the credit for 2003 as well as 2002, but Port gets it.

WINNERS AND LOSERS

When we look at the GM Rating, the *sine qua non* questions are, "Which general managers manipulated their teams into postseason play, and which ones manipulated their teams out of postseason play?"

As a yardstick, we can say a GM "made the difference" when he improved his team's short-term BFW/PW by more games than the number of games by which the team qualified for the postseason. The converse would also be true for teams failing to reach postseason play: If a GM's short-term moves cost his team more than the number of games by which the team missed the playoffs, it's reasonable to hold the GM accountable.

Between 1999 and 2003, there were 150 team seasons played, and 40 teams qualified for postseason play. The GMs of 15 of those 40 teams—that's 38 percent of the field—did in fact improve their teams short term by the threshold figure. Here's the honor roll:

1999

Steve Phillips, Mets, +12.20 (Mets won the wild card in a playoff with Cincinnati)

2000

Walt Jocketty, St. Louis, +19.40 (Cardinals won their division by 10 games)

Steve Phillips, Mets, +8.80 (Mets won the wild card by 8 games over Los Angeles)

Ron Schueler, White Sox, +8.70 (Sox won the AL Central by 5 games over Cleveland)

Billy Beane, Oakland, +7.20 (A's won the division by a half game over Seattle)

Pat Gillick, Seattle, +1.00 (Mariners won the wild card by 1 game over Cleveland)

2001

Walt Jocketty, St. Louis, +12.00 (Cardinals tied Houston for the NL Central; won the wild card by 3 games over San Francisco)

Gerry Hunsicker, Houston, +8.30 (Astros tied St. Louis for the NL Central; won the wild card by 3 games over San Francisco)

John Schuerholz, Atlanta, +4.70 (Braves won the NL East by 2 games over Philadelphia)

2002

Brian Sabean, San Francisco, +17.90 (Giants won the NL wild card by 11 and a half games over Houston)

Brian Cashman, Yankees, +11.00 (Yankees won the AL East by 10 and a half games over Boston)

Bill Stoneman, Anaheim, +6.20 (Angels won the AL wild card by 6 games over Boston)

2003

Larry Beinfest, Florida, +7.50 (Marlins won the NL wild card by 4 games over Houston)

Theo Epstein, Boston, +4.10 (Red Sox won the AL wild card by 2 games over Seattle)

Billy Beane, Oakland, +3.40 (A's won the AL West by 3 games over Seattle)

Beane (2000 and 2003) and Jocketty (2000 and 2001) can personally claim credit for having manipulated their teams into postseason play twice in the past five years. Ten others—Beinfest, Cashman, Epstein, Gillick, Hunsicker, Phillips, Sabean, Schuerholz, Schueler, and Stoneman—can say they did it once. Beinfest and Stoneman, of course, get extra credit, because once in the playoffs, their teams won world titles.

But if GMs can manipulate their teams *into* the playoffs, they can also manipulate their teams *out* of them. Fortunately for GMs, that doesn't appear to happen nearly as often. Between 1999 and 2003, only six times has a general manager cost his team enough games in the standings to deprive it of postseason play. Curiously, four of the six are also among the ten men who got credit for having *won* postseason spots. Here are the six:

2000

Bill Stoneman, Anaheim, −10.90 (Angels finished 9.5 games behind AL West-champion Oakland, and 9 games behind wild-card champion Seattle)

2001

Brian Sabean, San Francisco, −5.20 (Giants finished 2 games behind NL West-champion Arizona)

Kevin Malone, Los Angeles, −8.90 (Dodgers finished 6 games behind NL West-champion Arizona)

2003

J. P. Ricciardi, Toronto, −12.70 (Blue Jays finished 9 games behind wild-card champion Boston)

Gerry Hunsicker, Houston, −1.80 (Astros finished 1 game behind NL Central-champion Cubs)

Walt Jocketty, St. Louis, −9.40 (Cardinals finished 3 games behind NL Central-champion Cubs)

12

OUTGUESSING PARK EFFECTS

"Every park plays a major role in shaping the statistics of those who play there. That is not a theory. It is a fact." Bill James made that statement in a 1983 *Sport* magazine article examining the impact of what had come to be called "park effects." And when Bill James speaks on matters related to baseball statistics, his is the voice of God.

Which in a sense makes the rest of this chapter heresy. So read on at your own risk, fellow sinners. Two decades after its rise to popularity, the time is at hand to question whether in its worship of park effects the Holy Mother Church of Baseball Strategy pays homage to a ne'er-do-well.

That which statisticians commonly characterize as park effect certainly measures something. As far back as the mid 1970s, the game's best mathematical minds—James himself, Craig Wright, and Pete Palmer—working independently, developed the concept of a park effect, which they defined as the impact a particular facility has on run production. The essence of the theory is so simple that its importance hasn't even been seriously questioned. Suppose you have a slugger of good but not Bonds-ish abilities, a Larry Walker, for example. You play him for four seasons—let's take 1991–94—in the dead air of Montreal, then four more seasons—1995–98—in the slugger's paradise that is Coors Field. Presumably Walker benefits from the change if for no other reason than that Coors is a friendlier park in which to hit than Olympic. That's a park effect. The extent of the effect can be measured by comparing the player's performance against the league-wide performances in those same settings.

Here are Walker's cumulative statistics for those four-year periods:

	AB	H	2B	HR	RBI	AVG	SLG	OBA
1991–94 (Olympic)	1,900	557	129	80	329	.293	.487	.364
1995–98 (Coors)	1,788	599	141	126	356	.335	.643	.405

We can stipulate that there's nothing at all wrong with the top line. Any manager would be content to feature in his lineup a player who averages 20 homers and 82 RBIs a season with a .293 batting average. But look at the striking improvement on the bottom line: hits, doubles, and homers significantly up, and all on 112 fewer at bats; a dramatic increase in batting, slugging, and on-base average.

Those keen on park effects would nod knowingly and attribute Walker's improvement in some substantial portion to Coors. By every measure, Coors is a hitter's paradise, a fact that is not really in dispute anywhere, including here. How much of a role did Coors play in Walker's development? Well, during the four years in question, run production at Coors Field was about 55 percent more robust than elsewhere. Between 1991 and 1994, run production at Olympic Stadium in Montreal suffered through about a 6 percent depression. If Walker was really a 6 percent better hitter between 1991 and 1994 than his statistics indicated, but a 55 percent worse hitter between 1995–98 than the numbers suggest, then it's possible that the move to Coors accounted for the major portion of the improvement in his statistical line.

Which is why, advocates of park effects argue, you need to pay close attention to that particular statistic when you evaluate talent for possible acquisition. Otherwise, they point out, you may think the free agent you're signing to a multimillion dollar contract is the Mike Hampton who posted a 3.14 ERA in 2000 in Shea Stadium rather than the Mike Hampton who had ERAs of 5.41 and 6.15 in 2001 and 2002 in Coors.

You can discuss a park effect on any of several aspects of offense: home runs, batting average, hits, extra base hits, and strikeouts among them. But because it is at the heart of the game, the *sine qua non* of park effects is runs scored. When you talk about a park's true effect on offense, that's what you ought to be discussing. All else is essentially trivia.

WHAT MAKES A PARK EFFECT?

The formula for calculating a park's effect on run production is well beyond fifth-grade math. But in its essentials, it amounts to this: Add up all the runs scored by both teams in a given park. Then add up all the runs scored by the home team and that team's opponents in all that team's road games. (Interleague games have to be deleted when the teams do not meet home and home, a necessary component to getting an accurate park effect.) Then calculate the ratio of runs scored by both teams in the games played in the park being measured against the number of runs scored in the road games. The result—with 100 being neutral—is the park effect.

It is an utterly logical argument, designed, according to James in that same *Sport* magazine article, to measure the impact of five physical characteristics. The characteristics are:

1. Dimensions: How large is the park? Does it inflate or depress home run totals? Does it favor a lefty or a righty?
2. Visibility: How is the lighting? How is the hitting background? These factors can logically influence strikeout totals.
3. Foul territory: Is it expansive (as in the Oakland Coliseum) or relatively sparse (as at Wrigley Field)? The difference could theoretically amount to a couple of extra outs per game.
4. Playing surfaces: Does it have a natural grass surface or artificial turf? And in either case, is the surface fast or slow? Whatever the answer, it will impact the number of hits that do or do not get through the infield.

5. Climate: How high above sea level is the park? The higher the better for hitters. Coors, at roughly one mile up, is easily the big league champ in this respect. Second is Atlanta at a relatively trifling fifth of a mile. Cool temperatures act to depress batting skills; wind can obviously either depress or inflate offense on a daily basis.

Taken together, these five characteristics share one central attribute: Relatively speaking, they do not, in and of themselves, succumb to the whims of the home team's talent, or lack of same. Ballparks don't get any higher or lower, they don't move from climate to climate, the infield grass is (presumably) cut at the same level. While changes in dimension or playing surface do occur, they are infrequent, are not influenced by whether the good guys are at bat or in the field, and are pretty well documented over time.

COORS AND DEVIANT BEHAVIOR: I

There is, at least theoretically, a hierarchy to ballparks, those that are pitchers' places and those that favor offense, and in constructing a team it logically follows that it is important to recognize the distinction. For the record, here is the 2003 hierarchy, starting with the most pitcher-friendly park, and proceeding along the offensive scale.

San Diego	82
Los Angeles	83
Oakland	85
Philadelphia	86
Cleveland	87
Anaheim	89
Atlanta	90
Detroit	90
New York Yankees	92
St. Louis	92
Baltimore	93

Chicago Cubs	95
Florida	95
Tampa Bay	95
Cincinnati	96
Chicago W. Sox	96
Seattle	96
New York Mets	99
Pittsburgh	100
San Francisco	100
Minnesota	101
Milwaukee	104
Houston	106
Boston	108
Toronto	115
Texas	123
Colorado	125
Arizona	126
Kansas City	131
Montreal (Olympic)	137
Montreal (Bithorn)	155

Having spelled out the components of park effects, let's toy with a more substantive question: Is it actually useful information to those charged with constructing a team?

Generally speaking, the five conditions first outlined by Bill James in his groundbreaking *Sport* magazine article—dimension, visibility, foul territory, surface, and climate—share one common and binding trait: They are fixed and immutable. (The occasional exception here is weather, where there can be year-to-year variations, although we would not expect those to be profound.) In other words, it does not matter whether the home team is a bunch of fence busters or pansyweights, whether the pitching staff is led by Greg Maddux or Mike Maddux. The formula for park effect theoretically renders it substantially immune from such changeable influences.

GOOD OLD UNCHANGING WRIGLEY

Purely for purposes of statistical analysis—calculating the real difference between one group of Larry Walker's seasons and a second group—park effect is unassailable. But to be meaningful as a team-building tool, since GMs are interested in upcoming performance, it must reliably predict the future, not simply quantify the past. We can perform two real-life tests as a gauge of the validity of this premise insofar as it impacts team-building. The first is the Wrigley Field test.

Say you leave a park utterly alone—the way, for instance Wrigley Field has been left alone—over a period of decades. In such a laboratory setting, assuming park effect to be a useful predictor of performance, the park effect on run production ought to be relatively constant.

Wrigley is in fact a good case study because baseball is played there essentially as it has been played for a half century. In fact, Phil Lowry's widely praised 1985 book on ballpark histories, *Green Cathedrals,* documented only two dimension changes at Wrigley since 1938. In 1957, the distance from home plate to the backstop was shortened by two feet. Then in 1982, it was restored to its former distance. In 1970, a wire basket was added atop the existing brick wall. The field has always been grass, the wind has always been brisk, and the temperatures have always been changeable. (There have been two changes of note since *Green Cathedrals*; the addition of lights in the mid 1980s, and the addition of three more rows of seats behind home plate in 2004, reducing foul territory.)

In such a laboratory-type park, one might expect that a graph of the park's effect on run production to look like a relatively straight line, allowing for those seasonal fluctuations attributable to random chance. In assessing the predictive power of park effects for team-building purposes, it's especially important for that pattern to be reasonably constant. The graph below represents the actual year-by-year variation in park effects for Wrigley Field between 1992 and 2003.

Something different from the predictable mode we anticipated, what we in fact get when we graph Wrigley's park effect is a line rather resembling a roller coaster, complete with some fairly substantial dips

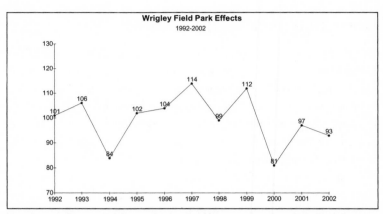

Between 1992 and 2002, the park effect at Wrigley Field varied by 33 points, from a low of 81 in 2000 to a high of 114 in 1997.

and climbs. In 1994, for example, Wrigley's park effect was 84, meaning that it depressed offense by 16 percent. A mere three seasons later, in 1997, Wrigley inflated offense by 14 percent, a variation of 30 percent, about twice the maximum amount that ought to be explicable. In 1999, Wrigley inflated offense by 12 percent; in 2000, it depressed it by 19 percent. Now many things happened to the fortunes of the Cubs between 1994 and 1997, but none of them involved either the dimensions, foul territory, visibility, or playing surfaces at Wrigley. That leaves only the wind, which is infamous at Wrigley. But is it infamous enough to account for a 31 percent swing in the park effect? One of the aspects of park effects we're going to explore in greater depth momentarily is the role played by other parks in its calculation. But in this instance, it isn't easy to attribute such fluctuations to changes in other parks. Between 1993 and 1994, the only adjustment of consequence to the physical setting in any of the fourteen National League parks in which the Cubs played involved an adjustment to the outfield fences at the Florida Marlins' Joe Robbie Stadium. That impacted exactly seven Chicago Cubs games.

Following the run production depression of 1994, the Wrigley park effect rebounded by a full 18 percent in 1995. Coors Field opened in 1995, a fact which—with its park effect of 164—was certain to tug to some extent on the effects of other parks. But here is the problem with attributing the rebound of Wrigley's park effect in whole or in part to the debut of Coors: Because it is based on a comparison of run production at home versus on the road, *park effect is a zero-sum number*. Introducing a great new hitter's paradise into the equation—one, for instance, with a park effect of 164—ought to depress the park effects everywhere else. In other words, during the year Coors opened, one would have expected Wrigley's park effect to deflate. Instead, it rose by about 18 percent.

Such occurrences, even though true, might theoretically be explained as anomalies, except that they are not. One of the virtues of Lowry's book is that, since it catalogs every change made to every park and playing surface, it allows us to itemize any adjustment to a park effect that might be attributable to one of those five factors. The graph below is a look at the park effects chart for Wrigley Field across a longer, two-decade period between the mid 1960s and mid 1980s. Over that period, not a single physical change involving dimension,

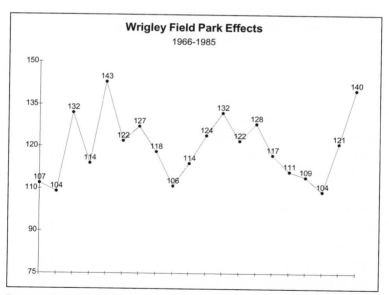

Between 1966 and 1985, the playing characteristics of Wrigley in Chicago remained unchanged. It was consistently a hitter's park. Even so, the park effects varied by 37.5 percent, from a low of 104 (in 1967 and 1983) to a high of 143 (in 1970).

visibility, foul territory, surface, or climate occurred at Wrigley that would modify, in any direction, the park's effect on offense.

Again, the sudden changes are, for team-building purposes, dramatic. In 1967, Wrigley Field inflated offense by only 4 percent; in 1968, the same park inflated offense by 32 percent. A year later the figure was back to 14 percent; a year after that and it was 43 percent. If this is the natural range of motion of a park effect—the workings of random chance—then is there any point in trying to build your team around a park . . . or, if you are a GM, in even knowing what the park effect is?

THE SPORTSMAN'S ANOMALY

There is a second informative test we may perform, one that can be called the Sportsman's Park Anomaly, which sheds a lot of light on the context in which park effects must be understood. Between 1920 and 1953, Sportsman's Park—later known as Busch Stadium and located at Grand and Dodier in St. Louis—simultaneously played host to two Major League teams, the National League Cardinals and the American League Browns. For many of those three decades and change, the fortunes of those teams could not have been more different: the Cardinals won nine pennants, the Browns won just one . . . and they lost the 1944 World Series to the Cardinals. Over those same years, the Browns managed to finish in the AL second division two dozen times, more than three times as often as the Cards.

But their differences are not of interest here; what is of interest is the park effect of Sportsman's Park during those thirty-three cohabited seasons. Because if the park—which is to say the physical facility and related environmental conditions—truly is the influence projected by park effect, then we would have reason to expect it to be roughly consistent in games played by both the Browns and Cards during those years. None of the five factors commonly recognized as park effects could be altered for one as opposed to the other. St. Louis was as hot, windy, or rainy a town for one team's games as for another's, the infield was as baked for one as for the other, and if the fences were moved, they were moved for both. Beyond that, the period 1920 to 1953 is an era of remarkable stability in Major League park construction. There are no franchise moves at all, relatively few dimensional adjustments, and just a handful of new facilities—Yankee Stadium and Municipal Stadium in Cleveland being the noteworthy ones. The only change of true significance: the introduction of night baseball, which occurred at various dates around the league between 1935 and 1948.

In short, we would expect a graph of the lines indicating the park effects for those two teams during those two years to run—with reasonable allowances for night ball and random chance—both parallel and constant. Having said that, here is the actual graph of the park effects for the St. Louis Cardinals and St. Louis Browns between the years 1920 and 1953:

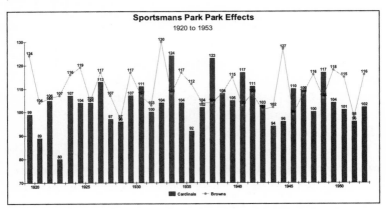

Over the thirty-three-year period, the park effect at Sportsman's Park averaged 114 when the Browns played there, but 107 when the Cardinals played there, an average difference of 6 percent in a park that was always identically outfitted for each team.

But the most striking element of the chart is the wide variations in occurring both within seasons and within teams.

In 1920, the park effect at Sportsman's Park was 99—giving pitchers a 5 percent advantage—when the Cardinals were at home. But when the Browns hit town, Sportsman's became one of the game's great offensive parks, giving hitters a 24 percent advantage.

The difference was 27 percent in 1923, 15 percent in 1925, and 26 percent in 1933. That season, Sportsman's favored offense by a tepid 4 percent when National League teams played there. But on the days when AL clubs swung into town, they swung big; at a 30 percent boost to run production, for AL teams (but not NL teams) in 1933, Sportsman's became one of the great batting parks of all time.

The very next year, Sportsman's pivoted, favoring offense by 24 percent during National League games, but by only 8 percent during American League games. That change is not explicable within the confines of the commonly understood definition of park effect.

In 1938, National League teams again enjoyed a big offensive advantage. For them, Sportsman's produced runs at a rate 23 percent above the norm; for American Leaguers, Sportsman's favored offense by a modest 4 percent.

In 1940, Sportsman's was again an American League hitter's park, by a margin of 15 percent. In 1941, it favored the National League hitters by 17 percent. American League hitters returned to favor by 27 percent in 1945, a season in which Sportsman's Park depressed National League offense by 4 percent. In 1948, Sportsman's was a perfectly neutral park for National League teams, but for American Leaguers it inflated offense by 16 percent.

In the thirty-three seasons the park hosted dual occupancy, the two teams' games produced park effects that differed by 20 percent or more five times. The ratings varied from a low of 80 for National Leaguers in 1923 to a high of 130 for American Leaguers in 1933.

Variations of the Sportsman's Anomaly exist in other locales. The Yankees and Mets shared Shea Stadium for two seasons in the 1970s during the renovation of Yankee Stadium. During those two seasons, Shea was a neutral park for one of the teams and a pitcher's park for the other—and the identities switched between the two seasons. In 1974, Shea's park effect was 90 when the Yankees played there—indicative of a pitcher's park—but 98 when the Mets were at home. In 1975, the park effect was 99 for the Yanks but only 89 for the Mets.

The Phillies and Athletics shared Shibe Park in Philadelphia for sixteen seasons between the late 1930s and mid 1950s. When the

Phillies played there, Shibe was consistently a neutral park with a tendency to favor pitching. In all sixteen seasons, the park effect for Phillies games fell between 89 and 100. But for Athletics games, the range was substantially wider, ranging from a low of 84 (in 1950) to a high of 124 just two seasons later. That's a forty-point swing for the same team in the same park within two seasons.

How can this be explained? Well, mathematicians can actually explain it fairly easily. That's because they understand that park effects actually expresses nothing more than a ratio: the ratio of runs scored by the home and visiting teams in one park measured against all other parks. How does that help mathematicians explain the ability of Sportsman's Park to be great for hitters when the Browns play there but great for pitchers when the Cards play there? Simple again; Sportsman's Park is only half the picture. The other half includes all the other ballparks in which the Cardinals and Browns (plus their opponents) spent half their seasons—and those ballparks were almost entirely different every year. The Browns never played in Wrigley Field or Braves Field, just as the Cardinals never played in Tiger Stadium or Griffith Stadium. Viewing park effects in that light, it's no trick for a mathematician to see perfect harmony in Sportsman's playing 6 percent more favorably to offense when the Browns were home than when the Cardinals were. All that tells a mathematician is that National League parks of the period must have been a lot more hitter-friendly than American League parks. In other words, park effect is quite noticeably relative.

METAPHYSICAL PARK EFFECTS

But is relativism the only reason why the St. Louis Browns and their American League opponents did score runs in Sportsman's Park at a rate 30 percent above the rate at which those same teams scored runs elsewhere? Could anything else account for such a change?

Variations in pitching rotations could create part of the swing. If in a given season Pedro Martinez's turn never comes up when the Boston Red Sox visit New York, but if he opposes them two or three

times in Boston, how much of an impact will that have on what we refer to as the "park effect"? Such a chance-based variation hardly seems
likely to be that significant, and the question is not likely to be answered without much more research.

In *Total Baseball* (1984), John Thorn and Pete Palmer suggested
that part of the answer might not be physical at all, but psychological.
We might lump these together as "metaphysical park effects." Drawing on a 1980 study by Robert Kingsley, they suggested that the attitude of the players, and specifically the way the park changes their
view of how the game must be played in order to win, should also be
considered as part of the equation. If that is the case, then managerial
style may also be considered a "park effect." In order to test that premise, let's review one of our earlier charts, but this time consider it in
the context of managerial changes.

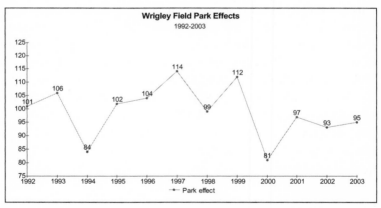

Between 1992 and 2002, the park effect at Wrigley Field varied by 33 points, from
a low of 81 in 2000 to a high of 114 in 1997.

In 1992, the manager of the Chicago Cubs was Jim Lefebvre.
Lefebvre also managed the Cubs in 1993. Prior to the 1994 season,
however, he was replaced by Tom Trebelhorn. Trebelhorn was in turn
replaced by Jim Riggleman for 1995. Riggleman continued at the
Cubs helm until 2000, when he was replaced by Don Baylor.

Can we chart any relationship between managerial moves and park effects? Perhaps. When Trebelhorn managed, park effects at Wrigley nose-dived. During Riggleman's tenure, they resumed their prior levels. Baylor's first season in 2000 again produced a very subdued park effect. It recovered some in 2001, but still not to the usual levels.

Wind? Nope. In 2000, wind patterns at Wrigley were essentially unchanged from the previous season. So let's ask a more provocative question: Could there have been something in the way Tom Trebelhorn or Don Baylor managed a ball game that tended to depress Wrigley Field's park effect? A quick glance at additional evidence is highly contradictory. Review again the graph of park effects at Wrigley Field between 1966 and 1985. Between 1966 and 1972, when the manager was Leo Durocher, Wrigley's park effect varied wildly, between 104 and 143. But between 1977 and 1979, when Herman Franks drew up home-team strategy, it assumed a more stable pattern, varying between 122 and 132. Lee Elia followed Franks as manager for two seasons during which the park effect fell to 109 and 104. One assumes Elia managed differently from Franks; perhaps that's a factor in the decline. Jim Frey followed Elia in 1984 and 1985 and the park effect soared, to 121 and then 140.

A few years ago, a retired professor named Willie Runquist advanced his own explanation as to why park effect doesn't work as a predictive tool, suggesting that the answer lies in what he called a confusion of "genuine park effects with differences in overall level of home team performance." False park effects mask as real ones, he concluded, due to no other reason than the overall superiority of the home team. Here is his explanation in three paragraphs:

Assume that there are two teams, the Sluggers and the Wimps, who play each other in identical indoor stadiums. Because of travel, etc., each team scores 5 percent more runs at home and 5 percent fewer on the road. Note that this is not a "park effect," but a "home cooking effect" that exists in both parks.

The Sluggers overall score 600 runs, 315 at Slugger Stadium and 285 of them at Wimps Field. On the other hand, the Wimps score 400 runs, 210 at home and 190 when they play in Slugger Stadium.

The conventional method for calculating park effects looks at the total number of runs scored by both teams in both parks. In Slugger Stadium, the two teams score 315 + 190 = 505 runs, and in Wimps Field the two teams score 285 + 210 = 495 runs. Via this method, Slugger Stadium appears to be a hitter's park, while Wimps Field appears to be a pitcher's park. We have "created" an apparent park effect when in fact there is none. There is only a general home team advantage and overall differences between the two teams' ability to score runs.

This does not mean, Runquist emphasizes, that park effects do not exist; rather, that they can be biased beyond recognition (and, presumably, beyond functional value) by the home team's overall level of performance.

COORS AND DEVIANT BEHAVIOR: II

Since we know that a park effect exists, a fair question is whether this phenomenon is changing. In the late 1960s and early 1970s, an entire new class of "cookie cutter" parks were constructed, in St. Louis, Philadelphia, Cincinnati, and Pittsburgh. In each case they replaced a sort of quirky old park that might have been expected to have a substantial park effect. Did the introduction of these cookie cutter parks homogenize park effects in the National League? Did we trend toward sameness in substance as well as in style?

Since all four of the cookie cutters opened between 1966 and 1971—and all in the National League—any standardization ought to show up in the league's park effects for those seasons. In 1966, the year Busch Memorial Stadium in St. Louis opened, the standard deviation for National League park effects was 12.53. We can use that as a baseline for comparison. It fell to 11.4 in 1967, then rose in 1968 to 17.8. In 1969, it fell again, all the way to 6.52, meaning that in 1969 it made very, very little difference in run production—almost coincidental difference—where a National League game was played. Remember, that was the season before most of the big changes in parks.

In midseason 1970, Riverfront Stadium in Cincinnati and Three Rivers Stadium in Pittsburgh replaced Crosley Field and Forbes Field; each of the replacements was a far less quirky, more standardized park. Yet in 1970, the standard deviation for National League park effects rebounded from its compressed state of the season before to a more robust 15.99, a figure suggesting that in 1970 it made a big difference indeed in run production where a game was played. Veterans Stadium in Philadelphia, the fourth cookie cutter park, opened in April of 1971. That season the standard deviation for National League park effects was 12.03, almost exactly where it was when Busch Stadium dawned the cookie cutter era in 1966.

Here are the standard deviations for National League park effects for the succeeding five seasons: 14.65, 16.74, 10.66, 10.31, 17.14. This is not the neatest grouping of numbers one might ever hope to see, but neither does it suggest either mathematical anarchy or, more to the point, homogenization of park effects in the National League.

Let's fast-forward now to the 1990s. Superficially, the standard deviation of National League park effects for the 1993 through 2003 seasons appears to suggest that the site of a game makes a significant difference. Here are the numbers:

1993	15.51
1994	13.43
1995	21.01
1996	22.01
1997	11.84
1998	19.28
1999	18.57
2000	20.49
2001	16.61
2002	15.65
2003	15.30

But there is a trick in here: In 1993, the National League began playing baseball in Denver, with the extreme park effects that emanate out of its mile-high location. Below is the table for the standard deviation of all National League parks except the one in Denver for the years between 1993 and 2003:

1993	6.27
1994	10.56
1995	12.26
1996	9.96
1997	7.99
1998	11.38
1999	8.53
2000	11.54
2001	11.12
2002	12.75
2003	14.45

The opening of a new stadium in Houston—like Coors, a hitter's park—may have influenced the increase for the 2000 through 2003 seasons. Still, historically, these are not unusually high standard deviations, and they suggest that in the National League at least something is at work to actually homogenize the impact of park effect. Is that something Coors Field? Remember what we noted earlier in this chapter: Park effect is a zero-sum number. As Coors' park effect detaches itself by an unheard-of factor of three (and sometimes four) standard deviations from all of the league's other parks, is it reducing their relationship with one another to a matter of slightly lesser significance? Perhaps what an entire generation of cookie cutter parks failed to do is taking place now, except at a (geographically) higher level.

BUILDING FOR YOUR PARK

Of all possible study topics concerning park effect, the most pertinent is this: Should teams be built around their park? If you've got a hitter's park, are you better off to corral a stable of sluggers, or to look even harder for pitching? In a pitcher's park, do teams constructed around pitching flourish? Is a balanced approach better? Or does it even matter?

Since the evidence amply demonstrates that park effect is not a predictable physical quantity, but also contains elements outside a GM's control—some of them metaphysical, others pertaining to foreign parks—the honest answer almost certainly is, "It doesn't matter." After all, what's the point of worrying whether to shape the Cleveland Indians to the confines of Jacobs Field when the park effect at Jacobs Field itself has ranged between 87 and 114 just since 1994? For heaven's sake, which park would you build the team for: Jacobs the hitter's park or Jacobs the pitcher's park?

But in cases where the general tendency of the park is well established, the idea of building toward or away from that may still be valid if there is evidence that doing so will improve a team's chances of winning. And while the numbers often do vary too greatly to be of substantial value, it is nonetheless a fair statement that some Major League parks tend to fit broad categories of classification.

The best way to analyze the reliability of the characteristics of Major League parks would be to perform a standard deviation test on each. Since the park effect at Minute Maid is influenced by factors as diverse and distant as the opening of the Great American Ballpark, not even a standard deviation test will offer a certain guidepost. But carefully analyzed—and we'll try to analyze carefully—the data may provide some suggestions.

Here's the test. For each current Major League ballpark except Great American (which only opened in 2003), we've calculated both the average park effect and the standard deviation either since the park's opening or since 1994, whichever was most recent. The higher the average, obviously, the more hitter-friendly the park. But the higher the standard deviation, the less reliable the characterization.

As a rule of thumb, hitter's parks show a greater variance than pitcher's parks. Of the 29 parks included in the survey, six had an average park effect above 106, suggesting a hitter's park. But in four of those cases, the standard deviation of the park effects was 10 or better, suggesting that the rating is, let us be kind, fluid. The two exceptions, by the way, were both very new parks—Minute Maid in Houston and PNC in Pittsburgh—where only four and three years' worth of data exist. Time will tell whether the park effects of those two stadiums also turn out to be volatile.

In contrast, there were seven parks with average park effects below 94, and in none of those seven cases did the standard deviation top 10. The highest was Network Associates in Oakland, with a 9.2 deviation, but the average standard deviation of those parks was below 6. So as a general proposition, pitcher's parks seem to be more reliably so than hitter's parks.

What follows is the most reasonable characterization I can make of each park, including the average park effect between 1994 and 2003 and the standard deviation.

Reliably hitter's parks: Coors Field (Colorado), 151.9, 15.7; Minute Maid (Houston), 111.8, 4.9. Coors has the widest range of park effects of any Major League park—a high of 172 and a low of 125—but at these altitudes we are only debating degrees of hitter-friendliness. Minute Maid's standard deviation is the lowest for any park with an effect above 100; with a minimum park effect to date of 106, it has to date given no indication that it is anything other than the hitter's paradise it is commonly viewed as.

Usually hitter's parks: Bank One (Phoenix), 111.2, 11.0; Kauffman (Kansas City), 110.6, 12.4; The Ballpark at Arlington (Texas), 110.0, 10.0; PNC Park (Pittsburgh), 106.3, 5.3. After two seasons as essentially a neutral park, Bank One is probably moving toward being viewed as a more reliably hitter's park. Kauffman has simply been all over the place, ascribable in part but not in whole to some significant park-related changes. Its park effect was 118 in 1994, falling to 92 in 1995, then climbing as high as 131 in 2003. Kauffman has been reliably a hitter's park for the past four seasons; in another season or two we may view it as reliably a hitter's park. Arlington is just kind of funky. Its rating was 114 in 2000, but that fell to 99 in 2001, then climbed to 123 in 2002 and again in 2003. PNC's three seasons include one in which it was a decided hitter's park, another in which it was a borderline hitter's park, and a third in which it was perfectly neutral.

Reliably neutral: Fenway Park (Boston), 103.6, 5.3; Metrodome (Minnesota), 103.5, 6.5; Skydome (Toronto), 101.4, 6.4; Tropicana (Tampa Bay), 100.0, 4.0; Busch Stadium (St. Louis), 99.2, 5.1; Turner Field (Atlanta), 96.7, 6.1. Tropicana is the second most predictable park in the majors, with just one rating (and that in its initial season) that was not between 95 and 100. Busch is nearly as reliable a neutral park, although it has been a pitcher's park in 2002 and 2003. In six of the past ten seasons, Fenway's park effect has been between 94 and 106, a reasonable standard for designating a neutral park. The three exceptions were all minor, twice to 107 and then in 2003 to 108. The Metrodome and Skydome don't look alike, but they play alike. Both have been neutral parks with deviations in the 6.5 range that is about average for a big league park over a decade. Two pitcher-friendly seasons since its 1997 opening intimate against Turner's neutrality, but with an overall 96.7 average and a moderate variation, it is a fairly reliable neutral park.

Unreliably neutral: Olympic (Montreal), 105.8, 14.1; Jacobs (Cleveland), 100.6, 8.1; Edison (Anaheim), 99.9, 7.8; Veterans (Philadelphia), 99.6, 12.2; Yankee Stadium (New York Yankees), 93.9, 7.3; Wrigley (Chicago Cubs), 98.1, 10.1; U.S. Cellular (Chicago White Sox), 97.2, 8.2; Pro Player (Florida), 85.1, 9.5. GMs trying to build teams around these parks are on a fool's errand. To use the recently departed Veterans Stadium as an example, in its final ten seasons it rated above 106 three times, below 94 five times, and between 99 and 105 twice. To say that its average for that period was 99.6 is saying nothing of consequence. We think of Pro Player as a pitcher's park, and it generally is. But in 1994 the park effect was 121. Yankee Stadium may be the toughest park of all to characterize. Although never a good hitter's park (its high park effect for the decade is 103), the stadium produces effects that are inconsistent. Twice since 1994 it has been an extreme pitcher's park, with ratings low in the 80s in '94 and again in '99. On the other hand, four times since 1995 Yankee

Stadium has produced a park effect between 101 and 103. As for Olympic, *sacre bleu!* In 2003, its park effect was 137, a 58-point stretch just since 1998, when the park effect was 79, and a 38-point leap even from 2002. Part of the explanation may lie in the Expos playing fewer than the normal number of home games in Montreal in 2003, and therefore destabilizing the numbers. But c'mon, 38 and 58 points.

Often pitcher-friendly: Camden Yards (Baltimore), 94.9, 7.8; Shea Stadium (New York Mets), 94.8, 7.5. It's almost fair to class Camden with pitcher's parks; after a 113 in 1994, its rating has only topped 93 once since 1998. The same is almost as true of Shea, with two ratings above 93 since 1998.

Reliably pitcher's parks: Dodger Stadium (Los Angeles), 82.8, 4.3; Qualcomm (San Diego), 86.4, 6.9; Pac Bell (San Francisco), 88.6, 7.4; Safeco (Seattle), 88.6, 5.1; Comerica (Detroit), 88.8, 1.6; Network Associates (Oakland), 91.3, 9.2. For the most part, these parks are widely and accurately understood to favor pitchers. In the forty-three seasons collectively played in them since 1994, the parks produced thirty-six ratings below 94, and only one above 106—a 108 at Network Associates in 1997. Despite that rating, five other seasons with park effects in the 80s establish that facility's identity beyond question. Since its opening in 2000, Comerica has been the most consistent park in the majors, with all ratings between 86 and 90. The 1.6 deviation for its park factor is almost impossibly low to maintain. Even so, since that deviation is still half the next lowest deviation of any park, it's safe to say that Comerica will remain a pitcher's park unless they bring the fences in a lot more than they have.

Check back in a few years: Miller Field (Milwaukee), 99.3, 5.9. Although the data suggest neutrality, the numbers are too fragmentary after three years to draw that conclusion. Miller had two seasons modestly favoring offense, with park ratings of 103 and 104. In the third season, however, it rated 91, a very pitcher-friendly number. Miller's identity so far defies characterization.

13

As I Was Saying . . .

A summary of eight guidelines for managers and six more for general managers from The Book.

FOR MANAGERS

Steal more frequently, but with fewer players. A good marker for being a successful base stealer is a 75 percent success rate. In 2003, thirty-seven major leaguers attained that success rate with at least ten attempts. Collectively, they accounted for 810 stolen bases, and only got caught 166 times. But for the most part, neither they nor their managers took particular advantage of their skill. Only four (Crawford, Pierre, Podsednik, and Roberts) actually attempted as many as 50 steals. Meanwhile, the MLB steal success rate was 69 percent. In short, the wrong people are trying to steal too many bases, and the right people aren't trying to steal enough.

Use the ball and strike count to your advantage. Batters should aggressively work the strike zone for hittable pitches until they have two strikes on them. At that point, their philosophy must become a lot more defensive.

Fall in love with switch-hitters only selectively. After they open a roster slot for a twelfth pitcher, teams turn to switch-hitters out of a belief that one guy can take the place of two. The result—carrying both a twelfth-best pitcher and a guy who can't hit from at least one side of the plate—doesn't sound appealing. A more logical approach would be to tell the pitching coach to muddle through with eleven arms, then find a platoon of two decent (perhaps even good?) hitters. You know, like they did in the old days . . . 1993.

Pitching's magic number: 115. Distinguish between good starters and truly good starters . . . then treat the truly good ones as the useful commodities they are. They do not wear down, they improve with work. If they are having good games, their performance does not decline to the point where a relief pitcher is a better bet until the 115-pitch mark . . . and then only if it's a closer.

The false worship of that which is new. In which inning are the most runs scored? The answer, widely known, is the first inning. One widely understood reason is the offense's ability to set up its lineup to maximize production. A second is the prospect that a pitcher is not yet fully prepared to pitch in game conditions. There could be several reasons for this: inadequate warmup, the need to adjust to the mound, or to an umpire's strike zone. Why would one assume that a new pitcher in the seventh, eighth, or ninth inning would defy the trend that is so commonly understood and accepted of pitchers in the first inning? No need to answer: That's a rhetorical question.

Use a hierarchical rotation. . . . A pitcher only has value when he pitches. Most teams today use a five-man rotation, and that is NOT the same as using their best pitchers on four days rest. A more hierarchical approach that included a five-day rotation for a team's aces would put those pitchers on the field two to three more starts per season. Since we've already established that the best pitchers tend to improve their performance with work, the fact that those starts would come at the expense of the lesser-quality fourth and fifth pitching slots would reduce the team earned run average and yield more victories.

. . . . Not a hierarchical bullpen. The hierarchical bullpen is another matter entirely. Simply put, it ought to be scrapped, with managers according themselves the leeway to make game-based decisions. This can be demonstrated statistically to be no threat to performance, and it would reduce salaries by abolishing the mystical job of "set-up man" and, in several cases, "closer." A corollary point: Almost no closer is worth really big money, because closers are not reliable from season to season, and because there is a large chance that you can pull somebody out of the system to do what most closers do. Yes, there are occasional exceptions. Eric Gagne is one, so is Mariano Rivera. And that's about it. Here's the full list of pitchers who saved at least ten games in each season between 1999 and 2004: Armando Benitez, Troy Percival, and Mariano Rivera.

The dawn of bullpen awareness. Fascinatingly, there were signs as 2004 drew along that this reality of the bullpen might finally be setting in. Late in June, David Leonhardt of the *New York Times* noted that about 16 percent of the appearances of "closers" were occurring with men on base, up from 12 percent in 2003. That means they weren't automatically coming in at the start of the ninth inning, as had been established practice. Closers were also pitching more than one inning slightly more frequently. He quoted Chris Antonetti, assistant general manager of the Cleveland Indians, as observing a greater "situational awareness" . . . a desire to "use your best relievers at the most critical, highly leveraged point in the game." Bill James brought some of that same philosophy to his job as an executive with the Boston Red Sox. "Using your relief ace to protect a three-run lead," James was quoted as saying, "is like a business using a top executive to negotiate fire insurance." The Sox were widely roasted in 2003 after the Sox pen underperformed, and especially after the debacle against New York in the postseason. But Boston's problem wasn't the logic; it was that in the great relief corps crapshoot, they had no luck. James's philosophy was correct.

FOR GENERAL MANAGERS

Favor your rotation. Teams that make a payroll priority of starting pitching, or those that take a balanced approach to payroll, seem to reap benefits from that decision. What about "hitting teams?" Clubs that pay an inordinate amount to their projected three-four-five batters may have fun—fans dig the long ball—but they do not win. There were twenty-two such teams between 1999 and 2003, but only two— the 2000 Giants and 2002 Athletics—played in the postseason. Their average winning percentage is about 47 percent, their average salary about $64.08 million for the period.

Money isn't everything . . . at the moment. Sorry, GMs, but you cannot cry poverty as a rationale for finishing fourth or fifth. Bill Stoneman, Larry Beinfest, Terry Ryan, and Billy Beane have undermined your argument on the field, and it doesn't fare much better in the computer, either. In the contemporary game—by which we mean since about 2000—the relationship between a team's payroll and its on-field performance has become quite neutral. As recently as 2001, that relationship could be expressed as 31 percent; that is, we could think of payroll as 31 percent of the reason why a team did what it did. That's well below levels of the late 1990s, when there was a suffocating 60 to 80 percent relationship between what a team paid and how it did. In 2003, the relationship was below 50 percent. That might be changing. The 2004 relationship climbed back to about 52 percent, suggesting we may be near a return to the days when money rules.

No superstar is worth the money they get, but overpay anyway. Just use some judgment. To use a contemporary example, Carlos Beltran is arguably the best center fielder in the majors. From a money standpoint, that makes him worth about $8 million. You may pay twice that, but at least he delivers quality. If Mike Piazza comes available, he is another matter. In 2003, Piazza earned $15.5 million, in return for which he produced $2.9 million in Earned Value, a deficit of about $12 million. His many supporters will find this hard to swallow, but in 2003 he was the fourteenth most valuable catcher in the NL. When stars come onto the market, you run into these types of overpayment problems all the time. Virtually all stars are grossly overpaid. The average fifteen-year-plus player got about a $6 million salary in 2003, in return for which he produced an EV of about half that much. But $3 million is still a very good EV; you could win a lot of pennants with a core of players producing $3 million in EV. The problem that tends to plague losing teams is their inability to judge which overpaid players will still yield good value, and which will not. The issue is complicated by the fact that these judgments often have to be made on a multi-season basis.

There is no superstar learning curve. When in June of 2004 the Kansas City Royals traded their best player, Beltran, for three prospects, the deal was roundly lamented as a comment on the financial condition of the game. Beltran was to become a free agent at season's end, and the Royals, who run a tight ship, had no hope of re-signing him. Faced with that reality, Royals' GM Allard Baird took the best deal he could get. In retrospect, Baird's real error was his failure to lock Beltran into a multi-season deal as soon as he showed superstar promise. Had he done so, it might have cost him some money early on, but it would have secured Beltran's future as an organizational building block. Superstars show their ability early in their careers. The prudent GM will prioritize locking them up on terms that are favorable both to them and the team.

Build for the long term, and build through signings. Joe Garagiola, Jr., built the Arizona Diamondbacks up literally from nothing in 1997 to the world's championship in 2001. Between 2000 and 2001, all of Garagiola's moves improved the D-Backs barely at all. Yet the groundwork he had already laid—acquiring Curt Schilling, Randy Johnson, and Luis Gonzalez—laid the bedrock for that world's title. The pre-2001 Garagiola moves can be said to have made that 2001 Arizona team nearly twenty-one games better in the standings than they otherwise would have been. As a measure of the potential long-term impact of player moves, this is not unusual. The only GMs since 1999 who have helped their teams short term by an average of five games or more per season have been former Boston executive Dan Duquette (+5.58), and the Yankees' Brian Cashman (+5.04). By contrast fifteen general managers have averaged a long-term improvement to their teams in excess of five games for the past five seasons, and the figure is often much in excess. For the 2002 season, ironically the year he was fired from his position, Duquette's previous deals made the Boston Red Sox twenty-nine games better in the standings than they otherwise would have been.

Farming? Be patient . . . and be alert for crop failure. Few teams—the Minnesota Twins are an exception—build themselves up over time through their farm systems. There may be a bit of self-fulfilling prophecy to this—teams that are already close to contention tend to prefer veteran players to relying on their farms—but the record is clear. Short term, it is next to impossible to turn a team around with youngsters. The 2003 Arizona Diamondbacks improved by 8.4 games due to their system products . . . and still finished sixteen and a half games back. The last playoff-bound team that relied heavily on its farm products was the 2001 St. Louis Cardinals, whose rookie class consisted of several warm bodies and Albert Pujols.

PLATOON COEFFICIENT

The platoon coefficient may be calculated either for an individual player, a team, or a manager.

To determine a player's platoon coefficient, you must first know the percentage of games in which that player's team faced right-handed and left-handed starting pitching. (Typically right-handers start between 70 and 75 percent of games.) Subtract the percentage of the player's starts versus same-side pitching from the percentage of games played by the team against pitchers who threw the same way; the result, expressed as a percentage, is the player's platoon coefficient.

Example: In 1999, Todd Walker, a left-hand hitter, started 133 games for the Minnesota Twins, 117 against right-handed pitchers and 16 against left-hand pitchers. Walker made 12.0 percent of his starts against left-handers. The Twins played 22.9 percent of their games (37 of 161) against left-handed starters. Walker's platoon coefficient is 12 percent–22.9 percent or 10.9 percent.

Example: Ken Griffey, Jr., who bats left-handed, started 160 games for Seattle, 125 against right-handers and 35 against left-handers. Griffey thus made 21.9 percent of his starts against left-handers. The Mariners played 21.6 percent of their games against left-handed starters. Griffey's platoon coefficient is 21.9 percent–21.6 percent, or +.3 percent. In a strict sense, Griffey was reverse platooned, since the only two games he missed were both against right-handers. As the numbers suggest, however, that characterization is meaningless.

The more negative a player's platoon coefficient, the more significant his platoon role. A player's platoon coefficient cannot exceed his team's platoon coefficient.

TACTICIAN RATINGS

1999

AL Mgr.	Team	Sac.	Steal	Steal2	H&R	Overall
Howe	Oak.	0.537	0.489	0.489	0.697	0.553
Hargrove	Cle.	0.531	0.558	0.558	0.530	0.544
Muser	KC	0.474	0.572	0.572	0.493	0.528
Miller	Bal.	0.480	0.522	0.522	0.568	0.523
Piniella	Sea.	0.519	0.555	0.555	0.433	0.516
Fregosi	Tor.	0.531	0.532	0.532	0.442	0.509
Oates	Tex.	0.561	0.503	0.503	0.447	0.504
Williams	Bos.	0.502	0.472	0.472	0.544	0.498
Torre	NYY	0.508	0.481	0.481	0.520	0.498
Collins	Ana.	0.481	0.458	0.458	0.580	0.494
Manuel J	CWS	0.465	0.514	0.514	0.457	0.488
Parrish	Det.	0.528	0.454	0.454	0.479	0.479
Rothschild	TB	0.484	0.447	0.447	0.528	0.477
Zimmer	NYY	0.404	0.490	0.490	0.517	0.475
Kelly	Min.	0.487	0.496	0.496	0.368	0.462
Maddon	Ana.	0.504	0.455	0.455	0.395	0.452

NL Mgr.	Team	Sac.	Steal	Steal2	H&R	Overall
Francona	Phi	0.533	0.561	0.561	0.523	0.545
Showalter	Ari.	0.535	0.560	0.560	0.515	0.543
Valentine	NYM	0.582	0.512	0.512	0.564	0.543
Cox	Atl.	0.506	0.498	0.498	0.649	0.538
LaRussa	SL	0.485	0.529	0.529	0.599	0.536
Johnson D	LA	0.540	0.512	0.512	0.547	0.528
Bochy	SD	0.421	0.519	0.519	0.596	0.514
Dierker	Hou.	0.500	0.496	0.496	0.541	0.508
McKeon	Cin.	0.504	0.541	0.541	0.436	0.506
Lefebvre	Mil.	0.546	0.517	0.517	0.416	0.499

Lamont	Pit.	0.513	0.517	0.517	0.401	0.487
Garner	Mil.	0.493	0.509	0.509	0.431	0.486
Baker	SF	0.486	0.475	0.475	0.422	0.465
Boles	Fla.	0.469	0.480	0.480	0.418	0.462
Alou	Mtl.	0.528	0.417	0.417	0.471	0.458
Riggleman	ChC	0.446	0.415	0.415	0.527	0.451
Leyland	Pit.	0.413	0.445	0.445	0.439	0.436

2000

AL Mgr.	Team	Sac.	Steal	Steal2	H&R	Avg.
Manuel C	Cle.	0.514	0.561	0.561	0.536	0.543
Torre	NYY	0.496	0.491	0.491	0.675	0.538
Muser	KC	0.531	0.566	0.566	0.490	0.538
Manuel J	CWS	0.526	0.539	0.539	0.490	0.524
Oates	Tex.	0.505	0.434	0.434	0.687	0.515
Scioscia	Ana.	0.510	0.468	0.468	0.536	0.496
Piniella	Sea.	0.532	0.500	0.500	0.446	0.495
Rothschild	TB	0.482	0.483	0.483	0.528	0.494
Garner	Det.	0.481	0.501	0.501	0.491	0.494
Williams	Bos.	0.545	0.430	0.430	0.552	0.489
Kelly	Min.	0.459	0.487	0.487	0.523	0.489
Fregosi	Tor.	0.459	0.528	0.528	0.414	0.482
Hargrove	Bal.	0.489	0.482	0.482	0.412	0.466
Howe	Oak.	0.470	0.531	0.531	0.226	0.440

NL Mgr.	Team	Sac.	Steal	Steal2	H&R	Avg.
Baker	SF	0.561	0.492	0.492	0.703	0.562
Francona	Phi.	0.521	0.568	0.568	0.543	0.550
Cox	Atl.	0.499	0.533	0.533	0.509	0.519
LaRussa	SL	0.491	0.463	0.463	0.649	0.517
Bell	Col.	0.513	0.501	0.501	0.541	0.514
Showalter	Ari.	0.415	0.506	0.506	0.602	0.507
Dierker	Hou.	0.489	0.505	0.505	0.510	0.502
McKeon	Cin.	0.475	0.532	0.532	0.463	0.501
Bochy	SD	0.475	0.524	0.524	0.460	0.496
Boles	Fla.	0.486	0.554	0.554	0.374	0.492
Baylor	ChC	0.521	0.526	0.526	0.374	0.487
Lamont	Pit.	0.475	0.502	0.502	0.464	0.486
Valentine	NYM	0.530	0.433	0.433	0.484	0.470
Alou	Mtl.	0.516	0.402	0.402	0.547	0.467
Johnson D	LA	0.502	0.510	0.510	0.328	0.463
Lopes	Mil.	0.483	0.457	0.457	0.448	0.461

2001

AL Mgr.	Team	Sac.	Steal	Steal2	H&R	Avg.
McRae	TB	0.509	0.497	0.497	0.756	0.565
Piniella	Sea.	0.501	0.582	0.582	0.674	0.585
Kelly	Min.	0.491	0.495	0.495	0.614	0.524
Torre	NYY	0.490	0.543	0.543	0.568	0.536
Muser	KC	0.475	0.509	0.509	0.531	0.506
Martinez	Tor.	0.440	0.534	0.534	0.555	0.516
Williams	Bos.	0.511	0.452	0.452	0.643	0.515
Manuel J	CWS	0.507	0.488	0.488	0.571	0.514
Hargrove	Bal.	0.491	0.517	0.517	0.489	0.504
Narron	Tex.	0.441	0.552	0.552	0.386	0.483
Manuel C	Cle.	0.546	0.475	0.475	0.526	0.506
Scioscia	Ana.	0.489	0.499	0.499	0.582	0.517
Garner	Det.	0.473	0.496	0.496	0.457	0.481
Howe	Oak.	0.442	0.507	0.507	0.449	0.476
Oates	Tex.	0.609	0.503	0.503	0.402	0.504
Kerrigan	Bos.	0.474	0.350	0.350	0.302	0.369
Rothschild	TB	0.609	0.506	0.506	0.000	0.405

NL Mgr.	Team	Sac.	Steal	Steal2	H&R	Avg.
LaRussa	SL	0.541	0.545	0.545	0.792	0.606
Alou	Mtl.	0.526	0.542	0.542	0.638	0.562
Bochy	SD	0.456	0.563	0.563	0.519	0.525
Bowa	Phi.	0.522	0.578	0.578	0.421	0.525
Brenly	Ari.	0.510	0.492	0.492	0.631	0.531
Baylor	ChC	0.548	0.491	0.491	0.478	0.502
Cox	Atl.	0.504	0.490	0.490	0.507	0.498
Boles	Fla.	0.586	0.566	0.566	0.359	0.519
Baker	SF	0.452	0.435	0.435	0.674	0.499
Boone	Cin.	0.481	0.495	0.495	0.458	0.482
Perez	Cin.	0.466	0.486	0.486	0.609	0.512
Valentine	NYM	0.548	0.437	0.437	0.494	0.479
Lopes	Mil.	0.487	0.489	0.489	0.509	0.494
Torborg	Mtl.	0.496	0.488	0.488	0.359	0.458
Bell	Col.	0.483	0.536	0.536	0.412	0.492
Tracy	LA	0.455	0.513	0.513	0.399	0.470
McClendon	Pit.	0.458	0.423	0.423	0.408	0.428
Dierker	Hou.	0.484	0.427	0.427	0.332	0.418

2002

AL Mgr.	Team	Sac.	Steal	Steal2	H&R	Avg.
Scioscia	Ana.	0.528	0.499	0.499	0.625	0.538
Tosca	Tor.	0.495	0.519	0.519	0.612	0.536
Manuel J	CWS	0.513	0.507	0.507	0.451	0.495
Howe	Oak.	0.533	0.499	0.499	0.413	0.486
Piniella	Sea.	0.449	0.504	0.504	0.615	0.518
Pena	KC	0.470	0.466	0.466	0.534	0.484
Little	Bos.	0.460	0.531	0.531	0.441	0.491
Hargrove	Bal.	0.453	0.499	0.499	0.468	0.480
Pujols	Det.	0.429	0.423	0.423	0.646	0.480
Torre	NYY	0.477	0.519	0.519	0.445	0.490
McRae	TB	0.483	0.497	0.497	0.480	0.489
Gardenhire	Min.	0.530	0.401	0.401	0.340	0.418
Narron	Tex.	0.514	0.463	0.463	0.426	0.467
Manuel C	Cle.	0.501	0.365	0.365	0.527	0.440
Martinez	Tor.	0.425	0.594	0.594	0.147	0.440
Mizerock	KC	0.614	0.661	0.661	0.281	0.554
Muser	KC	0.614	0.537	0.537	0.702	0.598
Skinner	Cle.	0.557	0.515	0.515	0.864	0.613

NL Mgr.	Team	Sac.	Steal	Steal2	H&R	Avg.
Baylor	ChC	0.552	0.585	0.585	0.548	0.568
LaRussa	SL	0.520	0.494	0.494	0.613	0.530
Tracy	LA	0.508	0.531	0.531	0.483	0.513
Baker	SF	0.504	0.573	0.573	0.504	0.539
Cox	Atl.	0.487	0.486	0.486	0.624	0.521
Torborg	Fla.	0.454	0.521	0.521	0.549	0.511
Valentine	NYM	0.490	0.496	0.496	0.521	0.501
Boone	Cin.	0.488	0.507	0.507	0.456	0.490
Brenly	Ari.	0.498	0.490	0.490	0.607	0.521
Hurdle	Col.	0.538	0.487	0.487	0.479	0.498
Williams	Hou.	0.480	0.532	0.532	0.352	0.474
Bowa	Phi.	0.457	0.520	0.520	0.385	0.471
Robinson	Mtl.	0.510	0.476	0.476	0.423	0.471
McClendon	Pit.	0.448	0.468	0.468	0.487	0.468
Royster	Mil.	0.457	0.485	0.485	0.597	0.506
Bochy	SD	0.484	0.454	0.454	0.563	0.489
Bell	Col.	0.610	0.476	0.476	0.423	0.496
Kimm	ChC	0.476	0.482	0.482	0.487	0.482
Lopes	Mil.	0.542	0.441	0.441	0.403	0.457

2003

AL Mgr.	Team	Sac.	Steal	Steal2	H&R	Avg.
Melvin	Sea.	0.504	0.532	0.532	0.667	0.559
Piniella	TB	0.442	0.551	0.551	0.637	0.545
Macha	Oak.	0.448	0.553	0.553	0.616	0.543
Torre	NYY	0.546	0.534	0.534	0.507	0.530
Hargrove	Bal.	0.532	0.509	0.509	0.561	0.528
Pena	KC	0.531	0.529	0.529	0.477	0.517
Little	Bos.	0.458	0.511	0.511	0.567	0.512
Tosca	Tor.	0.534	0.426	0.426	0.572	0.490
Scioscia	Ana.	0.507	0.485	0.485	0.477	0.489
Showalter	Tex.	0.506	0.516	0.516	0.375	0.478
Gardenhire	Min.	0.480	0.486	0.486	0.399	0.463
Trammell	Det.	0.532	0.435	0.435	0.415	0.454
Manuel J	CWS	0.519	0.519	0.519	0.253	0.453
Wedge	Cle.	0.468	0.418	0.418	0.480	0.446

NL Mgr.	Team	Sac.	Steal	Steal2	H&R	Avg.
Bowa	Phi.	0.440	0.518	0.518	0.710	0.547
LaRussa	SL	0.528	0.523	0.523	0.581	0.539
Yost	Mil.	0.504	0.521	0.521	0.592	0.535
McClendon	Pit.	0.509	0.508	0.508	0.609	0.534
Cox	Atl.	0.484	0.549	0.549	0.517	0.525
McKeon	Fla.	0.534	0.456	0.456	0.652	0.525
Baker	ChC	0.546	0.510	0.510	0.492	0.515
Robinson	Mtl.	0.524	0.523	0.523	0.474	0.511
Tracy	LA	0.488	0.501	0.501	0.526	0.504
Torborg	Fla.	0.531	0.550	0.550	0.323	0.489
Alou	SF	0.531	0.428	0.428	0.565	0.488
Howe	NYM	0.531	0.504	0.504	0.407	0.487
Brenly	Ari.	0.471	0.485	0.485	0.502	0.486
Miley	Cin.	0.434	0.458	0.458	0.554	0.476
Boone	Cin.	0.474	0.533	0.533	0.356	0.474
Bochy	SD	0.495	0.480	0.480	0.424	0.470
Williams	Hou.	0.513	0.500	0.500	0.360	0.468
Hurdle	Col.	0.467	0.458	0.458	0.356	0.435

REGRESSION THEORY STANDINGS*

1995

	Team	Payroll	Proj. wins	Actual wins	Notes
AL East	Yankees	$55.90	85	79	
	Orioles	$46.90	80	71	
	Blue Jays	$41.90	77	56	
	Red Sox	$37.10	75	86	
	Tigers	$28.00	70	60	2
AL Cent.	Indians	$39.60	76	100	
	White Sox	$36.40	74	68	
	Royals	$28.10	70	70	
	Brewers	$17.20	64	65	2
	Twins	$14.50	62	56	2
AL West	Mariners	$37.30	75	79	
	Rangers	$35.70	74	74	
	Angels	$33.50	73	78	
	A's	$31.40	72	67	
NL East	Braves	$46.70	80	90	
	Phillies	$29.50	71	69	
	Marlins	$22.60	67	67	
	Mets	$13.00	61	69	1, 2
	Expos	$12.80	61	66	2
NL Cent.	Reds	$45.50	79	85	
	Astros	$33.60	73	76	
	Cubs	$33.40	73	73	
	Cardinals	$27.50	69	62	
	Pirates	$17.40	64	58	
NL West	Dodgers	$40.60	77	78	
	Rockies	$37.40	75	77	

*See note on regression theory, p. 184.

	Team	Payroll	Proj. wins	Actual wins	Notes
	Giants	$33.70	73	67	
	Padres	$25.00	68	70	

1. Best-performing low-revenue team
2. No faith and hope

1996

	Team	Payroll	Proj. wins	Actual wins	Notes
AL East	Yankees	$62.000	95	92	
	Orioles	$54.100	91	88	
	Red Sox	$39.800	84	85	
	Blue Jays	$28.400	79	74	
	Tigers	$17.700	74	53	2
AL Cent.	Indians	$48.300	89	99	
	White Sox	$45.000	87	85	
	Twins	$21.300	75	78	
	Royals	$19.900	75	75	
	Brewers	$11.400	70	80	2
AL West	Mariners	$42.700	86	85	
	Rangers	$38.300	84	90	
	Angels	$24.300	77	70	
	A's	$19.500	74	78	
NL East	Braves	$53.700	91	96	
	Phillies	$29.900	80	67	
	Marlins	$25.200	77	80	
	Mets	$24.900	77	71	
	Expos	$17.300	73	88	1
NL Cent.	Reds	$42.100	86	81	
	Cardinals	$36.600	83	88	
	Cubs	$29.300	79	76	
	Astros	$25.800	78	82	
	Pirates	$16.500	73	73	
NL West	Rockies	$37.500	83	83	
	Dodgers	$37.300	83	90	
	Giants	$35.000	82	68	
	Padres	$33.200	81	91	

1. Best-performing low-revenue team
2. No faith and hope

1997

	Team	Payroll	Proj. wins	Actual wins	Notes
AL East	Yankees	$65.000	93	96	
	Orioles	$61.500	92	98	

	Team	Payroll	Proj. wins	Actual wins	Notes
	Blue Jays	$44.000	83	76	
	Red Sox	$38.900	81	78	
	Tigers	$16.200	70	79	2
AL Cent.	Indians	$58.500	90	86	
	White Sox	$41.900	82	80	
	Royals	$35.200	79	67	
	Twins	$31.800	78	68	2
	Brewers	$26.200	75	78	2
AL West	Mariners	$48.100	85	90	
	Rangers	$43.700	83	77	
	Angels	$37.400	80	84	
	A's	$13.700	69	65	2
NL East	Marlins	$53.200	88	92	
	Braves	$52.800	88	101	
	Mets	$39.200	81	88	
	Phillies	$30.700	77	68	
	Expos	$18.500	71	78	2
NL Cent.	Cardinals	$48.100	85	73	
	Reds	$36.900	80	76	
	Astros	$34.200	79	84	
	Cubs	$25.700	75	68	
	Pirates	$12.000	68	79	1, 2
NL West	Dodgers	$48.700	86	88	
	Giants	$44.100	83	90	
	Rockies	$41.600	82	83	
	Padres	$36.900	80	76	

1. Best-performing low-revenue team
2. No faith and hope

1998

	Team	Payroll	Proj. wins	Actual wins	Notes
AL East	Orioles	$77.300	103	79	
	Yankees	$65.100	95	114	
	Red Sox	$59.500	92	92	
	Blue Jays	$31.000	75	88	1, 2
	Devil Rays	$27.700	73	63	2
AL Cent.	Indians	$63.100	94	89	
	Royals	$35.500	77	72	2
	White Sox	$35.200	77	80	2
	Twins	$27.900	73	70	2
	Tigers	$19.200	67	65	2
AL West	Rangers	$60.700	93	88	

	Team	Payroll	Proj. wins	Actual wins	Notes
	Angels	$47.900	85	85	
	Mariners	$43.900	82	76	
	A's	$17.900	67	74	2
NL East	Braves	$62.000	93	106	
	Mets	$58.700	91	88	
	Marlins	$14.700	75	54	2
	Phillies	$28.600	73	75	2
	Expos	$8.300	61	65	2
NL Cent.	Astros	$54.700	89	102	
	Cubs	$52.800	88	90	
	Cardinals	$51.000	87	83	
	Brewers	$32.500	75	74	2
	Reds	$21.700	69	77	2
	Pirates	$13.700	64	69	2
NL West	Dodgers	$62.800	94	83	
	Padres	$53.100	88	98	
	Giants	$49.100	86	89	
	Rockies	$42.200	81	77	
	D-Backs	$31.600	75	65	2

1. Best-performing low-revenue team
2. No faith and hope

1999

	Team	Payroll	Proj. wins	Actual wins	Notes
AL East	Yankees	$88.130	97	98	
	Red Sox	$71.720	91	94	
	Orioles	$70.810	90	78	
	Blue Jays	$48.160	81	84	
	Devil Rays	$37.810	77	69	
AL Cent.	Indians	$73.900	92	97	
	Tigers	$34.960	75	69	
	White Sox	$24.550	71	75	2
	Royals	$16.560	68	64	2
	Twins	$16.340	68	63	2
AL West	Rangers	$81.300	95	95	
	Angels	$49.890	82	70	
	Mariners	$44.370	79	79	
	A's	$24.150	71	87	2
NL East	Braves	$75.070	92	103	
	Mets	$71.330	90	97	
	Phillies	$30.520	74	77	
	Expos	$16.360	68	68	2
	Marlins	$15.150	67	64	2

NL Cent.	Astros	$55.560	84	97	
	Cubs	$55.370	84	67	
	Cardinals	$46.250	80	75	
	Brewers	$42.930	79	74	
	Reds	$42.140	78	96	1
	Pirates	$24.220	71	78	
NL West	Dodgers	$71.130	90	77	
	D-Backs	$70.370	90	100	
	Rockies	$54.390	83	72	
	Giants	$46.000	80	86	
	Padres	$45.930	80	74	

1. Best-performing low-revenue team
2. No faith and hope

2000

	Team	Payroll	Proj. wins	Actual wins	Notes
AL East	Yankees	$112.010	93	87	
	Red Sox	$90.540	88	85	
	Orioles	$59.270	82	74	
	Blue Jays	$54.080	81	83	
	Devil Rays	$51.480	80	69	
AL Cent.	Indians	$76.520	85	90	
	Tigers	$58.550	82	79	
	White Sox	$36.980	77	95	1
	Royals	$23.650	74	77	
	Twins	$14.690	72	69	
AL West	Rangers	$61.830	82	71	
	Mariners	$61.720	82	91	
	Angels	$53.050	80	82	
	A's	$32.170	76	91	
NL East	Braves	$94.400	89	95	
	Mets	$81.840	87	94	
	Phillies	$35.930	77	65	
	Expos	$27.620	75	67	
	Marlins	$25.110	75	79	
NL Cent.	Cardinals	$72.690	85	95	
	Astros	$50.530	80	72	
	Cubs	$50.310	80	65	
	Reds	$36.250	77	83	
	Pirates	$29.340	75	69	
	Brewers	$26.180	75	73	
NL West	Dodgers	$90.380	88	86	
	D-Backs	$73.870	85	85	

Rockies	$56.050	81	82	
Padres	$55.330	81	76	
Giants	$54.040	81	97	

1. Best-performing low-revenue team

2001

	Team	Payroll	Proj. wins	Actual wins	Notes
AL East	Yankees	$143.264	93	95	
	Red Sox	$122.620	89	82	
	Blue Jays	$83.978	82	80	
	Orioles	$82.343	82	63	
	Devil Rays	$57.634	77	62	
AL Cent.	Indians	$108.941	87	91	
	Twins	$42.349	81	85	
	White Sox	$66.616	79	83	
	Tigers	$57.863	77	66	
	Royals	$45.540	75	65	
AL West	Rangers	$98.710	85	73	
	Mariners	$90.924	83	116	
	Angels	$62.661	78	75	
	A's	$47.103	75	102	1
NL East	Braves	$103.600	86	88	
	Mets	$97.840	85	82	
	Marlins	$56.518	77	76	
	Phillies	$49.900	76	86	
	Expos	$43.500	74	68	
NL Cent.	Astros	$84.041	82	93	
	Cardinals	$82.715	82	93	
	Cubs	$81.808	82	88	
	Pirates	$65.983	79	62	
	Brewers	$62.133	78	68	
	Reds	$58.288	77	66	
NL West	Dodgers	$123.831	90	86	
	D-Backs	$99.153	85	92	
	Rockies	$89.671	83	73	
	Giants	$81.255	82	90	
	Padres	$44.072	74	79	

1. Best-performing low-revenue team

2002

	Team	Payroll	Proj. wins	Actual wins	Notes
AL East	Yankees	$175.327	104	103	
	Red Sox	$113.795	88	93	
	Orioles	$72.085	78	67	
	Blue Jays	$66.698	76	78	
	Devil Rays	$43.984	71	55	
AL Cent.	White Sox	$65.535	86	81	
	Indians	$90.428	82	74	
	Tigers	$75.324	78	55	
	Royals	$58.708	74	62	
	Twins	$53.666	73	94	
AL West	Rangers	$130.622	92	72	
	Mariners	$100.045	85	93	
	Angels	$77.184	79	99	
	A's	$65.878	76	103	1
NL East	Mets	$109.917	87	75	
	Braves	$110.770	87	101	
	Phillies	$72.240	78	80	
	Marlins	$53.103	73	69	
	Expos	$43.549	70	83	
NL Cent.	Cardinals	$96.113	84	97	
	Cubs	$88.838	82	67	
	Astros	$82.118	80	84	
	Reds	$62.397	75	78	
	Pirates	$63.701	75	72	
	Brewers	$58.190	74	56	
NL West	Dodgers	$120.009	90	92	
	D-Backs	$114.324	88	98	
	Giants	$96.222	84	95	
	Rockies	$80.035	80	73	
	Padres	$65.677	76	66	

1. Best-performing low-revenue team

2003

	Team	Payroll	Proj. wins	Actual wins	Notes
AL East	Yankees	$152.749	97	101	
	Red Sox	$99.947	87	95	
	Orioles	$73.878	82	71	
	Blue Jays	$51.269	77	86	
	Devil Rays	$19.630	71	63	
AL Central	Twins	$55.505	78	90	
	White Sox	$51.010	77	86	

	Tigers	$49.168	77	43	
	Indians	$48.584	77	68	
	Royals	$40.518	75	83	
AL West	Rangers	$103.491	87	71	
	Mariners	$86.959	84	93	
	Angels	$79.032	83	77	
	A's	$50.261	77	96	1
NL East	Mets	$117.176	90	66	
	Braves	$106.243	88	101	
	Phillies	$70.780	81	86	
	Expos	$51.949	77	83	
	Marlins	$49.050	77	91	
NL Central	Cardinals	$83.487	83	85	
	Cubs	$79.868	83	88	
	Astros	$71.040	81	87	
	Reds	$59.356	79	69	
	Pirates	$54.812	78	75	
	Brewers	$40.627	75	68	
NL West	Dodgers	$105.872	88	85	
	Giants	$82.852	83	100	
	D-Backs	$80.640	83	84	
	Rockies	$67.180	80	74	
	Padres	$47.928	76	64	

1. Best-performing low-revenue team

EARNED VALUE

Earned Value is a figure, expressed in dollars, which represents the amount a player contributed to his team's success. It is computed based on position and is comparative with other players who played the same position in the same league during the same season. The higher a player's Earned Value, the more he contributed to his team's success. Players who exceeded the average Earned Value for the position were a net contributor. Earned Value can also be used to measure a player's contribution relative to his pay—a gauge of utilization of salary resources—but this can be misleading since a player may be significantly positive in this category yet well down the list in actual Earned Value.

To calculate Earned Value, a standardized player rating tool is necessary. I use TPR or TPI. It is also necessary to know the salary of all players. Finally, in order to avoid negative overall ratings at any particular position, an adjustment is added based on playing time. The adjustments for each position, which were suggested by Pete Palmer, are noted at the bottom of this sheet.

The formula for Earned Value is:

EV = (A – B) * (C) + (D)
where A = Adjusted TPR or TPI
    B = League Average Adjusted TPR or TPI
    C = Average League Salary at the position/League
       Average Adjusted TPR or TPI
    D = League Average Salary at the position

As an example, here is a calculation of Scott Rolen's Earned Value for 1998. Rolen's TPR was 5.1. His Adjusted TPR was 10.6. His salary was $750,000. The averaged Adjusted TPR for NL third basemen was 4.07. The average salary for NL third basemen was $1.536 million. The calculation is as follows:

Rolen's EV = (10.6 − 4.07) * (C) + (1.536)
Where C = 1.536/4.07 = .377747
Rolen's EV = (6.04 * .377747) + $1.536
or $3.818 million

That made Scott Rolen the most valuable third baseman in the National League in 1998.

Here are the position adjustments. All are based on plate appearances except for pitchers, whose adjustments are based on innings pitched.

First Base and Outfield

PA	Adj
600	4.50
550	4.13
500	3.75
450	3.38
400	3.00
350	2.63
300	2.25
250	1.88
200	1.50
150	1.13
100	0.75

Catcher

PA	Adj
600	5.50
550	5.04
500	4.58
450	4.11
400	3.65
350	3.20
300	2.75
250	2.29
200	1.82
150	1.38
100	0.94

Shortstop

PA	Adj
600	6.50
550	5.95
500	5.40
450	4.85
400	4.30
350	3.85
300	3.25
250	2.70
200	2.15
150	1.60
100	1.05

Second and Third Base

PA	Adj
600	5.00
550	4.60
500	4.16
450	3.75
400	3.29
350	2.90
300	2.50
250	2.10
200	1.64
150	1.25
100	0.85

Pitcher

IP	Adj
243	6.00
223	5.50
203	5.00
182	4.50
162	4.00
142	3.50
122	3.00
101	2.50
81	2.00
61	1.50
41	1.00
21	0.50

Here are the 2003 Earned Values for all Major League players with 100 or more plate appearances, 15 starts, 10 saves, or 50 innings pitched. Non-players are grouped by most frequently played position. Pitchers who made at least 15 starts are classified as starters. Those with at least 10 saves are classified as closers. Those in neither category are classified as "other pitchers." Also included in the ratings are those who played less than the minimum, but who were paid at least $500,000 more than the team average salary. Where salaries are not known, italics indicate an estimated salary. In most instances, these are rookies called up in mid-season for whom the Major League minimum is applicable. Numbers in parentheses are negative.

Earned Values are presented first by league and position, and secondly by team.

EARNED VALUES

2003 AL Position Players

Catcher	Team	Salary	Earned Value	Difference
Posada	NYY	$8.000	$5.367	($2.633)
Pierzynski	Min	$0.365	$3.642	$3.277
Hernandez	Oak	$1.888	$3.589	$1.701
Varitek	Bos	$4.700	$3.218	($1.482)

Molina B	Ana	$1.425	$2.779	$1.354
Myers	Tor	$0.800	$2.012	$1.212
Olivo	CWS	$0.300	$1.773	$1.473
Hall	TB	$0.300	$1.752	$1.452
Bard	Cle	$0.302	$1.721	$1.419
Wilson	Tor	$0.316	$1.318	$1.002
Inge	Det	$0.315	$1.218	$0.903
Davis	Sea	$1.000	$1.160	$0.160
Diaz	Tex	$1.838	$1.138	($0.700)
Fordyce	Bal	$3.500	$1.112	($2.388)
DiFelice	KC	$0.625	$1.070	$0.445
Mayne	KC	$2.750	$1.006	($1.744)
Wilson	Sea	$3.500	$0.927	($2.573)
Martinez V	Cle	$0.300	$0.837	$0.537
Alomar, Jr	CWS	$0.700	$0.699	($0.001)
Gil	Bal	$0.330	$0.625	$0.295
Mirabelli	Bos	$0.805	$0.543	($0.262)
Laker	Cle	$0.400	$0.466	$0.066
Flaherty	NYY	$0.750	$0.286	($0.464)
Valentin Ja	TB	$0.305	$0.286	($0.019)
Greene	Tex	$0.750	$0.223	($0.527)
Molina J	Ana	$0.320	($0.243)	($0.563)
Cash	Tor	$0.300	($0.402)	($0.702)
Wallbeck	Det	$0.400	($0.825)	($1.225)

First Base	Team	Salary	Earned Value	Difference
Delgado	Tor	$18.700	$8.671	($10.029)
Giambi Ja	NYY	$11.429	$6.279	($5.150)
Johnson	NYY	$0.364	$5.033	$4.669
Millar	Bos	$2.000	$4.983	$2.983
Olerud	Sea	$7.700	$4.884	($2.816)
Lee	TB	$0.500	$4.385	$3.885
Mientkiewicz	Min	$1.750	$4.111	$2.361
Conine	Bal	$3.450	$3.538	$0.088
Pena	Det	$0.310	$3.140	$2.830
Spiezio	Ana	$4.250	$2.915	($1.335)
Hatteberg	Oak	$1.750	$2.891	$1.141
Texeira	Tex	$0.750	$2.816	$2.066
Broussard	Cle	$0.303	$1.794	$1.491
Konerko	CWS	$6.250	$1.769	($4.481)
Harvey	KC	$0.300	$1.744	$1.444
Daubach	CWS	$0.450	$0.997	$0.547
Wooten	Ana	$0.338	$0.548	$0.210

Lopez	KC	$0.300	$0.449	$0.149
Quinlan	Ana	$0.300	$0.249	($0.051)

Second Base	**Team**	**Salary**	**Earned Value**	**Difference**
Soriano	NYY	$0.800	$3.565	$2.765
Hudson	Tor	$0.313	$3.382	$3.069
Boone	Sea	$8.000	$3.275	($4.725)
Elli	Oak	$0.308	$2.943	$2.635
Young	Tex	$0.415	$2.653	$2.238
Walker	Bos	$3.450	$1.990	($1.460)
Roberts	Bal	$0.300	$1.973	$1.673
Kennedy	Ana	$2.270	$1.803	($0.467)
Morris	Det	$0.400	$1.575	$1.175
Relaford	KC	$0.900	$1.268	$0.368
Anderson	TB	$0.600	$1.103	$0.503
Hairston	Bal	$1.550	$0.846	($0.704)
Phillips	Cle	$0.301	$0.829	$0.528
Jimenez	CWS	$0.170	$0.788	$0.618
Alomar R	CWS	$3.920	$0.622	($3.298)
Hocking	Min	$1.000	$0.390	($0.610)
Menechino	Oak	$0.335	$0.269	($0.066)
Jackson D	Bos	$0.625	$0.187	($0.438)
Rivas	Min	$0.340	$0.149	($0.191)
Berg	Tor	$0.450	$0.062	($0.388)
Gil B	Ana	$0.725	($0.021)	($0.746)
Gomez	Min	$0.500	($0.062)	($0.562)
Perez A	TB	$0.300	($0.145)	($0.445)
McDonald	Cle	$0.315	($0.191)	($0.506)
Febles	KC	$0.775	($0.191)	($0.966)

Shortstop	**Team**	**Salary**	**Earned Value**	**Difference**
Rodriguez	Tex	$22.000	$10.977	($11.023)
Garciaparra	Bos	$11.000	$8.782	($2.218)
Tejada	Oak	$5.125	$8.022	$2.897
Valentin	CWS	$5.000	$6.966	$1.966
Berroa	KC	$0.303	$6.502	$6.199
Lugo	TB	$0.750	$5.109	$4.359
Jeter	NYY	$15.600	$4.391	($11.209)
Bordick	Tor	$1.000	$4.264	$3.264
Woodward	Tor	$0.775	$4.095	$3.320
Cruz	Bal	$1.000	$3.926	$2.926
Amezaga	Ana	$0.300	$3.673	$3.373
Guillen	Sea	$2.500	$3.462	$0.962

Graffanino	CWS	$0.675	$3.293	$2.618
Vizquel	Cle	$5.500	$3.124	($2.376)
Santiago	Det	$0.307	$2.575	$2.268
McLemore	Sea	$3.150	$2.406	($0.744)
Infante	Det	$0.300	$2.153	$1.853
Guzman	Min	$2.525	$1.984	($0.541)
Peralta	Cle	$0.300	$1.773	$1.473
Ordonez	TB	$6.500	$1.647	($4.853)
Sanchez	Sea	$0.650	$1.013	$0.363
Eckstein	Ana	$0.425	$0.296	($0.129)
Almonte	NYY	$0.300	$0.296	($0.004)
Wilson	NYY	$0.700	$0.211	($0.489)
Gutierrez	Cle	$3.917	($0.338)	($4.255)

Third Base	Team	Salary	Earned Value	Difference
Mueller	Bos	$2.100	$6.792	$4.692
Chavez	Oak	$3.675	$6.683	$3.008
Blalock	Tex	$0.303	$4.939	$4.636
Koskie	Min	$3.400	$4.431	$1.031
Blake	Cle	$0.330	$3.487	$3.157
Randa	KC	$4.500	$3.022	($1.478)
Crede	CWS	$0.315	$2.906	$2.591
Hinske	Tor	$0.600	$2.804	$2.204
Glaus	Ana	$7.250	$2.179	($5.071)
Batista	Bal	$6.400	$1.961	($4.439)
Ventura	NYY	$3.600	$1.743	($1.857)
Rolls	TB	$0.300	$1.743	$1.443
Boone A	NYY	$1.147	$1.482	$0.335
Halter	Det	$2.150	$1.380	($0.770)
Munson	Det	$1.700	$1.090	($0.610)
Zeile	NYY	$0.945	$0.683	($0.262)
Sandberg	TB	$0.300	$0.618	$0.318
Bloomquist	Sea	$0.300	$0.247	($0.053)
Hillenbrand	Bos	$0.148	($0.109)	($0.257)
Sadler	Tex	$0.400	($0.109)	($0.509)
Cirillo	Sea	$6.725	($0.436)	($7.161)
Easley	TB	$0.400	($0.545)	($0.945)

Left Field	Team	Salary	Earned Value	Difference
Ramirez	Bos	$20.000	$7.632	($12.368)
Anderson	Ana	$5.350	$7.585	$2.235
Stewart	Tor-Min	$6.200	$5.404	($0.796)
Mora	Bal	$1.725	$5.238	$3.513

Lee	CWS	$4.200	$5.120	$0.920
Winn	Sea	$3.300	$4.930	$1.630
Matsui	NYY	$6.000	$4.646	($1.354)
Jones J	Min	$2.750	$4.006	$1.256
Crawford	TB	$0.300	$3.508	$3.208
Ibanez	KC	$3.000	$3.508	$0.508
Catalanotto	Tor	$2.200	$3.176	$0.976
Bigbie	Bal	$0.300	$2.892	$2.592
Lawton	Cle	$6.750	$2.465	($4.285)
Monroe	Det	$0.300	$2.441	$2.141
Spencer	Cle-Tex	$0.600	$1.612	$1.012
McMillon	Oak	$0.500	$1.067	$0.567
Rivera	NYY	$0.500	$0.877	$0.377
Long	Oak	$2.175	$0.806	($1.369)
Mench	Tex	$0.328	$0.616	$0.289
Jones J	Tex	$0.300	$0.237	($0.063)
Petrick	Det	$0.500	$0.142	($0.358)
Piatt	Oak-TB	$0.322	$0.047	($0.275)
Brown D	KC	$0.310	($0.047)	($0.357)

Center Field	Team	Salary	Earned Value	Difference
Beltran	KC	$6.000	$8.413	$2.413
Cameron	Sea	$7.416	$7.057	($0.359)
Wells	Tor	$0.520	$6.648	$6.128
Everett	Tex-CWS	$9.150	$5.856	($3.294)
Bradley	Cle	$0.314	$5.753	$5.439
Baldelli	TB	$0.300	$5.523	$5.223
Matos	Bal	$0.300	$4.986	$4.686
Damon	Bos	$7.500	$4.705	($2.795)
Hunter	Min	$4.750	$4.603	($0.147)
Williams B	NYY	$12.357	$4.449	($7.908)
Byrnes	Oak	$0.300	$2.736	$2.436
Sanchez	Det	$0.225	$2.659	$2.434
Erstad	Ana	$7.250	$1.509	($5.741)
Figgins	Ana	$0.300	$1.509	$1.209
Rowand	CWS	$0.320	$1.457	$1.137
Crisp	Cle	$0.300	$1.125	$0.825
Owens	Ana	$0.925	$0.588	($0.337)
Glanville	Tex	$0.790	$0.409	($0.381)
Harris	CWS	$0.300	$0.332	$0.032
Greer	Tex	$7.000	($0.000)	($7.000)
Singleton	Oak	$1.200	($0.051)	($1.251)
Matthews	Bal	$0.297	($0.179)	($0.476)

Rios	CWS	$0.450	($0.256)	($0.706)
Torres	Det	$0.300	($0.281)	($0.581)
Christenson	Tex	$0.500	($0.486)	($0.986)

Right Field	Team	Salary	Earned Value	Difference
Ordonez	CWS	$9.000	$9.344	$0.344
Huff	TB	$0.325	$8.222	$7.897
Nixon	Bos	$4.000	$7.288	$3.288
Salmon	Ana	$9.900	$7.226	($2.674)
Suzuki	Sea	$4.667	$7.226	$2.559
Gerut	Cle	$0.300	$5.668	$5.368
Gibbons	Bal	$0.375	$5.232	$4.857
Davanon	Ana	$0.300	$4.641	$4.341
Gonzalez	Tex	$13.000	$3.800	($9.200)
Mondesi	NYY	$8.970	$3.769	($5.201)
Kielty	Min-Tor	$0.325	$3.675	$3.350
Guiel	KC	$0.300	$3.644	$3.344
Higginson	Det	$11.850	$2.678	($9.172)
Johnson R	Tor	$0.300	$2.616	$2.316
Mohr	Min	$0.315	$2,398	$2.083
Tucker	KC	$2.750	$1.993	($0.757)
Garcia	NYY	$0.900	$1.588	$0.688
Escobar	Cle	$0.300	$1.184	$0.884
Kapler	Bos	$3.425	$1.152	($2.273)
Nix	Tex	$0.300	$1.028	$0.728
Mabry	Sea	$0.600	$0.561	($0.039)
Guillen J	Oak	$0.200	$0.280	$0.080
Cuddyer	Min	$0.303	$0.062	($0.241)
Dye	Oak	$11.667	($0.903)	($12.570)

Des. Hitter	Team	Salary	Earned Value	Difference
Young D	Det	$6.750	$11.299	$4.549
Thomas	CWS	$5.000	$10.285	$5.285
Martinez	Sea	$4.000	$9.308	$5.308
Ortiz	Bos	$1.250	$8.185	$6.935
Palmeiro	Tex	$9.000	$7.533	($1.467)
Durazo	Oak	$1.065	$6.084	$5.019
Sweeney	KC	$11.000	$5.179	($5.821)
Phelps	Tor	$0.320	$4.889	$4.569
Fullmer	Ana	$1.000	$3.187	$2.187
LeCroy	Min	$0.313	$2.934	$2.621
Surhoff	Bal	$1.000	$2.789	$1.789
Segui	Bal	$7.000	$2.723	($4.277)

Hafner	Cle	$0.302	$2.680	$2.378
Burks	Cle	$7.167	$2.173	($4.994)
Grieve	TB	$5.500	$1.738	($3.762)
Sierra	Tex-NYY	$0.600	$1.666	$1.066
Witt K	Det	$0.300	$1.557	$1.257
Martin	TB	$0.300	$0.978	$0.678
Morneau	Min	$0.300	$0.217	($0.083)
Belle	Bal	$13.000	$0.000	($13.000)
Palmer	Det	$8.500	($1.738)	($10.238)

2003 NL Position Players

Catcher	Team	Salary	Earned Value	Difference
Lopez	Atl	$7.000	$9.423	$2.423
LoDuca	LA	$2.637	$8.323	$5.686
Rodriguez I	Fla	$10.000	$7.768	($2.232)
Lieberthal	Phi	$7.250	$6.282	($0.968)
Kendall	Pit	$8.571	$6.242	($2.329)
Schneider	Mtl	$0.310	$4.954	$4.644
Ausmus	Hou	$5.500	$4.934	($0.566)
Miller	ChC	$2.700	$4.756	$2.056
Santiago	SF	$1.775	$3.874	$2.099
Hammock	Ari	$0.300	$3.389	$3.089
Matheny	SL	$3.250	$3.280	$0.030
Johnson	Col	$7.000	$3.121	($3.879)
LaRue	Cin	$1.250	$3.121	$1.871
Piazza	NYM	$15.571	$2.963	($12.608)
Torrealba	SF	$0.312	$2.398	$2.086
Wilson	NYM	$0.315	$2.269	$1.954
Osik	Mil	$0.455	$2.071	$1.616
Pratt	Phi	$0.850	$1.962	$1.112
Moeller	Ari	$0.300	$1.873	$1.573
Barajas	Ari	$0.300	$1.803	$1.503
Ross	LA	$0.300	$1.625	$1.325
Perez E	Mil	$0.500	$1.585	$1.085
Barrett	Mtl	$2.600	$1.575	($1.025)
Ojeda	SD	$0.300	$1.367	$1.067
Estalella	Col	$0.500	$1.070	$0.570
Stinnett	Phi	$1.300	$0.912	($0.388)
Bako	ChC	$0.750	$0.515	($0.235)
Widger	SL	$0.500	$0.337	($0.163)
Zaun	Hou-Col	$1.200	$0.079	($1.121)
Redmond	Fla	$1.050	$0.040	($1.010)

Hundley	LA	$6.500	$0.000	($6.500)
Blanco	Atl	$1.300	($0.119)	($1.419)
Bennett	SD	$0.700	($0.644)	($1.344)

First Base	Team	Salary	Earned Value	Difference
Helton	Col	$10.600	$17.100	$6.500
Sexson	Mil	$5.125	$12.452	$7.327
Thome	Phi	$11.167	$11.954	$0.787
Lee D	Fla	$4.250	$10.625	$6.375
Bagwell	Hou	$13.000	$9.795	($3.205)
Klesko	SD	$5.500	$7.097	$1.597
Martinez	SL	$7.500	$5.396	($2.104)
Baerga	Ari	$0.500	$5.188	$4.688
Snow	SF	$6.850	$5.188	($1.662)
Phillips	NYM	$0.300	$3.984	$3.684
Casey	Cin	$5.600	$3.652	($1.948)
Nevin	SD	$5.000	$3.445	($1.555)
Karros	ChC	$8.375	$3.030	($5.345)
Cordero	Mtl	$0.600	$2.947	$2.347
Simon	Pit-ChC	$1.475	$2.822	$1.347
Overbay	Ari	$0.300	$2.781	$2.481
Franco J	Atl	$0.600	$2.656	$2.056
Fick	Atl	$1.000	$2.449	$1.449
Galarraga	SF	$0.500	$2.449	$1.949
Choi	ChC	$0.305	$2.158	$1.853
Hillenbrand	Ari	$0.261	$2.034	$1.773
McGriff	LA	$3.750	$1.909	($1.841)
Hansen	SD	$0.550	$1.702	$1.152
Clark T	NYM	$0.500	$1.287	$0.787
Ventura	LA	$1.400	$0.581	($0.819)
Coomer	LA	$0.500	$0.249	($0.251)
Rivera C	Pit	$0.300	($0.083)	($0.383)
Franco M	Atl	$0.800	($0.249)	($1.049)
Grace	Ari	$1.750	($0.291)	($2.041)
Young K	Pit	$6.625	($0.996)	($7.621)
Vaughn	NYM	$17.167	($1.162)	($18.329)

Second Base	Team	Salary	Earned Value	Difference
Giles M	Atl	$0.317	$5.406	$5.089
Loretta	SD	$1.250	$4.270	$3.020
Grudzielanek	ChC	$5.500	$4.186	($1.314)
Castillo L	Fla	$4.850	$4.029	($0.821)
Polanco	Phi	$2.875	$3.825	$0.950

Kent	Hou	$7.500	$3.704	($3.796)
Durham	SF	$5.200	$3.157	($2.043)
Cora	LA	$1.150	$2.977	$1.827
Vidro	Mtl	$5.500	$2.947	($2.553)
Belliard	Col	$0.475	$2.526	$2.051
Perez	SF	$1.500	$2.105	$0.605
Spivey	Ari	$0.432	$1.979	$1.547
Young	Mil-SF	$2.000	$1.900	($0.100)
Jimenez	Cin	$0.175	$1.864	$1.689
Cabrera	LA	$0.435	$1.744	$1.309
Martinez R	ChC	$0.800	$1.383	$0.583
Kata	Ari	$0.300	$1.323	$1.023
DeRosa	Atl	$0.340	$1.203	$0.863
Reboulet	Pit	$0.400	$1.143	$0.743
McEwing	NYM	$0.600	$1.022	$0.422
Nunez	Pit	$0.675	$1.022	$0.347
Ginter	Mil	$0.301	$0.962	$0.661
Castro	Cin	$0.800	$0.902	$0.102
Hart	SL	$0.300	$0.842	$0.542
Hall	Mil	$0.300	$0.752	$0.452
Reese	Pit	$2.500	$0.752	($1.748)
Alomar	NYM	$4.080	$0.662	($3.418)
Utley	Phi	$0.300	$0.631	$0.331
Vina	SL	$5.333	$0.421	($4.912)
Lockhart	SD	$0.500	$0.391	($0.109)
Punto	Phi	$0.300	$0.271	($0.029)
Cairo	SL	$0.850	($0.060)	($0.910)
Mateo	Mtl	$0.300	($0.090)	($0.390)
Bell	NYM	$0.550	($0.271)	($0.821)
Fox	Fla	$0.800	($0.391)	($1.191)

Shortstop	Team	Salary	Earned Value	Difference
Furcal	Atl	$2.200	$5.131	$2.931
Cabrera	Mtl	$3.300	$4.962	$1.662
Renteria	SL	$6.500	$4.906	($1.594)
Gonzalez	ChC	$5.750	$4.539	($1.211)
Gonzalez A	Fla	$1.700	$3.975	$2.275
Rollins	Phi	$0.450	$3.722	$3.272
Cintron	Ari	$0.300	$3.299	$2.999
Everett	Hou	$0.300	$3.101	$2.801
Uribe	Col	$0.300	$3.073	$2.773
Iztouris	LA	$0.335	$3.017	$2.682
Wilson J	Pit	$0.335	$2.791	$2.456

Aurilia	SF	$6.250	$2.199	($4.051)
Vazquez	SD	$0.315	$2.171	$1.856
Clayton	Mil	$1.500	$1.523	$0.023
Reyes J	NYM	$0.300	$1.466	$1.166
Larkin	Cin	$9.000	$1.410	($7.590)
Vizcaino	Hou	$2.000	$0.649	($1.351)
Womack	Ari-Col-ChC	$6.000	$0.254	($5.746)
Lopez F	Cin	$0.334	$0.141	($0.193)
Olmedo	Cin	$0.300	$0.113	($0.187)
Mordecai	Fla	$0.500	$0.029	($0.471)
Meares	Pit	$3.790	$0.000	($3.790)
Sanchez	NYM	$0.650	($0.056)	($0.706)

Third Base	Team	Salary	Earned Value	Difference
Rolen	SL	$7.625	$6.861	($0.764)
Lowell	Fla	$3.700	$5.265	$1.565
Ramirez	Pit-ChC	$3.000	$4.866	$1.866
Burroughs	SD	$3.020	$4.308	$1.288
Ensberg	Hou	$0.300	$4.300	$4.000
Boone A	Cin	$2.553	$4.140	$1.587
Beltre	LA	$3.700	$3.829	$0.129
Castilla	Atl	$5.000	$3.510	($1.490)
Wigginton	NYM	$0.303	$2.633	$2.330
Stynes	Col	$0.750	$2.593	$1.843
Hernandez	Col-ChC-Pit	$1.000	$2.473	$1.473
Helms	Mil	$0.575	$2.282	$1.707
Alfonzo	SF	$4.000	$2.074	($1.926)
Bellhorn	ChC-Col	$0.465	$1.995	$1.530
Counsell	Ari	$2.517	$1.755	($0.762)
Carroll	Mtl	$0.300	$1.675	$1.375
Perez	Phi	$0.550	$1.675	$1.125
Branyan	Cin	$0.395	$1.628	$1.233
Feliz	SF	$0.325	$1.548	$1.223
Merloni	SD	$0.300	$1.237	$0.937
Bell	Phi	$3.200	$1.117	($2.083)
Zeile	Mtl	$0.555	$0.838	$0.283
Blum	Hou	$1.500	$0.790	($0.710)
Mackowiak	Pit	$0.322	$0.758	$0.436
Norton	Col	$0.600	$0.599	($0.001)
Williams M	Ari	$10.000	$0.519	($9.481)
Larson	Cin	$0.308	($0.119)	($0.427)
Tatis	Mtl	$6.500	($0.119)	($6.619)

Harris	ChC-Fla	$0.800	($0.199)	($0.999)
Guzman	Mtl	$0.300	($0.359)	($0.659)

Left Field	Team	Salary	Earned Value	Difference
Bonds	SF	$15.500	$12.773	($2.727)
Pujols	SL	$0.900	$12.213	$11.313
Giles	Pit-SD	$8.833	$8.346	($0.487)
Berkman	Hou	$3.500	$6.921	$3.421
Jenkins	Mil	$5.188	$6.641	$1.453
Gonzalez L	Ari	$4.000	$6.514	$2.514
Jones C	Atl	$13.333	$6.005	($7.328)
Floyd	NYM	$6.500	$5.191	($1.309)
Payton	Col	$1.850	$4.987	$3.137
Wilkerson	Mtl	$0.315	$4.911	$4.596
Alou	ChC	$9.500	$4.478	($5.022)
Dunn	Cin	$0.400	$4.249	$3.849
White R	SD	$5.500	$3.359	($2.141)
Hollandsworth	Fla	$1.500	$2.824	$1.324
Burnitz	NYM-LA	$12.167	$2.799	($9.368)
Burrell	Phi	$1.250	$2.366	$1.116
Cabrera	Fla	$0.300	$1.985	$1.685
Michaels	Phi	$0.305	$1.883	$1.578
Bay	SD-Pit	$0.300	$1.272	$0.972
Perez T	NYM	$0.313	$1.247	$0.934
Gonzalez R	NYM	$0.300	$1.018	$0.718
Conine	Fla	$0.800	$0.967	$0.167
Hammonds	Mil-SF	$8.200	$0.941	($7.259)
Stenson	Cin	$0.300	$0.865	$0.565
Banks	Fla	$0.300	$0.738	$0.438
Calloway	Mtl	$0.300	$0.636	$0.336
Kinkade	LA	$0.320	$0.229	($0.091)
O'Leary	ChC	$0.750	$0.127	($0.623)
Macias	Mtl	$0.825	($0.025)	($0.850)
Kapler	Col	$2.500	($0.407)	($2.907)

Center Field	Team	Salary	Earned Value	Difference
Edmonds	SL	$8.333	$8.345	$0.012
Podsednik	Mil	$0.300	$5.932	$5.632
Jones	Atl	$12.000	$5.490	($6.510)
Lofton	Pit-ChC	$1.025	$4.870	$3.845
Pierre	Fla	$1.000	$4.693	$3.693
Kotsay	SD	$4.450	$4.560	$0.110

Byrd	Phi	$0.300	$4.117	$3.817
Wilson	Col	$6.500	$4.073	($2.427)
Grissom	SF	$1.875	$3.984	$2.109
Finley	Ari	$4.250	$3.918	($0.332)
Biggio	Hou	$9.750	$3.453	($6.297)
Patterson	ChC	$0.365	$2.169	$1.804
Ledee	Phi	$0.850	$1.837	$0.987
Griffey	Cin	$12.500	$1.793	($10.707)
Redman	Pit	$0.350	$1.771	$1.421
Matthews	SD	$0.603	$1.638	$1.035
Chavez	Mtl	$0.300	$1.284	$0.984
Roberts	LA	$0.400	$1.151	$0.751
Sanchez	Mil	$0.115	$0.908	$0.793
Freel	Cin	$0.300	$0.576	$0.276
Goodwin	ChC	$0.635	$0.553	($0.082)
Duncan	NYM	$0.300	$0.376	$0.076
Taylor	Cin	$0.334	$0.199	($0.135)
Pena	Cin	$0.788	($0.066)	($0.854)

Right Field	Team	Salary	Earned Value	Difference
Sheffield	Atl	$11.417	$11.218	($0.199)
Hidalgo	Hou	$8.500	$9.646	$1.146
Abreu	Phi	$9.100	$8.876	($0.224)
Guerrero V	Mtl	$11.500	$7.365	($4.135)
Cruz	SF	$2.500	$7.273	$4.773
Guillen J	Cin	$0.300	$6.348	$6.048
Sosa	ChC	$16.000	$6.194	($9.806)
Green S	LA	$15.667	$5.794	($9.873)
Sanders	Pit	$1.000	$5.763	$4.763
Encarnacion	Fla	$3.450	$5.177	$1.727
Walker	Col	$12.667	$4.777	($7.890)
Drew	SL	$3.700	$4.623	$0.923
Stairs	Pit	$4.345	$3.445	($0.910)
Wilson C	Pit	$0.327	$4.006	$3.679
Kearns	Cin	$0.350	$3.883	$3.533
Vander Wal	Mil	$0.550	$3.852	$3.302
Perez	SL	$0.500	$2.928	$2.428
Clark	Mil	$0.313	$2.774	$2.461
Nady	SD	$0.750	$2.712	$1.962
Cedeno	NYM	$4.875	$2.650	($2.225)
Palmeiro	SL	$0.700	$2.620	$1.920
Buchanan	SD	$0.325	$2.342	$2.017
Mondesi	Ari	$4.030	$1.510	($2.520)

Dellucci	Ari	$0.690	$1.387	$0.697
Bautista	Ari	$3.000	$0.678	($2.322)
Merced	Hou	$1.700	$0.616	($1.084)
Mateo	Cin	$0.340	$0.123	($0.217)
Reyes R	Col	$0.300	$0.062	($0.238)
Robinson	SL	$0.320	$0.000	($0.320)
Bragg	Atl	$0.450	($0.586)	($1.036)
McCracken	Ari	$1.750	($0.986)	($2.736)

2003 AL Pitchers

15+ starts	Team	Salary	Earned Value	Difference
Loaiza	CWS	$0.500	$7.925	$7.425
Hudson	Oak	$2.700	$7.561	$4.861
Halladay	Tor	$3.825	$7.198	$3.373
Zito	Oak	$1.000	$6.471	$5.471
Martinez P	Bos	$15.500	$6.398	($9.102)
Moyer	Sea	$6.500	$6.398	($0.102)
Mussina	NYY	$12.000	$6.034	($5.966)
Mulder	Oak	$2.650	$6.034	$3.384
Colon	CWS	$8.250	$5.744	($2.506)
May D	KC	$0.450	$5.017	$4.567
Sabathia	Cle	$1.100	$4.799	$3.699
Franklin	Sea	$0.425	$4.799	$4.374
Pineiro	Sea	$0.440	$4.726	$4.286
Clemens	NYY	$10.100	$4.653	($5.447)
Wells	NYY	$3.250	$4.653	$1.403
Buehrle	CWS	$0.445	$4.508	$4.063
Santana Jo	Min	$0.335	$4.508	$4.173
Thomson	Tex	$1.300	$4.290	$2.990
Wakefield	Bos	$4.000	$4.144	$0.144
Anderson	Cle-KC	$1.500	$4.144	$2.644
Pettite	NYY	$11.500	$4.072	($7.428)
Ponson	Bal	$2.932	$3.853	$0.921
Lowe	Bos	$3.625	$3.853	$0.228
Radke	Min	$8.750	$3.781	($4.969)
Escobar	Tor	$3.900	$3.781	($0.119)
Gonzalez	TB	$0.300	$3.635	$3.335
Zambrano	TB	$0.300	$3.635	$3.335
Lohse	Min	$0.330	$3.563	$3.233
Lilly	Oak	$0.335	$3.563	$3.228
Johnson	Bal	$2.900	$3.417	$0.517
Garland	CWS	$0.375	$3.417	$3.042

Affeldt	KC	$0.313	$3.345	$3.032
Hentgen	Bal	$1.200	$3.272	$2.072
Rogers	Min	$2.000	$3.272	$1.272
Garcia	Sea	$6.875	$3.199	($3.676)
Lackey	Ana	$0.315	$2.908	$2.593
Meche	Sea	$0.325	$2.908	$2.583
Cornejo	Det	$0.303	$2.690	$2.387
Burkett	Bos	$5.500	$2.618	($2.882)
Davis	Cle	$0.300	$2.472	$2.172
Sosa	TB	$0.300	$2.399	$2.099
Hernandez R	KC	$0.306	$2.181	$1.875
Washburn	Ana	$3.875	$2.109	($1.766)
Westbrook	Cle	$0.306	$2.109	$1.803
Sele	Ana	$8.167	$1.963	($6.204)
Reed	Min	$8.000	$1.818	($6.182)
Hendrickson	Tor	$0.302	$1.745	$1.443
George	KC	$0.304	$1.672	$1.369
Traber	Cle	$0.301	$1.600	$1.299
Snyder	KC	$0.300	$1.454	$1.154
Benoit	Tex	$0.300	$1.454	$1.154
Lidle	Tor	$5.350	$1.454	($3.896)
Helling	Bal	$0.890	$1.236	$0.346
Bell	TB	$0.300	$1.236	$0.936
Appier	Ana-KC	$11.500	$1.164	($10.336)
Weaver	NYY	$4.150	$1.164	($2.986)
Ortiz	Ana	$2.267	$1.091	($1.176)
Valdes	Tex	$2.500	$1.091	($1.409)
Wright	CWS	$0.325	$0.945	$0.620
Lopez	Bal	$0.325	$0.873	$0.548
Mays	Min	$4.150	$0.873	($3.277)
Kennedy	TB	$0.300	$0.873	$0.573
Park	Tex	$13.000	$0.727	($12.273)
Daal	Bal	$3.000	$0.727	($2.273)
Maroth	Det	$0.309	$0.655	$0.346
Rodriguez	Cle	$0.302	$0.509	$0.207
Knotts	Det	$0.305	$0.509	$0.204
Milton	Min	$6.000	$0.509	($5.491)
Bonderman	Det	$0.300	$0.437	$0.137
Bernero	Det	$0.314	$0.437	$0.123
Erickson	Bal	$7.030	$0.000	($7.030)
Lewis	Tex	$0.303	($0.218)	($0.521)

Closer	Team	Salary	Earned Value	Difference
Foulke	Oak	$6.000	$7.123	$1.123
Rivera	NYY	$10.500	$6.233	($4.267)
Hasegawa	Sea	$1.800	$4.749	$2.949
Cordero	Tex	$0.900	$4.551	$3.651
Marte	CWS	$0.330	$4.353	$4.023
Guardado	Min	$2.700	$4.254	$1.554
Gordon	CWS	$1.400	$3.957	$2.557
Kim	Bos	$1.600	$3.661	$2.061
Baez	Cle	$5.125	$2.968	($2.157)
MacDougal	KC	$0.301	$2.869	$2.568
Lopez A	Tor	$0.300	$2.671	$2.371
Carter	TB	$0.300	$2.473	$2.173
Percival	Ana	$7.833	$2.276	($5.557)
Urbina	Tex	$2.250	$1.583	($0.667)
Julio	Bal	$0.350	$1.088	$0.738
Sasaki	Sea	$8.000	$0.989	($7.011)
Politte	Tor	$0.845	$0.791	($0.054)
Patterson	Det	$2.500	$0.495	($2.005)
Koch	CWS	$4.250	$0.198	($4.052)

50+IP	Team	Salary	Earned Value	Difference
Hawkins	Min	$3.000	$3.374	$0.374
Shields	Ana	$0.305	$3.129	$2.824
Karsay	NYY	$5.000	$2.515	($2.485)
Bradford	Oak	$0.331	$2.331	$2.000
Rodriguez	Ana	$0.313	$2.209	$1.896
Levine	TB-KC	$0.400	$2.086	$1.686
Hammond	NYY	$2.200	$1.963	($0.237)
Colome	TB	$0.300	$1.963	$1.663
Gobble	KC	$0.300	$1.963	$1.663
Rincon R	Oak	$1.700	$1.902	$0.202
Weber	Ana	$0.375	$1.840	$1.465
Rincon J	Min	$0.320	$1.779	$1.459
Stanford	Cle	$0.300	$1.779	$1.479
Donnelly	Ana	$0.325	$1.656	$1.331
Riske	Cle	$0.314	$1.656	$1.342
Ligtenberg	Bal	$1.200	$1.656	$0.456
DuBose	Bal	$0.300	$1.595	$1.295
Walker	Det	$0.360	$1.595	$1.235
Ryan	Bal	$0.763	$1.595	$0.832
Timlin	Bos	$1.850	$1.534	($0.316)
Contreras	NYY	$5.500	$1.534	($3.966)

Mateo	Sea	$0.303	$1.534	$1.231
Nelson	Sea-NYY	$3.983	$1.534	($2.449)
Dickey	Tex	$0.300	$1.534	$1.234
Soriano	Sea	$0.300	$1.472	$1.172
Glover	CWS-Ana	$0.330	$1.472	$1.142
Leskanic	KC	$1.850	$1.472	($0.378)
Kershner	Tor	$0.300	$1.411	$1.111
Embree	Bos	$3.000	$1.141	($1.589)
Harper	TB	$0.300	$1.350	$1.050
Harden	Oak	$0.300	$1.350	$1.050
Towers	Tor	$0.800	$1.350	$0.550
Rhodes	Sea	$3.500	$1.350	($2.150)
Sparks	Det-Oak	$4.500	$1.288	($3.212)
Schoenweis	Ana-CWS	$1.425	$1.288	($0.137)
Grimsley	KC	$2.000	$1.288	($0.712)
Shouse	Tex	$0.300	$1.288	$0.988
Carrasco	KC	$0.300	$1.166	$0.866
Lima	KC	$0.300	$1.166	$0.866
Lyon	Bos	$0.309	$1.104	$0.795
Lee	Cle	$0.301	$1.104	$0.803
Wilson	KC	$0.311	$1.104	$0.793
Mulholland	Cle	$0.500	$1.043	$0.543
Boyd	Cle	$0.300	$1.043	$0.743
Hitchcock	NYY	$3.480	$0.982	($2.498)
Osuna	NYY	$2.400	$0.920	($1.480)
Miller	Tor	$0.305	$0.920	$0.615
Walker	Tor	$0.425	$0.920	$0.495
Halama	Oak	$0.750	$0.859	$0.109
Fultz	Tex	$0.600	$0.859	$0.259
Bauer	Bal	$0.325	$0.859	$0.534
Romero	Min	$0.325	$0.859	$0.534
Spurling	Det	$0.305	$0.798	$0.493
Powell	Tex	$3.250	$0.675	($2.575)
Roney	Det	$0.300	$0.552	$0.252
Suppan	Bos	$0.500	$0.552	$0.052
Davis D	Tex-Tor	$0.330	$0.491	$0.161
Mecir	Oak	$3.217	$0.307	($2.910)
Mounce	Tex	$0.300	$0.307	$0.007
Fossum	Bos	$0.325	$0.245	($0.080)
Moss	Bal	$0.700	$0.245	($0.455)
Ledezma	Det	$0.300	$0.123	($0.177)
Mendoza	Bos	$2.900	$0.061	($2.839)
Wickman	Cle	$6.000	$0.000	($6.000)

Wohlers	Cle	$2.600	$0.000	($2.600)
Sturtze	Tor	$1.000	($0.123)	($1.123)
Callaway	Tex	$0.300	($0.981)	($1.281)

2003 NL Pitchers

15+ starts	Team	Salary	Earned Value	Difference
Prior	ChC	$1.450	$7.784	$6.334
Hernandez	Mtl	$3.825	$7.627	$3.802
Brown	LA	$15.714	$7.155	($8.559)
Vazquez	Mtl	$6.000	$6.998	$0.998
Schmidt	SF	$5.937	$6.998	$1.061
Zambrano	ChC	$0.340	$6.919	$6.579
Nomo	LA	$7.750	$6.683	($1.067)
Wood	ChC	$6.190	$6.369	$0.179
Webb	Ari	$0.300	$5.976	$5.676
Ortiz	Atl	$4.662	$5.425	$0.763
Wells	Pit	$0.370	$5.347	$4.977
Williams	SL	$6.000	$5.347	($0.653)
Schilling	Ari	$10.000	$5.032	($4.968)
Trachsel	NYM	$3.000	$4.954	$1.954
Maddux	Atl	$14.750	$4.875	($9.875)
Willis	Fla	$0.300	$4.875	$4.575
Batista	Ari	$3.375	$4.796	$1.421
Hampton	Atl	$13.625	$4.796	($8.829)
Redding	Hou	$0.300	$4.796	$4.496
Ohka	Mtl	$0.340	$4.639	$4.299
Suppan	Pit	$0.346	$4.246	$3.900
Clement	ChC	$4.000	$4.167	$0.167
Beckett	Fla	$1.725	$4.167	$2.442
Millwood	Phi	$9.900	$4.167	($5.733)
Morris	SL	$10.500	$4.167	($6.333)
Miller	Hou	$0.525	$4.010	$3.485
Oswalt	Hou	$0.500	$4.010	$3.510
Redman	Fla	$2.150	$3.931	$1.781
Lawrence	SD	$0.625	$3.853	$3.228
Wolf	Phi	$2.375	$3.774	$1.399
Oliver	Col	$0.350	$3.695	$3.345
Seo	NYM	$0.300	$3.695	$3.395
Eaton	SD	$0.350	$3.695	$3.345
Ramirez	Atl	$0.300	$3.617	$3.317
Leiter A	NYM	$8.000	$3.617	($4.383)

Pavano	Fla	$1.500	$3.538	$2.038
Penny	Fla	$1.875	$3.460	$1.585
Sheets	Mil	$0.428	$3.381	$2.953
Chacon	Col	$0.300	$3.302	$3.002
Williams	SF	$0.300	$3.302	$3.002
Jennings	Col	$0.325	$3.224	$2.899
Day	Mtl	$0.301	$3.224	$2.923
Glavine	NYM	$11.000	$3.224	($7.776)
Dessens	Ari	$3.000	$3.145	$0.145
Peavy	SD	$0.305	$3.066	$2.761
Villone	Hou	$0.500	$2.831	$2.331
Myers	Phi	$0.300	$2.831	$2.531
Padilla	Phi	$0.425	$2.831	$2.406
Johnson	Ari	$15.000	$2.752	($12.248)
Stephenson	SL	$0.800	$2.752	$1.952
Perez	LA	$3.400	$2.673	($0.727)
Ishii	LA	$2.575	$2.595	$0.020
D'Amico	Pit	$0.750	$2.595	$1.845
Vargas	Mtl	$0.300	$2.516	$2.216
Wilson	Cin	$0.500	$2.359	$1.859
Rueter	SF	$5.866	$2.359	($3.507)
Tomko	SL	$3.300	$2.202	($1.098)
Robertson	Hou	$0.300	$2.044	$1.744
Torres	Pit	$0.325	$2.044	$1.719
Ponson	SF	$1.318	$1.887	$0.569
Moss	SF	$1.550	$1.808	$0.258
Cook A	Col	$0.300	$1.651	$1.351
Graves	Cin	$5.000	$1.494	($3.506)
Kinney	Mil	$0.318	$1.494	$1.176
Fogg	Pit	$0.322	$1.494	$1.172
Reynolds	Atl	$0.400	$1.415	$1.015
Dreifort	LA	$12.400	$1.337	($11.063)
Franklin	Mil	$0.315	$1.258	$0.943
Duckworth	Phi	$0.325	$1.022	$0.697
Estes	ChC	$3.000	$0.944	($2.056)
Benson	Pit	$4.300	$0.944	($3.356)
Foppert	SF	$0.300	$0.944	$0.644
Perez	SD-Pit	$0.305	$0.865	$0.560
Burnett	Fla	$2.500	$0.786	($1.714)
Astacio	NYM	$7.000	$0.786	($6.214)
Simontacchi	SL	$0.315	$0.629	$0.314
Dempster	Cin	$3.250	$0.472	($2.778)
Rusch	Mil	$4.250	$0.393	($3.857)

Jarvis	SD	$3.000	$0.236	($2.764)
Hernandez O	Mtl	$4.100	$0.000	($4.100)
Haynes	Cin	$2.500	($0.079)	($2.579)
Neagle	Col	$9.000	($0.315)	($9.315)

Closers	Team	Salary	Earned Value	Difference
Gagne	LA	$0.550	$9.779	$9.229
Wagner	Hou	$8.000	$8.645	$0.645
Smoltz	Atl	$10.667	$7.795	($2.872)
Mantei	Ari	$7.083	$5.385	($1.698)
Borowski	ChC	$0.410	$5.244	$4.834
Worrell	SF	$2.000	$4.535	$2.535
Beck	SD	$0.400	$4.110	$3.710
Looper	Fla	$1.600	$3.968	$2.368
Tavarez	Pit	$0.750	$3.685	$2.935
Valverde	Ari	$0.300	$3.685	$3.385
Benitez	NYM	$4.657	$3.685	($0.972)
Kolb	Mil	$0.300	$3.685	$3.385
Urbina	Fla	$2.250	$3.118	$0.868
Jimenez	Col	$3.600	$2.976	($0.624)
Reitsma	Cin	$0.400	$2.976	$2.576
Williamson	Cin	$1.070	$2.976	$1.906
Isringhausen	SL	$7.250	$2.693	($4.557)
Biddle	Mtl	$0.320	$2.551	$2.231
DeJean	Mil-SL	$1.700	$1.842	$0.142
Hoffman	SD	$9.600	$0.709	($8.891)
Nen	SF	$8.750	$0.000	($8.750)
Williams M	Pit-Phi	$3.500	($1.134)	($4.634)
Mesa	Phi	$5.200	($2.551)	($7.751)

50+IP	Team	Salary	Earned Value	Difference
Villareal	Ari	$0.300	$2.771	$2.471
Mota	LA	$0.675	$2.505	$1.830
Dotel	Hou	$1.600	$2.345	$0.745
Ayala	Mtl	$0.300	$2.292	$1.992
Cormier	Phi	$2.983	$2.238	($0.745)
Alvarez	LA	$0.500	$2.132	$1.632
Quantrill	LA	$3.333	$1.972	($1.361)
Weathers	NYM	$3.733	$1.812	($1.921)
Fuentes	Col	$0.300	$1.759	$1.459
Shuey	LA	$3.917	$1.705	($2.212)
Linebrink	Hou-SD	$0.400	$1.492	$1.092
Herges	SD-SF	$0.400	$1.492	$1.092

Heredia F	Cin	$0.497	$1.492	$0.995
Reed S	Col	$0.600	$1.439	$0.839
Lidge	Hou	$0.300	$1.439	$1.139
Stone	Hou	$0.325	$1.439	$1.114
Adams	Phi	$2.900	$1.439	($1.461)
Brower	SF	$0.300	$1.439	$1.139
Rodriguez	SF	$3.167	$1.439	($1.728)
Remlinger	ChC	$2.633	$1.386	($1.247)
Farnsworth	ChC	$0.600	$1.332	$0.732
Wendell	Phi	$3.350	$1.332	($2.018)
Silva	Phi	$0.310	$1.279	$0.969
Kline	SL	$1.800	$1.279	($0.521)
Speier	Col	$0.850	$1.226	$0.376
Eldred	SL	$0.500	$1.226	$0.726
Kieschnick	Mil	$0.300	$1.172	$0.872
Randolph	Ari	$0.300	$1.119	$0.819
Mercker	Atl-Cin	$0.400	$1.119	$0.719
Riedling	Cin	$0.350	$1.119	$0.769
Lopez	Col	$0.300	$1.119	$0.819
Davis	Mil	$0.300	$1.119	$0.819
Estrella	Mil	$0.300	$1.119	$0.819
Eischen	Mtl	$0.750	$1.066	$0.316
Tucker	Mtl	$0.210	$1.066	$0.856
Hermanson	SF-SL	$0.400	$1.066	$0.666
Ainsworth	SF	$0.302	$1.066	$0.764
Miceli	Col-Hou	$0.350	$1.013	$0.663
King	Atl	$0.600	$0.959	$0.359
Sullivan	Cin	$1.400	$0.959	($0.441)
Eyre	SF	$0.725	$0.959	$0.234
Hodges	Atl	$0.300	$0.906	$0.606
Martin	LA	$0.300	$0.906	$0.606
Leskanic	Mil	$1.850	$0.906	($0.944)
Meadows	Pit	$0.300	$0.906	$0.606
Tejera	Fla	$0.300	$0.853	$0.553
Wheeler	NYM	$0.300	$0.853	$0.553
Phelps	Fla	$0.300	$0.799	$0.499
Matthews	SD	$0.350	$0.799	$0.449
Alfonseca	ChC	$4.000	$0.746	($3.254)
Reith	Cin	$0.300	$0.746	$0.446
Obermuller	Mil	$0.300	$0.746	$0.446
Zerbe	SF	$0.317	$0.746	$0.429
Munro	Hou	$0.305	$0.746	$0.441
Stark	Col	$0.310	$0.693	$0.383

Beimel	Pit	$0.322	$0.693	$0.371
Hackman	SD	$0.345	$0.693	$0.348
Hernandez	Atl	$0.600	$0.640	$0.040
de los Santos	Mil-Phi	$0.925	$0.640	($0.285)
Bong	Atl	$0.300	$0.586	$0.286
White G	Cin	$1.600	$0.586	($1.014)
Haren	SL	$0.300	$0.480	$0.180
Patterson	Ari	$0.300	$0.426	$0.126
Roa	Col-Phi-SD	$0.315	$0.426	$0.111
Ashby	LA	$8.500	$0.320	($8.180)
Boehringer	Pit	$1.500	$0.320	($1.180)
Fassero	SL	$1.250	$0.266	($0.984)
Elarton	Col	$0.300	$0.107	($0.193)
Cruz	ChC	$0.340	$0.053	($0.287)
Vizcaino	Mil	$0.370	$0.053	($0.317)
Cruz N	Col	$0.700	$0.053	($0.647)
Heilman	NYM	$0.300	($0.160)	($0.460)
Jones T	Col	$3.000	($0.213)	($3.213)
Almanza	Fla	$0.775	($0.213)	($0.988)
Nathan	SF	$0.300	($0.266)	($0.566)
Wright	SD-Atl	$0.725	($0.426)	($1.151)

2003 EARNED VALUES BY TEAM

American League

ANAHEIM ANGELS

Player	Salary	Earned Value	Difference
Anderson	$5.350	$7.585	$2.235
Salmon	$9.900	$7.226	($2.674)
Davanon	$0.300	$4.641	$4.341
Amezaga	$0.300	$3.673	$3.373
Fullmer	$1.000	$3.187	$2.187
Shields	$0.305	$3.129	$2.824
Spiezio	$4.250	$2.915	($1.335)
Lackey	$0.315	$2.908	$2.593
Molina B	$1.425	$2.779	$1.354
Percival	$7.833	$2.276	($5.557)
Rodriguez	$0.313	$2.209	$1.896
Glaus	$7.250	$2.179	($5.071)
Washburn	$3.875	$2.109	($1.766)

Sele	$8.167	$1.963	($6.204)
Weber	$0.375	$1.840	$1.465
Kennedy	$2.270	$1.803	($0.467)
Donnelly	$0.325	$1.656	$1.331
Erstad	$7.250	$1.509	($5.741)
Figgins	$0.300	$1.509	$1.209
Ortiz	$2.267	$1.091	($1.176)
Appier	$9.550	$0.967	($8.583)
Glover	$0.145	$0.798	$0.653
Schoenweis	$0.855	$0.675	($0.180)
Owens	$0.925	$0.588	($0.337)
Wooten	$0.338	$0.548	$0.210
Eckstein	$0.425	$0.296	($0.129)
Quinlan	$0.300	$0.249	($0.051)
Gil B	$0.725	($0.021)	($0.746)
Molina J	$0.320	($0.243)	($0.563)
	$76.953	$62.044	($14.909)

BALTIMORE ORIOLES

Player	Salary	Earned Value	Difference
Mora	$1.725	$5.238	$3.513
Matos	$0.300	$4.986	$4.686
Cruz	$1.000	$3.926	$2.926
Ponson	$2.932	$3.853	$0.921
Conine	$3.450	$3.538	$0.088
Johnson	$2.900	$3.417	$0.517
Hentgen	$1.200	$3.272	$2.072
Bigbie	$0.300	$2.892	$2.592
Surhoff	$1.000	$2.789	$1.789
Segui	$7.000	$2.723	($4.277)
Gibbons	$0.375	$2.323	$1.948
Roberts	$0.300	$1.973	$1.673
Batista	$6.400	$1.961	($4.439)
Ligtenberg	$1.200	$1.656	$0.456
DuBose	$0.300	$1.595	$1.295
Ryan	$0.763	$1.595	$0.832
Helling	$0.890	$1.236	$0.346
Fordyce	$3.500	$1.112	($2.388)
Julio	$0.350	$1.088	$0.738
Lopez	$0.325	$0.873	$0.548
Bauer	$0.325	$0.859	$0.534
Hairston	$1.550	$0.846	($0.704)

Daal	$3.000	$0.727	($2.273)
Gil	$0.330	$0.625	$0.295
Moss	$0.700	$0.245	($0.455)
Belle	$13.000	$0.000	($13.000)
Erickson	$7.030	$0.000	($7.030)
Matthews	$0.297	($0.179)	($0.476)
	$62.442	$55.169	($7.273)

BOSTON RED SOX

Player	Salary	Earned Value	Difference
Garciaparra	$11.000	$8.782	($2.218)
Ortiz	$1.250	$8.185	$6.935
Ramirez	$20.000	$7.632	($12.368)
Nixon	$4.000	$7.288	$3.288
Mueller	$2.100	$6.792	$4.692
Martinez P	$15.500	$6.398	($9.102)
Millar	$2.000	$4.983	$2.983
Damon	$7.500	$4.705	($2.795)
Wakefield	$4.000	$4.144	$0.144
Lowe	$3.625	$3.853	$0.228
Kim	$1.600	$3.661	$2.061
Varitek	$4.700	$3.218	($1.482)
Burkett	$5.500	$2.618	($2.882)
Walker	$3.450	$1.990	($1.460)
Timlin	$1.850	$1.534	($0.316)
Embree	$3.000	$1.411	($1.589)
Kapler	$3.425	$1.142	($2.283)
Lyon	$0.309	$1.104	$0.795
Suppan	$0.500	$0.552	$0.052
Mirabelli	$0.805	$0.543	($0.262)
Fossum	$0.325	$0.245	($0.080)
Jackson D	$0.625	$0.187	($0.438)
Mendoza	$2.900	$0.061	($2.839)
Hillenbrand	$0.148	($0.109)	($0.257)
	$100.112	$80.919	($19.193)

CHICAGO WHITE SOX

Player	Salary	Earned Value	Difference
Thomas	$5.000	$10.285	$5.285
Ordonez	$9.000	$9.344	$0.344

Loaiza	$0.500	$7.925	$7.425
Valentin	$5.000	$6.966	$1.966
Colon	$8.250	$5.744	($2.506)
Lee	$4.200	$5.120	$0.920
Buehrle	$0.445	$4.508	$4.063
Marte	$0.330	$4.353	$4.023
Gordon	$1.400	$3.957	$2.557
Garland	$0.375	$3.417	$3.042
Graffanino	$0.675	$3.293	$2.618
Crede	$0.315	$2.906	$2.591
Everett	$4.397	$2.864	($1.533)
Olivo	$0.300	$1.773	$1.473
Konerko	$6.250	$1.769	($4.481)
Rowand	$0.320	$1.457	$1.137
Daubach	$0.450	$0.997	$0.547
Wright	$0.325	$0.945	$0.620
Jimenez	$0.170	$0.788	$0.618
Alomar, Jr	$0.700	$0.699	($0.001)
Glover	$0.185	$0.674	$0.489
Alomar R	$3.920	$0.622	($3.298)
Schoenweis	$0.570	$0.613	$0.043
Harris	$0.300	$0.332	$0.032
Koch	$4.250	$0.198	($4.052)
Rios	$0.450	($0.256)	($0.706)
	$58.077	$81.293	$23.216

CLEVELAND INDIANS

Player	Salary	Earned Value	Difference
Bradley	$0.314	$5.753	$5.439
Gerut	$0.300	$5.668	$5.368
Sabathia	$1.100	$4.799	$3.699
Blake	$0.330	$3.487	$3.157
Anderson	$1.125	$3.345	$2.220
Vizquel	$5.500	$3.124	($2.376)
Baez	$5.125	$2.968	($2.157)
Hafner	$0.302	$2.680	$2.378
Davis	$0.300	$2.472	$2.172
Lawton	$6.750	$2.465	($4.285)
Burks	$7.167	$2.173	($4.994)
Westbrook	$0.306	$2.109	$1.803
Broussard	$0.303	$1.794	$1.491

Stanford	$0.300	$1.779	$1.479
Peralta	$0.300	$1.773	$1.473
Bard	$0.302	$1.721	$1.419
Riske	$0.314	$1.656	$1.342
Traber	$0.301	$1.600	$1.299
Escobar	$0.300	$1.184	$0.884
Spencer	$0.319	$1.138	$0.819
Crisp	$0.300	$1.125	$0.825
Lee	$0.301	$1.104	$0.803
Mulholland	$0.500	$1.043	$0.543
Boyd	$0.300	$1.043	$0.743
Martinez V	$0.300	$0.837	$0.537
Phillips	$0.301	$0.829	$0.528
Rodriguez	$0.302	$0.509	$0.207
Laker	$0.400	$0.466	$0.066
Wickman	$6.000	$0.000	($6.000)
Wohlers	$2.600	$0.000	($2.600)
McDonald	$0.315	($0.191)	($0.506)
Gutierrez	$3.917	($0.338)	($4.255)
	$46.594	$60.115	$13.521

DETROIT TIGERS

Player	Salary	Earned Value	Difference
Young D	$6.750	$11.299	$4.549
Pena	$0.310	$3.140	$2.830
Cornejo	$0.303	$2.690	$2.387
Higginson	$11.850	$2.678	($9.172)
Sanchez	$0.225	$2.659	$2.434
Santiago	$0.307	$2.575	$2.268
Monroe	$0.300	$2.441	$2.141
Infante	$0.300	$2.153	$1.853
Walker	$0.360	$1.595	$1.235
Morris	$0.400	$1.575	$1.175
Witt K	$0.300	$1.557	$1.257
Halter	$2.150	$1.380	($0.770)
Sparks	$3.790	$1.288	($2.502)
Inge	$0.315	$1.218	$0.903
Munson	$1.700	$1.090	($0.610)
Spurling	$0.305	$0.798	$0.493
Maroth	$0.309	$0.655	$0.346
Roney	$0.300	$0.552	$0.252

Knotts	$0.305	$0.509	$0.204
Patterson	$2.500	$0.495	($2.005)
Bonderman	$0.300	$0.437	$0.137
Bernero	$0.314	$0.437	$0.123
Petrick	$0.500	$0.142	($0.358)
Ledezma	$0.300	$0.123	($0.177)
Torres	$0.300	($0.281)	($0.581)
Walbeck	$0.400	($0.825)	($1.225)
Palmer	$8.500	($1.738)	($10.238)
	$43.693	$40.642	($3.051)

KANSAS CITY ROYALS

Player	Salary	Earned Value	Difference
Beltran	$6.000	$8.413	$2.413
Berroa	$0.303	$6.502	$6.199
Sweeney	$11.000	$5.179	($5.821)
May D	$0.450	$5.017	$4.567
Guiel	$0.300	$3.644	$3.344
Ibanez	$3.000	$3.508	$0.508
Affeldt	$0.313	$3.345	$3.032
Randa	$4.500	$3.022	($1.478)
MacDougal	$0.301	$2.869	$2.568
Hernandez R	$0.306	$2.181	$1.875
Tucker	$2.750	$1.993	($0.757)
Gobble	$0.300	$1.963	$1.663
Harvey	$0.300	$1.744	$1.444
George	$0.304	$1.672	$1.369
Leskanic	$1.850	$1.472	($0.378)
Snyder	$0.300	$1.454	$1.154
Anderson	$0.375	$1.309	$0.934
Grimsley	$2.000	$1.288	($0.712)
Relaford	$0.900	$1.268	$0.368
Carrasco	$0.300	$1.166	$0.866
Lima	$0.300	$1.166	$0.866
Wilson	$0.311	$1.104	$0.793
DiFelice	$0.625	$1.070	$0.445
Mayne	$2.750	$1.006	($1.744)
Levine	$0.116	$0.718	$0.602
Lopez	$0.300	$0.449	$0.149
Appier	$1.950	$0.197	($1.753)
Brown D	$0.310	($0.047)	($0.357)

| Febles | $0.775 | ($0.091) | ($0.866) |
| | $43.289 | $64.581 | $21.293 |

MINNESOTA TWINS

Player	Salary	Earned Value	Difference
Hunter	$4.750	$4.603	($0.147)
Santana Jo	$0.335	$4.508	$4.173
Koskie	$3.400	$4.431	$1.031
Guardado	$2.700	$4.254	$1.554
Mientkiewicz	$1.750	$4.111	$2.361
Jones J	$2.750	$4.006	$1.256
Radke	$8.750	$3.781	($4.969)
Pierzynski	$0.365	$3.642	$3.277
Lohse	$0.330	$3.563	$3.233
Hawkins	$3.000	$3.374	$0.374
Rogers	$2.000	$3.272	$1.272
Stewart	$2.960	$3.091	$0.131
LeCroy	$0.313	$2.934	$2.621
Kielty	$0.187	$2.454	$2.267
Mohr	$0.315	$2.398	$2.083
Guzman	$2.525	$1.984	($0.541)
Reed	$8.000	$1.818	($6.182)
Rincon J	$0.320	$1.779	$1.459
Mays	$4.150	$0.873	($3.277)
Romero	$0.325	$0.859	$0.534
Milton	$6.000	$0.509	($5.491)
Hocking	$1.000	$0.390	($0.610)
Morneau	$0.300	$0.217	($0.083)
Rivas	$0.340	$0.149	($0.191)
Cuddyer	$0.303	$0.062	($0.241)
Gomez	$0.500	($0.062)	($0.562)
	$57.668	$63.000	$5.332

NEW YORK YANKEES

Player	Salary	Earned Value	Difference
Giambi Ja	$11.429	$6.279	($5.150)
Rivera M	$10.500	$6.233	($4.267)
Mussina	$12.000	$6.034	($5.966)
Posada	$8.000	$5.367	($2.633)

Johnson	$0.364	$5.033	$4.669
Clemens	$10.100	$4.653	($5.447)
Wells	$3.250	$4.653	$1.403
Matsui	$6.000	$4.646	($1.354)
Williams B	$12.357	$4.449	($7.908)
Jeter	$15.600	$4.391	($11.209)
Pettite	$11.500	$4.072	($7.428)
Mondesi	$8.970	$3.769	($5.201)
Soriano	$0.800	$3.565	$2.765
Karsay	$5.000	$2.515	($2.485)
Hammond	$2.200	$1.963	($0.237)
Ventura	$3.600	$1.743	($1.857)
Garcia	$0.900	$1.588	$0.688
Contreras	$5.500	$1.534	($3.966)
Boone A	$1.147	$1.482	$0.335
Sierra	$0.336	$1.246	$0.910
Weaver	$4.150	$1.164	($2.986)
Hitchcock	$3.480	$0.982	($2.498)
Osuna	$2.400	$0.920	($1.480)
Rivera R	$0.500	$0.877	$0.377
Zeile	$0.945	$0.683	($0.262)
Nelson	$1.314	$0.405	($0.909)
Almonte	$0.300	$0.296	($0.004)
Flaherty	$0.750	$0.286	($0.464)
Wilson	$0.700	$0.211	($0.489)
	$144.092	$81.039	($63.053)

OAKLAND A'S

Player	Salary	Earned Value	Difference
Tejada	$5.125	$8.022	$2.897
Hudson	$2.700	$7.561	$4.861
Foulke	$6.000	$7.123	$1.123
Chavez	$3.675	$6.683	$3.008
Zito	$1.000	$6.471	$5.471
Durazo	$1.065	$6.084	$5.019
Mulder	$2.650	$6.034	$3.384
Hernandez	$1.888	$3.589	$1.701
Lilly	$0.335	$3.563	$3.228
Ellis	$0.308	$2.943	$2.635
Hatteberg	$1.750	$2.891	$1.141
Byrnes	$0.300	$2.736	$2.436
Bradford	$0.331	$2.331	$2.000

Rincon R	$1.700	$1.902	$0.202
Harden	$0.300	$1.350	$1.050
McMillon	$0.500	$1.067	$0.567
Halama	$0.750	$0.859	$0.109
Long	$2.175	$0.806	($1.369)
Mecir	$3.217	$0.307	($2.910)
Guillen J	$0.200	$0.280	$0.080
Menechino	$0.335	$0.269	($0.066)
Piatt	$0.254	$0.085	($0.169)
Singleton	$1.200	($0.051)	($1.251)
Sparks	$0.610	($0.061)	($0.671)
Dye	$11.667	($0.903)	($12.570)
	$50.035	$71.941	$21.906

SEATTLE MARINERS

Player	Salary	Earned Value	Difference
Martinez	$4.000	$9.308	$5.308
Suzuki	$4.667	$7.226	$2.559
Cameron	$7.416	$7.057	($0.359)
Moyer	$6.500	$6.398	($0.102)
Winn	$3.300	$4.930	$1.630
Olerud	$7.700	$4.884	($2.816)
Franklin	$0.425	$4.799	$4.374
Hasegawa	$1.800	$4.749	$2.949
Pineiro	$0.440	$4.726	$4.286
Meche	$0.325	$3.908	$3.583
Guillen	$2.500	$3.462	$0.962
Boone	$8.000	$3.275	($4.725)
Garcia	$6.875	$3.199	($3.676)
McLemore	$3.150	$2.406	($0.744)
Mateo	$0.303	$1.534	$1.231
Soriano	$0.300	$1.472	$1.172
Rhodes	$3.500	$1.350	($2.150)
Davis	$1.000	$1.160	$0.160
Nelson	$2.669	$1.129	($1.540)
Sanchez	$0.650	$1.013	$0.363
Sasaki	$8.000	$0.989	($7.011)
Wilson	$3.500	$0.927	($2.573)
Mabry	$0.600	$0.561	($0.039)
Bloomquist	$0.300	$0.247	($0.053)
Cirillo	$6.725	($0.436)	($7.161)
	$84.645	$80.273	($4.372)

TAMPA BAY DEVIL RAYS

Player	Salary	Earned Value	Difference
Huff	$0.325	$8.222	$7.897
Baldelli	$0.300	$5.523	$5.223
Lugo	$0.750	$5.109	$4.359
Lee	$0.500	$4.385	$3.885
Gonzalez	$0.300	$3.635	$3.335
Zambrano	$0.300	$3.635	$3.335
Crawford	$0.300	$3.508	$3.208
Carter	$0.300	$2.473	$2.173
Sosa	$0.300	$2.399	$2.099
Colome	$0.300	$1.963	$1.663
Hall	$0.300	$1.752	$1.452
Rolls	$0.300	$1.743	$1.443
Grieve	$5.500	$1.738	($3.762)
Ordonez	$6.500	$1.647	($4.853)
Levine	$0.284	$1.368	$1.084
Harper	$0.300	$1.350	$1.050
Bell	$0.300	$1.236	$0.936
Anderson	$0.600	$1.103	$0.503
Martin	$0.300	$0.978	$0.678
Kennedy	$0.300	$0.873	$0.573
Sandberg	$0.300	$0.618	$0.318
Valentin Ja	$0.305	$0.286	($0.019)
Piatt	$0.068	($0.038)	($0.106)
Perez A	$0.300	($0.145)	($0.445)
Easley	$0.400	($0.545)	($0.945)
	$19.732	$54.816	$35.084

TEXAS RANGERS

Player	Salary	Earned Value	Difference
Rodriguez	$22.000	$10.977	($11.023)
Palmeiro	$9.000	$7.533	($1.467)
Blalock	$0.303	$4.939	$4.636
Cordero	$0.900	$4.551	$3.651
Thomson	$1.300	$4.290	$2.990
Gonzalez	$13.000	$3.800	($9.200)
Everett	$4.753	$2.992	($1.761)
Texeira	$0.750	$2.816	$2.066
Young	$0.415	$2.653	$2.238
Sierra	$0.264	$2.245	$1.981

Urbina	$2.250	$1.583	($0.667)
Dickey	$0.300	$1.534	$1.234
Benoit	$0.300	$1.454	$1.154
Shouse	$0.300	$1.288	$0.988
Diaz	$1.838	$1.138	($0.700)
Valdes	$2.500	$1.091	($1.409)
Nix	$0.300	$1.028	$0.728
Fultz	$0.600	$0.859	$0.259
Park	$13.000	$0.727	($12.273)
Powell	$3.250	$0.675	($2.575)
Mench	$0.328	$0.616	$0.289
Spencer	$0.281	$0.569	$0.288
Glanville	$0.790	$0.409	($0.381)
Mounce	$0.300	$0.307	$0.007
Jones J	$0.300	$0.237	($0.063)
Greene	$0.750	$0.223	($0.527)
Greer	$7.000	$0.000	($7.000)
Davis D	$0.017	($0.012)	($0.029)
Sadler	$0.400	($0.109)	($0.509)
Lewis	$0.303	($0.218)	($0.521)
Christenson	$0.500	($0.486)	($0.986)
Callaway	$0.300	($0.981)	($1.281)
	$88.592	$58.728	($29.864)

TORONTO BLUE JAYS

Player	Salary	Earned Value	Difference
Delgado	$18.700	$8.671	($10.029)
Halladay	$3.825	$7.198	$3.373
Wells	$0.520	$6.648	$6.128
Phelps	$0.320	$4.889	$4.569
Bordick	$1.000	$4.264	$3.264
Woodward	$0.775	$4.095	$3.320
Escobar	$3.900	$3.781	($0.119)
Hudson	$0.313	$3.382	$3.069
Catalanotto	$2.200	$3.176	$0.976
Hinske	$0.600	$2.804	$2.204
Lopez A	$0.300	$2.671	$2.371
Johnson R	$0.300	$2.616	$2.316
Stewart	$3.240	$2.313	($0.927)
Myers	$0.800	$2.012	$1.212
Hendrickson	$0.302	$1.745	$1.443
Lidle	$5.350	$1.454	($3.896)

Kershner	$0.300	$1.411	$1.111
Towers	$0.800	$1.350	$0.550
Wilson	$0.316	$1.318	$1.002
Kielty	$0.138	$1.221	$1.083
Miller	$0.305	$0.920	$0.615
Walker	$0.425	$0.920	$0.495
Politte	$0.845	$0.791	($0.054)
Davis D	$0.313	$0.626	$0.313
Berg	$0.450	$0.062	($0.388)
Sturtze	$1.000	($0.123)	($1.123)
Cash	$0.300	($0.402)	($0.702)
	$47.637	$69.813	$22.176

National League

ARIZONA DIAMONDBACKS

Player	Salary	Earned Value	Difference
Gonzalez L	$4.000	$6.514	$2.514
Webb	$0.300	$5.976	$5.676
Mantei	$7.083	$5.385	($1.698)
Baerga	$0.500	$5.188	$4.688
Schilling	$10.000	$5.032	($4.968)
Batista	$3.375	$4.796	$1.421
Finley	$4.250	$3.918	($0.332)
Valverde	$0.300	$3.685	$3.385
Hammock	$0.300	$3.389	$3.089
Cintron	$0.300	$3.299	$2.999
Dessens	$3.000	$3.145	$0.145
Overbay	$0.300	$2.781	$2.481
Villareal	$0.300	$2.771	$2.471
Johnson	$15.000	$2.752	($12.248)
Hillenbrand	$0.261	$2.034	$1.773
Spivey	$0.432	$1.979	$1.547
Moeller	$0.300	$1.873	$1.573
Barajas	$0.300	$1.803	$1.503
Counsell	$2.517	$1.755	($0.762)
Mondesi	$4.030	$1.510	($2.520)
Dellucci	$0.690	$1.387	$0.697
Kata	$0.300	$1.323	$1.023
Randolph	$0.300	$1.119	$0.819
Bautista	$3.000	$0.678	($2.322)

Player	Salary	Earned Value	Difference
Williams M	$10.000	$0.519	($9.481)
Patterson	$0.300	$0.426	$0.126
Womack	$3.780	$0.412	($3.368)
Grace	$1.750	($0.291)	($2.041)
McCracken	$1.750	($0.986)	($2.736)
	$78.718	$74.172	($4.546)

ATLANTA BRAVES

Player	Salary	Earned Value	Difference
Sheffield	$11.417	$11.218	($0.199)
Lopez	$7.000	$9.423	$2.423
Smoltz	$10.667	$7.795	($2.872)
Jones C	$13.333	$6.005	($7.328)
Jones A	$12.000	$5.490	($6.510)
Ortiz	$4.662	$5.425	$0.763
Giles M	$0.317	$5.406	$5.089
Furcal	$2.200	$5.131	$2.931
Maddux	$14.750	$4.875	($9.875)
Hampton	$13.625	$4.796	($8.829)
Ramirez	$0.300	$3.617	$3.317
Castilla	$5.000	$3.510	($1.490)
Franco J	$0.600	$2.656	$2.056
Fick	$1.000	$2.449	$1.449
Reynolds	$0.400	$1.415	$1.015
DeRosa	$0.340	$1.203	$0.863
King	$0.600	$0.959	$0.359
Hodges	$0.300	$0.906	$0.606
Hernandez	$0.600	$0.640	$0.040
Bong	$0.300	$0.586	$0.286
Wright	$0.116	$0.346	$0.230
Mercker	$0.124	$0.240	$0.116
Blanco	$1.300	($0.119)	($1.419)
Franco M	$0.800	($0.249)	($1.049)
Bragg	$0.450	($0.586)	($1.036)
	$102.201	$83.137	($19.064)

CHICAGO CUBS

Player	Salary	Earned Value	Difference
Prior	$1.450	$7.784	$6.334
Zambrano	$0.340	$6.919	$6.579

Wood	$6.190	$6.369	$0.179
Sosa	$16.000	$6.194	($9.806)
Borowski	$0.410	$5.244	$4.834
Miller	$2.700	$4.756	$2.056
Gonzalez	$5.750	$4.539	($1.211)
Alou	$9.500	$4.478	($5.022)
Grudzielanek	$5.500	$4.186	($1.314)
Clement	$4.000	$4.167	$0.167
Karros	$8.375	$3.030	($5.345)
Ramirez	$1.140	$2.792	$1.652
Lofton	$0.390	$2.222	$1.832
Patterson	$0.365	$2.169	$1.804
Choi	$0.305	$2.158	$1.853
Remlinger	$2.633	$1.386	($1.247)
MartinezR	$0.800	$1.383	$0.583
Farnsworth	$0.600	$1.332	$0.732
Bellhorn	$0.260	$1.245	$0.985
Simon	$0.368	$1.245	$0.877
Estes	$3.000	$0.944	($2.056)
Alfonseca	$4.000	$0.746	($3.254)
Goodwin	$0.635	$0.553	($0.082)
Bako	$0.750	$0.515	($0.235)
Hernandez	$0.130	$0.160	$0.030
O'Leary	$0.750	$0.127	($0.623)
Cruz	$0.340	$0.053	($0.287)
Womack	$0.900	$0.045	($0.855)
Harris	$0.720	($0.303)	($1.023)
	$78.301	$76.4238	($1.863)

CINCINNATI REDS

Player	Salary	Earned Value	Difference
Guillen J	$0.300	$6.348	$6.048
Dunn	$0.400	$4.249	$3.849
Boone A	$2.553	$4.140	$1.587
Kearns	$0.350	$3.883	$3.533
Casey	$5.600	$3.652	($1.948)
LaRue	$1.250	$3.121	$1.871
Reitsma	$0.400	$2.976	$2.576
Williamson	$1.070	$2.976	$1.906
Wilson	$0.500	$2.359	$1.859
Jimenez	$0.175	$1.864	$1.689
Griffey	$12.500	$1.793	($10.707)

Branyan	$0.395	$1.628	$1.233
Graves	$5.000	$1.494	($3.506)
Heredia F	$0.497	$1.492	$0.995
Larkin	$9.000	$1.410	($7.590)
Riedling	$0.350	$1.119	$0.769
Sullivan	$1.400	$0.959	($0.441)
Castro	$0.800	$0.902	$0.102
Stenson	$0.300	$0.865	$0.565
Mercker	$0.276	$0.767	$0.491
Reith	$0.300	$0.746	$0.446
White G	$1.600	$0.586	($1.014)
Freel	$0.300	$0.576	$0.276
Dempster	$3.250	$0.472	($2.778)
Taylor	$0.334	$0.199	($0.135)
Lopez F	$0.334	$0.141	($0.193)
Mateo	$0.340	$0.123	($0.217)
Olmedo	$0.300	$0.113	($0.187)
Pena	$0.788	($0.066)	($0.854)
Haynes	$2.500	($0.079)	($2.579)
Larson	$0.308	($0.119)	($0.427)
	$53.470	$50.689	($2.781)

COLORADO ROCKIES

Player	Salary	Earned Value	Difference
Helton	$10.600	$17.100	$6.500
Payton	$1.850	$4.987	$3.137
Walker	$12.667	$4.777	($7.890)
Wilson	$6.500	$4.073	($2.427)
Oliver	$0.350	$3.695	$3.345
Chacon	$0.300	$3.302	$3.002
Jennings	$0.325	$3.224	$2.899
Johnson	$7.000	$3.121	($3.879)
Uribe	$0.300	$3.073	$2.773
Jimenez	$3.600	$2.976	($0.624)
Stynes	$0.750	$2.593	$1.843
Belliard	$0.475	$2.526	$2.051
Fuentes	$0.300	$1.759	$1.459
Cook A	$0.300	$1.651	$1.351
Reed S	$0.600	$1.439	$0.839
Speier	$0.850	$1.226	$0.376
Lopez	$0.300	$1.119	$0.819
Estalella	$0.500	$1.070	$0.570

Hernandez	$0.500	$0.798	$0.298
Bellhorn	$0.205	$0.750	$0.545
Womack	$1.320	$0.705	($0.615)
Stark	$0.310	$0.693	$0.383
Norton	$0.600	$0.599	($0.001)
Zaun	$0.340	$0.277	($0.063)
Miceli	$0.140	$0.266	$0.126
Elarton	$0.300	$0.107	($0.193)
Reyes R	$0.300	$0.062	($0.238)
Cruz N	$0.700	$0.053	($0.647)
Jones T	$3.000	($0.213)	($3.213)
Roa	$0.038	($0.277)	($0.315)
Neagle	$9.000	($0.315)	($9.315)
Kapler	$2.500	($0.407)	($2.907)
	$66.820	$66.809	($0.011)

FLORIDA MARLINS

Player	Salary	Earned Value	Difference
Lee D	$4.250	$10.625	$6.375
Rodriguez I	$10.000	$7.768	($2.232)
Lowell	$3.700	$5.265	$1.565
Encarnacion	$3.450	$5.177	$1.727
Willis	$0.300	$4.875	$4.575
Pierre	$1.000	$4.693	$3.693
Beckett	$1.725	$4.167	$2.442
Castillo L	$4.850	$4.029	($0.821)
Looper	$1.600	$3.986	$2.386
Gonzalez A	$1.700	$3.975	$2.275
Redman	$2.150	$3.931	$1.781
Pavano	$1.500	$3.538	$2.038
Penny	$1.875	$3.460	$1.585
Urbina	$2.250	$3.118	$0.868
Hollandsworth	$1.500	$2.824	$1.324
Cabrera	$0.300	$1.985	$1.685
Conine	$0.800	$0.967	$0.167
Tejera	$0.300	$0.853	$0.553
Phelps	$0.300	$0.799	$0.499
Burnett	$2.500	$0.786	($1.714)
Banks	$0.300	$0.738	$0.438
Harris	$0.080	$0.104	$0.024
Redmond	$1.050	$0.040	($1.010)
Mordecai	$0.500	$0.029	($0.471)

Almanza	$0.775	($0.213)	($0.988)
Fox	$0.800	($0.391)	($1.191)
	$49.555	$77.128	$27.573

HOUSTON ASTROS

Player	Salary	Earned Value	Difference
Bagwell	$13.000	$9.795	($3.205)
Hidalgo	$8.500	$9.646	$1.146
Wagner	$8.000	$8.645	$0.645
Berkman	$3.500	$6.921	$3.421
Ausmus	$5.500	$4.934	($0.566)
Redding	$0.300	$4.796	$4.496
Ensberg	$0.300	$4.300	$4.000
Miller	$0.525	$4.010	$3.485
Oswalt	$0.500	$4.010	$3.510
Kent	$7.500	$3.704	($3.796)
Biggio	$9.750	$3.453	($6.297)
Everett	$0.300	$3.101	$2.801
Villone	$0.500	$2.831	$2.331
Dotel	$1.600	$2.345	$0.745
Robertson	$0.300	$2.044	$1.744
Lidge	$0.300	$1.439	$1.139
Stone	$0.325	$1.439	$1.114
Blum	$1.500	$0.790	($0.710)
Munro	$0.305	$0.746	$0.441
Miceli	$0.210	$0.693	$0.483
Vizcaino	$2.000	$0.649	($1.351)
Merced	$1.700	$0.616	($1.084)
Linebrink	$0.133	$0.373	$0.240
Zaun	$0.860	($0.099)	($0.959)
	$67.408	$81.181	$13.773

LOS ANGELES DODGERS

Player	Salary	Earned Value	Difference
Gagne	$0.550	$9.779	$9.229
LoDuca	$2.637	$8.323	$5.686
Brown	$15.714	$7.155	($8.559)
Nomo	$7.750	$6.683	($1.067)
Green S	$15.667	$5.794	($9.873)
Beltre	$3.700	$3.829	$0.129

Iztouris	$0.335	$3.017	$2.682
Cora	$1.150	$2.977	$1.827
Perez	$3.400	$2.673	($0.727)
Ishii	$2.575	$2.595	$0.020
Mota	$0.675	$2.505	$1.830
Alvarez	$0.500	$2.132	$1.632
Quantrill	$3.333	$1.972	($1.361)
McGriff	$3.750	$1.909	($1.841)
Cabrera	$0.435	$1.744	$1.309
Shuey	$3.917	$1.705	($2.212)
Ross	$0.300	$1.625	$1.325
Dreifort	$12.400	$1.337	($11.063)
Roberts	$0.400	$1.151	$0.751
Martin	$0.300	$0.906	$0.606
Ventura	$1.400	$0.581	($0.819)
Ashby	$8.500	$0.320	($8.180)
Coomer	$0.500	$0.249	($0.251)
Kinkade	$0.320	$0.229	($0.091)
Hundley	$6.500	$0.000	($6.500)
Burnitz	$5.840	($0.102)	($5.942)
	$102.548	$71.088	($31.460)

MILWAUKEE BREWERS

Player	Salary	Earned Value	Difference
Sexson	$5.125	$12.452	$7.327
Jenkins	$5.188	$6.641	$1.453
Podsednik	$0.300	$5.932	$5.632
Vander Wal	$0.550	$3.852	$3.302
Kolb	$0.300	$3.685	$3.385
Sheets	$0.428	$3.381	$2.953
Clark	$0.313	$2.774	$2.461
Helms	$0.575	$2.282	$1.707
Osik	$0.455	$2.071	$1.616
Young	$1.700	$1.766	$0.066
Perez E	$0.500	$1.585	$1.085
Clayton	$1.500	$1.523	$0.023
Kinney	$0.318	$1.494	$1.176
Franklin	$0.315	$1.258	$0.943
Kieschnick	$0.300	$1.172	$0.872
Davis	$0.300	$1.119	$0.819
Estrella	$0.300	$1.119	$0.819
DeJean	$1.326	$1.077	($0.249)

Ginter	$0.301	$0.962	$0.661
Sanchez	$0.115	$0.908	$0.793
Leskanic	$1.850	$0.906	($0.944)
delosSantos	$0.851	$0.789	($0.062)
Hall	$0.300	$0.752	$0.452
Obermuller	$0.300	$0.746	$0.446
Rusch	$4.250	$0.393	($3.857)
Vizcaino	$0.370	$0.053	($0.317)
Hammonds	$2.296	($0.188)	($2.484)
	$30.426	$60.504	$30.078

MONTREAL EXPOS

Player	Salary	Earned Value	Difference
Hernandez	$3.825	$7.627	$3.802
Guerrero V	$11.500	$7.365	($4.135)
Vazquez	$6.000	$6.998	$0.998
Schneider	$0.310	$4.954	$4.644
Cabrera	$3.300	$4.942	$1.642
Wilkerson	$0.315	$4.911	$4.596
Ohka	$0.340	$4.639	$4.299
Day	$0.301	$3.224	$2.923
Cordero	$0.600	$2.947	$2.347
Vidro	$5.500	$2.947	($2.553)
Biddle	$0.320	$2.551	$2.231
Vargas	$0.300	$2.516	$2.216
Ayala	$0.300	$2.292	$1.992
Carroll	$0.300	$1.675	$1.375
Barrett	$2.600	$1.575	($1.025)
Chavez	$0.300	$1.284	$0.984
Eischen	$0.750	$1.066	$0.316
Tucker	$0.210	$1.066	$0.856
Zeile	$0.555	$0.838	$0.283
Calloway	$0.300	$0.636	$0.336
Hernandez O	$4.100	$0.000	($4.100)
Macias	$0.825	($0.025)	($0.850)
Mateo	$0.300	($0.090)	($0.390)
Tatis	$6.500	($0.119)	($6.619)
Guzman	$0.300	($0.359)	($0.659)
	$49.951	$65.460	$15.509

NEW YORK METS

Player	Salary	Earned Value	Difference
Floyd	$6.500	$5.191	($1.309)
Trachsel	$3.000	$4.954	$1.954
Phillips	$0.300	$3.984	$3.684
Seo	$0.300	$3.695	$3.395
Benitez	$4.657	$3.685	($0.972)
Leiter A	$8.000	$3.617	($4.383)
Glavine	$11.000	$3.224	($7.776)
Piazza	$15.571	$2.963	($12.608)
Burnitz	$6.327	$2.901	($3.426)
Cedeno	$4.875	$2.650	($2.225)
Wigginton	$0.303	$2.633	$2.330
Wilson	$0.315	$2.269	$1.954
Weathers	$3.733	$1.812	($1.921)
Reyes J	$0.300	$1.466	$1.166
Clark T	$0.500	$1.287	$0.787
Perez T	$0.313	$1.247	$0.934
McEwing	$0.600	$1.022	$0.422
Gonzalez R	$0.300	$1.018	$0.718
Wheeler	$0.300	$0.853	$0.553
Astacio	$7.000	$0.786	($6.214)
Alomar	$4.080	$0.662	($3.418)
Duncan	$0.300	$0.376	$0.076
Sanchez	$0.650	($0.056)	($0.706)
Heilman	$0.300	($0.160)	($0.460)
Bell	$0.550	($0.271)	($0.821)
Vaughn	$17.167	($1.162)	($18.329)
	$97.241	$50.646	($46.595)

PHILADELPHIA PHILLIES

Player	Salary	Earned Value	Difference
Thome	$11.167	$11.954	$0.787
Abreu	$9.100	$8.876	($0.224)
Lieberthal	$7.250	$6.282	($0.968)
Millwood	$9.900	$4.167	($5.733)
Byrd	$0.300	$4.117	$3.817
Polanco	$2.875	$3.825	$0.950
Wolf	$2.375	$3.774	$1.399
Rollins	$0.450	$3.722	$3.272
Myers	$0.300	$2.831	$2.531

Padilla	$0.425	$2.831	$2.406
Burrell	$1.250	$2.366	($1.116)
Cormier	$2.983	$2.238	($0.745)
Pratt	$0.850	$1.962	$1.112
Michaels	$0.305	$1.883	$1.578
Ledee	$0.850	$1.837	$0.987
Perez	$0.550	$1.675	$1.125
Adams	$2.900	$1.439	($1.461)
Wendell	$3.350	$1.332	($2.018)
Silva	$0.310	$1.279	$0.969
Bell	$3.200	$1.117	($2.083)
Duckworth	$0.325	$1.022	$0.697
Stinnett	$1.300	$0.912	($0.388)
Utley	$0.300	$0.631	$0.331
Roa	$0.120	$0.277	$0.157
Punto	$0.300	$0.271	($0.029)
Williams M	$1.400	($0.283)	($1.683)
de los Santos	$0.074	($0.309)	($0.383)
Mesa	$5.200	($2.551)	($7.751)
	$69.709	$69.477	($0.232)

PITTSBURGH PIRATES

Player	Salary	Earned Value	Difference
Giles	$6.980	$6.880	($0.100)
Kendall	$8.571	$6.242	($2.329)
Sanders	$1.000	$5.763	$4.763
Wells	$0.370	$5.347	$4.977
Stairs	$0.900	$4.345	$3.445
Suppan	$0.346	$4.246	$3.900
Wilson C	$0.327	$4.006	$3.679
Tavarez	$0.750	$3.685	$2.935
Ramirez	$1.860	$2.952	$1.092
Wilson J	$0.335	$2.791	$2.456
Lofton	$0.635	$2.647	$2.012
D'Amico	$0.750	$2.595	$1.845
Torres	$0.325	$2.044	$1.719
Redman	$0.350	$1.771	$1.421
Simon	$1.107	$1.577	$0.470
Fogg	$0.322	$1.494	$1.172
Hernandez	$0.370	$1.436	$1.066
Reboulet	$0.400	$1.143	$0.743
Nunez	$0.675	$1.022	$0.347

Bay	$0.276	$1.008	$0.732
Benson	$4.300	$0.944	($3.356)
Meadows	$0.300	$0.906	$0.606
Mackowiak	$0.322	$0.758	$0.436
Reese	$2.500	$0.752	($1.748)
Beimel	$0.322	$0.693	$0.371
Boehringer	$1.500	$0.320	($1.180)
Perez O	$0.055	$0.110	$0.055
Meares	$3.790	$0.000	($3.790)
Rivera C	$0.300	($0.083)	($0.383)
Williams M	$2.100	($0.709)	($2.809)
Young K	$6.625	($0.996)	($7.621)
	$48.763	$65.689	$16.926

SAN DIEGO PADRES

Player	Salary	Earned Value	Difference
Klesko	$5.500	$7.097	$1.597
Kotsay	$4.450	$4.560	$0.110
Burroughs	$3.020	$4.308	$1.288
Loretta	$1.250	$4.270	$3.020
Beck	$0.400	$4.110	$3.710
Lawrence	$0.625	$3.853	$3.228
Eaton	$0.350	$3.695	$3.345
Nevin	$5.000	$3.445	($1.555)
White R	$5.500	$3.359	($2.141)
Peavy	$0.750	$2.712	$1.962
Nady	$0.750	$2.712	$1.962
Buchanan	$0.325	$2.342	$2.017
Vazquez	$0.315	$2.171	$1.856
Giles	$1.853	$1.873	$0.020
Hansen	$0.550	$1.702	$1.152
Matthews	$0.603	$1.638	$1.035
Ojeda	$0.300	$1.367	$1.067
Merloni	$0.300	$1.237	$0.937
Linebrink	$0.267	$1.119	$0.852
Herges	$0.224	$0.858	$0.634
Matthews	$0.350	$0.799	$0.449
Perez O	$0.250	$0.755	$0.505
Hoffman	$9.600	$0.709	($8.891)
Hackman	$0.345	$0.693	$0.348
Lockhart	$0.500	$0.391	($0.109)
Roa	$0.158	$0.277	$0.119

Bay	$0.024	$0.265	$0.241
Jarvis	$3.000	$0.236	($2.764)
Bennett	$0.700	($0.644)	($1.344)
Wright	$0.609	($0.719)	($1.328)
	$47.423	$61.544	$14.121

SAN FRANCISCO GIANTS

Player	Salary	Earned Value	Difference
Bonds	$15.500	$12.773	($2.727)
Cruz	$2.500	$7.273	$4.773
Schmidt	$5.937	$6.998	$1.061
Snow	$6.850	$5.188	($1.662)
Worrell	$2.000	$4.535	$2.535
Grissom	$1.875	$3.984	$2.109
Santiago	$1.775	$3.874	$2.099
Williams	$0.300	$3.302	$3.002
Durham	$5.200	$3.157	($2.043)
Galarraga	$0.500	$2.449	$1.949
Torrealba	$0.312	$2.398	$2.086
Rueter	$5.866	$2.359	($3.507)
Aurilia	$6.250	$2.199	($4.051)
Perez	$1.500	$2.105	$0.605
Alfonzo	$4.000	$2.074	($1.926)
Ponson	$1.318	$1.887	$0.569
Moss	$1.550	$1.808	$0.258
Feliz	$0.325	$1.548	$1.223
Brower	$0.300	$1.439	$1.139
Rodriguez	$3.167	$1.439	($1.728)
Hammonds	$5.904	$1.130	($4.774)
Ainsworth	$0.302	$1.066	$0.764
Eyre	$0.725	$0.959	$0.234
Foppert	$0.300	$0.944	$0.644
Zerbe	$0.317	$0.746	$0.429
Hermanson	$0.224	$0.703	$0.479
Herges	$0.176	$0.688	$0.512
Young	$0.300	$0.135	($0.165)
Nen	$8.750	$0.000	($8.750)
Nathan	$0.300	($0.266)	($0.566)
	$84.323	$78.894	($5.429)

ST. LOUIS CARDINALS

Player	Salary	Earned Value	Difference
Pujols	$0.900	$12.213	$11.313
Edmonds	$8.333	$8.345	$0.012
Rolen	$7.625	$6.861	($0.764)
Martinez	$7.500	$5.396	($2.104)
Williams	$6.000	$5.347	($0.653)
Renteria	$6.500	$4.906	($1.594)
Drew	$3.700	$4.623	$0.923
Morris	$10.500	$4.167	($6.333)
Matheny	$3.250	$3.280	$0.330
Perez	$0.500	$2.928	$2.428
Stephenson	$0.800	$2.752	$1.952
Isringhausen	$7.250	$2.693	($4.557)
Palmeiro	$0.700	$2.620	$1.920
Tomko	$3.300	$2.202	($1.098)
Kline	$1.800	$1.279	($0.521)
Eldred	$0.500	$1.226	$0.726
Hart	$0.300	$0.842	$0.542
Simontacchi	$0.315	$0.629	$0.314
DeJean	$0.374	$0.624	$0.250
Haren	$0.300	$0.480	$0.180
Vina	$5.333	$0.421	($4.912)
Widger	$0.500	$0.337	($0.163)
Fassero	$1.250	$0.266	($0.984)
Hermanson	$0.176	$0.256	$0.080
Robinson	$0.320	$0.000	($0.320)
Cairo	$0.850	($0.060)	($0.910)
	$78.876	$74.633	($4.243)

THE GENERAL MANAGER RATING SYSTEM

To calculate a GM rating for any general manager, you must know the following:

1. The general manager's tenure.
2. The roster of players on the team at the time the GM became GM.
3. The dates and methods of player comings and goings—including trade, free agency, release, and promotion from within the system.
4. The seasonal BFWs or PWs for each player.

Here is an explanation of the terms.

1. "Acquired" means obtained via trade, sale, or via waiver from another Major League team in exchange for some consideration.
2. "Traded" means sent to another Major League team in a trade, sale, or waiver arrangement.
3. "Free Agent" means signed at the expiration of a previous contract, or following release from such a contract. Also included in this category are players re-signed or extended by the same team if those players are or would be qualified for free agent eligibility, or if they are signed to a multi-year sign contract.
4. "Product" means having played the equivalent of at least one season with the parent team's farm system. A player is no longer a product once he attains free agent eligibility, or signs a multi-year extension.

5. "FA Lost" means those players who left the organization as free agents or were released and subsequently played with another Major League team.

6. "Short-term" gain or loss is the BFW or PW gained or lost as a result of the movement (by any method) of a particular player either in the season during which a player is acquired or traded (if the move occurs in-season), or (if during the off-season) in the season immediately following.

7. "Long-term" gain represents the BFWs or PWs generated by a player in any season subsequent to the season of his acquisition for the duration of his current contract with the team, or until he attains free agent leverage, or until he signs a multi-season contract extension.

8. "Long-term" loss is calculated using a sliding scale of all the BFWs or PWs generated by players over the first five seasons subsequent to the season in which short-term loss is calculated. The sliding scale is as follows: 100 percent of BFW or PW in the first season of long-term loss, 80 percent in the second season, 60 percent in the third season, 40 percent in the fourth season, and 20 percent in the fifth season. Following the fifth season of long-term loss, no value is accrued. If the player is reacquired by the team during that period, calculation of long-term loss is halted.

9. "Residual rating" is the impact on a team of the moves made by a former GM. It is calculated on the same basis as long-term gain and loss.

The calculation formula is as follows:

1. Add the sum of all short-term acquisitions, all short-term player losses, all short-term free agent gains, all short-term free agent losses, and all short-term prospects for the season in question.

2. Add the sum of all long-term acquisitions, all long-term player losses, all long-term free agent gains, all long-term free agent losses, and all long-term prospect losses for the same season. (If a GM participated in a team formulation draft, he accrues long-term

points [but not short-term points] for the subsequent season performances of players he drafts as well. They are tabulated in the same fashion.) Divide this total by two.

3. The sum of these two steps is the GM rating for the season.

4. To calculate a general manager's rating over any period of seasons, divide the ratings in each category by the number of seasons and sum the totals. Note: Except in rare instances where he takes over in mid-season, a general manager cannot have a long-term rating in his first full season as a general manager. Therefore, when calculating a GM's career rating, divide his long-term scores by the number of seasons minus one.

5. In cases where a GM leaves an organization, acquisitions made by that GM continue to count as part of his residual rating until one of the following things happens: 1. Players who had been acquired by the departed GM are re-signed under terms outlined in the paragraph concerning free agents. 2. The GM who replaces the departed GM is himself replaced.

The table below lists the GM Ratings for the 1999–2003 seasons. Short-term ratings are listed first, then long-term ratings, then residual ratings.

SEASON BY SEASON GM RATINGS

2003

AMERICAN LEAGUE

Short Term

GM	Team	Acq.	Traded	FA Got	FA Lst.	Prod.	Total
Gillick	Sea	0.40	−0.70	7.00	3.70	−0.40	10.00
Cashman	NYY	0.10	0.00	1.30	3.20	−0.20	4.40
Epstein	Bos	−0.50	1.40	2.90	0.30	0.00	4.10
Beane	Oak	3.20	4.60	−2.40	−1.50	−0.50	3.40
Williams	CWS	2.10	−5.50	4.20	2.70	−0.40	3.10

Stoneman	Ana	0.00	0.50	1.90	−1.10	0.30	1.60
Shapiro	Cle	−0.30	0.00	−1.30	3.00	−1.30	0.10
Ryan	Min	1.10	2.80	−2.10	−1.90	−0.70	−0.80
LaMar	TB	−1.60	−0.10	−2.50	1.30	0.20	−2.70
Baird	KC	0.20	1.20	−3.40	0.00	−3.40	−5.40
Flanagan	Bal	−1.60	−0.20	−6.40	2.50	−0.40	−6.10
Ricciardi	Tor	−2.10	−1.10	−0.60	−6.10	−2.80	−12.70
Hart	Tex	−3.20	0.30	−3.10	−2.50	−4.30	−12.80
Dombrowski	Det	−4.90	1.00	−5.10	4.20	−9.50	−14.30

Long Term

GM	Team	Acq.	Traded	FA Got	FA Lst.	Prod.	Drafts	Total
Cashman	NYY	−2.00	3.80	18.20	4.30	1.20		25.50
Beane	Oak	3.60	4.70	2.70	−1.00	11.80		21.80
Gillick	Sea	−2.80	3.60	6.10	0.10	3.10		10.10
Baird	KC	−2.00	4.80	3.70	0.20	0.50		7.20
Ryan	Min	1.00	0.20	7.20	3.20	−8.80		2.80
Williams	CWS	−1.40	−2.30	9.80	−1.60	−1.70		2.80
Hart	Tex	−0.90	3.00	−1.40	−0.30	1.20		1.60
LaMar	TB	−2.10	0.90	0.00	2.10	−0.60		0.30
Epstein	Bos	——	——	——	——	——		0.00
Flanagan	Bal	——	——	——	——	——		0.00
Stoneman	Ana	−0.90	−1.00	−4.00	3.80	0.10		−2.00
Ricciardi	Tor	−0.90	−3.10	0.00	0.00	−1.60		−5.60
Shapiro	Cle	−3.50	−1.60	1.40	−0.30	−2.00		−6.00
Dombrowski	Det	−1.90	0.00	0.00	0.00	−8.80		−10.70

Residual

GM	Team	Acquired	Lost	Total
Port	Bos	15.00	−0.80	14.20
Ash	Tor	9.90	2.00	11.90
Melvin	Tex	8.00	3.90	11.90
Hart	Cle	5.00	−1.00	4.00
Robinson	KC	0.00	2.50	2.50
Schueler	CWS	0.90	1.60	2.50
Smith	Det	−0.90	3.30	2.40
Duquette	Bos	0.00	1.60	1.60
Watson	NYY	0.00	0.70	0.70
Gillick	Bal	0.00	−0.10	−0.10
Woodward	Sea	−0.60	−0.40	−0.20

| Bavasi | Ana | −0.40 | −1.50 | −1.90 |
| Thrift | Bal | −1.90 | −1.40 | −3.30 |

NATIONAL LEAGUE

Short Term

GM	Team	Acq.	Traded	FA Got	FA Lst.	Prod.	Total
Beinfest	Fla	2.70	−1.70	4.50	1.50	0.50	7.50
Garagiola	Ari	−1.30	−0.80	0.30	−0.50	8.40	6.10
Wade	Phi	−1.70	0.80	−1.10	2.50	0.60	1.10
Schuerholz	Atl	3.80	3.30	−4.50	−0.60	−1.00	1.00
Duquette	NYM	0.00	1.50	−0.10	0.00	−2.90	−1.50
Hunsicker	Hou	0.00	1.10	2.50	−5.20	−0.20	−1.80
Minaya	Mtl	0.70	−2.60	−1.10	0.70	0.20	−2.10
Phillips	NYM	0.00	−1.90	−0.80	0.80	−0.70	−2.60
Hendry	ChC	1.00	0.90	−3.10	−0.80	−1.20	−3.20
Towers	SD	0.60	3.40	−4.10	2.00	−5.50	−3.60
Littlefield	Pit	−1.40	−2.60	1.90	0.00	−1.60	−3.70
Bowden	Cin	0.60	0.60	−3.90	2.80	−4.60	−4.50
Evans	LA	−2.80	−2.00	−3.20	3.80	−1.00	−5.20
O'Dowd	Col	−3.00	−1.20	−1.70	1.90	−3.60	−7.60
Sabean	SF	0.10	−2.50	1.10	−4.60	−2.10	−8.00
Jocketty	SL	−2.60	0.60	−6.40	0.70	−1.70	−9.40
Melvin	Mil	−1.90	2.00	−5.80	−0.60	−5.10	−11.40
Interim	Cin	−3.60	−0.10	−3.80	0.00	−5.90	−13.40

Long Term

GM	Team	Acq.	Traded	FA Got	FA Lst.	Prod.	Drafts	Total
Schuerholz	Atl	3.10	0.80	10.90	5.90	8.30		29.00
Sabean	SF	0.00	4.80	13.00	2.20	2.80		22.80
Jocketty	SL	3.00	−1.00	5.80	2.00	6.80		16.60
Hunsicker	Hou	−0.10	0.80	6.40	−0.30	7.50		14.30
O'Dowd	Col	0.50	8.90	−1.80	1.20	1.50		10.30
Wade	Phi	3.30	2.10	4.60	1.00	−1.00		10.00
Phillips	NYM	−2.10	13.00	1.70	−2.50	−3.40		6.70
Beinfest	Fla	−0.30	0.60	0.10	1.90	1.70		4.00
Evans	LA	1.60	−5.10	4.80	0.50	0.00		1.80
Garagiola	Ari	−0.70	0.80	1.10	−1.00	1.50	−0.60	1.10
Duquette	NYM	——	——	——	——	——		0.00

Melvin	Mil	——	——	——	——	——	0.00
Interim	Cin	——	——	——	——	——	0.00
Littlefield	Pit	−0.30	−2.90	−0.30	0.00	0.20	−3.30
Minaya	Mtl	−4.20	0.40	0.00	0.00	0.00	−3.80
Hendry	ChC	0.00	−3.90	0.00	0.00	0.00	−3.90
Bowden	Cin	−4.10	−2.60	−3.40	1.80	4.20	−4.10
Towers	SD	−0.40	1.50	−1.00	−2.50	−1.70	−4.10

Residual

GM	Team	Acquired	Lost	Total
McPhail	ChC	15.10	3.70	18.80
Malone	LA	9.00	3.30	12.30
Beattie	Mtl	10.00	−3.30	6.70
Bonifay	Pit	0.00	1.20	1.20
Claire	LA	0.00	0.40	0.40
Taylor	Mil	−1.00	1.40	0.40
Lasorda	LA	0.00	0.30	0.30
Gephardt	Col	0.00	0.10	0.10
Lynch	ChC	0.00	−0.20	−0.20
Bando	Mil	0.00	−1.10	−1.10
Dombrowski	Fla	0.30	−2.20	−1.90

2002

AMERICAN LEAGUE

Short Term

GM	Team	Acq.	Traded	FA Got	FA Lst.	Prod.	Total
Cashman	NYY	1.20	−0.50	7.70	3.60	−1.00	11.00
Stoneman	Ana	2.30	0.00	2.90	−2.40	3.40	6.20
Smith	Det	−2.30	0.90	−2.60	5.50	0.00	1.50
Melvin	Tex	0.00	0.90	0.00	0.00	0.00	0.90
Williams	CWS	−2.50	1.40	6.80	−3.30	−1.70	0.70
Beane	Oak	3.50	2.60	1.60	−8.00	0.80	0.50
Port	Bos	0.80	0.00	−0.80	0.00	0.00	0.00
Gillick	Sea	−3.00	1.50	−1.00	0.70	0.10	−1.70
Duquette	Bos	−2.90	0.00	0.50	0.10	0.00	−2.30
Ryan	Min	−0.30	−0.40	−1.20	−0.60	0.10	−2.40
LaMar	TB	−0.20	0.20	0.00	1.50	−4.90	−3.40

Thrift	Bal	-2.40	0.30	-1.60	-0.20	0.20	-3.70
Ricciardi	Tor	-3.10	0.80	-1.70	1.10	-2.50	-5.40
Baird	KC	-1.70	0.70	-3.90	1.30	-3.30	-6.90
Dombrowski	Det	-5.50	1.60	-0.30	1.30	-5.50	-8.40
Hart	Tex	-3.70	-0.10	-4.10	1.10	-2.40	-9.20
Shapiro	Cle	-1.90	3.30	-4.30	-0.10	-6.60	-9.60

Long Term

GM	Team	Acq.	Traded	FA Got	FA Lst.	Prod.	Drafts	Total
Duquette	Bos	1.70	1.60	23.60	1.70	1.00		29.60
Melvin	Tex	7.20	4.70	0.00	3.60	0.00		15.50
Cashman	NYY	0.00	0.00	10.70	1.40	-0.30		11.80
Beane	Oak	0.00	-0.40	7.90	-2.20	5.50		10.80
Ryan	Min	4.10	-0.70	1.70	4.20	-0.50		8.80
Gillick	Sea	0.10	0.10	11.50	-8.60	2.30		5.40
Stoneman	Ana	3.20	-2.40	2.10	0.20	0.10		3.20
Baird	KC	-1.80	1.50	1.50	1.50	-1.10		1.60
Dombrowski	Det	——	——	——	——	——		0.00
Hart	Tex	——	——	——	——	——		0.00
Port	Bos	——	——	——	——	——		0.00
Ricciardi	Tor	——	——	——	——	——		0.00
Shapiro	Cle	——	——	——	——	——		0.00
Smith	Det	-3.20	3.80	-0.90	0.00	0.20		-0.10
Williams	CWS	0.00	0.80	1.30	0.50	-3.50		-0.90
Thrift	Bal	2.10	-4.00	0.50	-4.40	2.80		-3.00
LaMar	TB	-9.90	-6.60	-3.60	4.10	-4.00	-1.30	21.30

Residual

GM	Team	Acquired	Lost	Total
Bavasi	Ana	4.80	-0.20	4.60
Schueler	CWS	1.50	1.40	2.90
Watson	NYY	0.00	0.80	0.80
Alderson	Oak	0.00	0.40	0.40
Robinson	KC	-2.80	1.90	-0.90
Woodward	Sea	0.70	-2.20	-1.50
Gillick	Bal	-1.20	-0.60	-1.80
Ash	Tor	0.10	-3.20	-3.10
Hart	Cle	0.70	-6.00	-5.30

NATIONAL LEAGUE

Short Term

GM	Team	Acq.	Traded	FA Got	FA Lst.	Prod.	Total
Sabean	SF	0.00	2.80	15.10	1.10	−1.10	17.90
Hunsicker	Hou	2.30	1.80	4.40	5.70	−2.90	11.30
Littlefield	Pit	0.00	4.00	2.00	2.20	0.20	8.40
McPhail	ChC	1.30	3.40	1.20	1.00	1.10	8.00
Jocketty	SL	3.50	−1.10	1.40	2.50	0.60	6.90
Evans	LA	0.10	−0.10	0.80	4.10	−0.20	4.70
Schuerholz	Atl	1.00	2.70	2.30	−1.40	−0.20	4.40
Wade	Phi	2.70	−2.60	1.40	1.70	−0.70	2.50
Garagiola	Ari	−0.30	1.40	−1.80	−0.60	−0.60	−1.90
Minaya	Mtl	−0.70	−0.90	−1.70	0.90	0.10	−2.30
Bowden	Cin	−3.60	0.00	−1.60	0.00	2.60	−2.60
Hendry	ChC	−0.40	−0.40	−0.20	0.00	−3.30	−4.30
O'Dowd	Col	−6.20	1.30	−1.70	−0.40	1.10	−5.90
Phillips	NYM	−7.30	2.60	−3.30	−0.90	2.40	−6.50
Towers	SD	−3.10	−1.10	3.20	0.10	−7.80	−8.70
Taylor	Mil	−8.50	4.60	−5.20	−0.70	−2.80	−12.60
Beinfest	Fla	−5.30	−0.20	−2.20	−1.60	−3.50	−12.80

Long Term

GM	Team	Acq.	Traded	FA Got	FA Lst.	Prod.	Drafts	Total
Schuerholz	Atl	2.10	1.00	11.60	−0.10	1.90		16.50
Garagiola	Ari	2.60	2.70	4.60	−1.00	5.00	0.30	14.20
Hunsicker	Hou	−1.40	10.10	0.90	−3.80	4.70		10.50
Jocketty	SL	2.40	−0.90	4.70	1.80	2.10		10.10
Sabean	SF	0.00	−0.70	8.30	3.10	−1.30		9.40
Bowden	Cin	0.60	1.90	−3.60	4.40	3.30		6.60
McPhail	ChC	−0.30	3.40	1.20	1.60	−3.40		2.50
Wade	Phi	−2.90	−1.80	7.20	2.20	−2.50		2.20
O'Dowd	Col	−1.70	6.40	−1.90	4.60	−6.00		1.40
Beinfest	Fla	——	——	——	——	——		0.00
Evans	LA	——	——	——	——	——		0.00
Hendry	ChC	——	——	——	——	——		0.00
Minaya	Mtl	——	——	——	——	——		0.00
Littlefield	Pit	−0.90	0.50	0.00	0.00	0.00		−0.40
Taylor	Mil	−4.40	1.90	2.60	0.00	−1.00		−0.90

| Phillips | NYM | −1.00 | −1.90 | 4.20 | −3.10 | 0.00 | −1.80 |
| Towers | SD | −2.90 | −1.90 | 1.50 | −1.00 | −3.20 | −7.50 |

Residual

GM	Team	Acquired	Lost	Total
Beattie	Mtl	11.30	−0.70	10.60
Dombrowski	Fla	7.80	−0.40	7.40
Malone	LA	3.20	2.90	6.10
Gephardt	Col	3.10	−0.30	2.80
Bonifay	Pit	−2.50	3.80	1.30
Bando	Mil	0.00	0.90	0.90
Claire	LA	0.00	0.90	0.90
Lasorda	LA	0.00	0.40	0.40
McIlvaine	NYM	0.00	−0.20	−0.20
Thomas	Phi	0.00	−0.30	−0.30
Lynch	ChC	−5.10	−2.70	−7.80

2001

AMERICAN LEAGUE

Short Term

GM	Team	Acq.	Traded	FA Got	FA Lst.	Prod.	Total
Gillick	Sea	0.10	0.20	16.30	−8.00	1.10	9.70
Duquette	Bos	0.50	1.60	4.90	1.20	−3.60	4.60
Ash	Tor	−1.40	−1.10	1.20	3.80	1.30	3.80
Hart	Cle	−1.80	−1.50	7.30	−2.70	1.20	2.50
Cashman	NYY	−2.20	−0.20	4.90	−0.80	−2.80	−1.10
Melvin	Tex	−3.50	1.90	0.80	1.20	−1.90	−1.50
Stoneman	Ana	−0.30	1.60	−3.20	0.90	−1.50	−2.50
Beane	Oak	0.30	0.00	−1.60	−1.20	−0.70	−3.20
Williams	CWS	−0.90	2.60	−0.90	−1.10	−2.90	−3.20
Ryan	Min	−0.80	0.70	2.60	1.20	−8.50	−4.80
Baird	KC	0.40	1.40	−1.40	−1.10	−4.20	−4.90
LaMar	TB	−2.40	−2.10	−1.10	0.20	−0.20	−5.60
Thrift	Bal	0.10	1.20	−4.60	−3.40	−4.90	−11.60
Smith	Det	−4.90	0.30	0.10	−0.80	−9.50	−14.80

Long Term

GM	Team	Acq.	Traded	FA Got	FA Lst.	Prod.	Drafts	Total
Beane	Oak	0.30	1.40	13.10	0.20	9.80		24.80
Ryan	Min	−0.10	1.30	−0.10	1.00	4.50		6.60
Cashman	NYY	−1.80	−2.80	9.00	0.60	−0.40		4.60
Gillick	Sea	−0.80	0.20	9.10	0.00	−3.90		4.60
Stoneman	Ana	0.40	−3.20	2.80	2.30	0.40		2.70
Duquette	Bos	0.30	0.60	−1.60	0.60	1.50		1.40
Ash	Tor	2.30	−8.20	0.40	1.20	4.40		0.10
Hart	Cle	−4.40	2.00	5.20	−1.90	−0.80		0.10
Williams	CWS	——	——	——	——	——		0.00
Baird	KC	−1.10	−1.10	0.00	0.00	0.00		−2.20
Thrift	Bal	−1.30	−0.20	−1.20	−0.90	−0.20		−3.80
Melvin	Tex	−3.30	−0.40	3.60	−4.60	−0.50		−5.20
Smith	Det	0.50	−5.40	−2.50	0.20	−0.10		−7.30
LaMar	TB	−0.80	−2.90	−2.30	0.10	−5.20	−4.40	−15.50

Residual

GM	Team	Acquired	Lost	Total
Schueler	CWS	11.40	−2.10	9.40
Robinson	KC	−0.90	2.30	1.40
Watson	NYY	2.80	−1.80	1.00
Woodward	Sea	1.40	−0.50	0.90
Bavasi	Ana	3.30	−2.50	0.80
Alderson	Oak	−1.00	0.00	−1.00
Gillick	Bal	−4.70	−7.00	−11.70

NATIONAL LEAGUE

Short Term

GM	Team	Acq.	Traded	FA Got	FA Lst.	Prod.	Total
Jocketty	SL	3.00	1.40	1.00	1.00	5.60	12.00
Hunsicker	Hou	−0.90	2.80	1.80	1.90	2.70	8.30
O'Dowd	Col	−2.80	1.70	4.10	4.00	−1.10	5.90
Schuerholz	Atl	2.20	0.70	0.40	2.20	−0.80	4.70
Phillips	NYM	−1.60	3.10	0.80	2.50	−1.90	2.90
Garagiola	Ari	−0.40	0.00	5.30	−0.50	−3.90	0.50
Wade	Phi	−1.00	−0.20	1.40	2.30	−2.30	0.20
Taylor	Mil	0.00	2.30	1.30	0.50	−4.90	−0.80

Dombrowski	Fla	−5.10	−1.20	5.00	−0.10	0.10	−1.30
Bowden	Cin	−2.20	6.30	−4.80	0.50	−1.90	−2.10
Littlefield	Pit	−2.00	−0.10	0.00	0.00	−1.50	−3.60
McPhail	ChC	0.80	0.60	−3.30	0.40	−3.40	−4.90
Sabean	SF	−0.50	−1.30	2.60	−1.40	−4.60	−5.20
Towers	SD	−0.60	3.30	−3.10	−1.80	−5.50	−7.70
Malone	LA	−3.50	−0.20	−1.30	0.50	−4.40	−8.90
Bonifay	Pit	−3.90	0.10	−2.70	0.00	−3.00	−9.50
Beattie	Mtl	−6.10	−1.50	−2.50	0.50	−1.30	−10.90

Long Term

GM	Team	Acq.	Traded	FA Got	FA Lst.	Prod.	Drafts	Total
Garagiola	Ari	5.50	4.40	1.20	4.00	2.90	2.70	20.70
Malone	LA	1.90	8.40	2.60	0.30	2.80		16.00
Sabean	SF	−1.50	−2.60	16.50	0.40	−1.50		11.30
McPhail	ChC	1.30	−0.70	9.50	0.00	0.00		10.10
Jocketty	SL	3.80	0.10	−4.50	3.10	7.40		9.90
Towers	SD	−1.20	3.90	5.50	0.60	−0.10		8.70
Schuerholz	Atl	−2.40	−6.00	11.50	2.10	0.00		5.20
Wade	Phi	−1.70	−0.80	7.10	−1.40	1.90		5.10
Littlefield	Pit	——	——	——	——	——		0.00
Phillips	NYM	1.10	0.20	−0.90	0.80	−1.80		−0.60
Bonifay	Pit	2.10	3.20	−4.80	1.40	−2.60		−0.70
O'Dowd	Col	2.60	−1.90	−0.70	0.00	−1.90		−1.90
Hunsicker	Hou	3.70	−2.20	−0.90	−9.30	6.70		−2.00
Dombrowski	Fla	4.80	−5.60	−0.60	0.80	−1.50		−2.10
Bowden	Cin	−1.10	−1.30	−2.60	1.00	0.50		−3.50
Beattie	Mtl	−1.30	−2.70	1.00	1.60	−6.20		−7.60
Taylor	Mil	−3.80	−5.60	1.90	0.00	−0.30		−7.80

Residual

GM	Team	Acquired	Lost	Total
Bando	Mil	1.10	5.20	6.30
Lynch	ChC	1.10	3.60	4.70
Lasorda	LA	0.80	2.40	3.20
Gebhardt	Col	2.50	0.00	2.50
Thomas	Phi	−0.40	1.20	0.80
Quinn	SF	0.00	0.10	0.10
McIlvaine	NYM	0.00	−0.20	−0.20
Claire	LA	0.00	−1.80	−1.80

2000

AMERICAN LEAGUE

Short Term

GM	Team	Acq.	Traded	FA Got	FA Lst.	Prod.	Total
Duquette	Bos	−4.70	1.60	8.60	7.80	0.70	14.00
Schueler	CWS	4.90	3.80	2.40	−0.20	−2.20	8.70
Beane	Oak	−3.00	1.40	7.60	0.80	0.40	7.20
Ash	Tor	2.80	−0.50	1.80	0.50	−2.20	2.40
Baird	KC	0.30	0.60	0.00	0.40	0.00	1.30
Gillick	Sea	−0.30	−3.00	2.90	2.20	−0.80	1.00
Cashman	NYY	1.00	4.10	−3.00	1.10	−2.60	0.60
Smith	Det	0.20	0.80	0.60	0.70	−2.70	−0.40
Hart	Cle	−1.70	0.60	−0.50	1.60	−2.40	−2.40
LaMar	TB	1.30	−0.60	−4.80	0.90	−1.60	−4.80
Ryan	Min	−7.00	0.90	1.00	1.30	−3.40	−7.20
Melvin	Tex	−1.20	−1.20	−2.60	2.00	−5.50	−8.50
Stoneman	Ana	−4.50	−5.00	−2.20	1.40	−0.60	−10.90
Thrift	Bal	−2.40	−1.80	−2.20	−1.30	−3.60	−11.30
Robinson	KC	−4.60	0.90	−3.30	−2.20	−2.20	−11.40

Long Term

GM	Team	Acq.	Traded	FA Got	FA Lst.	Prod.	Drafts	Total
Hart	Cle	6.90	−7.10	10.60	2.20	−0.20		12.40
Beane	Oak	0.70	1.80	5.80	4.10	−0.70		11.70
Robinson	KC	2.10	−1.10	−0.60	9.30	0.70		10.40
Schueler	CWS	−0.40	−0.40	4.10	3.50	2.70		9.50
Smith	Det	5.50	2.40	1.20	−1.70	−0.10		7.30
Melvin	Tex	−0.80	8.40	2.20	−2.80	0.20		7.20
Cashman	NYY	−1.80	0.80	6.40	0.30	−0.70		5.00
Duquette	Bos	−1.20	−0.40	2.80	2.90	−2.00		2.10
LaMar	TB	−2.00	0.40	3.30	1.20	−1.90	0.00	1.00
Baird	KC	——	——	——	——	——		0.00
Gillick	Sea	——	——	——	——	——		0.00
Stoneman	Ana	——	——	——	——	——		0.00
Thrift	Bal	——	——	——	——	——		0.00
Ryan	Min	0.70	2.00	−0.40	0.40	−4.40		−1.70
Ash	Tor	1.60	0.90	−1.00	−1.70	−1.90		−2.10

Residual

GM	Team	Acquired	Lost	Total
Woodward	Sea	8.00	1.80	9.80
Watson	NYY	3.40	4.50	7.90
Bavasi	Ana	9.90	−2.50	7.40
Gillick	Bal	−3.00	4.00	1.00
Michael	NYY	0.00	0.40	0.40
Hemond	Bal	0.00	0.30	0.30
Alderson	Oak	−1.90	1.30	−0.60
Klein	Det	0.00	−0.60	−0.60

NATIONAL LEAGUE

Short Term

GM	Team	Acq.	Traded	FA Got	FA Lst.	Prod.	Total
Jocketty	SL	11.40	4.80	−2.30	3.10	2.40	19.40
Phillips	NYM	−1.10	2.80	5.80	3.20	−1.90	8.80
Malone	LA	−0.60	3.80	1.80	0.90	0.70	6.60
Schuerholz	Atl	−0.40	5.00	−4.20	4.90	0.40	5.70
Dombrowski	Fla	−0.30	4.90	−0.90	1.10	−1.10	3.70
Sabean	SF	3.20	−0.30	−0.20	2.60	−1.80	3.50
Garagiola	Ari	1.80	1.20	−0.10	1.00	−0.40	3.50
O'Dowd	Col	5.30	−0.30	−1.50	1.50	−2.20	2.80
Bowden	Cin	−0.70	−1.60	3.80	1.40	−0.50	2.40
McPhail	ChC	0.20	−0.20	−0.40	0.00	0.00	−0.40
Bonifay	Pit	−0.90	3.50	−1.40	1.80	−5.10	−2.10
Taylor	Mil	−0.30	−5.10	3.60	0.90	−3.40	−4.30
Towers	SD	−1.40	3.70	−5.40	−1.90	−1.50	−6.50
Wade	Phi	−4.20	−1.40	−0.60	−0.80	−1.20	−8.20
Beattie	Mtl	−1.50	1.60	−4.80	−0.20	−4.90	−9.80
Hunsicker	Hou	−1.60	−5.40	−5.20	2.40	−0.10	−9.90
Lynch	ChC	−6.40	−1.80	−0.60	3.30	−7.40	−12.90

Long Term

GM	Team	Acq.	Traded	FA Got	FA Lst.	Prod.	Drafts	Total
Sabean	SF	3.50	2.70	19.30	3.50	0.40		29.40
Schuerholz	Atl	0.10	−4.00	12.80	0.00	5.30		14.20
Jocketty	SL	−3.00	6.10	2.50	5.00	2.30		12.90

Bowden	Cin	3.50	0.00	−0.30	4.00	4.10		11.30
Phillips	NYM	7.90	−4.10	−1.60	3.70	0.70		6.60
Bonifay	Pit	2.40	0.60	−1.50	1.30	2.70		5.50
Malone	LA	1.40	1.10	2.40	0.20	0.30		5.40
Lynch	ChC	−0.60	2.80	2.90	2.30	−3.60		3.80
Towers	SD	2.90	5.60	0.70	−4.90	−1.10		3.20
Garagiola	Ari	−2.20	0.90	7.40	1.00	−0.40	−4.50	2.20
McPhail	ChC	——	——	——	——	——		0.00
O'Dowd	Col	——	——	——	——	——		0.00
Taylor	Mil	——	——	——	——	——		0.00
Hunsicker	Hou	−0.30	−5.30	3.50	−4.10	1.90		−4.30
Beattie	Mtl	−1.00	−5.60	5.20	−2.00	−1.80		−5.20
Wade	Phi	−0.80	1.30	−5.10	1.40	−2.90		−6.10
Dombrowski	Fla	−0.40	−16.10	0.40	2.30	1.70		−12.10

Residual

GM	Team	Acquired	Lost	Total
Lasorda	LA	5.40	4.00	9.40
Bando	Mil	−4.60	5.80	1.20
Malone	Mtl	−0.20	1.20	1.00
Claire	LA	0.00	0.90	0.90
Thomas	Phi	0.30	0.50	0.80
Quinn	SF	−1.00	1.40	0.40
Smith	SD	0.00	0.40	0.40
Gebhardt	Col	5.30	−5.20	0.10
Watson	Hou	0.00	−1.00	−1.00
McIlvaine	NYM	−0.50	−1.70	−2.20

1999

AMERICAN LEAGUE

Short Term

GM	Team	Acq.	Traded	FA Got	FA Lst.	Prod.	Total
Cashman	NYY	0.60	−1.60	11.90	0.80	−1.40	10.30
Beane	Oak	1.10	2.40	6.20	−1.30	1.10	9.50
Duquette	Bos	1.30	1.00	6.30	−2.10	−0.50	6.00
LaMar	TB	−0.50	2.40	0.00	1.50	−1.90	1.50
Ash	Tor	1.80	−0.50	−2.30	0.30	1.30	0.60

Melvin	Tex	0.40	−0.50	−2.10	0.40	1.40	−0.40
Hart	Cle	−1.20	−3.40	4.80	−2.40	−1.50	−3.70
Robinson	KC	−1.90	0.30	−2.10	2.20	−2.50	−4.00
Bavasi	Ana	−3.20	−1.90	−3.90	2.20	−0.10	−6.90
Woodward	Sea	−1.10	1.60	−5.60	−2.20	−0.50	−7.80
Smith	Det	−2.80	−2.20	−0.90	0.70	−3.10	−8.30
Gillick	Bal	−2.20	0.10	3.90	−9.00	−1.40	−8.60
Schueler	CWS	2.40	−0.80	1.00	−5.30	−6.50	−9.20
Ryan	Min	0.00	1.00	−1.50	−0.90	−12.80	−14.20

Long Term

GM	Team	Acq.	Traded	FA Got	FA Lst.	Prod.	Drafts	Total
Gillick	Bal	0.60	2.40	11.90	−0.80	−4.00		10.10
Melvin	Tex	2.50	−0.60	7.70	1.00	−1.80		8.80
Hart	Cle	6.50	−5.00	8.80	−1.20	−3.20		5.90
Duquette	Bos	3.90	−2.60	0.20	−1.40	4.70		4.80
Cashman	NYY	1.00	2.30	1.30	0.00	0.00		4.60
Robinson	KC	0.50	4.80	−1.80	−1.60	2.30		4.20
Ryan	Min	−0.70	1.90	3.00	0.90	−3.00		2.10
Ash	Tor	−0.20	−2.60	6.70	−0.90	−2.00		1.00
Woodward	Sea	−3.40	−9.00	8.90	3.20	1.00		0.70
Smith	Det	2.20	−0.40	0.20	0.90	−3.50		−0.60
LaMar	TB	2.10	−1.30	0.00	0.00	0.10	−3.30	−2.40
Schueler	CWS	2.30	0.60	−1.70	1.00	−7.40		−5.20
Bavasi	Ana	−2.10	0.40	1.90	0.70	−6.30		−5.40
Beane	Oak	0.40	−1.40	−1.60	−2.90	−1.70		−7.20

Residual

GM	Team	Acquired	Lost	Total
Watson	NYY	4.00	2.00	6.00
Klein	Det	0.00	1.60	1.60
Michael	NYY	0.00	1.00	1.00
Grieve	Tex	0.00	0.30	0.30
Gillick	Tor	0.00	0.00	0.00
McPhail	Min	0.00	−0.10	−0.10
Hemond	Bal	0.00	−0.30	−0.30
Alderson	Oak	−1.60	−6.80	−8.40

NATIONAL LEAGUE

Short Term

GM	Team	Acq.	Traded	FA Got	FA Lst.	Prod.	Total
Garagiola	Ari	3.20	−0.80	8.10	1.30	0.50	12.30
Phillips	NYM	4.10	−0.80	7.30	3.10	−1.50	12.20
Bonifay	Pit	2.90	1.60	3.80	0.90	0.30	9.50
Sabean	SF	0.20	0.30	6.20	−1.20	1.60	7.10
Bowden	Cin	4.40	−4.20	−2.50	0.30	4.20	2.20
Beattie	Mtl	−0.40	−0.10	3.90	−0.40	−4.50	−1.50
Malone	LA	−3.50	−0.70	2.30	1.20	−0.80	−1.50
Schuerholz	Atl	2.00	1.60	−3.90	−0.50	−1.30	−2.10
Wade	Phi	−4.80	0.20	1.50	2.90	−2.60	−2.80
Hunsicker	Hou	0.50	−2.30	1.10	−3.50	−0.10	−4.30
Jocketty	SL	−1.40	−3.90	0.60	3.50	−3.50	−4.70
Gebhardt	Col	−1.80	0.50	−0.80	−0.90	−2.20	−5.20
Dombrowski	Fla	−1.00	0.40	−2.10	−0.40	−3.30	−5.60
Lynch	ChC	−4.00	0.90	−0.80	3.90	−6.10	−6.10
Towers	SD	3.60	6.10	−1.90	−5.50	−8.50	−6.20
Bando	Mil	1.40	1.60	−3.00	−3.10	−4.30	−7.40

Long Term

GM	Team	Acq	Traded	FA Got	FA Lst.	Prod.	Drafts	Total
Schuerholz	Atl	−1.10	1.80	11.70	0.80	9.70		22.90
Bowden	Cin	3.10	1.20	3.60	8.90	2.60		19.40
Hunsicker	Hou	4.50	−6.30	12.90	−1.70	4.10		13.50
Towers	SD	2.70	4.10	2.90	−0.90	−0.30		8.50
Garagiola	Ari	3.40	1.20	1.00	0.00	−1.60	4.40	8.40
Wade	Phi	−0.30	3.80	3.50	−0.20	−0.20		6.60
Phillips	NYM	0.60	−0.10	2.30	0.00	−0.20		2.60
Jocketty	SL	1.90	−1.50	2.60	2.20	−4.00		1.20
Malone	LA	0.00	0.00	0.00	−0.20	−0.30		−0.50
Gebhardt	Col	−2.70	−2.90	2.40	1.60	−2.20		−3.80
Bonifay	Pit	−1.90	0.00	0.40	−1.80	−1.20		−4.50
Beattie	Mtl	−3.30	−6.30	−1.90	3.70	2.90		−4.90
Sabean	SF	−3.50	−0.20	−2.60	−0.10	0.80		−5.60
Bando	Mil	0.80	−2.00	−2.10	0.90	−6.40		−8.80
Dombrowski	Fla	−4.40	−7.60	1.90	3.20	−3.80		−10.70
Lynch	ChC	−4.30	−1.80	−3.00	−3.50	0.50	−12.10	

Residual

GM	Team	Acquired	Lost	Total
Smith	SD	0.00	3.40	3.40
Lasorda	LA	1.20	1.70	2.90
Thomas	Phi	2.50	0.20	2.70
Claire	LA	0.00	0.60	0.60
Himes	ChC	0.00	0.60	0.60
Duquette	Mtl	0.00	0.10	0.10
Quinn	SF	−1.10	1.00	−0.10
Maxville	SL	−0.30	0.00	−0.30
Malone	Mtl	1.20	−1.70	−0.50
Watson	Hou	0.00	−3.20	−3.20
McIlvaine	NYM	1.10	−4.80	−3.70

2004 DATA

(Note: In this section, all dollar figures are in millions.)

PAYROLL PROJECTED STANDINGS

In 2004, for the first time in several seasons, the influence of payroll ruled three teams out of consideration for the postseason even before the season started. Those three teams were the Orioles, Blue Jays, and Devil Rays, all in the AL East. The Minnesota Twins overperformed their lower-half payroll by fifteen games, setting the standard for the year. Here are the payroll projected standings and actual standings for the 2004 season.

	Team	Payroll	Proj. Wins	Actual Wins	
AL East	Yankees	$184.194	107	101	
	Red Sox	$127.299	94	98	
	Orioles	$51.623	77	78	2
	Blue Jays	$50.017	77	67	2
	D-Rays	$29.557	72	70	2
AL Central	White Sox	$66.213	80	83	
	Twins	$53.585	77	92	1
	Tigers	$46.832	76	72	
	Royals	$47.609	76	58	
	Indians	$34.319	73	80	
AL West	Angels	$100.535	88	91	
	Mariners	$81.516	84	63	
	A's	$59.426	79	92	
	Rangers	$55.050	78	89	

NL East	Mets	$96.661	87	71
	Phillies	$93.219	86	86
	Braves	$90.183	86	96
	Marlins	$42.143	75	83
	Expos	$41.198	75	67
NL Central	Cubs	$90.560	86	89
	Cardinals	$83.228	84	105
	Astros	$75.397	82	92
	Reds	$46.615	76	76
	Pirates	$32.228	73	72
	Brewers	$27.529	72	67
NL West	Dodgers	$92.902	86	93
	Giants	$82.019	84	91
	D-Backs	$69.781	81	51
	Rockies	$65.445	80	68
	Padres	$55.385	78	87

1. *Best-performing low-revenue team*

2. *No faith and hope*

2004 EARNED VALUES

For the first time since 1999, earned values moderated slightly in 2004. Although 57 percent of core Major League players still received salaries that were more than $1 million out of line with their performance, that was down from 64 percent in 2003. There were also fewer disparities at higher levels. The performance of 37 percent of players (down from 41 percent in 2003) varied from payroll by more than $2 million. In 2003, 50 percent of players overperformed their paychecks by $500,000 or more; in 2004, 46 percent did so. In 2003, 31 percent underperformed by $500,000 or more; in 2004, 29 percent did so.

The five highest earned values in 2004 were:

1. Todd Helton, Colorado, $14.500
2. Barry Bonds, San Francisco, $14.260
3. Pedro Guerrero, Anaheim, $13.894
4. Albert Pujols, St. Louis, $13.679
5. Ichiro Suzuki, Seattle, $11.847

The numbers of Helton and Pujols, on the previous page, as well as the list of the five greatest overperformances, below, are heavily influenced by the fact that the average National League first baseman was paid $5.067 million in 2004. That's $1 million more than the average salary for any other position in either league. That includes several—Jeff Bagwell, Shawn Green, Richie Sexson, and Mike Piazza—who substantially underperformed, driving up EV numbers for high-performance first basemen. Here is the list of the five highest overperformances of 2004:

1. Brad Lidge, Houston, $9.700
2. Travis Hafner, Cleveland, $9.136
3. Johann Santana, Minnesota, $8.694
4. Brad Wilkerson, Montreal, $8.106
5. Lyle Overbay, Milwaukee, $7.335

As might be expected to a team that operates on a $172 million payroll, the Yankees dominate the list of the greatest underperformances. At the salaries they make, it is almost impossible for them not to. In fact, of the five most overpaid in 2004, only Park could be said to have had a bad season. Here are the five greatest underperformers based on 2004 EV:

1. Rodriguez, New York Yankees, ($16.500)
2. Ramirez, Boston, ($13.879)
3. Jeter, New York Yankees, ($13.051)
4. Park, Texas, ($13.047)
5. Mussina, New York Yankees, ($12.855)

With A-Rod's move to third, there were renewed signs of a payroll "middle infield ghetto" in 2004. As noted, the highest-paid position in the NL was first base. That was also true ($4.071 million) in the AL. In the NL, center fielders, right fielders, starters, and closers made more than $3 million on average. In the AL, shortstops, left fielders, right fielders, and starters topped $3 million.

But second basemen averaged only $1.256 million in the AL, and just $1.562 million in the NL. If you removed Jeff Kent ($10 million) from the equation, the NL average fell to $1.313 million; if you removed Vidro ($7 million) as well, it fell to $1.141 million. NL shortstops earned $1.904 million on average. Even catchers tended to be paid more than that, and that's significant because since catching duties tend to be split, fewer catchers make big salaries.

AL shortstop remains the exception, but that's largely due to the presence of Jeter and Nomar. All by himself, Jeter's $18.6 million check raised the AL shortstop average from $2.34 million to $3.2 million. Traditionally, the evidence that GM's paid big money for the long ball could be found in left field and at first base. For the past few seasons, with the ascension of the Jeter–A-Rod–Nomar triumverate, that was not true. It is becoming true again.

Fittingly, the world champion Boston Red Sox had the highest earned value in 2004, at $84.04 million. That was about $1 million higher than the NL champion Cardinals—$83.03 million, and about $7 million higher than the Yankees ($76.759 million). In fact, that Yankees nearly became the first team in history to "waste" $100 million since their total EV was $95.586 million below their payroll.

Here are the 2004 earned values for all players with more than 100 plate appearances or more than 50 innings pitched. The first list is divided by league and position. A subsequent list presents 2004 EVs by team. (Data is presented in order of earned value. Negative amounts are in parentheses.)

EARNED VALUES

2004 AL Position Players

Catcher	Team	Salary	Earned Value	Difference
Rodriguez	Det	$7.000	$7.259	$0.259
Varitek	Bos	$6.900	$6.198	($0.702)
Posada	NYY	$9.000	$5.833	($3.167)
Martinez	Cle	$0.305	$5.065	$4.760
Lopez	Bal	$6.000	$4.023	($1.977)
Miller	Oak	$3.000	$2.697	($0.303)
Zaun	Tor	$0.500	$2.377	$1.877

Molina B	Ana	$2.025	$2.194	$0.169
Barajas	Tex	$0.500	$1.737	$1.237
Molina J	Ana	$0.335	$1.728	$1.393
Hall	TB	$0.320	$1.509	$1.189
Mauer	Min	$0.300	$1.500	$1.200
Melhuse	Oak	$0.358	$1.454	$1.096
Davis	Sea-CWS	$1.400	$1.088	($0.312)
Mirabelli	Bos	$0.825	$0.988	$0.163
Blanco	Min	$0.750	$0.960	$0.210
Burke	CWS	$0.300	$0.860	$0.560
Buck	KC	$0.300	$0.631	$0.331
Flaherty	NYY	$0.775	$0.585	($0.190)
Olivo	CWS-Sea	$0.320	$0.503	$0.183
Wilson	Sea	$3.500	$0.412	($3.088)
Cash	Tor	$0.302	$0.165	($0.137)
Laird	Tex	$0.300	$0.165	($0.135)
Alomar, Jr	CWS	$0.700	($0.109)	($0.809)
Santiago	KC	$2.150	($0.109)	($2.259)
Laker	Cle	$0.450	($0.146)	($0.596)
Fordyce	TB	$0.650	($0.292)	($0.942)

First Base	Team	Salary	Earned Value	Difference
Texeira	Tex	$2.625	$8.358	$5.733
Millar	Bos	$3.300	$7.719	$4.419
Konerko	CWS	$8.000	$7.598	($0.402)
Delgado	Tor	$19.700	$7.522	($12.178)
Palmeiro	Bal	$4.000	$6.990	$2.990
Broussard	Cle	$0.324	$6.352	$6.028
Pena	Det	$0.330	$5.972	$5.642
Hatteberg	Oak	$2.300	$5.926	$3.626
Martinez	TB	$7.500	$5.850	($1.650)
Sweeney	KC	$11.000	$4.863	($6.137)
Morneau	Min	$0.300	$4.483	$4.183
Harvey	KC	$0.318	$3.616	$3.298
Olerud	Sea-NYY	$7.700	$3.616	($4.084)
Erstad	Ana	$7.750	$3.571	($4.179)
Gload	CWS	$0.302	$2.857	$2.555
Giambi	NYY	$12.429	$2.051	($10.378)
Merloni	Cle	$0.560	$1.975	$1.415
Jacobson	Sea	$0.300	$1.869	$1.569
Clark	NYY	$0.750	$1.489	$0.739
McCarty	Bos	$0.500	$1.261	$0.761

Mientkiewicz	Min-Bos	$2.800	$0.608	($2.192)
Karros	Oak	$0.550	($0.078)	($0.628)
Kotchman	Ana	$0.300	($0.836)	($1.136)

Second Base	**Team**	**Salary**	**Earned Value**	**Difference**
Hudson	Tor	$0.322	$2.923	$2.601
Uribe	CWS	$0.350	$2.656	$2.306
Soriano	Tex	$5.400	$2.366	($3.034)
Bellhorn	Bos	$0.490	$2.290	$1.800
Belliard	Cle	$1.100	$2.175	$1.075
Infante	Det	$0.305	$1.969	$1.664
Rivas	Min	$1.500	$1.565	$0.065
Kennedy	Ana	$2.500	$1.549	($0.951)
Roberts	Bal	$0.345	$1.488	$1.143
Graffanino	KC	$1.100	$1.450	$0.350
Scutaro	Oak	$0.302	$1.393	$1.091
Harris	CWS	$0.319	$1.240	$0.921
Cairo	NYY	$0.900	$1.183	$0.283
McLemore	Oak	$0.600	$0.954	$0.354
Menechino	Oak-Tor	$0.400	$0.954	$0.554
Boone	Sea	$8.000	$0.763	($7.237)
Cuddyer	Min	$0.308	$0.725	$0.417
Sanchez	TB	$1.000	$0.649	($0.351)
Smith	Det	$0.300	$0.591	$0.291
Cantu	TB	$0.300	$0.515	$0.215
Punto	Min	$0.308	$0.324	$0.016
Vina	Det	$3.000	$0.324	($2.676)
Wilson	NYY	$0.700	$0.076	($0.624)
Gotay	KC	$0.300	$0.019	($0.281)

Shortstop	**Team**	**Salary**	**Earned Value**	**Difference**
Tejada	Bal	$5.000	$8.167	$3.167
Guillen	Det	$2.500	$7.326	$4.826
Jeter	NYY	$18.600	$5.549	($13.051)
Crosby	Oak	$0.301	$5.424	$5.123
Lugo	TB	$1.750	$4.801	$3.051
Vizquel	Cle	$6.000	$4.426	($1.574)
Guzman	Min	$3.725	$4.115	$0.390
Valentin	CWS	$5.000	$4.021	($0.979)
Young M	Tex	$0.450	$3.928	$3.478
Berroa	KC	$0.373	$2.681	$2.308
Eckstein	Ana	$2.150	$2.307	$0.157

Reese	Bos	$1.000	$2.182	$1.182
Gomez	Tor	$0.750	$1.777	$1.027
Cabrera	Bos	$2.000	$1.216	($0.784)
Garciaparra	Bos	$7.705	$0.935	($6.770)
Woodward	Tor	$0.775	$0.904	$0.129
Aurilia	Sea	$2.045	$0.686	($1.359)
Upton	TB	$0.300	$0.436	$0.136
Lopez	Sea	$0.300	($0.156)	($0.456)

Third Base	Team	Salary	Earned Value	Difference
Mora	Bal	$2.333	$6.657	$4.324
Chavez	Oak	$5.325	$5.668	$0.343
Rodriguez	NYY	$22.000	$5.470	($16.530)
Blake	Cle	$0.352	$4.350	$3.998
Huff	TB	$2.667	$4.086	$1.419
Blalock	Tex	$0.550	$3.691	$3.141
Figgins	Ana	$0.320	$3.361	$3.041
Koskie	Min	$4.500	$2.933	($1.567)
Randa	KC	$3.250	$2.808	($0.442)
Mueller	Bos	$2.100	$2.735	$0.635
Inge	Det	$0.340	$2.498	$2.158
Munson	Det	$1.488	$1.912	$0.424
Hinske	Tor	$0.900	$1.516	$0.616
Youkilis	Bos	$0.300	$1.477	$1.177
Crede	CWS	$0.340	$1.424	$1.084
Spiezio	Sea	$2.567	$1.246	($1.321)
Cabrera	Sea	$1.000	$1.187	$0.187
Relaford	KC	$0.900	$0.916	$0.016
Bloomquist	Sea	$0.325	$0.159	($0.166)
Blum	TB	$1.500	$0.132	($1.368)
Rolls	TB	$0.800	($0.362)	($1.162)

Left Field	Team	Salary	Earned Value	Difference
Matsui	NYY	$6.000	$7.149	$1.149
Lee	CWS	$4.200	$6.366	$2.166
Ramirez	Bos	$20.000	$6.121	($13.879)
Guillen	Ana	$5.350	$5.876	$0.526
Crawford	TB	$0.300	$5.680	$5.380
Gross	Tor	$3.300	$4.015	$0.715
Monroe	Det	$0.300	$3.893	$3.593
Ford	Min	$1.725	$3.648	$1.923
Stewart	Min	$2.750	$3.550	$0.800

Lawton	Cle	$6.750	$3.526	($3.224)
Guiel	KC	$3.000	$3.428	$0.428
Berg	Tor	$6.200	$2.840	($3.360)
White	Det	$0.600	$2.644	$2.044
Kielty	Oak	$2.175	$2.400	$0.225
Bigbie	Bal	$0.300	$2.008	$1.708
Ibanez	Sea	$0.322	$1.812	$1.490
Johnson	Tor	$2.200	$1.616	($0.584)
Byrnes	Oak	$0.500	$1.494	$0.994
Thames	Det	$0.500	$1.224	$0.724
Catalanotto	Tor	$2.300	$1.058	($1.242)
Dellucci	Tex	$0.328	$0.049	($0.279)
Young E	Tex	$0.300	($0.147)	($0.447)
Brown	KC	$0.310	($0.538)	($0.848)

Center Field	Team	Salary	Earned Value	Difference
Rowand	CWS	$0.340	$4.656	$4.316
Damon	Bos	$8.000	$4.616	($3.384)
Kotsay	Oak	$5.500	$4.616	($0.884)
Winn	Sea	$3.500	$4.460	$0.960
Baldelli	TB	$0.320	$3.795	$3.475
Wells	Tor	$0.870	$3.462	$2.592
Williams	NYY	$12.357	$3.443	($8.914)
Hunter	Min	$6.500	$3.384	($3.116)
Crisp	Cle	$0.319	$3.091	$2.772
Beltran	KC	$4.500	$3.091	($1.409)
DaVanon	Ana	$0.375	$2.895	$2.520
Anderson	Ana	$6.200	$2.719	($3.481)
DeJesus	KC	$0.300	$2.484	$2.184
Lofton	NYY	$3.100	$1.995	($1.105)
Sanchez	Det	$0.385	$1.565	$1.180
Nix	Tex	$0.300	$1.232	$0.932
Sizemore	Cle	$0.300	$0.880	$0.580
Matos	Bal	$0.975	$0.861	($0.114)
Escobar	Cle	$0.302	$0.802	$0.500
Logan	Det	$0.300	$0.743	$0.443
Bocachica	Sea	$0.400	$0.352	($0.048)

Right Field	Team	Salary	Earned Value	Difference
Guerrero	Ana	$11.000	$13.894	$2.894
Suzuki	Sea	$6.500	$11.847	$5.347
Sheffield	NYY	$13.000	$10.823	($2.177)

Cruz, Jr	TB	$2.500	$5.412	$2.912
Mench	Tex	$0.345	$5.375	$5.030
Higginson	Det	$8.850	$5.192	($3.658)
Gerut	Cle	$0.326	$4.863	$4.537
Dye	Oak	$11.667	$4.132	($7.535)
Jones	Min	$4.350	$4.095	($0.255)
Stairs	KC	$1.000	$3.913	$2.913
Hairston	Bal	$1.650	$3.876	$2.226
Matthews	Tex	$0.400	$3.876	$3.476
Surhoff	Bal	$0.800	$3.510	$2.710
Rios	Tor	$0.310	$3.181	$2.871
Ordonez	CWS	$14.000	$2.340	($11.660)
Nixon	Bos	$4.500	$1.792	($2.708)
Gibbons	Bal	$2.600	$1.317	($1.283)
Kapler	Bos	$0.750	$1.243	$0.493
Gonzalez	KC	$4.000	$0.658	($3.342)
Perez	CWS	$0.850	$0.512	($0.338)
Nunez	KC	$0.229	$0.439	$0.210
Jordan	Tex	$1.250	$0.000	($1.250)
Clark	Tor	$0.305	($0.073)	($0.378)
Borchard	CWS	$0.300	($0.731)	($1.031)

Des. Hitter	Team	Salary	Earned Value	Difference
Hafner	Cle	$0.316	$9.452	$9.136
Ortiz	Bos	$4.588	$8.480	$3.892
Durazo	Oak	$2.100	$7.450	$5.350
Thomas	CWS	$6.000	$4.652	($1.348)
Young	Det	$7.750	$3.887	($3.863)
Newhan	Bal	$0.300	$3.533	$3.233
Martinez	Sea	$3.000	$3.357	$0.357
Glaus	Ana	$9.900	$2.591	($7.309)
Sierra	NYY	$1.000	$1.826	$0.826
Offerman	Min	$0.500	$1.531	$1.031
Phelps	Tor-Cle	$0.342	$1.325	$0.983
Fullmer	Tex	$1.000	$1.031	$0.031
Pickering	KC	$0.310	$0.883	$0.573
Everett	CWS	$2.228	$0.854	($1.374)
Salmon	Ana	$9.900	$0.707	($9.193)
LeCroy	Min	$0.340	$0.677	$0.337
Perry	Tex	$1.700	$0.147	($1.553)
Fick	TB	$0.755	($0.353)	($1.108)

2004 AL Pitchers

Starting Pitcher	Team	Salary	Earned Value	Difference
Santana	Min	$1.600	$10.294	$8.694
Schilling	Bos	$12.000	$9.055	($2.945)
Buehrle	CWS	$3.500	$7.244	$3.744
Martinez	Bos	$17.500	$7.149	($10.351)
Westbrook	Cle	$0.925	$7.053	$6.128
Radke	Min	$10.765	$6.863	($3.902)
Drese	Tex	$0.350	$6.291	$5.941
Garcia	Sea-CWS	$6.875	$6.291	($0.584)
Lopez	Bal	$0.365	$6.195	$5.830
Rogers	Tex	$2.500	$5.910	$3.410
Escobar	Ana	$5.750	$5.719	($0.031)
Hudson	Oak	$5.000	$5.528	$0.528
Lilly	Tor	$1.900	$5.338	$3.438
Mulder	Oak	$4.450	$5.338	$0.888
Silva	Min	$0.340	$5.338	$4.998
Maroth	Det	$0.333	$5.052	$4.719
Zito	Oak	$3.000	$4.861	$1.861
Arroyo	Bos	$0.333	$4.766	$4.433
Harden	Oak	$0.300	$4.766	$4.466
Greinke	KC	$0.300	$4.670	$4.370
Garland	CWS	$2.300	$4.575	$2.275
Sabathia	Cle	$2.700	$4.575	$1.875
Batista	Tor	$3.600	$4.384	$0.784
Lieber	NYY	$2.700	$3.908	$1.208
Halladay	Tor	$6.000	$3.813	($2.187)
Lackey	Ana	$0.375	$3.813	$3.438
Vazquez	NYY	$9.000	$3.527	($5.473)
Wakefield	Bos	$4.350	$3.527	($0.823)
Brown	NYY	$15.714	$3.336	($12.378)
Franklin	Sea	$1.800	$3.336	$1.536
Redman	Oak	$2.000	$3.336	$1.336
Ponson	Bal	$3.000	$3.241	$0.241
Hendrickson	TB	$0.315	$3.145	$2.830
Hernandez	NYY	$0.500	$3.145	$2.645
Mussina	NYY	$16.000	$3.145	($12.855)
Washburn	Ana	$5.450	$3.145	($2.305)
Zambrano	TB	$0.217	$3.145	$2.928
Bonderman	Det	$0.330	$3.050	$2.720
Colon	Ana	$11.000	$2.859	($8.141)
Moyer	Sea	$7.000	$2.764	($4.236)
Cabrera	Bal	$0.300	$2.669	$2.369

Bedard	Bal	$0.300	$2.574	$2.274
Bush	Tor	$0.300	$2.574	$2.274
Gobble	KC	$0.304	$2.574	$2.270
Lohse	Min	$0.395	$2.478	$2.083
Pineiro	Sea	$3.000	$2.478	($0.522)
Bell	TB	$0.300	$2.383	$2.083
Loaiza	CWS-NYY	$4.000	$2.383	($1.617)
Robertson	Det	$0.305	$2.383	$2.078
Elarton	Cle	$0.356	$2.288	$1.932
Johnson	Det	$3.000	$2.192	($0.808)
Lowe	Bos	$4.500	$2.097	($2.403)
Meche	Sea	$1.950	$2.097	$0.147
Brazelton	TB	$0.300	$2.002	$1.702
Towers	Tor	$0.340	$2.002	$1.662
Contreras	NYY-CWS	$8.500	$1.906	($6.594)
Knotts	Det	$0.316	$1.906	$1.590
Lee	Cle	$0.303	$1.906	$1.603
Anderson	KC	$3.250	$1.811	($1.439)
May	KC	$1.750	$1.811	$0.061
Mulholland	Min	$0.350	$1.811	$1.461
Sele	Ana	$8.667	$1.811	($6.856)
Benoit	Tex	$0.335	$1.525	$1.190
Davis	Cle	$0.327	$1.525	$1.198
Schoenewis	CWS	$1.725	$1.430	($0.295)
Dickey	Tex	$0.338	$1.144	$0.806
Wood	KC	$0.300	$1.144	$0.844
Park	Tex	$14.000	$0.953	($13.047)
Miller	Tor	$0.300	$0.763	$0.463
Daal	Bal	$4.500	$0.000	($4.500)
Mays	Min	$5.750	$0.000	($5.750)
Jarvis	Sea	$4.250	($0.381)	($4.631)
Hentgen	Tor	$2.200	($0.477)	($2.677)

Closer	Team	Salary	Earned Value	Difference
Rivera	NYY	$10.890	$6.740	($4.150)
Cordero	Tex	$2.000	$6.038	$4.038
Foulke	Bos	$3.500	$5.509	$2.009
Nathan	Min	$0.440	$5.403	$4.963
Takatsu	CWS	$0.750	$4.449	$3.699
Rodriguez	Ana	$0.375	$3.602	$3.227
Baez	TB	$1.750	$2.966	$1.216
Frasor	Tor	$0.300	$2.754	$2.454
Percival	Ana	$7.833	$2.648	($5.185)

Guardado	Sea	$4.000	$2.436	($1.564)
Dotel	Oak	$1.647	$1.801	$0.154
Julio	Bal	$0.385	$1.801	$1.416
Affeldt	KC	$0.350	$1.377	$1.027
Urbina	Det	$0.500	$1.059	$0.559
Wickman	Cle	$6.000	$0.742	($5.258)
Koch	CWS	$6.375	$0.318	($6.057)
Patterson	Det	$2.800	$0.318	($2.482)

Other Pitchers	Team	Salary	Earned Value	Difference
Gordon	NYY	$3.500	$3.174	($0.326)
Rincon	Min	$0.330	$2.930	$2.600
Ryan	Bal	$1.275	$2.686	$1.411
Duchscherrer	Oak	$0.303	$2.258	$1.955
Shields	Ana	$0.375	$1.953	$1.578
Madritsch	Sea	$0.300	$1.892	$1.592
Marte	CWS	$0.500	$1.892	$1.392
Ortiz	Ana	$3.267	$1.892	($1.375)
Romero	Min	$0.820	$1.709	$0.889
Almanzar	Tex	$0.420	$1.648	$1.228
Villone	Sea	$1.000	$1.587	$0.587
Reyes	KC	$0.550	$1.526	$0.976
Speier	Tor	$1.600	$1.526	($0.074)
Yan	Det	$0.650	$1.526	$0.876
Riske	Cle	$1.025	$1.465	$0.440
Halama	TB	$0.600	$1.404	$0.804
Mahay	Tex	$0.500	$1.404	$0.904
Timlin	Bos	$2.500	$1.404	($1.096)
Carter	TB	$0.320	$1.343	$1.023
Parrish	Bal	$0.320	$1.343	$1.023
Walker	Det	$0.775	$1.343	$0.568
Gregg	Ana	$0.302	$1.282	$0.980
Harper	TB	$0.310	$1.282	$0.972
Betancourt	Cle	$0.305	$1.221	$0.916
Francisco	Tex	$0.300	$1.221	$0.921
Grimsley	KC-Bal	$1.000	$1.221	$0.221
Camp	KC	$0.300	$1.098	$0.798
Hammond	Oak	$2.400	$1.098	($1.302)
Miller	Cle	$0.300	$1.037	$0.737
Quantrill	NYY	$3.000	$1.037	($1.963)
Adams	Tor-Bos	$1.700	$0.976	($0.724)
Roa	Min	$0.320	$0.976	$0.656
Mecir	Oak	$2.877	$0.915	($1.962)

Brocail	Tex	$0.350	$0.854	$0.504
Levine	Det	$0.825	$0.854	$0.029
Putz	Sea	$0.300	$0.854	$0.554
Embree	Bos	$3.000	$0.793	($2.207)
Bradford	Oak	$0.965	$0.671	($0.294)
Chulk	Tor	$0.300	$0.671	$0.371
Politte	CWS	$0.800	$0.671	($0.129)
Sullivan	KC	$2.100	$0.671	($1.429)
Adkins	CWS	$0.301	$0.610	$0.309
Bauer	Bal	$0.335	$0.610	$0.275
Fultz	Min	$0.550	$0.610	$0.060
Ledezma	Det	$0.300	$0.610	$0.310
Groom	Bal	$3.000	$0.549	($2.451)
Mateo	Sea	$0.345	$0.549	$0.204
Sosa	TB	$0.313	$0.549	$0.236
Tadano	Cle	$0.300	$0.549	$0.249
Cotts	CWS	$0.301	$0.488	$0.187
Durbin	Cle	$0.269	$0.488	$0.219
Riley	Bal	$0.310	$0.488	$0.178
Hasegawa	Sea	$2.750	$0.427	($2.323)
Powell	Tex	$3.500	$0.427	($3.073)
Sturtze	NYY	$0.330	$0.427	$0.097
Wasdin	Tex	$0.330	$0.366	$0.036
White	Cle	$0.330	$0.366	$0.036
Borkowski	Bal	$0.300	$0.305	$0.005
DuBose	Bal	$0.305	$0.061	($0.244)
Greisinger	Min	$0.310	$0.000	($0.310)
Ligtenberg	Tor	$2.000	$0.000	($2.000)
Zimmerman	Tex	$4.467	$0.000	($4.467)
Gonzalez	TB	$1.700	($0.062)	($1.762)
Waechter	TB	$0.300	($0.123)	($0.423)

2004 NL Position Players

Catcher	Team	Salary	Earned Value	Difference
Kendall	Pit	$8.571	$7.783	($0.788)
Estrada	Atl	$0.313	$6.482	$6.169
Hernandez	SD	$2.938	$5.053	$2.115
Barrett	ChC	$1.550	$4.891	$3.341
Lieberthal	Phi	$7.500	$4.043	($3.457)
LoDuca	LA-Fla	$4.067	$3.764	($0.303)
Matheny	SL	$4.000	$3.427	($0.573)
Schneider	Mtl	$0.350	$3.380	$3.030
LaRue	Cin	$2.600	$3.078	$0.478

Pierzynski	SF	$3.500	$2.451	($1.049)
Johnson	Col	$9.000	$2.207	($6.793)
Torrealba	SF	$0.334	$1.487	$1.153
Moeller	Mil	$0.370	$1.452	$1.082
Ojeda	SD	$0.305	$1.371	$1.066
Snyder	Ari	$0.300	$1.324	$1.024
Phillips	NYM	$0.318	$1.278	$0.960
Redmond	Fla	$0.840	$1.150	$0.310
Wilson	NYM	$0.715	$1.138	$0.423
Ausmus	Hou	$1.000	$1.103	$0.103
Diaz	Mtl	$2.588	$1.022	($1.566)
Hammock	Ari	$0.315	$0.836	$0.521
Valentin	Cin	$0.500	$0.836	$0.336
Closser	Col	$0.300	$0.743	$0.443
Molina	SL	$0.300	$0.627	$0.327
Greene	Col	$0.550	$0.371	($0.179)
Perez E	Atl	$0.625	$0.209	($0.416)
Pratt	Phi	$0.875	$0.162	($0.713)
Chavez	Hou	$0.315	$0.093	($0.222)
Castro	Fla	$0.400	($0.186)	($0.586)
Mayne	Ari-LA	$0.800	($0.209)	($1.009)
Ross	LA	$0.310	($0.372)	($0.682)
Bako	ChC	$0.865	($0.883)	($1.748)
Brito	Ari	$0.300	($0.953)	($1.253)
Bennett	Mil	$0.300	($1.255)	($1.555)

First Base	Team	Salary	Earned Value	Difference
Helton	Col	$11.600	$14.500	$2.900
Pujols	SL	$7.000	$13.679	$6.679
Thome	Phi	$12.167	$9.302	($2.865)
Wilkerson	Mtl	$0.375	$8.481	$8.106
Lee	ChC	$6.167	$7.661	$1.494
Overbay	Mil	$0.326	$7.661	$7.335
Nevin	SD	$8.500	$7.524	($0.976)
Casey	Cin	$6.800	$6.840	$0.040
Snow	SF	$1.500	$6.539	$5.039
Bagwell	Hou	$16.000	$6.156	($9.844)
Feliz	SF	$0.850	$4.856	$4.006
Green	LA	$16.667	$4.651	($12.016)
Piazza	NYM	$16.071	$3.762	($12.309)
Hillenbrand	Ari	$2.600	$3.734	$1.134
Choi	Fla-LA	$0.310	$3.666	$3.356
Franco	Atl	$0.750	$3.598	$2.848

LaRoche	Atl	$0.300	$2.367	$2.067
Sexson	Ari	$8.725	$1.847	($6.878)
Saenz	LA	$0.350	$1.436	$1.086
Ward	Pit	$0.350	$1.436	$1.086
Johnson	Mtl	$1.250	$1.067	($0.183)
Ventura	LA	$1.200	$0.999	($0.201)
Zeile	NYM	$1.000	$0.862	($0.138)
Simon	Pit	$0.739	($1.026)	($1.765)

Second Base	Team	Salary	Earned Value	Difference
Loretta	SD	$2.500	$5.391	$2.891
Kent	Hou	$10.000	$4.084	($5.916)
Polanco	Phi	$3.950	$3.354	($0.596)
Giles	Atl	$0.430	$3.262	$2.832
Castillo	Fla	$4.667	$3.104	($1.563)
Durham	SF	$7.200	$2.973	($4.227)
Womack	SL	$0.300	$2.723	$2.423
Cora	LA	$1.300	$2.478	$1.178
Jimenez	Cin	$1.615	$2.342	$0.727
Miles	Col	$0.300	$2.233	$1.933
Hernandez	LA	$0.500	$1.765	$1.265
Vidro	Mtl	$7.000	$1.716	($5.284)
Grudzielanek	ChC	$2.500	$1.579	($0.921)
Walker	ChC	$1.750	$1.520	($0.230)
Spivey	Mil	$2.367	$1.471	($0.896)
Castillo	Pit	$0.300	$1.411	$1.111
Ginter	Mil	$0.383	$1.247	$0.864
Gonzalez	Col	$0.300	$1.144	$0.844
Green N	Atl	$0.300	$1.144	$0.844
Carroll	Mtl	$0.310	$1.089	$0.779
Hairston	Ari	$0.300	$1.089	$0.789
Easley	Fla	$0.300	$1.002	$0.702
Hill	Pit	$0.315	$0.981	$0.666
Utley	Phi	$0.300	$0.981	$0.681
Hall	Mil	$0.310	$0.975	$0.665
Kata	Ari	$0.315	$0.844	$0.529
Reyes	NYM	$0.308	$0.567	$0.259
Anderson	SL	$0.600	$0.436	($0.164)
Keppinger	NYM	$0.300	$0.409	$0.109
Alomar	Ari	$0.659	$0.354	($0.305)
McEwing	NYM	$0.500	$0.354	($0.146)
Nunez	Pit	$0.625	$0.354	($0.271)
Macias	ChC	$0.750	$0.294	($0.456)

Green A	Ari	$0.300	$0.028	($0.272)
Garcia	NYM	$0.800	($0.027)	($0.827)

Shortstop	Team	Salary	Earned Value	Difference
Wilson	Pit	$1.850	$5.423	$3.573
Furcal	Atl	$3.700	$4.561	$0.861
Renteria	SL	$7.250	$3.396	($3.854)
Matsui	NYM	$5.033	$2.788	($2.245)
Rollins	Phi	$2.425	$2.788	$0.363
Clayton	Col	$0.650	$2.737	$2.087
Iztouris C	LA	$0.359	$2.686	$2.327
Everett	Hou	$0.370	$2.585	$2.215
Gonzalez A	Fla	$2.800	$2.509	($0.291)
Perez	SF-ChC	$2.750	$2.179	($0.571)
Cintron	Ari	$0.335	$2.053	$1.718
Cruz	SF	$0.300	$2.027	$1.727
Larkin	Cin	$0.700	$1.901	$1.201
Counsell	Mil	$3.167	$1.774	($1.393)
Vizcaino	Hou	$1.200	$1.749	$0.549
Cabrera	Mtl	$4.000	$1.723	($2.277)
Lopez	Cin	$0.300	$1.368	$1.068
Martinez	ChC	$0.900	$1.267	$0.367
Luna	SL	$0.300	$0.862	$0.562
Gonzalez A	ChC-Mtl-SD	$5.750	$0.836	($4.914)
Garciaparra	ChC	$3.795	$0.811	($2.984)
Delgado	NYM	$0.300	$0.786	$0.486
Garcia	Atl	$0.313	$0.380	$0.067
Izturis M	Mtl	$0.300	$0.329	$0.029
Greene	SD	$0.301	$0.000	($0.301)
Vazquez	SD	$0.343	($0.025)	($0.368)

Third Base	Team	Salary	Earned Value	Difference
Rolen	SL	$8.625	$8.475	($0.150)
Beltre	LA	$5.000	$8.044	$3.044
Lowell	Fla	$6.500	$5.386	($1.114)
Freel	Cin	$0.320	$4.740	$4.420
Ramirez	ChC	$6.000	$4.740	($1.260)
Castilla	Col	$2.100	$4.525	$2.425
Bell	Phi	$4.400	$4.237	($0.163)
Jones	Atl	$15.333	$3.950	($11.383)
Tracy	Ari	$0.300	$3.203	$2.903
Lamb	Hou	$0.352	$2.586	$2.234
Batista	Mtl	$1.500	$2.514	$1.014

Burroughs	SD	$0.340	$2.514	$2.174
Wigginton	NYM-Pit	$0.316	$2.413	$2.097
Ensberg	Hou	$0.380	$2.126	$1.746
Wright	NYM	$0.300	$1.724	$1.424
Branyan	Mil	$0.350	$1.472	$1.122
Castro	Cin	$1.000	$1.221	$0.221
Olson	Ari	$0.300	$0.682	$0.382
Aurilia	SD	$1.105	$0.539	($0.566)
Helms	Mil	$1.688	$0.503	($1.185)
Hummel	Cin	$0.300	$0.180	($0.120)
Perez	Phi	$0.750	$0.180	($0.570)
DeRosa	Atl	$0.725	$0.144	($0.581)
Stynes	Pit	$0.750	$0.036	($0.714)
Alfonzo	SF	$6.500	($0.036)	($6.536)
Larson	Cin	$0.318	($0.036)	($0.354)
Harris	Fla	$0.400	($0.108)	($0.508)

Left Field	Team	Salary	Earned Value	Difference
Bonds	SF	$18.000	$14.260	($3.740)
Dunn	Cin	$0.445	$7.315	$6.870
Alou	ChC	$9.500	$5.648	($3.852)
Conine	Fla	$3.000	$4.468	$1.468
Bay	Pit	$0.305	$4.421	$4.116
Klesko	SD	$6.000	$4.421	($1.579)
Burrell	Phi	$4.250	$4.028	($0.222)
Biggio	Hou	$3.000	$3.611	$0.611
Jenkins	Mil	$8.738	$3.611	($5.127)
Gonzalez	Ari	$8.250	$3.032	($5.218)
Floyd	NYM	$6.500	$2.870	($3.630)
Marrero	Atl	$3.000	$2.755	($0.245)
Werth	LA	$0.303	$2.639	$2.336
Sledge	Mtl	$0.300	$2.593	$2.293
Thomas	Atl	$0.300	$2.477	$2.177
Mabry	SL	$0.400	$2.292	$1.892
Long	SD	$3.575	$2.176	($1.399)
Valent	NYM	$0.300	$2.083	$1.783
Holliday	Col	$0.300	$1.944	$1.644
Roberts	LA	$0.686	$1.643	$0.957
Spencer	NYM	$0.538	$1.481	$0.943
Lankford	SL	$0.650	$1.204	$0.554
Lane	Hou	$0.308	$1.042	$0.734
Taguchi	SL	$1.200	$0.671	($0.529)
Palmeiro	Hou	$0.750	$0.579	($0.171)

Mondesi	Pit	$0.866	$0.509	($0.357)
Wise	Atl	$0.325	$0.393	$0.068
Bragg	SD-Cin	$0.400	$0.324	($0.076)
McCracken	Ari	$1.548	$0.301	($1.247)
Hocking	Col	$0.650	$0.231	($0.419)
Grabowski	LA	$0.301	$0.116	($0.185)
Williams	NYM	$0.500	$0.046	($0.454)
Goodwin	ChC	$0.650	($0.139)	($0.789)

Center Field	Team	Salary	Earned Value	Difference
Edmonds	SL	$9.333	$10.471	$1.138
Jones	Atl	$12.500	$6.221	($6.279)
Beltran	Hou	$4.500	$5.313	$0.813
Bradley	LA	$1.730	$5.210	$3.480
Finley	Ari-LA	$7.000	$4.873	($2.127)
Pierre	Fla	$2.400	$4.769	$2.369
Cameron	NYM	$4.333	$4.717	$0.384
Payton	SD	$1.500	$4.406	$2.906
Patterson	ChC	$0.480	$4.043	$3.563
Grissom	SF	$2.125	$3.940	$1.815
Podsednik	Mil	$0.400	$3.421	$3.021
Griffey	Cin	$12.500	$3.369	($9.131)
Michaels	Phi	$0.335	$2.747	$2.412
Chavez	Mtl	$0.350	$2.644	$2.294
Redman	Pit	$0.321	$2.514	$2.193
Ledee	Phi-SF	$1.225	$1.555	$0.330
Terrero	Ari	$0.300	$0.803	$0.503
Wilson	Col	$9.000	$0.622	($8.378)
Freeman	Col	$0.300	$0.052	($0.248)
Byrd	Phi	$0.355	$0.026	($0.329)
Glanville	Phi	$0.550	($0.181)	($0.731)

Right Field	Team	Salary	Earned Value	Difference
Drew	Atl	$4.200	$9.802	$5.602
Abreu	Phi	$10.600	$9.698	($0.902)
Berkman	Hou	$6.500	$8.968	$2.468
Giles	SD	$8.833	$5.882	($2.951)
Cabrera	Fla	$0.320	$6.569	$6.249
Wilson	Pit	$1.150	$5.005	$3.855
Burnitz	Col	$1.250	$4.797	$3.547
Walker	Col-SL	$12.667	$4.119	($8.548)
Clark	Mil	$0.376	$4.067	$3.691
Sosa	ChC	$16.000	$4.015	($11.985)

Pena	Cin	$0.345	$3.884	$3.539
Rivera	Mtl	$0.312	$3.545	$3.233
Tucker	SF	$1.500	$3.285	$1.785
Sanders	SL	$2.000	$3.207	$1.207
Mackowiak	Pit	$0.335	$3.076	$2.741
Mohr	SF	$0.343	$3.076	$2.733
Hidalgo	Hou-NYM	$12.500	$2.946	($9.554)
Bautista	Ari	$4.000	$2.529	($1.471)
Sweeney	Col	$0.400	$2.086	$1.686
Hollandsworth	ChC	$1.000	$2.007	$1.007
Grieve	Mil-ChC	$0.700	$1.538	$0.838
Encarnacion	LA-Fla	$3.565	$1.512	($2.053)
Buchanan	SD-NYM	$0.650	$0.834	$0.184
Kearns	Cin	$0.400	$0.834	$0.434
Hammonds	SF	$1.000	$0.574	($0.426)
Cruz	Cin	$0.350	$0.443	$0.093
Cedeno	SL	$5.375	$0.417	($4.958)
DeVore	Ari	$0.300	$0.261	($0.039)
Everett	Mtl	$2.272	$0.261	($2.011)
Garcia	NYM	$0.588	$0.209	($0.379)
Hawpe	Col	$0.300	$0.157	($0.143)
Pellow	Col	$0.310	($0.156)	($0.466)

2004 NL Pitchers

Starting Pitcher	Team	Salary	Earned Value	Difference
Johnson	Ari	$16.000	$9.444	($6.556)
Hernandez	Mtl	$6.000	$8.404	$2.404
Sheets	Mil	$2.425	$8.318	$5.893
Zambrano	ChC	$0.450	$7.625	$7.175
Schmidt	SF	$7.937	$7.538	($0.399)
Pavano	Fla	$3.800	$7.365	$3.565
Clemens	Hou	$5.000	$7.018	$2.018
Oswalt	Hou	$3.250	$6.931	$3.681
Peavy	SD	$0.350	$6.671	$6.321
Glavine	NYM	$10.766	$6.412	($4.354)
Davis	Mil	$0.450	$5.545	$5.095
Marquis	SL	$0.525	$5.458	$4.933
Maddux	ChC	$6.000	$5.285	($0.715)
Leiter	NYM	$10.296	$5.199	($5.097)
Wright	Atl	$0.850	$5.112	$4.262
Webb	Ari	$0.335	$5.025	$4.690
Weaver	LA	$6.250	$4.852	($1.398)

Thomson	Atl	$2.250	$4.765	$2.515
Clement	ChC	$6.000	$4.765	($1.235)
Perez	Pit	$0.321	$4.765	$4.444
Kennedy	Col	$0.320	$4.592	$4.272
Carpenter	SL	$0.300	$4.505	$4.205
Perez	LA	$5.000	$4.419	($0.581)
Trachsel	NYM	$5.000	$4.419	($0.581)
Ortiz	Atl	$6.200	$4.245	($1.955)
Wells	SD	$1.250	$4.072	$2.822
Penny	Fla-LA	$3.725	$3.986	$0.261
Hampton	Atl	$14.625	$3.899	($10.726)
Willis	Fla	$0.353	$3.899	$3.546
Williams	SL	$8.000	$3.726	($4.274)
Lima	LA	$0.500	$3.639	$3.139
Tomko	SF	$1.200	$3.639	$2.439
Wood	ChC	$8.000	$3.552	($4.448)
Beckett	Fla	$1.509	$3.466	$1.957
Lawrence	SD	$0.925	$3.466	$2.541
Rusch	ChC	$0.500	$3.292	$2.792
Jennings	Col	$0.340	$3.292	$2.952
Milton	Phi	$9.000	$3.292	($5.708)
Wilson	Cin	$3.500	$3.119	($0.381)
Miller	Hou	$3.400	$3.119	($0.281)
Lidle	Cin-Phi	$2.750	$3.032	$0.282
Rueter	SF	$6.133	$3.032	($3.101)
Day	Mtl	$0.315	$2.946	$2.631
Wolf	Phi	$4.375	$2.946	($1.429)
Eaton	SD	$1.925	$2.946	$1.021
Suppan	SL	$1.000	$2.946	$1.946
Estes	Col	$0.600	$2.686	$2.086
Burnett	Fla	$2.500	$2.686	$0.186
Morris	SL	$12.500	$2.686	($9.814)
Byrd	Atl	$7.000	$2.599	($4.401)
Prior	ChC	$3.150	$2.599	($0.551)
Kim	Mtl	$0.303	$2.599	$2.296
Fogg	Pit	$0.342	$2.599	$2.257
Wells	Pit	$2.575	$2.599	$0.024
Williams	SF	$0.308	$2.599	$2.291
Ohka	Mtl	$2.338	$2.426	$0.088
Alvarez	LA	$1.500	$2.339	$0.839
Hermanson	SF	$0.800	$2.253	$1.453
Ishii	LA	$2.975	$2.166	($0.809)
Millwood	Phi	$11.000	$2.079	($8.921)

Pettitte	Hou	$5.500	$1.906	($3.594)
Harang	Cin	$0.360	$1.733	$1.373
Santos	Mil	$0.300	$1.646	$1.346
Seo	NYM	$0.320	$1.646	$1.326
Myers	Phi	$0.363	$1.646	$1.283
Padilla	Phi	$2.600	$1.646	($0.954)
Valdes	SD-Fla	$0.800	$1.560	$0.760
Patterson	Mtl	$0.310	$1.385	$1.075
Obermueller	Mil	$0.314	$1.213	$0.899
Capuano	Mil	$0.305	$1.213	$0.908
Armas	Mtl	$2.100	$1.126	($0.974)
Sparks	Ari	$0.500	$1.040	$0.540
Munro	Hou	$0.350	$1.040	$0.690
Benson	Pit-NYM	$6.150	$0.866	($5.284)
Acevedo	Cin	$0.340	$0.347	$0.007
Redding	Hou	$0.395	$0.173	($0.222)
Neagle	Col	$9.000	$0.000	($9.000)
Fossum	Ari	$0.345	($0.173)	($0.518)
Cook	Col	$0.350	($0.347)	($0.697)
Vogelsong	Pit	$0.312	($0.433)	($0.745)
Haynes	Cin	$2.500	($1.213)	($3.713)
Nomo	LA	$9.000	($3.119)	($12.119)

Closer	Team	Salary	Earned Value	Difference
Lidge	Hou	$0.360	$10.060	$9.700
Benitez	Fla	$3.500	$8.719	$5.219
Gagne	LA	$5.000	$8.216	$3.216
Hawkins	ChC	$3.000	$6.204	$3.204
Cordero	Mtl	$0.300	$5.869	$5.569
Isringhausen	SL	$7.750	$5.869	($1.881)
Looper	NYM	$2.000	$5.701	$3.701
Hoffman	SD	$2.500	$5.533	$3.033
Mesa	Pit	$0.800	$5.198	$4.398
Smoltz	Atl	$11.667	$5.030	($6.637)
Kolb	Mil	$1.500	$4.192	$2.692
Wagner	Phi	$8.000	$4.024	($3.976)
Worrell	Phi	$2.750	$4.024	$1.274
Graves	Cin	$6.000	$2.012	$3.988
Aquino	Ari	$0.300	$1.845	$1.545
Dotel	Hou	$1.153	$1.845	$0.692
Herges	SF	$1.10	$0.336	($0.764)
Nen	SF	$9.150	$0.000	($9.150)
Chacon	Col	$1.850	($1.844)	($3.694)

Mantei	Ari	$7.000	($2.347)	($9.347)
Biddle	Mtl	$1.950	($2.850)	($4.800)

Other Pitchers	Team	Salary	Earned Value	Difference
Ayala	Mtl	$0.318	$2.873	$2.555
Mota	LA-Fla	$0.300	$2.246	$1.946
Torres	Pit	$0.775	$2.141	$1.366
Otsuka	SD	$0.700	$1.985	$1.285
Madson	Phi	$0.300	$1.933	$1.633
Tavarez	SL	$1.600	$1.828	$0.228
Linebrink	SD	$0.326	$1.776	$1.450
Brower	SF	$0.663	$1.724	$1.061
Alfonseca	Atl	$1.350	$1.619	$0.269
Rodriguez	SF-Phi	$0.300	$1.567	$1.267
Cruz	Atl	$0.370	$1.462	$1.092
Koplove	Ari	$0.330	$1.358	$1.028
Reed	Col	$0.600	$1.358	$0.758
Carrera	LA	$0.300	$1.306	$1.006
Miceli	Hou	$0.600	$1.306	$0.706
Cormier	Phi	$3.000	$1.254	($1.746)
Lowry	SF	$0.300	$1.254	$0.954
Stanton	NYM	$3.000	$1.254	($1.746)
Fassero	Col/Ari	$0.500	$1.149	$0.649
King	SL	$0.900	$1.149	$0.249
Dessens	Ari-LA	$4.000	$1.097	($2.903)
Kline	SL	$1.700	$1.097	($0.603)
Tucker	Mtl	$0.330	$1.045	$0.715
Backe	Hou	$0.300	$0.992	$0.692
Bottalico	NYM	$0.400	$0.992	$0.592
Jones	Cin-Phi	$0.500	$0.992	$0.492
Ramirez	Atl	$0.330	$0.992	$0.662
Vizcaino	Mil	$0.550	$0.992	$0.442
Sanchez	LA	$0.305	$0.940	$0.635
Eldred	SL	$0.900	$0.888	($0.012)
Harrikkala	Col	$0.300	$0.888	$0.588
Meadows	Pit	$0.625	$0.888	$0.263
Mercker	ChC	$1.200	$0.888	($0.312)
Reitsma	Atl	$0.950	$0.888	($0.062)
Vargas	Mtl	$0.308	$0.888	$0.580
Wright	Col	$0.500	$0.888	$0.388
Burba	Mil-SF	$0.440	$0.836	$0.396
Adams	Mil	$0.300	$0.783	$0.483
Grybowski	Atl	$0.378	$0.783	$0.405

Weathers	NYM-Fla	$3.933	$0.783	($3.150)
Wheeler	NYM-Hou	$0.300	$0.783	$0.483
Ginter	NYM	$0.320	$0.731	$0.411
Walker	SF	$0.450	$0.731	$0.281
Bennett	Mil	$0.300	$0.627	$0.327
Choate	Ari	$0.326	$0.627	$0.301
Farnsworth	ChC	$1.400	$0.627	($0.773)
Eyre	SF	$1.000	$0.575	($0.425)
Randolph	Ari	$0.323	$0.575	$0.252
Witasick	SD	$1.750	$0.575	($1.175)
Telemaco	Phi	$0.525	$0.522	($0.003)
Wise	Mil	$0.300	$0.522	$0.222
Dreifort	LA	$12.400	$0.470	($11.930)
Norton	Cin	$0.304	$0.418	$0.114
Bump	Fla	$0.305	$0.366	$0.061
Burnett	Pit	$0.300	$0.366	$0.066
Hancock	Phi-Cin	$0.300	$0.366	$0.066
VanPoppel	Cin	$0.300	$0.366	$0.066
Wagner	Cin	$0.303	$0.366	$0.063
Downs	Mtl	$0.315	$0.313	($0.002)
Harville	Hou	$0.291	$0.313	$0.022
Franklin	SF	$0.360	$0.261	($0.099)
Oliver	Fla-Hou	$0.500	$0.261	($0.239)
Riedling	Cin	$0.650	$0.261	($0.389)
Boehringer	Pit	$2.000	$0.209	($1.791)
Grabow	Pit	$0.300	$0.209	($0.091)
Hernandez	Phi	$0.750	$0.157	($0.593)
Kinney	Mil	$0.314	$0.104	($0.210)
Stone	Hou-SD	$0.395	$0.052	($0.343)
Mitre	ChC	$0.305	($0.052)	($0.357)
Claussen	Cin	$0.300	($0.313)	($0.613)

2004 EARNED VALUES BY TEAM

American League

ANAHEIM ANGELS

Player	Salary	Earned Value	Difference
Guerrero	$11.000	$13.894	$2.894
Guillen	$5.350	$5.876	$0.526
Escobar	$5.750	$5.719	($0.031)
Lackey	$0.375	$3.813	$3.438

Rodriguez	$0.375	$3.602	$3.227
Erstad	$7.750	$3.571	($4.179)
Figgins	$0.320	$3.361	$3.041
Washburn	$5.450	$3.145	($2.305)
DaVanon	$0.375	$2.895	$2.520
Colon	$11.000	$2.859	($8.141)
Anderson	$6.200	$2.719	($3.481)
Percival	$7.833	$2.648	($5.185)
Glaus	$9.900	$2.591	($7.309)
Eckstein	$2.150	$2.307	$0.157
Molina B	$2.025	$2.194	$0.169
Shields	$0.375	$1.953	$1.578
Ortiz	$3.267	$1.892	($1.375)
Sele	$8.667	$1.811	($6.856)
Molina J	$0.335	$1.728	$1.393
Kennedy	$2.500	$1.549	($0.951)
Gregg	$0.302	$1.282	$0.980
Salmon	$9.900	$0.707	($9.193)
Kotchman	$0.300	($0.836)	($1.136)
	$101.499	**$71.280**	**($30.219)**

Baltimore Orioles

Player	Salary	Earned Value	Difference
Tejada	$5.000	$8.167	$3.167
Lopez	$0.365	$5.830	$5.465
Mora	$2.333	$4.324	$1.991
Lopez	$6.000	$4.023	($1.977)
Hairston	$1.650	$3.876	$2.226
Newhan	$0.300	$3.533	$3.233
Surhoff	$0.800	$3.510	$2.710
Ponson	$3.000	$3.241	$0.241
Palmeiro	$4.000	$2.990	($1.010)
Ryan	$1.275	$2.686	$1.411
Cabrera	$0.300	$2.669	$2.369
Bedard	$0.300	$2.574	$2.274
Bigbie	$0.300	$2.008	$1.708
Julio	$0.385	$1.801	$1.416
Roberts	$0.345	$1.488	$1.143
Parrish	$0.320	$1.343	$1.023
Gibbons	$2.600	$1.317	($1.283)
Matos	$0.975	$0.861	($0.114)
Bauer	$0.335	$0.610	$0.275

Groom	$3.000	$0.549	($2.451)
Riley	$0.310	$0.488	$0.178
Borkowski	$0.300	$0.305	$0.005
Grimsley	$0.570	$0.183	($0.387)
DuBose	$0.305	$0.061	($0.244)
Daal	$4.500	$0.000	($4.500)
	$39.568	**$58.437**	**$18.869**

BOSTON RED SOX

Player	Salary	Earned Value	Difference
Schilling	$12.000	$9.055	($2.945)
Ortiz	$4.588	$8.480	$3.892
Millar	$3.300	$7.719	$4.419
Martinez	$17.500	$7.149	($10.351)
Varitek	$6.900	$6.198	($0.702)
Ramirez	$20.000	$6.121	($13.879)
Foulke	$3.500	$5.509	$2.009
Arroyo	$0.333	$4.766	$4.433
Damon	$8.000	$4.616	($3.384)
Wakefield	$4.350	$3.527	($0.823)
Mueller	$2.100	$2.735	$0.635
Bellhorn	$0.490	$2.290	$1.800
Reese	$1.000	$2.182	$1.182
Lowe	$4.500	$2.097	($2.403)
Nixon	$4.500	$1.792	($2.708)
Youkilis	$0.300	$1.477	$1.177
Timlin	$2.500	$1.404	($1.096)
McCarty	$0.500	$1.261	$0.761
Kapler	$0.750	$1.243	$0.493
Cabrera	$2.000	$1.216	($0.784)
Mirabelli	$0.825	$0.988	$0.163
Garciaparra	$7.705	$0.935	($6.770)
Embree	$3.000	$0.793	($2.207)
Mientkiewicz	$0.924	$0.304	($0.620)
Adams	$0.660	$0.183	($0.477)
	$112.225	**$84.040**	**($28.185)**

CHICAGO WHITE SOX

Player	Salary	Earned Value	Difference
Konerko	$8.000	$7.598	($0.402)
Buehrle	$3.500	$7.244	$3.744

Lee	$4.200	$6.366	$2.166
Rowand	$0.340	$4.656	$4.316
Thomas	$6.000	$4.652	($1.348)
Garland	$2.300	$4.575	$2.275
Takatsu	$0.750	$4.449	$3.699
Valentin	$5.000	$4.021	($0.979)
Garcia	$3.437	$3.813	$0.375
Gload	$0.302	$2.857	$2.555
Loaiza	$2.680	$2.764	$0.084
Uribe	$0.350	$2.656	$2.306
Ordonez	$14.000	$2.340	($11.660)
Marte	$0.500	$1.892	$1.392
Schoenewis	$1.725	$1.430	($0.295)
Contreras	$2.800	$1.430	($1.370)
Crede	$0.340	$1.424	$1.084
Harris	$0.319	$1.240	$0.921
Burke	$0.300	$0.860	$0.560
Everett	$2.228	$0.854	($1.374)
Olivo	$0.320	$0.677	$0.357
Politte	$0.800	$0.671	($0.129)
Adkins	$0.301	$0.610	$0.309
Perez	$0.850	$0.512	($0.338)
Cotts	$0.301	$0.488	$0.187
Koch	$6.375	$0.318	($6.057)
Davis	$0.462	$0.147	($0.315)
Alomar, Jr	$0.700	($0.109)	($0.809)
Borchard	$0.300	($0.731)	($1.031)
	$69.480	**$69.704**	**$0.223**

CLEVELAND INDIANS

Player	Salary	Earned Value	Difference
Hafner	$0.316	$9.452	$9.136
Westbrook	$0.925	$7.053	$6.128
Broussard	$0.324	$6.352	$6.028
Martinez	$0.305	$5.065	$4.760
Gerut	$0.326	$4.863	$4.537
Sabathia	$2.700	$4.575	$1.875
Vizquel	$6.000	$4.426	($1.574)
Blake	$0.352	$4.350	$3.998
Lawton	$6.750	$3.526	($3.224)
Crisp	$0.319	$3.091	$2.772
Elarton	$0.356	$2.288	$1.932

Belliard	$1.100	$2.175	$1.075
Merloni	$0.560	$1.975	$1.415
Lee	$0.303	$1.906	$1.603
Davis	$0.327	$1.525	$1.198
Riske	$1.025	$1.465	$0.440
Betancourt	$0.305	$1.221	$0.916
Miller	$0.300	$1.037	$0.737
Phelps	$0.085	$0.890	$0.805
Sizemore	$0.300	$0.880	$0.580
Escobar	$0.302	$0.802	$0.500
Wickman	$6.000	$0.742	($5.258)
Tadano	$0.300	$0.549	$0.249
Durbin	$0.269	$0.488	$0.219
White	$0.330	$0.366	$0.036
Laker	$0.450	($0.146)	($0.596)
	$30.629	**$70.916**	**$40.287**

DETROIT TIGERS

Player	Salary	Earned Value	Difference
Guillen	$2.500	$7.326	$4.826
Rodriguez	$7.000	$7.259	$0.259
Pena	$0.330	$5.972	$5.642
Higginson	$8.850	$5.192	($3.658)
Maroth	$0.333	$5.052	$4.719
Monroe	$0.300	$3.893	$3.593
Young	$7.750	$3.887	($3.863)
Bonderman	$0.330	$3.050	$2.720
White	$0.600	$2.644	$2.044
Inge	$0.340	$2.498	$2.158
Robertson	$0.305	$2.383	$2.078
Johnson	$3.000	$2.192	($0.808)
Infante	$0.305	$1.969	$1.664
Munson	$1.488	$1.912	$0.424
Knotts	$0.316	$1.906	$1.590
Sanchez	$0.385	$1.565	$1.180
Yan	$0.650	$1.526	$0.876
Walker	$0.775	$1.343	$0.568
Thames	$0.500	$1.224	$0.724
Urbina	$0.500	$1.059	$0.559
Levine	$0.825	$0.854	$0.029
Logan	$0.300	$0.743	$0.443
Ledezma	$0.300	$0.610	$0.310

Smith	$0.300	$0.591	$0.291
Vina	$3.000	$0.324	($2.676)
Patterson	$2.800	$0.318	($2.482)
	$44.082	**$67.292**	**$23.210**

KANSAS CITY ROYALS

Player	Salary	Earned Value	Difference
Sweeney	$11.000	$4.863	($6.137)
Greinke	$0.300	$4.670	$4.370
Stairs	$1.000	$3.913	$2.913
Harvey	$0.318	$3.616	$3.298
DeJesus	$0.300	$3.484	$3.184
Guiel	$3.000	$3.428	$0.428
Beltran	$4.500	$3.091	($1.409)
Randa	$3.250	$2.808	($0.442)
Berroa	$0.373	$2.681	$2.308
Gobble	$0.304	$2.574	$2.270
Anderson	$3.250	$1.811	($1.439)
May	$1.750	$1.811	$0.061
Reyes	$0.550	$1.526	$0.976
Graffanino	$1.100	$1.450	$0.350
Affeldt	$0.350	$1.377	$1.027
Wood	$0.300	$1.144	$0.844
Camp	$0.300	$1.098	$0.798
Relaford	$0.900	$0.916	$0.016
Pickering	$0.310	$0.883	$0.573
Grimsley	$0.430	$0.793	$0.363
Sullivan	$2.100	$0.671	($1.429)
Gonzalez	$4.000	$0.658	($3.342)
Buck	$0.300	$0.631	$0.331
Nunez	$0.229	$0.439	$0.210
Gotay	$0.300	$0.019	($0.281)
Santiago	$2.150	($0.109)	($2.259)
Brown	$0.310	($0.538)	($0.848)
	$42.974	**$49.708**	**$6.734**

MINNESOTA TWINS

Player	Salary	Earned Value	Difference
Santana	$1.600	$10.294	$8.694
Radke	$10.765	$6.863	($3.902)

Nathan	$0.440	$5.403	$4.963
Silva	$0.340	$5.338	$4.998
Morneau	$0.300	$4.483	$4.183
Guzman	$3.725	$4.115	$0.390
Jones	$4.350	$4.095	($0.255)
Ford	$1.725	$3.648	$1.923
Stewart	$2.750	$3.550	$0.800
Hunter	$6.500	$3.384	($3.116)
Koskie	$4.500	$2.933	($1.567)
Rincon	$0.330	$2.930	$2.600
Lohse	$0.395	$2.478	$2.083
Mulholland	$0.350	$1.811	$1.461
Romero	$0.820	$1.709	$0.889
Rivas	$1.500	$1.565	$0.065
Offerman	$0.500	$1.531	$1.031
Mauer	$0.300	$1.500	$1.200
Roa	$0.320	$0.976	$0.656
Blanco	$0.750	$0.960	$0.210
Cuddyer	$0.308	$0.725	$0.417
LeCroy	$0.340	$0.677	$0.337
Fultz	$0.550	$0.610	$0.060
Punto	$0.308	$0.324	$0.016
Mientkiewicz	$1.876	$0.304	($1.572)
Mays	$5.750	$0.000	($5.750)
Greisinger	$0.310	$0.000	($0.310)
	$51.702	**$72.206**	**$20.504**

NEW YORK YANKEES

Player	Salary	Earned Value	Difference
Sheffield	$13.000	$10.823	($2.177)
Matsui	$6.000	$7.149	$1.149
Rivera	$10.890	$6.674	($4.216)
Posada	$9.000	$5.833	($3.167)
Jeter	$18.600	$5.549	($13.051)
Rodriguez	$22.000	$5.470	($16.530)
Lieber	$2.700	$3.908	$1.208
Vazquez	$9.000	$3.527	($5.473)
Williams	$12.357	$3.443	($8.914)
Brown	$15.714	$3.336	($12.378)
Gordon	$3.500	$3.174	($0.326)
Hernandez	$0.500	$3.145	$2.645
Mussina	$16.000	$3.145	($12.855)

Giambi	$12.429	$2.051	($10.378)
Lofton	$3.100	$1.995	($1.105)
Sierra	$1.000	$1.826	$0.826
Clark	$0.750	$1.489	$0.739
Olerud	$3.080	$1.200	($1.880)
Cairo	$0.900	$1.183	$0.283
Quantrill	$3.000	$1.037	($1.963)
Flaherty	$0.775	$0.585	($0.190)
Sturtze	$0.330	$0.427	$0.097
Wilson	$0.700	$0.076	($0.624)
Loaiza	$1.320	($0.095)	($1.415)
Contreras	$5.700	($0.191)	($5.891)
	$172.345	**$76.759**	**($95.586)**

OAKLAND A'S

Player	Salary	Earned Value	Difference
Durazo	$2.100	$7.450	$5.350
Hatteberg	$2.300	$5.926	$3.626
Chavez	$5.325	$5.668	$0.343
Hudson	$5.000	$5.528	$0.528
Crosby	$0.301	$5.424	$5.123
Mulder	$4.450	$5.338	$0.888
Zito	$3.000	$4.861	$1.861
Harden	$0.300	$4.766	$4.466
Kotsay	$5.500	$4.616	($0.884)
Dye	$11.667	$4.132	($7.535)
Redman	$2.000	$3.336	$1.336
Miller	$3.000	$2.697	($0.303)
Kielty	$2.175	$2.400	$0.225
Duchscherrer	$0.303	$2.258	$1.955
Dotel	$1.647	$1.801	$0.154
Byrnes	$0.500	$1.494	$0.994
Melhuse	$0.358	$1.454	$1.096
Scutaro	$0.302	$1.393	$1.091
Hammond	$2.400	$1.098	($1.302)
McLemore	$0.600	$0.954	$0.354
Mecir	$2.877	$0.915	($1.962)
Bradford	$0.965	$0.671	($0.294)
Karros	$0.550	($0.076)	($0.626)
Menechino	$0.400	($0.172)	($0.572)
	$58.020	**$73.932**	**$15.912**

SEATTLE MARINERS

Player	Salary	Earned Value	Difference
Suzuki	$6.500	$11.847	$5.347
Winn	$3.500	$4.460	$0.960
Garcia	$3.438	$3.813	$0.375
Martinez	$3.000	$3.357	$0.357
Franklin	$1.800	$3.336	$1.536
Moyer	$7.000	$2.764	($4.236)
Pineiro	$3.000	$2.478	($0.522)
Guardado	$4.000	$2.436	($1.564)
Olerud	$4.620	$2.416	($2.204)
Meche	$1.950	$2.097	$0.147
Madritsch	$0.300	$1.892	$1.592
Jacobson	$0.300	$1.869	$1.569
Ibanez	$0.322	$1.812	$1.490
Villone	$1.000	$1.586	$0.586
Spiezio	$2.567	$1.246	($1.321)
Cabrera	$1.000	$1.187	$0.187
Putz	$0.300	$0.854	$0.554
Davis	$0.938	$0.851	($0.087)
Boone	$8.000	$0.763	($7.237)
Aurilia	$2.045	$0.686	($1.359)
Mateo	$0.345	$0.549	$0.204
Hasegawa	$2.750	$0.427	($2.323)
Wilson	$3.500	$0.412	($3.088)
Bocachica	$0.400	$0.352	($0.048)
Bloomquist	$0.325	$0.159	($0.166)
Lopez	$0.300	($0.156)	($0.456)
Olivo	$0.106	($0.265)	($0.371)
Jarvis	$4.250	($0.381)	($4.631)
	$67.556	**$52.847**	**($14.709)**

TAMPA BAY DEVIL RAYS

Player	Salary	Earned Value	Difference
Martinez	$7.500	$5.850	($1.650)
Crawford	$0.300	$5.680	$5.380
Cruz, Jr	$2.500	$5.412	$2.912
Lugo	$1.750	$4.801	$3.051
Huff	$2.667	$4.086	$1.419
Baldelli	$0.320	$3.795	$3.475
Hendrickson	$0.315	$3.145	$2.830

Zambrano	$0.217	$3.145	$2.928
Baez	$1.750	$2.966	$1.216
Bell	$0.300	$2.383	$2.083
Brazelton	$0.300	$2.002	$1.702
Hall	$0.320	$1.509	$1.189
Halama	$0.600	$1.404	$0.804
Carter	$0.320	$1.343	$1.023
Harper	$0.310	$1.282	$0.972
Sanchez	$1.000	$0.649	($0.351)
Sosa	$0.313	$0.549	$0.236
Cantu	$0.300	$0.515	$0.215
Upton	$0.300	$0.436	$0.136
Blum	$1.500	$0.132	($1.368)
Gonzalez	$1.700	($0.062)	($1.762)
Waechter	$0.300	($0.123)	($0.423)
Fordyce	$0.650	($0.292)	($0.942)
Fick	$0.755	($0.353)	($1.108)
Rolls	$0.800	($0.362)	($1.162)
	$27.087	**$49.892**	**$22.805**

TEXAS RANGERS

Player	Salary	Earned Value	Difference
Texeira	$2.625	$8.358	$5.733
Drese	$0.350	$6.291	$5.941
Cordero	$2.000	$6.038	$4.038
Rogers	$2.500	$5.910	$3.410
Mench	$0.345	$5.375	$5.030
Young M	$0.450	$3.928	$3.478
Matthews	$0.400	$3.876	$3.476
Blalock	$0.550	$3.691	$3.141
Soriano	$5.400	$2.366	($3.034)
Barajas	$0.500	$1.737	$1.237
Almanzar	$0.420	$1.648	$1.228
Benoit	$0.335	$1.525	$1.190
Mahay	$0.500	$1.404	$0.904
Nix	$0.300	$1.232	$0.932
Francisco	$0.300	$1.221	$0.921
Dickey	$0.338	$1.144	$0.806
Fullmer	$1.000	$1.031	$0.031
Park	$14.000	$0.953	($13.047)
Brocail	$0.350	$0.854	$0.504
Powell	$3.500	$0.427	($3.073)

Wasdin	$0.330	$0.366	$0.036
Laird	$0.300	$0.165	($0.135)
Perry	$1.700	$0.147	($1.553)
Dellucci	$0.328	$0.049	($0.279)
Jordan	$1.250	$0.000	($1.250)
Zimmerman	$4.467	$0.000	($4.467)
Young E	$0.300	($0.147)	($0.447)
	$44.838	**$59.589**	**$14.752**

TORONTO BLUE JAYS

Player	Salary	Earned Value	Difference
Delgado	$19.700	$7.522	($12.178)
Lilly	$1.900	$5.338	$3.438
Batista	$3.600	$4.384	$0.784
Gross	$3.300	$4.015	$0.715
Halladay	$6.000	$3.813	($2.187)
Wells	$0.870	$3.462	$2.592
Rios	$0.310	$3.181	$2.871
Hudson	$0.322	$2.923	$2.601
Berg	$6.200	$2.840	($3.360)
Frasor	$0.300	$2.754	$2.454
Bush	$0.300	$2.574	$2.274
Zaun	$0.500	$2.377	$1.877
Towers	$0.340	$2.002	$1.662
Gomez	$0.750	$1.777	$1.027
Johnson	$2.200	$1.616	($0.584)
Speier	$1.600	$1.526	($0.074)
Hinske	$0.900	$1.516	$0.616
Menechino	$0.360	$1.088	$0.728
Catalanotto	$2.300	$1.058	($1.242)
Adams	$1.044	$1.037	($0.007)
Woodward	$0.775	$0.904	$0.129
Miller	$0.300	$0.763	$0.463
Chulk	$0.300	$0.671	$0.371
Phelps	$0.257	$0.435	$0.178
Cash	$0.302	$0.165	($0.137)
Ligtenberg	$2.000	$0.000	$2.000)
Clark	$0.305	($0.073)	($0.378)
Hentgen	$2.200	($0.477)	($2.677)
	$59.235	**$59.191**	**($0.044)**

National League

ARIZONA DIAMONDBACKS

Player	Salary	Earned Value	Difference
Johnson	$16.000	$9.444	($6.556)
Webb	$0.335	$5.025	$4.690
Hillenbrand	$2.600	$3.734	$1.134
Tracy	$0.300	$3.203	$2.903
Gonzalez	$8.250	$3.020	($5.230)
Finley	$4.690	$2.911	($1.779)
Bautista	$4.000	$2.529	($1.471)
Cintron	$0.335	$2.053	$1.718
Sexson	$8.725	$1.847	($6.878)
Aquino	$0.300	$1.845	$1.545
Koplove	$0.330	$1.358	$1.028
Snyder	$0.300	$1.324	$1.024
Hairston	$0.300	$1.089	$0.789
Sparks	$0.500	$1.040	$0.540
Dessens	$3.238	$0.992	($2.246)
Kata	$0.315	$0.844	$0.529
Hammock	$0.315	$0.836	$0.521
Terrero	$0.300	$0.803	$0.503
Olson	$0.300	$0.682	$0.382
Choate	$0.326	$0.627	$0.301
Randolph	$0.323	$0.575	$0.252
Mayne	$0.536	$0.371	($0.165)
Alomar	$0.659	$0.354	($0.305)
McCracken	$1.548	$0.301	($1.247)
DeVore	$0.300	$0.261	($0.039)
Green A	$0.300	$0.028	($0.272)
Fassero	$0.003	$0.000	($0.003)
Fossum	$0.345	($0.173)	($0.518)
Brito	$0.300	($0.953)	($1.253)
Mantei	$7.000	($2.347)	($9.347)
	$63.073	**$43.623**	**($19.450)**

ATLANTA BRAVES

Player	Salary	Earned Value	Difference
Drew	$4.200	$9.802	$5.602
Estrada	$0.313	$6.482	$6.169

Jones A	$12.500	$6.221	($6.279)
Wright	$0.850	$5.112	$4.262
Smoltz	$11.667	$5.030	($6.637)
Thomson	$2.250	$4.765	$2.515
Furcal	$3.700	$4.561	$0.861
Ortiz	$6.200	$4.245	($1.955)
Jones C	$15.333	$3.950	($11.383)
Hampton	$14.625	$3.899	($10.726)
Franco	$0.750	$3.598	$2.848
Giles	$0.430	$3.262	$2.832
Marrero	$3.000	$2.755	($0.245)
Byrd	$7.000	$2.599	($4.401)
Thomas	$0.300	$2.477	$2.177
LaRoche	$0.300	$2.367	$2.067
Alfonseca	$1.350	$1.619	$0.269
Cruz	$0.370	$1.462	$1.092
Green N	$0.300	$1.144	$0.844
Ramirez	$0.330	$0.992	$0.662
Reitsma	$0.950	$0.888	($0.062)
Grybowski	$0.378	$0.783	$0.405
Wise	$0.325	$0.393	$0.068
Garcia	$0.313	$0.380	$0.067
Perez	$0.625	$0.209	($0.416)
DeRosa	$0.725	$0.144	($0.581)
	$89.084	**$79.139**	**($9.945)**

CHICAGO CUBS

Player	Salary	Earned Value	Difference
Lee	$6.167	$7.661	$1.494
Zambrano	$0.450	$7.625	$7.175
Hawkins	$3.000	$6.204	$3.204
Alou	$9.500	$5.648	($3.852)
Maddux	$6.000	$5.285	($0.715)
Barrett	$1.550	$4.891	$3.341
Clement	$6.000	$4.765	($1.235)
Ramirez	$6.000	$4.740	($1.260)
Patterson	$0.480	$4.043	$3.563
Sosa	$16.000	$4.015	($11.985)
Wood	$8.000	$3.552	($4.448)
Rusch	$0.500	$3.307	$2.807
Prior	$3.150	$2.599	($0.551)
Hollandsworth	$1.000	$2.007	$1.007

Grudzielanek	$2.500	$1.579	($0.921)
Walker	$1.750	$1.520	($0.230)
Martinez	$0.900	$1.267	$0.367
Mercker	$1.200	$0.888	($0.312)
Garciaparra	$3.795	$0.811	($2.984)
Gonzalez	$3.853	$0.750	($3.103)
Perez	$0.850	$0.730	($0.120)
Farnsworth	$1.400	$0.627	($0.773)
Grieve	$0.200	$0.600	$0.400
Macias	$0.750	$0.294	($0.456)
Mitre	$0.305	($0.052)	($0.357)
Goodwin	$0.650	($0.139)	($0.789)
Bako	$0.865	($0.883)	($1.748)
	$86.815	**$74.334**	**($12.481)**

CINCINNATI REDS

Player	Salary	Earned Value	Difference
Dunn	$0.445	$7.315	$6.870
Casey	$6.800	$6.840	$0.040
Freel	$0.320	$4.740	$4.420
Pena	$0.345	$3.884	$3.539
Griffey	$12.500	$3.369	($9.131)
Wilson	$3.500	$3.119	($0.381)
LaRue	$2.600	$3.078	$0.478
Jimenez	$1.615	$2.342	$0.727
Graves	$6.000	$2.012	($3.988)
Larkin	$0.700	$1.901	$1.201
Harang	$0.360	$1.733	$1.373
Lidle	$1.942	$1.568	($0.374)
Lopez	$0.300	$1.368	$1.068
Castro	$1.000	$1.221	$0.221
Valentin	$0.500	$0.836	$0.336
Kearns	$0.400	$0.834	$0.434
Jones	$0.500	$0.732	$0.232
Cruz	$0.350	$0.443	$0.093
Norton	$0.304	$0.418	$0.114
VanPoppel	$0.300	$0.366	$0.066
Wagner	$0.303	$0.366	$0.063
Acevedo	$0.340	$0.347	$0.007
Hancock	$0.258	$0.315	$0.057
Riedling	$0.650	$0.261	($0.389)
Hummel	$0.300	$0.180	($0.120)

Player	Salary	Earned Value	Difference
Larson	$0.318	($0.036)	($0.354)
Bragg	$0.150	($0.047)	($0.197)
Claussen	$0.300	($0.313)	($0.613)
Haynes	$2.500	($1.213)	($3.713)
	$45.900	**$47.979**	**$2.079**

COLORADO ROCKIES

Player	Salary	Earned Value	Difference
Helton	$11.600	$14.500	$2.900
Burnitz	$1.250	$4.797	$3.547
Kennedy	$0.320	$4.592	$4.272
Castilla	$2.100	$4.525	$2.425
Jennings	$0.340	$3.292	$2.952
Walker	$9.000	$3.128	($5.872)
Clayton	$0.650	$2.737	$2.087
Estes	$0.600	$2.686	$2.086
Miles	$0.300	$2.244	$1.944
Johnson	$9.000	$2.207	($6.793)
Sweeney	$0.400	$2.086	$1.686
Holliday	$0.300	$1.944	$1.644
Reed S	$0.600	$1.358	$0.758
Gonzalez	$0.300	$1.144	$0.844
Fassero	$0.497	$0.992	$0.495
Harrikkala	$0.300	$0.888	$0.588
Wright	$0.500	$0.888	$0.388
Closser	$0.300	$0.743	$0.443
Wilson	$9.000	$0.622	($8.378)
Greene	$0.550	$0.371	($0.179)
Hocking	$0.650	$0.231	($0.419)
Hawpe	$0.300	$0.157	($0.143)
Freeman	$0.300	$0.052	($0.248)
Neagle	$9.000	$0.000	($9.000)
Pellow	$0.310	($0.156)	($0.466)
Cook	$0.350	($0.347)	($0.697)
Chacon	$1.850	($1.844)	($3.694)
	$60.667	**$53.837**	**($6.830)**

FLORIDA MARLINS

Player	Salary	Earned Value	Difference
Benitez	$3.500	$8.719	$5.219
Pavano	$3.800	$7.365	$3.565

Cabrera	$0.320	$6.569	$6.249
Lowell	$6.500	$5.386	($1.114)
Pierre	$2.400	$4.769	$2.369
Conine	$3.000	$4.468	$1.468
Willis	$0.353	$3.899	$3.546
Penny	$2.498	$2.986	$0.488
Choi	$0.207	$3.488	$3.281
Beckett	$1.509	$3.466	$1.957
Castillo	$4.667	$3.104	($1.563)
Burnett	$2.500	$2.686	$0.186
Gonzalez	$2.800	$2.609	($0.191)
Redmond	$0.840	$1.150	$0.310
Easley	$0.300	$1.002	$0.702
Encarnacion	$1.176	$0.761	($0.415)
LoDuca	$1.342	$0.650	($0.692)
Valdes	$0.264	$0.611	$0.347
Bump	$0.305	$0.366	$0.061
Mota	$0.108	$0.157	$0.049
Weathers	$0.696	$0.052	($0.644)
Harris	$0.400	($0.108)	($0.508)
Oliver	$0.404	($0.110)	($0.514)
Castro	$0.400	($0.186)	($0.586)
	$40.289	**$63.859**	**$23.570**

HOUSTON ASTROS

Player	Salary	Earned Value	Difference
Lidge	$0.360	$10.060	$9.700
Berkman	$6.500	$8.968	$2.468
Clemens	$5.000	$7.018	$2.018
Oswalt	$3.250	$6.931	$3.681
Bagwell	$16.000	$6.156	($9.844)
Beltran	$4.500	$5.313	$0.813
Kent	$10.000	$4.084	($5.916)
Biggio	$3.000	$3.611	$0.611
Miller	$3.400	$3.119	($0.281)
Lamb	$0.352	$2.586	$2.234
Everett	$0.370	$2.585	$2.215
Hidalgo	$8.250	$2.346	($5.904)
Ensberg	$0.380	$2.126	$1.746
Pettitte	$5.500	$1.906	($3.594)
Dotel	$1.153	$1.845	$0.692
Vizcaino	$1.200	$1.749	$0.549

Miceli	$0.600	$1.306	$0.706
Ausmus	$1.000	$1.103	$0.103
Munro	$0.350	$1.040	$0.690
Lane	$0.308	$1.042	$0.734
Backe	$0.300	$0.992	$0.692
Palmeiro	$0.750	$0.579	($0.171)
Harville	$0.291	$0.313	$0.022
Redding	$0.395	$0.173	($0.222)
Weathers	$1.311	$0.105	($1.206)
Chavez	$0.315	$0.093	($0.222)
Wheeler	$0.065	$0.052	($0.013)
Oliver	$0.096	($0.005)	($0.101)
Stone	$0.144	($0.314)	($0.458)
	$75.140	**$76.882**	**$1.742**

LOS ANGELES DODGERS

Player	Salary	Earned Value	Difference
Gagne	$5.000	$8.216	$3.216
Beltre	$5.000	$8.044	$3.044
Bradley	$1.730	$5.210	$3.480
Weaver	$6.250	$4.852	($1.398)
Green	$16.667	$4.651	($12.016)
Perez	$5.000	$4.419	($0.581)
Lima	$0.500	$3.639	$3.139
LoDuca	$2.725	$3.113	$0.388
Iztouris	$0.359	$2.686	$2.327
Werth	$0.303	$2.639	$2.336
Cora	$1.300	$2.478	$1.178
Alvarez	$1.500	$2.339	$0.839
Ishii	$2.975	$2.166	($0.809)
Mota	$0.192	$2.089	$1.897
Finley	$2.310	$1.768	($0.542)
Hernandez	$0.500	$1.765	$1.265
Roberts	$0.686	$1.643	$0.957
Saenz	$0.350	$1.436	$1.086
Carrera	$0.300	$1.306	$1.006
Ventura	$1.200	$0.999	($0.201)
Sanchez	$0.305	$0.940	$0.635
Encarnacion	$2.389	$0.751	($1.638)
Dreifort	$12.400	$0.470	($11.930)
Grabowski	$0.301	$0.116	($0.185)
Penny	$1.227	$0.087	($1.140)

Dessens	$0.762	$0.052	($0.710)
Ross	$0.310	($0.372)	($0.682)
Mayne	$0.264	($0.697)	($0.961)
Choi	$0.103	($0.958)	($1.061)
Nomo	$9.000	($3.119)	($12.119)
	$81.908	**$62.728**	**($19.180)**

MILWAUKEE BREWERS

Player	Salary	Earned Value	Difference
Sheets	$2.425	$8.318	$5.893
Overbay	$0.326	$7.661	$7.335
Davis	$0.450	$5.545	$5.095
Kolb	$1.500	$4.192	$2.692
Clark	$0.376	$4.067	$3.691
Jenkins	$8.738	$3.611	($5.127)
Podsednik	$0.400	$3.421	$3.021
Counsell	$3.167	$1.774	($1.393)
Santos	$0.300	$1.646	$1.346
Branyan	$0.350	$1.472	$1.122
Spivey	$2.367	$1.471	($0.896)
Moeller	$0.370	$1.452	$1.082
Ginter	$0.383	$1.247	$0.864
Obermueller	$0.314	$1.213	$0.899
Capuano	$0.305	$1.213	$0.908
Vizcaino	$0.550	$0.992	$0.442
Hall	$0.310	$0.975	$0.665
Grieve	$0.500	$0.939	$0.439
Burba	$0.406	$0.836	$0.430
Adams	$0.300	$0.783	$0.483
Wise	$0.300	$0.522	$0.222
Helms	$1.688	$0.503	($1.185)
Kinney	$0.314	$0.104	($0.210)
Bennett	$0.300	($1.255)	($1.555)
	$26.439	**$52.702**	**$26.263**

MONTREAL EXPOS

Player	Salary	Earned Value	Difference
Wilkerson	$0.375	$8.481	$8.106
Hernandez	$6.000	$8.404	$2.404
Cordero	$0.300	$5.869	$5.569
Rivera	$0.312	$3.545	$3.233

Schneider	$0.350	$3.380	$3.030
Day	$0.315	$2.946	$2.631
Ayala	$0.318	$2.873	$2.555
Chavez	$0.350	$2.644	$2.294
Kim	$0.303	$2.599	$2.296
Sledge	$0.300	$2.593	$2.293
Batista	$1.500	$2.514	$1.014
Ohka	$2.338	$2.426	$0.088
Cabrera	$4.000	$1.723	($2.277)
Vidro	$7.000	$1.716	($5.284)
Patterson	$0.310	$1.386	$1.076
Armas	$2.100	$1.126	($0.974)
Carroll	$0.310	$1.089	$0.779
Johnson	$1.250	$1.067	($0.183)
Tucker	$0.330	$1.045	$0.715
Diaz	$2.588	$1.022	($1.566)
Vargas	$0.308	$0.888	$0.580
Izturis	$0.300	$0.329	$0.029
Downs	$0.315	$0.313	($0.002)
Everett	$2.272	$0.261	($2.011)
Gonzalez	$1.438	$0.112	($1.326)
Biddle	$1.950	($2.850)	($4.800)
	$37.232	**$57.501**	**$20.269**

NEW YORK METS

Player	Salary	Earned Value	Difference
Glavine	$10.766	$6.412	($4.354)
Looper	$2.000	$5.701	$3.701
Leiter	$10.296	$5.199	($5.097)
Cameron	$4.333	$4.717	$0.384
Trachsel	$5.000	$4.419	($0.581)
Piazza	$16.071	$3.762	($12.309)
Floyd	$6.500	$2.870	($3.630)
Matsui	$5.033	$2.788	($2.245)
Wigginton	$0.212	$2.219	$2.007
Valent	$0.300	$2.083	$1.783
Wright	$0.300	$1.724	$1.424
Seo	$0.320	$1.646	$1.326
Spencer	$0.538	$1.481	$0.943
Phillips	$0.318	$1.278	$0.960
Stanton	$3.000	$1.254	($1.746)

Wilson	$0.715	$1.138	$0.423
Benson	$2.030	$1.034	($0.996)
Bottalico	$0.400	$0.992	$0.592
Zeile	$1.000	$0.862	($0.138)
Delgado	$0.300	$0.786	$0.486
Ginter	$0.320	$0.731	$0.411
Hidalgo	$4.250	$0.600	($3.650)
Reyes	$0.308	$0.567	$0.259
Weathers	$1.926	$0.471	($1.455)
Buchanan	$0.220	$0.417	$0.197
Keppinger	$0.300	$0.409	$0.109
McEwing	$0.500	$0.354	($0.146)
Wheeler	$0.300	$0.235	($0.065)
Garcia	$0.588	$0.209	($0.379)
Williams	$0.500	$0.046	($0.454)
Garcia	$0.800	($0.027)	($0.827)
	$79.444	**$56.377**	**($23.067)**

PHILADELPHIA PHILLIES

Player	Salary	Earned Value	Difference
Abreu	$10.600	$9.698	($0.902)
Thome	$12.167	$9.302	($2.865)
Bell	$4.400	$4.237	($0.163)
Lieberthal	$7.500	$4.043	($3.457)
Burrell	$4.250	$4.028	($0.222)
Wagner	$8.000	$4.024	($3.976)
Worrell	$2.750	$4.024	$1.274
Polanco	$3.950	$3.354	($0.596)
Milton	$9.000	$3.292	($5.708)
Wolf	$4.375	$2.946	$1.429
Rollins	$2.425	$2.788	$0.363
Michaels	$0.335	$2.747	$2.412
Millwood	$11.000	$2.079	($8.921)
Ledee	$0.820	$1.976	$1.156
Madson	$0.300	$1.933	$1.633
Myers	$0.363	$1.646	$1.283
Padilla	$2.600	$1.646	($0.954)
Lidle	$0.808	$1.306	$0.498
Cormier	$3.000	$1.254	($1.746)
Utley	$0.300	$0.981	$0.681
Rodriguez	$0.100	$0.627	$0.527

	Salary	Earned Value	Difference
Telemaco	$0.525	$0.522	($0.003)
Perez	$0.750	$0.180	($0.570)
Pratt	$0.875	$0.162	($0.713)
Hernandez	$0.750	$0.157	($0.593)
Jones	$0.152	$0.157	$0.005
Byrd	$0.355	$0.026	($0.329)
Glanville	$0.550	($0.181)	($0.731)
Hancock	$0.042	($0.210)	($0.252)
	$93.042	**$68.744**	**($24.298)**

PITTSBURGH PIRATES

Player	Salary	Earned Value	Difference
Kendall	$8.571	$7.783	($0.788)
Wilson J	$1.850	$5.423	$3.573
Mesa	$0.800	$5.198	$4.398
Wilson C	$1.150	$5.005	$3.855
Perez	$0.321	$4.765	$4.444
Bay	$0.305	$4.421	$4.116
Mackowiak	$0.335	$3.076	$2.741
Fogg	$0.342	$2.599	$2.257
Wells	$2.575	$2.599	$0.024
Redman	$0.321	$2.514	$2.193
Benson	$4.120	$2.499	($1.621)
Torres	$0.775	$2.141	$1.366
Ward	$0.350	$1.436	$1.086
Castillo	$0.300	$1.411	$1.111
Hill	$0.315	$0.981	$0.666
Meadows	$0.625	$0.888	$0.263
Mondesi	$0.866	$0.509	($0.357)
Burnett	$0.300	$0.366	$0.066
Nunez	$0.625	$0.354	($0.271)
Grabow	$0.300	$0.209	($0.091)
Boehringer	$2.000	$0.209	($1.791)
Wigginton	$0.104	$0.122	$0.018
Stynes	$0.750	$0.036	($0.714)
Vogelsong	$0.312	($0.433)	($0.745)
Simon	$0.739	($1.026)	($1.765)
	$29.051	**$53.085**	**$24.034**

SAN DIEGO PADRES

Player	Salary	Earned Value	Difference
Nevin	$8.500	$7.524	($0.976)
Giles	$8.833	$6.882	($1.951)
Peavy	$0.350	$6.671	$6.321
Hoffman	$2.500	$5.533	$3.033
Loretta	$2.500	$5.391	$2.891
Hernandez	$2.938	$5.053	$2.115
Klesko	$6.000	$4.421	($1.579)
Payton	$1.500	$4.406	$2.906
Wells	$1.250	$4.072	$2.822
Lawrence	$0.925	$3.466	$2.541
Eaton	$1.925	$2.946	$1.021
Burroughs	$0.340	$2.514	$2.174
Long	$3.575	$2.176	($1.399)
Otsuka	$0.700	$1.985	$1.285
Linebrink	$0.326	$1.776	$1.450
Ojeda	$0.305	$1.371	$1.066
Witasick	$1.750	$0.575	($1.175)
Aurilia	$1.105	$0.539	($0.566)
Buchanan	$0.430	$0.417	($0.013)
Valdes	$0.536	$0.262	($0.274)
Bragg	$0.250	$0.186	($0.064)
Stone	$0.251	$0.157	($0.094)
Greene	$0.301	$0.000	($0.301)
Vazquez	$0.343	($0.025)	($0.368)
Gonzalez	$0.459	($0.026)	($0.485)
	$47.892	**$68.272**	**$20.380**

SAN FRANCISCO GIANTS

Player	Salary	Earned Value	Difference
Bonds	$18.000	$14.260	($3.740)
Schmidt	$7.937	$7.538	($0.399)
Snow	$1.500	$6.539	$5.039
Feliz	$0.850	$4.856	$4.006
Grissom	$2.125	$3.940	$1.815
Tomko	$1.200	$3.639	$2.439
Tucker	$1.500	$3.285	$1.785
Mohr	$0.343	$3.076	$2.733
Rueter	$6.133	$3.032	($3.101)
Durham	$7.200	$2.973	($4.227)

Williams	$0.308	$2.599	$2.291
Pierzynski	$3.500	$2.451	($1.049)
Hermanson	$0.800	$2.253	$1.453
Cruz D	$0.300	$2.027	$1.727
Brower	$0.663	$1.724	$1.061
Torrealba	$0.334	$1.487	$1.153
Perez	$1.900	$1.399	($0.501)
Lowry	$0.300	$1.254	$0.954
Rodriguez	$0.200	$0.888	$0.688
Walker	$0.450	$0.731	$0.281
Eyre	$1.000	$0.575	($0.425)
Hammonds	$1.000	$0.574	($0.426)
Herges	$1.100	$0.336	($0.764)
Franklin	$0.360	$0.261	($0.099)
Nen	$9.150	$0.000	($9.150)
Alfonzo	$6.500	($0.036)	($6.536)
Burba	$0.034	($0.052)	($0.086)
Ledee	$0.405	($0.416)	($0.821)
	$75.092	**$71.193**	**($3.899)**

ST. LOUIS CARDINALS

Player	Salary	Earned Value	Difference
Pujols	$7.000	$13.679	$6.679
Edmonds	$9.333	$10.471	$1.138
Rolen	$8.625	$8.475	($0.150)
Isringhausen	$7.750	$5.869	($1.881)
Marquis	$0.525	$5.458	$4.933
Carpenter	$0.300	$4.505	$4.205
Williams	$8.000	$3.726	($4.274)
Matheny	$4.000	$3.427	($0.573)
Renteria	$7.250	$3.396	($3.854)
Sanders	$2.000	$3.207	$1.207
Suppan	$1.000	$2.946	$1.946
Womack	$0.300	$2.723	$2.423
Morris	$12.500	$2.686	($9.814)
Mabry	$0.400	$2.292	$1.892
Tavarez	$1.600	$1.828	$0.228
Lankford	$0.650	$1.204	$0.554
King	$0.900	$1.149	$0.249
Kline	$1.700	$1.097	($0.603)
Walker	$3.667	$0.991	($2.676)
Eldred	$0.900	$0.888	($0.012)

Luna	$0.300	$0.862	$0.562
Taguchi	$1.200	$0.671	($0.529)
Molina	$0.300	$0.627	$0.327
Anderson	$0.600	$0.436	($0.164)
Cedeno	$5.375	$0.417	($4.958)
	$86.175	**$83.030**	**($3.145)**

2004 GM RATINGS

In 2004, the best short-term score was turned in by world champion prodigy Theo Epstein . . . almost.

Epstein did have a fine season, one in which he could take credit for improving the Sox by 9 and one-half games short-term. Since Boston qualified for the postseason by the margin of 7 games over Oakland, it's reasonable to assert that Epstein maneuvered the Sox toward their world championship. The acquisition of Curt Schilling, reflected in Epstein's +4.20 short-term acquisitions score. The signing of free agent Keith Foulke was a second key.

But two GMs did better than Epstein's +9.5. The top short-term score (+14.10) was posted by the duo of Mike Flanagan and Jim Beattie in Baltimore. Flanagan-Beattie signed Miguel Tejada and Javier Lopez, re-signed Melvin Mora, and either released or lost to free agency eight other players, all eight of whom delivered bad 2004 seasons for their new teams. Among the offenders Baltimore had the sagacity to rid itself of were pitchers Pat Hentgen and Jason Johnson (a combined 10-24), and infielder Tony Batista (.241 with Montreal).

In St. Louis, Walt Jocketty rebounded from a frankly awful 2003 season with a +11.30 short-term score in 2004 that was the best in the National League. It was the third time in five seasons (2000 and 2001 being the others) that Jocketty stood first short-term among NL GMs.

Epstein wasn't the only GM who could claim credit for taking his team to the playoffs. In Anaheim, Bill Stoneman's work improved the Angels by 7.9 games; they won the AL West over Oakland by 1 game. In the NL West, rookie Dodger GM Paul DePodesta's 6.4 short-term score was second only to Jocketty. DePodesta's Dodgers won the division by 1 game over San Francisco. Meanwhile in Houston, since-retired GM Gerry Hunsicker aided the Astros by 5.7 games short term. They won the wild card by 1 game.

There were losers, as well, in 2004. GM Brian Sabean cost the Giants 2 games in the standings in 2004; they missed out on the division and wild card by 1 game. In Oakland, the oft-ballyhooed Billy Beane actually hurt the A's to the tune of 6.5 games short term in 2004. Since Oakland lost out on the division title by just 1 game, Beane's dealings can be said to have been the difference.

Here are the 2004 GM ratings. Short-term ratings are first, followed by long-term and residual ratings for GMs no longer with the teams they impacted.

GM RATINGS

2004

AMERICAN LEAGUE

Short Term

GM	Team	Acq.	Traded	FA Got	FA Lst.	Prod.	Total
Flanagan-Beattie	Bal	−0.90	1.20	7.00	8.90	−2.10	14.10
Epstein	Bos	4.20	2.60	2.80	0.40	−0.50	9.50
Stoneman	Ana	−0.10	0.00	5.00	2.70	0.30	7.90
Dombrowski	Det	5.50	0.10	0.70	0.10	−1.30	5.10
Ryan	Min	1.00	2.10	−2.50	−2.70	1.30	−0.80
Ricciardi	Tor	0.10	1.80	−3.30	−0.10	0.20	−1.30
Cashman	NYY	2.70	0.60	1.20	−5.00	−1.30	−1.80
Williams	CWS	−2.50	1.60	5.30	−1.80	−5.20	−2.60
Hart	Tex	1.40	−4.40	−3.80	5.00	−1.00	−2.80
Beane	Oak	0.60	−1.90	2.30	−10.60	3.10	−6.50
Shapiro	Cle	−2.80	0.20	−4.50	0.30	−1.30	−8.10
LaMar	TB	−4.50	−2.20	−4.30	4.40	−2.90	−9.50
Baird	KC	−4.60	−1.80	−5.90	1.00	0.10	−11.20
Bavasi	Sea	−2.40	−1.40	0.10	−3.10	−6.10	−12.90

Long Term

GM	Team	Acq.	Traded	FA Got	FA Lst.	Prod.	Total
Ryan	Min	5.80	4.30	1.20	−1.50	2.60	12.40
Shapiro	Cle	1.90	3.10	−0.70	−3.10	5.30	6.50
Epstein	Bos	1.50	1.40	1.70	1.20	0.00	5.80
Dombrowski	Det	−2.70	4.60	0.30	2.80	0.30	5.30
Beane	Oak	1.60	6.70	−0.50	−4.90	2.00	4.90
Cashman	NYY	−1.20	−4.90	8.30	2.60	0.00	4.80
Stoneman	Ana	−3.60	−0.70	−2.50	3.90	4.60	1.70
Williams	CWS	−2.20	−0.50	5.70	0.80	−2.20	1.60
Hart	Tex	1.80	−1.90	0.50	−2.80	2.70	0.30
Bavasi	Sea	—	—	—	—	—	0.00
LaMar	TB	−1.90	0.20	−1.10	0.50	1.80	−0.50
Ricciardi	Tor	−1.00	4.50	−5.20	1.20	−1.40	−1.90
Flanagan-Beattie	Bal	−0.80	−1.10	1.00	0.00	−1.40	−2.30
Baird	KC	0.00	1.70	−2.70	3.70	−6.30	−3.60

Residual

GM	Team	Acquired	Lost	Total
Port	Bos	8.50	1.60	10.10
Smith	Det	0.30	2.30	2.60
Melvin	Tex	−0.20	2.00	1.80
Robinson	KC	1.70	0.00	1.70
Ash	Tor	1.20	0.00	1.20
Schueler	CWS	−0.10	1.30	1.20
Thrift	Bal	−0.50	1.60	1.10
Bavasi	Ana	−0.20	1.10	0.90
Hart	Cle	0.60	0.10	0.70
Duquette	Bos	0.00	0.20	0.20
Gillick	Sea	−9.60	−2.40	−12.00

NATIONAL LEAGUE

Short Term

GM	Team	Acq.	Traded	FA Got	FA Lst.	Prod.	Total
Jocketty	SL	2.80	−6.00	13.60	0.50	0.40	11.30
DePodesta	LA	1.40	3.10	0.50	1.20	0.20	6.40
Hendry	ChC	−1.60	2.20	4.00	3.30	−1.70	6.20
Hunsicker	Hou	2.70	1.50	1.40	0.20	−0.10	5.70
Schuerholz	Atl	7.60	−3.00	2.10	0.80	−2.40	5.10
Towers	SD	−2.10	1.10	4.70	0.40	−1.10	3.00
Duquette	NYM	−1.10	5.00	−3.40	1.60	−1.60	0.50

Wade	Phi	0.40	0.80	−2.80	−1.10	2.10	−0.60
Sabean	SF	−2.80	−2.60	−1.00	5.10	−1.00	−2.30
Minaya	Mtl	−3.80	2.70	−3.30	−1.30	−0.30	−6.00
Beinfest	Fla	−1.30	3.00	−0.80	−3.70	−4.60	−7.40
O'Dowd	Col	0.50	−7.90	−4.20	4.60	−0.70	−7.70
Littlefield	Pit	−2.60	0.00	−1.10	−0.70	−4.90	−9.30
O'Brien	Cin	−3.40	−0.50	−5.90	−0.90	−1.40	−12.10
Melvin	Mil	−2.20	0.60	−11.40	1.50	−2.30	−13.80
Garagiola	Ari	−5.30	0.40	−7.00	2.70	−8.80	−18.00

Long Term

GM	Team	Acq.	Traded	FA Got	FA Lst.	Prod.	Total
Schuerholz	Atl	1.50	4.90	3.50	−1.70	4.30	12.50
Jocketty	SL	0.00	−2.00	11.20	2.40	−0.50	11.10
Sabean	SF	0.00	1.10	13.60	−3.50	−0.10	11.10
Melvin	Mil	−1.20	1.80	1.70	0.40	1.50	4.20
Towers	SD	2.30	−3.60	2.30	1.50	0.90	3.40
Garagiola	Ari	−1.40	−0.20	1.90	2.10	−1.60	0.80
Hendry	ChC	1.60	−3.10	0.30	1.60	0.00	0.40
Minaya	Mtl	−1.50	−0.80	0.00	−0.10	2.40	0.00
DePodesta	LA	—	—	—	—	—	0.00
O'Brien	Cin	—	—	—	—	—	0.00
Beinfest	Fla	−0.40	−1.60	3.50	−2.50	0.60	−0.40
Hunsicker	Hou	0.60	2.20	3.80	−11.70	4.30	−0.80
Wade	Phi	1.20	−6.70	9.20	0.50	−5.60	−1.40
O'Dowd	Col	−6.00	3.10	5.20	−0.40	−3.70	−1.80
Duquette	NYM	0.00	−2.20	0.00	0.00	−1.50	−3.70
Littlefield	Pit	−0.40	−5.50	−0.60	2.40	−0.70	−4.80

Residual

GM	Team	Acquired	Lost	Overall
McPhail	ChC	6.40	2.60	9.00
Taylor	Mil	4.50	3.10	7.60
Bonifay	Pit	4.80	1.00	5.80
Phillips	NYM	2.50	3.10	5.60
Malone	LA	0.00	3.40	3.40
Dombrowski	Fla	1.80	0.50	2.30
Evans	LA	1.10	−0.10	1.00
Lynch	ChC	0.00	−0.40	−0.40
Beattie	Mtl	−1.90	0.70	−1.20
Bowden	Cin	−8.20	2.30	−5.90